REPRESENTATION OF MINORITY GROUPS IN THE U.S.

Implications for the Twenty-First Century

Edited by
Charles E. Menifield

Copyright © 2001 by
Charles E. Menifield

Austin & Winfield, Publishers
4720 Boston Way
Lanham, Maryland 20706

12 Hid's Copse Rd.
Cumnor Hill, Oxford OX2 9JJ

Library of Congress Cataloging-in-Publication Data

Representation of minority groups in the U.S. : implications for
the twenty-first century / edited by Charles E. Menifield.
p.   cm
Includes bibliographical references and index.
1. Political participation—United States. 2. Minorities—
United States—Political activity. 3. Women in politics—
United States. 4. Representative government and representation—
United States. 5. Elections—United States. I. Menifield, Charles.
JK1764 .R46 2001   328.73'0734—dc21   2001033767 CIP

ISBN 1-57292-163-3 (cloth : alk. paper)
ISBN 1-57292-164-1 (pbk. : alk. paper)

Dedication

To my mother, Betty Jean Menifield, who taught me that I should respect other people, regardless to whether or not I subscribe to their philosophy. To my father, may you rest in peace, despite suffering the imperfections of man, you were always a good father and provider. You set a good and positive example for me. Most importantly, to my daughter and football buddy Tiffany, I hope one day that I can make you as proud of me as I am of you. You are a very strong, beautiful, young lady. I love you dearly.

Contents

Preface

Without question, our society has witnessed a dramatic transformation during the post Voting Rights Act era with regards to minority representation and behavior at every level of government. In fact, Congress, most state assemblies, and the courts have experienced significant changes in their racial and gender identity, particularly over the last 20 years. Arguably, some of these changes can be attributed to the Civil Rights Act of 1964, the Voting Rights Act of 1965 and its amendments, and the decision rendered by the Supreme Court in *Thornburg v. Gingles* (1986).

It is the purpose of this research to assess the changes that have occurred with respect to the descriptive and substantive representation of women, African Americans, Latinos, Asian Americans, and American Indians in the U.S. political system from 1965 to the present. To accomplish this purpose, each institutionally oriented chapter first provides the reader with detailed demographic and behavioral facts concerning minority groups in the political system. Second, representation of these groups are assessed through discussions of partisanship, ideology, policy impact, role orientations, leadership, committee assignment, bill cosponsorship, and voting behavior. In addition, the role and affect of redistricting and affirmative action on representation are discussed in two separate chapters.

We hope that our discussion of these major minority groups will help the reader better understand and appreciate the growth of these groups and the many techniques that they employ to better represent their constituents, despite the problems and many obstacles that have been placed in their paths. Lastly, we hope that our work will facilitate more research on minority groups.

Acknowledgements

I am very grateful to all of my colleagues and friends who took the time to write the individual chapters in this volume. It took us about a year, but we succeeded in finishing the task at hand. In addition, I would like to thank Dr. Dannie Harrison, Dean of the College of Business and Public Affairs at Murray State University who encouraged me to pursue the project; Dr. Douglas Feig, Professor of Political Science at Mississippi State University, who provided me with an assistant; and Kiffany Rudd, my assistant who made phone calls, searched the web, coded data, and found articles and books. Your services were invaluable.

Finally, I would like to thank Dr. Robert West, former Book Editor at *University Press of America*, for all of his suggestions on making this project a success.

CHAPTER 1

Minority Representation in the Twenty-First Century: An Introduction

Charles E. Menifield

Representation is one of the most pervasive and important processes that occur in a democratic society. In the U. S. federal government, this function has been laid primarily upon those who are elected from individual states to form Congress. States have mimicked the organizational structure of Congress by electing representatives to serve in their general assemblies. Although the idea of representation is certainly not new, the breadth of the concept has indeed evolved as society and government have become more socially, culturally, and politically diverse. Today, we see many different races and ethnic backgrounds in Congress, state legislative assemblies and other elected and appointed government positions. Arguably, some of these changes can be attributed to the Civil Rights Act of 1964, the Voting Rights Act of 1965 (VRA) and its amendments, and the decision rendered by the Supreme Court in *Thornburg v. Gingles* (1986).

It is the main purpose of this book to examine the affects of these and other changes on the descriptive and substantive representation of minority groups (gender and racial) in the various institutions that represent our government today at the federal, state, and local level. Although each of these chapters centers on the concept of representation in the post VRA period and exhibit similar characteristics, each of them is different. Gender and race specific chapters at both levels examine representation from both a descriptive and substantive perspective using various methodologies. Tertiary chapters cover subjects ranging from redistricting to non-voter representation to affirmative action. Data used in the research were taken from a variety of different sources. These include, but are not limited to the following publications and organizations. Full citations are found within the respective chapters.

Almanac of American Politics
Biographical Directory of Congress
Black Americans in Congress
Black Elected Officials: A Statistical Analysis
Book of the States
Center for American Women and Politics
Committees in the U.S. Congress
Congressional Quarterly
Congressional Research Service (CRS)
Council on State Governments
Current Population Survey
General Social Survey
Hispanic American Almanac
Hispanic Americans in Congress
Minorities and Women in State and Local Governments
National Asian American Political Almanac
National Committee for an Effective Congress
National Asso. of Latino Elected and Appointed Officials
National Election Study
National Hispanic Leadership Agenda
National Journal
Politics in America
State Government web sites
Statistical Record of Native North Americans
U.S. Census Bureau
U.S. Statistical Abstract
Washington Post Poll on Race Relations
U.S. Equal Employment Opportunity Commission

Manuscript Layout

Chapters two through four of the text consider African Americans[1], women, and Latinos[2] in Congress respectively. Each of these three chapters provides a plethora of descriptive data. In addition, substantive representation is considered through an examination of committee assignments, leadership assignments, roll call analysis, and other designs. Chapters five and six consider American Indians and Asian Americans primarily at the federal level. However, given the small number of Asian American and American Indian elected officials, the authors of these chapters also consider these groups at the state and local level. While chapter five gives special attention to bill sponsorship when considering substantive representation, chapter six focuses on the use of tribal governments to solve the problems and represent American Indians. Chapter seven examines class, race and the representation of minority political attitudes while looking at the voter, non-voter paradox. Chapter eight completes Part I of the book, Representation at the Federal Level, with an exposition on legislative redistricting and how it has affected representation from a historical perspective.

Part II of the book examines minority group representation at the state and local level. Chapters nine, ten and eleven examine African Americans, women and Hispanics respectively. Similar to the gender and race specific chapters in part one, each of these chapters provide demographic data on the groups along with an assessment of their ability to substantively represent their constituents. Chapter twelve assesses the occupational status of women relative to other groups in the south from 1975-1995, while chapter thirteen presents a case study examination of affirmative action in Mississippi using EEOC data. Chapter fourteen considers bill cosponsorship as a means to the adequate representation of African Americans and women in particular at the state and local level. Lastly, chapter fifteen concludes the text.

Important Questions

Although we consider many perplexing questions in these chapters, several epitomize what our broad goals are. 1) Have minority groups achieved descriptive representation in Congress, state legislatures, state executive offices, local governments and in the bureaucracy? 2) Have minority elected officials been able to substantively represent minority constituents? 3) Have non-minority elected officials represented minority groups effectively? 4.) How successful are the coalitions that minority group form with those in the majority? 5) From an ideological perspective, are all minority groups the same? If so, do these groups pursue similar legislation? 6) What is the future of minority representation in the twenty-first century?

Research Methodology

Unlike the earliest research on representation, which focused on descriptive issues, scholars today tend to center their analysis on substantive representation issues. Our approach however integrates both styles. We note several advantages to conducting descriptive analysis. First, according to the United States Bureau of the Census, the minority population in the U.S. is increasing at a phenomenal rate. For example, the Hispanic population is expected to surpass that of African Americans by the year 2010 (http://www.census.gov/population/www/projections/popproj.html). Both of these groups are growing at a rate faster than that of white Americans. Therefore, the political implications for both groups, given their political behavior, are very significant. Second, the number of minorities elected to public office has continued to increase with each election cycle. As a result, the potential policy impact continues to increase. Hence, the potential for these minority elected officials to substantively represent their constituents likewise increases. However, we do not argue that minority policy makers only represent other minorities, nor do we argue that minority groups need a minority representative to achieve substantive representation (Swain 1993; Whitby 1997; Endersby and Menifield 2000). On the contrary, we simply argue that an increase in the descriptive representation of any minority group may indeed lead to an increase in substantive representation for that minority group. Therefore, it is necessary to consider both concepts to fully appreciate how the groups are represented.

Representation: A Myth?

Representation in simple terms is a legislative function whereby elected or appointed officials attempt to exemplify the beliefs and views of their constituents through various types of behavior patterns. Pitkin (1969), a pioneer in the field, examined the classic literature seeking definitions of representation. She concluded that the classic definitions proposed by Burke, Hobbes, and Mill fell short of explaining what representation is today. Hobbes was likewise sharply criticized for his concept of authorization representation (a man who acts for another and has been given authority to act by another) as was Mill for his argument regarding an expert representative (one who portrays his constituents as having certain desires or views). Hobbes also failed to indicate how the sovereign consulted the citizens to determine their needs or protects their interests. These definitions also fell short in that they worked within the parameters of a black box, where no one actually knows how representation takes place (Pitkin 1969). Pitkin (1967) posited that representation is an activity whereby policy makers are responsive to their constituents. Through successful responsiveness, the chances of conflict between the two are kept at a minimum.

Pitkin's criticisms of these normative theorists were furthered by Eulau (1967) and Pennock and Chapman (1968) who argued that despite the passage of time, a clear-cut definition of representation cannot be made. In particular, Eulau criticized Burke's idea of representation because of its poor application in the modern world.

Burke, in writing about the British House of Commons states:

> The king is the representative of the people; so are the lords; so are the judges. They all are trustees for the people, as well as the commons; because no power is given for the sole sake of the holder; and although government certainly is an institution of divine authority, yet its forms, and the persons who administer it, all originate from the people.

Eulau (1967) centered his analysis on responsiveness and responsibility on the part of the policy-maker. Although similar in context to Burke's ideas of a trustee (a representative who votes as to his/her own conscience and best judgement), he envisioned the role of the representor as one who had expertise, therefore capable of determining what course of action was best for the people. In fact, he said, "government and legislation are matters of reason and judgement, and not of inclination" and "your representative owes you not his industry only, but his judgment" (Pitkin 1969, p. 175).

Wahlke (1971) however, partially agreed with Burke when he argued that the majority of citizens do not have specific policy demands or opinions on issues that may affect them. Nor do citizens attempt to convey the opinions that they do have to their representatives (see also Miller and Stokes 1963). In addition to behaving as trustee, a representative may also behave as a delegate where constituency opinion is reflected in his/her behavior or a politico where the representative chooses between the previous two behavioral typologies as the circumstance change.

Eulau and Karps (1977) expanded the definition of representation by emphasizing that legislators have four areas of concern. First, they argued that a legislator has a service responsibility to particular constituents. This included pursuing and securing legislation that brought benefits to these constituents. Second, legislators had an allocation responsibility to their entire district. In this case, legislators were responsible for securing legislation that would benefit their entire district. The third area was policy responsiveness. Legislators were expected to mingle with their constituents and find out what legislation their constituents' needed or desired. The final area emphasized by Eulau and Karps (1977) was symbolic responsiveness. Symbolic responsiveness builds trust and confidence within constituents that their policy-makers were able to represent them.

Swain (1993) indicated that "descriptive representation can be examined by comparing the incidence of particular demographic characteristics in the population-for example, race, gender, religion, occupation, or age-with those of the representative" (1993, p. 5). However, she also noted, as does others (Whitby 1997; Endersby and Menifield 2000) that demographic similarities between a legislator and his or her constituents do not translate to substantive representation. On the contrary, substantive representation is the ability of the legislator to respond effectively to the demands of constituents (see also Grofman 1982; and Pinderhughes 1987).

Although the current literature clearly emphasizes the merits of substantive representation, we certainly cannot forget the merits of descriptive representation as elucidated by Mansbridge (1999). In an exceptional piece on minority representation, she strongly expounded the values of descriptive representation. First, she indicated that "communication is impaired, often by distrust between the elected officials and their constituents" (p. 652). Essentially, when history is examined, it shows that a person who has experienced the legacy of a group of people can also appreciate what they are going through as an elected or appointed official. Whereas one who does not have that legacy may not be able to fully comprehend and win the trust of the group. Hence, the interests of the minority group fail to crystallize because of distrust and a lack of communication by the citizens to their elected official. The he is not from here and does not care about us attitude may prevail. Next, she indicated that descriptive representation creates a social meaning for the ability to rule. Historically, minority groups have not made binding decisions for minorities because they lack positions of power to do so. However, the ability to elect someone who exhibits demographic characteristics similar to your own provides symbolic rewards for minority citizens. This is exacerbated and legitimized when placed into the context of past overt discrimination. Mansbridge (1999) basically argued that history has a reinforcing quality when it comes to politics. Voters want to see someone who looks like them in office. Black voters tend to support black candidates and Hispanic voters tend to support Hispanic candidates. Although the support of women candidates by other women changes based on the office, region, and other factors, women tend to support other women. Why? Because they exhibit certain basic characteristics that the voter can immediately correlate with. Although Swain (1993) and others seriously question the ability of minority congressmen to substantively represent their constituents, it does not eliminate the fact that minority groups in general feel a kinship to those who exhibit similar demographic characteristics. Darcy, Welch, and Clark stated, "women have knowledge and insights into some matters that men do not have" (1987, p.12). Similar comparisons were made between Hispanic congressmen and the cultural connection that they have with their Hispanic constituents (Vega 1993). Mansbridge (1999) suggested that this relationship existed among all minority groups. Although the voter may sacrifice substantive benefits for this descriptive representation, these probable benefits do not outweigh the historical context.

Important Legislation Affecting Minority Representation

Although there were many pieces of legislation, such as the Civil Rights Acts, and individuals, such as Lyndon Baines Johnson and Martin Luther King Jr., that had positive affects on increasing the representation of minorities in elected and appointed positions, two particular pieces come to the forefront: The Voting Rights Act of 1965 (and the subsequent amendments) and the Supreme Court's decision in *Thornburg v. Gingles* (1986). Without these two political decisions, it is questionable what the face of our governmental institutions would look like today.

Racial minorities were given the right to vote in 1870 (15th amendment) and women in 1920 (19th amendment), but it was not until the 1960s that enforcing legislation was passed solidifying this right to racial minorities. History does however show us that women have also benefited from this legislation.

In 1940, about 3% of the African American voting age population in the south were registered to vote. By 1964, 43% of the group were registered to vote. However, registration did not lead to a dramatic increase in voting behavior, nor did it lead to a dramatic increase in the election of African American candidates (Menifield and Julian 1998). Despite the passage of the Civil Rights Act of 1964, which made literacy tests illegal for determining voting rights, and a strong Civil Rights Movement in the south, white resistance prevailed. In 1964, President Lyndon Johnson, along with efforts from the Southern Leadership Conference, began a campaign to remove the barriers that have been put into place by white political leaders in the south. Their efforts culminated in the passage of the Voting Rights Act of 1965 (VRA). Section 4 of the Act completely removed the literacy test, which had been put into place to prevent African Americans from voting. This Section was further strengthened in 1975 when an additional language minority trigger formula was added. Section 5 required all states to clear their voting statutes with the Attorney General or the U.S. District Court (Davidson 1994).

Sections 6 and 7 of the VRA gave the Attorney General much needed authority to appoint federal officials as examiners to ensure that legally qualified persons were free to register in all elections. Further, Section 8 gave the Attorney General the authority to send observers to ensure that these qualified voters could indeed vote in the elections. Lastly, Section 9 provided the detail for challenging the list of eligible voters drawn up by the federal examiners. Other parts of the Act allowed the registrars to enforce the 24th amendment, which abolished the poll tax (Davidson 1994).

Probably the most important component added to the VRA of 1965 came in 1982 when Congress voted to amend the Act forbidding vote dilution. Although changes in registration and voting patterns were prominent, this amendment to Section 2 of the amendment prevented state legislatures from passing laws that would provide fewer opportunities for protected classes from participating in the process and to select the person of their choice.

In 1986, the Supreme Court further expanded Section 2 of the VRA. In rendering the majority decision in *Thornburg v. Gingles* (1986), Justice William Brenan indicated that the Court had adopted several new criteria in determining minority dilution. First, he indicated that the minority group in an area must be large and geographically compact in order to constitute a majority in at least one single member district. Second, the group must be politically cohesive. Lastly, the majority vote must also be politically cohesive so as to defeat the minority candidate. Following this decision, many state and local governments created at least one district where minorities could elect another minority candidate. By so doing, these states staved off possible lawsuits.

When the Voting Rights Act of 1965 was passed, there were only 70 African Americans who held political office in the southern states covered by the Act. In the early 1980s, this number had increased to more than 2,500. By 1997, there were 8,656 African Americans holding elected offices (Bositis 1999).

Increases were also seen in the number of Latino representatives in Congress and state and local governments. For example, there were 3 Hispanics in Congress in 1965 and 17 in 1996 (Santos and Huerta 2001). At the state level, there were 114 Hispanic state legislators in 1985 and 186 in 2000 (NALEO 2000). Even more drastic increases have been seen among women in elected positions, particularly at the congressional level where they have more than doubled in the last thirty years.

Conclusion

This textbook does not attempt to answer every possible question concerning the representation of minority groups in the U.S. political system. Nor does it attempt to bring to closure the concept of representation. On the contrary, we want to stimulate further interest in the subject and encourage scholarly dialogue in an area of the discipline that is very dynamic.

References

Bositis, David. 1999. *Black Elected Officials: A Statistical Summary 1993-1997*. Washington, D.C.: Joint Center for Political and Economic Studies.

Darcy, R., Susan Welch and Janet Clark. 1987. *Women, Elections, and Representation*. Longman: NY, New York.

Davidson, Chandler. 1994. "The Recent Evolution of Voting Rights Law Affecting Racial and Language Minorities." In *Quiet Revolution in the South: The Impact of the Voting Rights Act 1965-1990*. eds. Chandler Davidson and Bernard Grofman. NJ: Princeton University Press.

Endersby, James W. and Charles E. Menifield. 2000. "Representation, Ethnicity, and Congress: Black and Hispanic Representatives and Constituencies." In *Black and Multiracial Politics in America*, eds. Yvette Alex-Assensoh and Lawrence Hanks. New York, NY: New York University Press.

Eulau, Heinz. 1967. "Changing Views of Representation." In *Contemporary Political Science: Toward Empirical Theory.* ed. Ithiel de Sola Pool. NY: McGraw Hill.

Eulau, Heinz and Paul D. Karps. 1977. "The Puzzle of Representation: Specifying Components of Responsiveness." *Legislative Studies Quarterly* 2: 233-254.

Grofman, Bernard. 1982. "Should Representatives Be Typical of Their Constituents?" In *Representation and Redistricting Issues.* ed. Bernard Grofman. Lexington, MA: Lexington Books.

http://www.census.gov/population/www/projections/popproj.html

Mansbridge, Jane. 1999. "Should Blacks Represent Blacks and Women Represent Women? A Contingent "Yes." *The Journal of Politics* 61: 628-657.

Menifield, Charles E. 1996. "Influence of Minority Groups in Congress: The Black, Women's Issues and Hispanic Caucuses." Doctoral dissertation completed at the University of Missouri-Columbia.

Miller, Warren, and Donald Stokes. 1963. "Constituency Influence in Congress." *American Political Science Review* 57:45-56.

NALEO (National Association of Latino Elected and Appointed Officials). 2000. "Latino Elected Officials in Top Positions." http://www.naleo.org/

Santos, Adolfo and Carlos Huerta. 2001. "Latino Representation in Congress." In *Minority Representation in Congress in the Twenty First Century,* ed. Charles E. Menifield. Lanham, MD: University Press of America.

Swain, Carol. 1993. *Black Faces, Black Interests: The Representation of African Americans in Congress.* Cambridge: Harvard University Press.

Pennock, J. Roland and John W. Chapman. 1968. *Representation.* NY: Atherton Press.

Pinderhughes, Diane. 1987. *Race and Ethnicity in Chicago Politics.* IL: University of Illinois Press.

Pitkin, Hanna. 1967. *The Concept of Representation.* Berkeley, CA: University of California Press.

Pitkin, Hanna F. 1969. *Representation.* New York, NY: Atherton Press.

Thornburg v. Gingles, 478 U.S. 30 (1986)

Vega, Arturo. 1993. "Variations and Sources of Group Cohesiveness in the Black and Hispanic Congressional Caucuses." *Latino Studies Journal* 14: 79-92.

Wahlke, John C. 1971. "Policy Demands and System Support: The Role of the Represented." *British Journal of Political Science* 1:271-290.

Whitby, Kenneth J. 1997. *The Color of Representation.* University of Michigan Press: Ann Arbor.

Notes

1 The terms black and African American are used interchangeably throughout the book.

2 Although all Americans of Spanish descent are not from the same country or region of the globe, we use the terms Latino and Hispanic interchangeably.

CHAPTER 2

African American Representation in Congress: Then and Now

Charles E. Menifield and Charles E. Jones

In 1870, the first three African Americans were elected to serve in Congress. Hiram Revels of Mississippi was elected to the Senate while Joseph Rainey of South Carolina and Jefferson Long of Georgia were elected to the House of Representatives. All three members joined the ranks of the Republican Party. By 1875, eight African Americans occupied seats in Congress. However, the tide began to change with subsequent elections. The number of African Americans dropped dramatically at the close of Reconstruction. Almost one hundred years would pass before there were more than seven African Americans in Congress (Whitby 1997; Singh 1998). During this period, Congress reverted back to a predominantly white male institution.

This chapter documents African American representation in Congress in the pre and post Voting Rights Act era. In conducting our analysis, we first provide a historical overview of African American representation in Congress beginning in 1960. This section examines the influx of African Americans who have been elected to Congress. Next, we put forth a framework to address the implications that the proliferation of black legislators poses for the purposive racial orientation of the Congressional Black Caucus (CBC). We then assess the ideological orientation and voting behavior of African American members of Congress. Lastly, we utilize OLS regression analysis to determine the impact of CBC membership on the voting behavior of caucus members.

Proliferation of African American Congressional Representation

Five years prior to the passage of the Voting Rights Act of 1965, there were four African Americans in Congress. Table 2-1 documents the proliferation of black lawmakers at the national level from 1960 thru 2000. As the table indicates, African Americans, Hispanics and women all enjoyed electoral success at the congressional level during this period. The number of women in Congress has particularly grown since 1990. This new found electoral success enjoyed by African American and Hispanic candidates was the direct result of legislative redistricting following the 1990 census and the Supreme Court's decision in *Thornburg v. Gingles* (1986). The court indicated that purposely diluting minority voting strength was unconstitutional. As a result of that decision, congressional districts were redrawn to include a large number of African American voters in particular districts. The election of 1992 was a historical milestone for minority representation in Congress. Each group, African Americans, Hispanics and women significantly increased the size of their respective legislative delegations.

The positive role that the Supreme Court played in the expansion of black representatives ceased in 1993 when the composition of the court changed. The views of the court regarding legislative redistricting became more conservative. The first among many cases was *Shaw v. Reno* (1992) where the Court ruled that purposely creating a majority minority district may in fact infringe upon the rights of white voters. Since that decision, the court has continued to render verdicts that have dismantled or substantially changed these districts all over the country. Fortunately, only a couple of African American and Hispanic congressmen have lost their seats thus far, as a result of these decisions (See Chapter 8 for a full discussion of these cases).

Table 2-1 Minority Representation in Congress

	1960	1965	1970	1975	1980	1985	1990	1995	2000
Afr. American	4	6	10	18	16	20	24	39	38
Women	20	13	15	19	23	25	28	55	65
Hispanic	3	5	6	7	7	10	11	17	18
Total	27	24	31	42	46	59	64	114	121

Note: Contiguous U.S. only.

Sources: Kanellos, Nicolas. 1997. *The Hispanic American Almanac.* (ed) 2nd Edition. Gale Publishers: Detroit, MI. Whicker, Marcia L. and Lois Duke Whitaker. 1999. "Women in Congress." In *Women in Politics: Outsiders or Insiders.* (ed.) Lois Duke Whitaker. Upper Saddle River, NJ. *Statistical Abstract of the United States*: U.S. Bureau of the Census: Washington, D.C. Various Issues.

Table 2-2 indicates that African Americans have maintained the same level of congressional representation during periods of a divided government in which the President was Republican and at least one house of Congress was controlled by Republicans. The table also shows that the greatest percentage growth occurred while Democrats controlled the House and Senate in 1992.

Table 2-2 African American Congressional Representation 1960-1998

Cong.	Year	President	Congress Controlled by	# of African Americans	% of Total
86th	1960	Kennedy (D)	Dem. (H&S)	4	0.9%
87th	1962	Kennedy (D)	Dem. (H&S)	4	0.9
88th	1964	Johnson (D)	Dem. (H&S)	6	1.4
89th	1966	Johnson (D)	Dem. (H&S)	6	1.4
90th	1968	Nixon ®	Dem. (H&S)	10	2.3
91st	1970	Nixon ®	Dem. (H&S)	10	2.3
92nd	1972	Nixon ®	Dem. (H&S)	15	3.4
93rd	1974	Ford ®	Dem. (H&S)	16	3.7
94th	1976	Carter (D)	Dem. (H&S)	18	4.1
95th	1978	Carter (D)	Dem. (H&S)	17	3.9
96th	1980	Reagan ®	Dem. (H&S)	16	3.7
97th	1982	Reagan ®	Dem. (H) Rep. (S)	18	4.1
98th	1984	Reagan ®	Dem. (H) Rep. (S)	21	4.8
99th	1986	Reagan ®	Dem. (H) Rep. (S)	21	4.8
100th	1988	Bush ®	Dem. (H) Rep. (S)	23	5.3
101st	1990	Bush ®	Dem. (H&S)	24	5.5
102nd	1992	Clinton (D)	Dem. (H&S)	25	5.7
103rd	1994	Clinton (D)	Dem. (H&S)	39	9.0
104th	1996	Clinton (D)	Rep. (H&S)	38	8.7
105th	1998	Clinton (D)	Rep. (H&S)	38	8.7

Note: This table excludes non-voting minority representatives from the Virgin Islands and Guam.

Sources: Bositis, David A. 1998. *Black Elected Officials: A Statistical Summary 1993-1997*. Joint Center for Political and Economic Studies: Washington, D.C. Menifield, Charles E. and Frank Julian. 1998. "Changing the Face of Congress: African-Americans in the Twenty-First Century. *Western Journal of Black Studies* 22, p. 18-30.

Representation of Minority Groups in the U.S.

Every state in the Deep South, except Arkansas, has elected at least one African American member to Congress. In fact, the number of African American congressmen from southern states increased to 12 members from 1990 to 1995 following the *Thornburg v. Gingles* decision (See Table 2-3). California and New York consistently have had the largest number of African American congressmen. Over half of remaining states have only one African American member of Congress. Although African Americans as a group do not tend to support or run under the Republican banner, two Republican African Americans were elected to serve in Congress in the 1990s. Gary Franks of Connecticut served from 1991-1996 and J.C. Watts

Table 2-3 Geographical Distribution of African American Congressional Representatives – 1960-2000

	1960	1965	1970	1975	1980	1985	1990	1995	2000
Alabama	0	0	0	0	0	0	0	1	1
California	0	1	1	3	3	4	4	4	4
Connecticut*	0	0	0	0	0	0	0	1	0
Dist. of Columbia	0	0	0	1	1	1	1	1	1
Florida	0	0	0	0	0	0	0	3	3
Georgia	0	0	0	1	0	0	1	3	3
Illinois	1	1	1	2	2	2	3	4	3
Indiana	0	0	0	0	0	1	0	0	1
Louisiana	0	0	0	0	0	0	0	2	1
Maryland	0	0	0	1	1	1	1	2	2
Massachusetts	0	0	1	1	0	0	0	0	0
Michigan	1	2	2	2	2	2	2	2	2
Mississippi	0	0	0	0	0	0	1	1	1
Missouri	0	0	1	1	1	2	2	1	1
New Jersey	0	0	0	0	0	0	1	1	1
New York	1	1	2	2	2	3	4	4	4
North Carolina	0	0	0	0	0	0	0	2	2
Ohio	0	0	1	1	1	1	1	1	1
Oklahoma*	0	0	0	0	0	0	0	1	1
Pennsylvania	1	1	1	1	1	1	1	1	1
South Carolina	0	0	0	0	0	0	0	1	1
Tennessee	0	0	0	1	1	1	1	1	1
Texas	0	0	0	1	1	1	1	1	2
Virginia	0	0	0	0	0	0	0	1	1
Total	4	6	10	18	16	20	24	39	38

Republican Member

Sources: Singh, Robert. 1998. The Congressional Black Caucus: Racial Politics in the U.S. Congress. *Sage: Thousand Oaks, CA. Congressional Black Caucus Membership Directory. www.freenet.tlh.fl.us/~tacot1bm/cbcdir.html.*

Table 2-4 African Americans in Congress, by Gender

	1960	1965	1970	1975	1980	1985	1990	1995	2000
Male	4	6	9	14	14	19	23	29	25
Female	0	0	1	4	2	1	1	10	13
Total	4	6	10	18	16	20	24	39	38

Sources: Singh, Robert. 1998. The Congressional Black Caucus: Racial Politics in the U.S. Congress. *Sage: Thousand Oaks, CA.* Statistical Abstract of the United States. *U.S. Bureau of the Census: Washington, D.C. Various Issues.*

of Oklahoma was elected in 1995 and continues to serve. Both are members of the House of Representatives (see Appendix 1-1 for a complete listing of all African Americans in Congress since 1965).

Although African American men outnumber African American women, the number of African American women increased more than ten fold from 1960 to 2000 (see Table 2-4). Similar to African American men, five of the ten women elected after 1990 were from the southern and southwestern states. This increase was not only limited to African American women. The number of women in Congress doubled from 1989 (28) to 2000 (56).

Ironically, when we considered the actual population of states where there are significant numbers of African Americans, we found that states with the largest percentages of African Americans have the fewest representatives in Congress. One third of Mississippi's and Louisiana's population and nearly one third of South Carolina's population is African American. However, each of these states has only one African American representative in Congress (See Table 2-5).

Similarly, although African Americans comprise over one quarter of Alabama's population, the state has only one African American representative. Georgia is the one exception to this apparent trend. The state's population is 28% percent African American and has three African American representatives (Menifield and Julian 1998). However, the major difference between Georgia and the other Deep South states is the addition of a large metropolitan area with a substantial number of African American voters. Hence, it is a lot more difficult to dilute the African American vote. The ability to create a fairly homogenous ethnic district is a lot more difficult to create when the African American voters are dispersed. The creation of such a district would more than likely not satisfy the Department of Justice or the Supreme Court if a suit were filed.

Table 2-5 States with Large African American Populations, by African Americans in Congress (1995 pop. data)

	Total Pop. (000)	% African. American	# of Cong. Districts (1998)	# of African American Representatives (1998)
Alabama	4,253	26%	7	1
California	31,589	8	52	4
Connecticut	3,275	9	6	0
DC	554	64	1	1
Florida	14,166	15	23	3
Georgia	7,201	28	11	3
Illinois	11,830	15	20	3
Indiana	5,804	8	10	1
Louisiana	4,342	42	5	1
Maryland	5,042	27	8	1
Massachusetts	6,074	6	10	0
Michigan	9,549	14	16	2
Mississippi	2,697	36	5	1
Missouri	5,324	11	9	1
New Jersey	7,945	15	13	1
New York	18,136	18	31	4
North Carolina	7,195	22	12	2
Ohio	11,151	11	19	1
Oklahoma	3,278	8	6	1
Pennsylvania	12,072	10	21	1
South Carolina	3,673	30	6	1
Tennessee	5,256	16	9	1
Texas	18,724	12	30	2
Virginia	6,618	20%	11	1

Source: U.S. Bureau of the Census, www.census.gov/populations/socdemo/voting/96cps/tab4A.txt.

Paradoxically, the proliferation of African American congressional legislators poses a threat to institutionalized African American congressional participation. Specifically, congressional observers (Swain 1992; Steel 1993; Katz 1993) suggest that the emergence of a new wave of African American politicians had political priorities that will ultimately undermine the racial raison d'etre of the Congressional Black Caucus. In order to explore fully the ramifications of the influx of African American members of the Congress, we first discuss the role of the Congressional Black Caucus as a mechanism for collective African American political action.

The CBC: A Racial Congressional Subgroup

The Congressional Black Caucus (CBC), a bipartisan racially based informal organization, constitutes the embodiment of African American collective participation in the congressional process. The organization reflects the congressional manifestation of the transformation from protest to electoral politics by African American political actors. The primary objective of the CBC is "to serve as legislative advocates in the U.S. Congress and to represent the interests of a national constituency, while addressing the concerns of our particular districts" (Jones 1987a, 221). The at-large African American community in the United States is that national constituency.

Formally organized in 1971, the CBC is generally viewed as one of the more liberal informal organizations that populated the congressional arena in the early 1970's (Cohodas 1985, 75). In the midst of rampant decentralization and the dispersion of power spawned by a bevy of internal rule changes, congressional observers witnessed the proliferation of informal organizations defined as "identifiable, self-conscious relatively stable units of interacting members whose relationships are not officially prescribed by statutes and rules" (Fiellin 1962,76). The prevalence of informal organizations in the contemporary Congress was, in large part, due to the power vacuums and policy voids created by the congressional reforms of the 1970s (Stevens, Mulhollan, and Rundquist 1981).

However, the formation of the Congressional Black Caucus was a by-product of external political forces rather than the internal legislative dynamics that characterized the development of traditional congressional subgroups (Smith 1981a; Barnett 1975). Racial caucuses like the CBC are manifestations of the black power concept that rest upon the premise of independent collective action (Carmichael and Hamilton 1967). Smith documents the proliferation of racial caucuses after the enunciation of the black power political strategy in 1966 (Smith 1981b, 436).

In the case of the CBC, the organization promotes the aggregate interests of African Americans in the congressional process. This critical function is sharpened by the national standing of the members of the Congressional Black Caucus. CBC members are the highest-ranking African American elected officials in the country, holding positions in the central policy-making body of the nation. By virtue of its political status, the CBC assumes extra-leadership obligations on behalf of the African American populace. Indeed, a leadership void within the African American political officialdom was a contributing factor in the formation of the CBC (Henry 1977).

Heretofore, the Congressional Black Caucus has constituted the institutionalization of African American participation in the congressional process. "Institutionalization" implies goal-consensus, permanence, internal complexity and the regularity of rules and procedures (Polsby 1968). The continuity of the CBC — an existence that spans two decades and other organizational attributes such as goal-agreement, governing procedures, specializations of tasks, auxiliary support mechanisms, and fund raising capabilities reflect the reutilization of collective African American participation in Congress (Barnett 1977).

The organizational components of this racial legislative subgroup include a thirty eight-member body with a permanent three-member staff, the Congressional Black Caucus Foundation (CBCF), and the Congressional Black Caucus Political Action Committee (CBC PAC). The CBC is guided by a leadership hierarchy that consists of a chairperson, vice-chair, secretary, and treasurer. CBC officers are elected on an annual basis via secret ballot. Members meet weekly to formulate policy positions that are reached by a two-thirds vote; however, official CBC positions are not binding on dissenting members.

Membership in the CBC requires that African American congressional members perform extra-legislative responsibilities and duties. First, constituency service tasks of CBC members usually transcend their "formal geographical constituencies" (Fenno 1978, 1-8). The CBC membership is often inundated with casework requests from African Americans who do not reside in their constitutionally prescribed districts. The Black Coaches Association's petition for the CBC to intervene in a dispute over the reduced scholarship policy of the NCAA during the 1994 basketball season is but one such example. In addition, CBC members also chair organizational task forces and coordinate "Brain Trusts" which are advisory councils of policy experts.

Membership dues of $5000 annually finance CBC operations. A three-person staff directed by an executive director assists Caucus activities. The CBC staff provides legislative and media services to the membership, although its functions were significantly reduced in response to new procedures regulating informal organizations adopted by the House of Representatives in 1982.

The expansion of the functions of the Congressional Black Caucus Foundation was also an artifact of the 1982 rule change. The Foundation now sponsors a congressional fellowship program for scholars and grad-

uate students, conducts policy research, and coordinates the highly successful annual CBC "Legislative Weekend." The "Legislative Weekend"
is the primary fund raising event of the CBC, drawing from the largess
of the nation's corporate sector and the expanded post-civil rights
African American middle class. The ambitious plans of the CBC PAC
have never fully materialized. Initially conceived to finance the campaigns of African American office-seekers, the CBC PAC has yet to
amass the necessary funds to fulfill its objective.

A recent organizational adaptation has been the addition of an
associate membership core. In 1988, the CBC adopted a restrictive
membership policy for white members of Congress (CBCF 1992, 71).
Under the associate membership policy, non-black members pay
reduced membership fees ($1000) and enjoy limited voting and partici-
pation privileges. The adoption of the associate membership component
partially modifies the organization's unofficial racially exclusive policy.
Although the formal regulations of the CBC do not prohibit white members, a long-standing informal policy has precluded their participation.
The CBC rejected the formal request for membership in 1976 by Pete
Stark, a white Congressman from California. The CBC's refusal to
admit Stark was consistent with the imperatives of the black power
political concept.

Over the course of its twenty-year existence, the accrual of seniority has permitted the CBC membership to acquire an array of institutional power positions in the House. At the time of his resignation to
assume the directorship of the United Negro College Fund in 1991,
William F. Gray (PA-2) occupied the third highest ranking position in
the chamber. Before his election to the majority whip position, Gray also
chaired the Budget Committee in the 99th and 100th Congresses. Other
former CBC members who chaired full standing committees include
Augustus Hawkins (CA-29), Education and Labor Committee (99th-
101st); Robert Nix (PA-2), Post Office and Civil Service (95th); and
Parren Mitchell (MD-7), Small Business (97th-99th). During the 102nd
Congress (1991-92), CBC members chaired four standing committees
and one select committee. Table 2-6 shows the total number of African
American committee chairs and vice chairs in the House of
Representatives from 1972-2000 (92nd-106th Congress). As the table
shows, the number of committee chairs reached a crescendo in1986 and
has since dropped. However, the relegation to ranking member is merely a function of the shift of power from Democrats to Republicans.

Table 2-6 African American Leadership on Committees in the House of Representatives by Congress

Congress	C.C.	R.M.	S.C.	R.M2.	# of Comm. in House	% Leaders in House
1972 92nd	0	0	3	0	15	3.4
1974 93rd	1	0	5	0	15	3.4
1976 94th	1	0	9	0	17	3.9
1978 95th	1	0	10	0	17	3.9
1980 96th	1	0	11	0	15	3.4
1982 97th	1	0	15	0	17	3.9
1984 98th	6	0	13	0	20	4.6
1986 99th	7	0	17	0	20	4.6
1988 100th	5	0	16	0	22	5.1
1990 101st	4	0	13	0	23	5.3
1992 102nd	3	0	15	0	25	5.7
1994 103rd	0	4	0	9	38	8.7
1996 104th	0	4	0	9	38	8.7
1998 105th	0	3	0	14	38	8.7
2000 106th	0	4	0	13	37	8.5

Note: Non-voting members are not included in the # in House category. C.C.= Committee Chair, R.M.=Ranking Minority, S.C. Subcommittee Chair, R.M2= Ranking Minority on the Subcommittee.

Sources: Data for the 106th-96th Congress is from *Politics in America*, Congressional Quarterly: Washington, D.C. Data for the 91st – 95th Congress is from *the Almanac of America Politics*. 1980. E.P. Dutton: NY.

In contrast to the era of the pre-reform Congress, the power and prerogative of committee chairpersons are now constrained by party caucus rules. Consequently, CBC members who head committees are precluded from acting unilaterally on behalf of the collective interest of African Americans. This vortex of cross-pressures provides a useful framework for analyzing the future role of the CBC.

The Vortex of Political Cross-Pressures: An Analytical Framework

Our understanding of the influx of the CBC membership is informed when viewed through the prism of conflicting political objectives. On the one hand, consistent with its racial collective raison d'etre, the CBC promotes the aggregate interests of the African American community. However, this political pursuit is often impaired by atomistic legislative dynamics that encourage individual political behavior. The CBC is confronted with the vexing task of securing racial collective outcomes without succumbing to the individualistic dictates of the congressional process, for to yield to these atomistic influents would render the CBC a muted version of its black power imperative.

The institutional arrangement of Congress sets in motion an inevitable host of cross-pressures, conflicting demands, and divided loyalties that routinely confront members. Clem (1989, 12-13) observes that "Congress receives unremitting pressure from several sources, each of which has expectations that produce divergent, contradictory directions." The internal constraints stemming from the dualist pressures inherent in Congress undergird recent assessments of the CBC.

For example, Swain (1992, 128) writes, "It is difficult to anticipate the future of the Caucus, but as more and more African-Americans climb the leadership structure, it seems likely that it will cease being an organization geared primarily toward advancing a black agenda," while congressional scholar Norman Ornstein proposes that "as you have people moving up to real policy power . . . to a degree you will get a redefinition of the role of the Caucus" (Pianin 1987, A16). These appraisals are, no doubt, rooted in the implicit assumption that the gravitational pull of atomistic legislative factors will compel CBC members to conform to conventional congressional behavior. Competing constituency pressures (Fiorina 1974), an adherence to institutional commitments (Fears 1985; Kenworthy 1989), and divergent political styles (Cohen 1987; Henry 1992) are all dynamics that are thought to ultimately weaken the racial collective purpose of the CBC.

The salience of constituency casework is a well-documented facet of legislative life (Froman 1967). Serving one's constituency constitutes an important component of the formal linkage mechanism between citizen and legislator. Campaign strategies, legislative expertise, and staff allocations are structured around this important legislative task. Constituency service provides a cornerstone for the reelection efforts of congressional members (Mayhew 1974).

Historically, the homogeneity of congressional districts represented by African American members of Congress minimized the tension between articulating the policy objectives of their perspective districts and those of the national African American populace. However, a recent trend toward greater diversification of CBC-held districts has led to speculations of CBC future divisiveness (Katz 1993). An increase in both majority-white districts and rural southern congressional jurisdictions occupied by

CBC members may undermine the shared outlook of the membership. Kenworthy (1989, A22) observes that "the future members who are also likely to come from multi-race districts far different from those of many older black lawmakers are less wedded to the tenets and politics that have traditionally bound the caucus together." The vote of Mike Espy, the former Secretary of Agriculture and the first African American elected (1986) to Congress from Mississippi since Reconstruction, in support of the position of the National Rifle Association reflects the cross-pressures of a heterogeneous CBC constituency.

Another equally troublesome cross-current for the CBC emanates from the acquisition of institutional power positions. As CBC members are absorbed into the leadership positions of the House, they are confronted with the task of fulfilling the prerequisites of institutional positions and also promoting the collective objectives of the CBC. The power of the Democratic Caucus to appoint committee chairs accentuates the importance of effective leadership in these positions. Committee chairmen are expected to forge coalitions and produce legislation consistent with party interests or risk losing their positions. Congressional scholar Norman Ornstein predicts that "if a black chairman can't pull together a coalition, and people say he wasn't persuasive or skillful, the power can backfire. Democrats will simply vote him out of office" (Fears 1985, 909). The leadership style of former CBC member William F. Gray exhibited a sensitivity to this dilemma. Under his chairmanship of the Budget Committee, Gray voted "present" rather than voting in the affirmative for the CBC alternative budget proposal.

Similarly, the emergence of a new generation of African American politicians also threatens the CBC's original mission of promoting the collective interest of African Americans. Martin Kilson, a prominent student of African American politics, describes this new wave of African American elected officials as transethnic politicians (Kilson 1989, 528-530). Transethnic politicians stress management and political skills over oratory ability. Kilson (1989, 529) suggests that a central precept of this style of leadership is a political maturation, which entails the avoidance of racially confrontational politics. Congressional observers (Cohen 1987; Broder 1989) contend that this new generation of African American congressional members offers a more pragmatic and consensus-oriented approach to government than the first wave of African American elected officials. Cohen (1987, 2432) writes that the new generation of African American congressional members "are pragmatic, articulate and young. They have government and business experience, not solely the civil rights profiles." Hence, the divergent political style of the transethnic legislator represents another potential distraction to the racial collective orientation of the CBC. In short, the atomistic dynamics of a highly fragmented Congress may foster political behaviors among CBC members that "obscure the reasons for institutionalizing a racially based political caucus and thus undermine their legitimacy" (Barnett 1977a, 23).

Thus far, we contend that the debate surrounding the future role of the CBC has been uneven and narrow. A critical missing component of this discussion is the racial imperatives of African American leadership which rest on the premise that a common experience of racial subordination exists among people of African descent in the United States. African American political leaders are, therefore, expected to assume extra-leadership responsibilities. Chief among these duties is representing the collective interests of African Americans. The special obligation of African American leadership emanating from this shared history of racial oppression fortifies the CBC's pursuit of a racial collective agenda.

Despite early vacillation over its proper role, the CBC membership has consistently operated as a mechanism of constructive opposition on behalf of African Americans outside their formal constituencies. The performance of this important informal group function, constructive opposition by CBC members, stems from the membership's acceptance of its legislative responsibilities that transcend the boundaries of individual constituencies. A CBC member comments on this leadership obligation: "You do wear two hats in that you don't just represent the constituents of your district, you feel a responsibility to represent blacks on a national basis" (Jones 1987a, 228). This collective leadership outlook predates the creation of the CBC. Adam Clayton Powell, who first entered the House of Representatives in 1945, recalled, "As soon as I was elected to Congress my mail involving cases for me to handle, people for me to see, came in such large quantities from behind the color curtain of America that the work of my own constituents had to suffer" (Powell 1971, 73). The persistence of this tradition partially accounts for the African American congressional delegation's participation in racialized political action. Despite divergent political styles and generational replacements, every individual of African descent to serve in Congress since the formation of the CBC in 1971 (with one exception) has formally joined the racial legislative subgroup.

Moreover, the coalescing bond that unites CBC members stems from the unique condition of African Americans, a predicament that often entails innovative political strategies and tactics. One of the founding members of the CBC recalled that the African American congressional delegation preferred to form a separate racial legislative unofficial group rather than work through the Democratic Study Group, a liberal-based informal organization. The member explained that "the DSG is fine, but we felt that there were certain issues on which we have a special interest because of the black experience. The [CBC] was to give us a better bargaining position" (Adair 1977, 21).

The collective political disposition of the CBC is further reinforced by the national status of the organization within the black political officialdom. The prestige and resources of national office situate the CBC prominently within the African American leadership hierarchy. The CBC performs vital roles in both the Black Leadership Forum and Black Leadership Roundtable, two post-civil rights coalition-based configurations designed to maximize the political influence of African Americans (Jones 1987b, 523). However, the CBC's legitimacy and status among the constellation of black political and civil rights organizations largely rest on its continual articulation and enactment of group interests.

We suggest that the shared experience of African Americans and the attendant leadership requisites arising from that history provide a countervailing balance to the fragmented dynamics of Congress. Smith (1981a, 17) astutely observes that "whether blacks form racially exclusive organizations and pursue race specific issues in the policy process is more a function of the imperatives of the black condition in the United States than the wishes of black political elites." The failure to properly locate the CBC in this broader context overlooks important solidarity factors that reinforce collective political action. Furthermore, the neglect to recognize the nexus between the subordinate status of African Americans and the extra-leadership responsibilities spawned by this material reality often results in circumscribed assessments of African American congressional behavior. A case in point is a positive commentary on Julian Dixon by noted congressional observer David Broder. Broder extols the alternative leadership style of Dixon, a style which eschews racially based politics (Broder 1989, A9). However, Broder glosses over the discrepancy between the alleged cross-racial approach of Dixon and the fact that Dixon once chaired the CBC, a racial based informal organization. Moreover, the short-lived covenant between the CBC and the Louis Farrakhan-led Nation of Islam was a political coalition (Duke 1993, A3) contrary to transethnic precepts. The gravitational pull of racial leadership obligations may partially account for such inconsistencies.

In sum, we argue that the aforementioned racial solidarity factors stimulate collective political behavior among CBC members. The racial imperatives of African American leadership function to deflect, temper, and sometimes negate the atomistic dynamics of congressional politics. This is not to suggest that racial solidarity factors are omnipotent and, therefore, immunize African Americans legislators from the fragmented forces of Congress. Rather, we merely assert that the intensity of these factors is often minimized by congressional observers. We now turn to an assessment of the ideological orientation and voting behavior of African American members of Congress.

Ideology and Voting Behavior

Research shows that descriptive representation does not necessarily translate to substantive representation (Swain 1993). However, before one can determine the impact a legislative subgroup has on legislation, it is important to determine the extent to which group members share similar ideological orientations. Key vote data drawn from the *National Journal* indicate that African American members of Congress constitute the most distinct liberal bloc within the House of Representatives. Tables 2-7 thru 2-9 show that the African American lawmakers are at the minimum 10 percentage points more liberal than Democrats, Republicans, Women and Hispanic legislators in the three policy areas considered during the four years: 1984, 1989, 1994 and 1999.

Table 2-7 Liberal Ideological Ratings on Economic Policy

	1984	1989	1994	1999
African Am.	83%	87%	80%	81%
Democrats	66	68	66	73
Republicans	20	20	15	22
Women	54	54	59	60
Hispanics	69	68	65	70

Table 2-8 Liberal Ideological Ratings on Social Policy

	1984	1989	1994	1999
African Am.	84%	86%	83%	81%
Democrats	64	66	68	71
Republicans	23	24	21	27
Women	57	59	66	69
Hispanics	70	69	67	70

Table 2-9 Liberal Ideological Ratings on Foreign Policy

	1984	1989	1994	1999
African Am.	86%	87%	76%	83%
Democrats	63	66	67	74
Republicans	20	21	18	25
Women	55	56	63	64
Hispanics	61	65	58	71

Another important asset of a legislative subgroup is voting cohesion. Using voting data on key legislation, we conduct cohesion analysis for African Americans, Democrats, Republicans, Women and Hispanics in Congress for: 1977, 1981, 1989 and 1999. Our findings show that African American congressmen are the most cohesive of all these groups (see tables 2-10 thru 2-12). They are the most cohesive on economic and social policy. With the exception of four cases, African Americans are more than ten percentage points higher than any other group in every category for every four years (see also Gile and Jones 1996 and Jones 1987c). The data in these tables reaffirm a very important point that was made regarding the CBC and its ability to represent the interest of African Americans in the country. By voting as a bloc on legislation suggests a lot of agreement within the Caucus. For example, the cohesion level scores on social policy consistently ranges in the 91%-96% level for each year of the analysis. Statistics show that African Americans, as a group, benefit from social programs. However, not all African American congressmen represent black constituents that may benefit from these programs. On the contrary, the per capita income for African American citizens in Mississippi is drastically different from those in Prince Georges County Maryland and Kansas City Missouri. Lastly, women have commonly exhibited extremely high levels of cohesion when it comes to social policy regardless of party identification. Table 2-11 shows that even women are not as homogenous as the African American delegation.

Table 2-10 Voting Cohesion on Economic Policy

	1977	1981	1989	1999
African Am.	90%	98%	97%	94%
Democrats	68	74	81	85
Republicans	85	92	85	81
Women	77	61	72	82
Hispanics	62	66	85	82

Table 2-11 Voting Cohesion on Social Policy

	1977	1981	1989	1999
African Am.	91%	92%	96%	95%
Democrats	65	68	78	80
Republicans	78	79	79	82
Women	77	66	80	87
Hispanics	74	72	84	74

Table 2-12 Voting Cohesion on Foreign Policy

	1977	1981	1989	1999
African Am.	86%	94%	97%	85%
Democrats	64	64	73	74
Republicans	79	76	86	82
Women	81	64	74	73
Hispanics	64	74	79	63

Despite its increasing diversity, the CBC still remains the most identifiable ideological – liberal cohesive voting bloc in Congress. The high levels of voting cohesion exhibited by the African American legislative delegation indicates that black law makers have not completely succumbed to the atomistic dynamics of Congress.

OLS Regression Analysis

We also decided to use an OLS regression model to test our theory because the previous analysis did not provide us with enough information to determine whether or not Caucus membership would play the same role when other more traditional variables are considered. Maybe black congressmen behave and vote the way that they do because of their liberal orientation rather than their membership in a racially based organization. Although party identification and ideological rating scores are typically used in voting behavior models, we also considered membership in the Hispanic and Women's Issues Caucus because of their minority status.

Race and gender are not used in most of our models because of multi-collinearity issues. Rather than using all three types of voted considered previously, we decided to use only the social and economic policy votes because these votes have the highest cohesion scores among Caucus members and because they have the greatest impact on African Americans.

Table 2-13 through 2-16 show that ADA score and Presidential Support score coefficients are strong predictors of social and economic policy voting behavior in all of the models at the .01 level of significance. The Black Caucus coefficients are also significant in each model at the .01 level with the exception of one model (the standard errors are in parenthesis). The Hispanic Caucus and Women's Issues variables do not appear to have an impact on the voting behavior of African Americans in the Congressional Black Caucus. The R^2 values and the F-Test values are also high in each model. This suggests that the amount of variability in the voting behavior can be explained/predicted by the independent variables.

Essentially, the regression analysis shows that the Caucus variable is quite robust. Membership in the caucus has a strong impact on the members of the Black Caucus. The organization is quite obviously seen and used as a tool by the members to represent the interests of African Americans. This includes individual district constituents and the national African American constituency throughout the country.

Table 2-13 OLS Regression Model: Black Caucus Voting Behavior in 1977

	Economic	Social
Intercept	-0.31 (0.03)	-0.22 (0.03)
Party ID (1=Dem., 0=Rep.)	0.24*** (0.02)	0.08*** (0.02)
ADA (0-100)	0.00*** (0.00)	0.00*** (0.00)
Presidential Support (0-100)	0.01*** (0.00)	-0.01*** (0.00)
Black Caucus	0.23*** (0.05)	0.22*** (0.05)
- (1=Memb., 0=Non-Memb.)		
Women's Issues Caucus	0.03 (0.05)	0.06 (0.04)
- (1=Memb., 0=Non-Memb.)		
Hispanic Caucus	0.21*** (0.08)	0.06 (0.07)
- (1=Memb., 0=Non-Memb.)		
R^2	.76	.72
F-Test Value	220.91	185.22

*p<.10; **p<.05; ***p<.01

Table 2-14 OLS Regression Model: Black Caucus Voting Behavior in 1981

	Economic	Social
Intercept	1.30 (0.03)	1.27 (0.34)
Party ID (1=Dem., 0=Rep.)	-0.24*** (0.02)	0.01 (0.02)
ADA (0-100)	-0.00*** (0.00)	0.00*** (0.00)
Presidential Support (0-100)	-0.01*** (0.00)	-0.02*** (0.00)
Black Caucus	0.06* (0.03)	0.12*** (0.04)
- (1=Memb., 0=Non-Memb.)		
Women's Issues Caucus	0.04 (0.03)	0.11*** (0.04)
- (1=Memb., 0=Non-Memb.)		
Hispanic Caucus	0.08 (0.05)	0.11 (0.07)
- (1=Memb., 0=Non-Memb.)		
R^2	.90	.75
F-Test Value	623.81	162.47

*p<.10; **p<.05; ***p<.01

Table 2-15 OLS Regression Model: Black Caucus Voting Behavior in 1989

	Economic	Social
Intercept	0.75 (0.07)	0.53 (0.09)
Gender	-0.04 (0.03)	-0.01 (0.04)
Party ID (1=Dem., 0=Rep.)	-0.14*** (0.02)	0.03 (0.02)
ADA (0-100)	0.00*** (0.00)	0.01*** (0.00)
Presidential Support (0-100)	-0.01*** (0.00)	-0.01*** (0.00)
Black Caucus	0.04** (0.02)	0.07** (0.03)
- (1=Memb., 0=Non-Memb.)		
Women's Issues Caucus	-0.04 (0.03)	0.06 (0.05)
- (1=Memb., 0=Non-Memb.)		
Hispanic Caucus	0.04 (0.03)	0.05 (0.04)
- (1=Memb., 0=Non-Memb.)		
R^2	.94	.85
F-Test Value	991.99	331.67

*p<.10; **p<.05; ***p<.01

Table 2-16 OLS Regression Model: Black Caucus Voting Behavior in 1993

	Economic	*Social*
Intercept	0.31 (0.03)	-0.22 (0.03)
Party ID (1=Dem., 0=Rep.)	0.24*** (0.02)	0.08*** (0.02)
ADA (0-100)	0.00*** (0.00)	0.00*** (0.00)
Presidential Support (0-100)	0.01*** (0.00)	-0.01*** (0.00)
Black Caucus	0.23*** (0.05)	0.22*** (0.05)
- (1=Memb., 0=Non-Memb.)		
Women's Issues Caucus	0.03 (0.05)	0.06 (0.04)
- (1=Memb., 0=Non-Memb.)		
Hispanic Caucus	0.21 (0.08)	0.06 (0.07)
- (1=Memb., 0=Non-Memb.)		
R^2	.76	.72
F-Test Value	220.91	185.22

*p<.10; **p<.05; ***p<.01

Implications and Conclusions

Since 1960, the size of the African American congressional delegation has significantly expanded from the mere four members to an all
time high of forty members in 1992. This unprecedented growth in
African American congressional representation includes the first African
American woman, Carol Mosely-Brown (D-IL.) who served in the
United State Senate. Following a positive Supreme Court Decision in
1986, the early 1990s produced the most African Americans in Congress
despite subsequent decisions from the Court that had negative affects on
the creation of majority minority districts.

As the number of African Americans has grown, both men and
women, so has the number of committee chair and vice chair positions.
The number of chairs increased to 7 along with 17 vice chairs in 1986.
Despite the fact that the number of chairs has decreased, African
American congressmen remain the ranking minority leaders on a number of committees. If policy making occurs as it is commonly accepted, the ability to represent increases as chair and leadership positions
are coveted.

Lastly, the research shows that the Congressional Black Caucus
has been the preeminent legislative organization that has advocated legislation that benefits all African Americans in the U.S. Despite a new
breed of African Americans taking office, this objective transcends each
of their individual agendas. The validity of this statement is reinforced

when different types of legislation are considered. The CBC is the most liberal organization in Congress and has consistently maintained high levels of voting cohesion. This is abundantly true when economic and social policies are considered. Both of which are clearly important to African Americans given their overall economic status. Cohesion and representation within Congress takes on an entirely new meaning when put into the context of other variables that traditionally explain voting behavior. Each of our regression models show that membership in the Caucus has an affect on the voting behavior of the caucus members on both social and economic policy. This was found to be true even when party identification and ideology are included in the model. The influx of new members did not change the behavior of the organization. In fact, the analysis clearly suggests that the cohesiveness of the organization and the impact of the organization on the behavior of the members have increased with the influx of new members.

Without question, it will take the effort of all congressmen to represent the interests of the country (Swain 1993; Endersby and Menifield 2000). More importantly, we show that the efforts of African American congressmen have no equal when the goals of the Congressional Black Caucus are considered. Their efforts to secure legislation for minorities are paramount to achieving social and economic parity. Without these efforts, it is questionable how African Americans will be represented in the twenty-first century.

References

Adair, Augustus A. 1977. *Black Legislative Influence in Federal Policy Decisions: The Congressional Black Caucus*, 1971-1975." Unpublished Doctoral Dissertation. Johns Hopkins University.

Almanac of America Politics. 1980. E.P. Dutton: NY.

Barnett, Marguerite R. 1975. "The Congressional Black Caucus." *Academy of Political Science Proceedings* 32: 34-50.

Barnett, Marguerite R. 1977. "The Congressional Black Caucus and the Institutionalization of Black Politics." *Journal of Afro-American Issues* 5: 201-226.

Bositis, David A. 1994. *The Congressional Black Caucus in the 103rd Congress.* Joint Center for Political and Economic Studies: Washington, D.C.

Bositis, David A. 1998. *Black Elected Officials: A Statistical Summary 1993-*

1997. Joint Center for Political and Economic Studies: Washington,
D.C.

Broder, David S. 1989. "On House Ethics, The Leading Light of Julian
Dixon." *Virginian-Pilot and Ledger-Star* April 12:A9.

Carmichael, Stokely. and Charles V. Hamilton. 1967. *Black Power: The
Politics of Liberation in America.* New York: Vintage Books.

Clay, William. 1993. *Just Permanent Interests: Black Americans in Congress,
1870-1991.* Amistad Press: NY, NY.

Clem, Alan L. 1989. *Congress: Power, Processes, and Politics.* Pacific Grove,
CA: Brooks/Cole Publishing Co.

Cohen, Richard. 1987. "New Breed for Black Caucus." *National Journal* 19:
2432-2435.

Cohodas, Nadine. 1985. "Black House Members Striving for Influence."
Congressional Quarterly Weekly Report April 13: 675-681.

Duke, Lynne. 1993. "Congressional Black Caucus and Nation of Islam Agree on
Alliance." *The Washington Post* September 17:A3.

Endersby, James W. and Charles E. Menifield. 2000. "Representation, Ethnicity,
and Congress: Black and Hispanic Representatives and Constituencies."
In *Black and Multiracial Politics in America.* (eds) Yvette Marie Alex-
Assensoh and Lawrence J. Hanks. NYU Press: NY.

Fears, D. C. 1985. "A Time of Testing for Black Caucus as Its Members Rise to
Power in
House." *National Journal* 17:909-911.

Fenno, Richard R. Jr. 1978. *Home Style: House Members in Their Districts.*
Boston, MA: Little, Brown and Co.

Fiellin, Allan. 1962. "The Function of Informal Groups in Legislative
Institutions." *The Journal of Politics* 24:75-90.

Fiorina, Morris P. 1974. *Representatives, Roll Calls, and Constituencies.*
Lexington, MA: D. C. Heath, Lexington Books.

Froman, Lewis. 1967. *The Congressional Process: Strategies, Rules and
Procedures.* Boston: Little, Brown and Co.

Gile, Roxanne L., and Charles E. Jones. 1996. "Congressional Racial
Solidarity." *Journal of Black Studies.* 25: 622-641.

Henry, Charles P. 1992. "Black Leadership and the Deracialization of Politics."
*Crisis_*100: 38-42.

Henry, Charles P. 1977. "Legitimizing Race in Congressional Politics."
American Politics Quarterly 5:149-176.

Http://www.census.gov/populations/socdemo/voting/96cps/tab4A.txt (1998).

Jones, Charles E. 1987a "An Overview of the Congressional Black Caucus:

1970-1985." In *Readings in American Political Issues*. (eds) Franklyn D. Jones and Michael O. Adams. Kendall Hunt: Dubuque, IA.

_____. 1987b. "Testing A Legislative Strategy: The Congressional Black Caucus Action-Alert Communications Network." *Legislative Studies Quarterly* 12: 521-536.

_____. 1987c. "United We Stand, Divided We Fall: An Analysis of the Congressional Black Caucus' Voting Behavior, 1975-1980." *Phylon* 48: 26-37.

Kanellos, Nicolas, 1997. *The Hispanic American Almanac*. (ed) 2nd Edition. Gale Publishers: Detroit, MI.

Katz, Jeffrey L. 1993. "Growing Black Caucus May Have New Voice." *Congressional Quarterly Weekly Report* January 2:5-11.

Kenworthy, Tom. 1989. "Congressional Black Caucus: New Circumstances After 20 Years." *The Washington Post* September 17: A1, A23.

Kilson, Martin. 1989. "Problems of Black Politics." *Dissent* 36: 526-34.

Levy, Arthur B, and Susan Stoudinger. 1976. "Sources of Voting Cues for the Congressional Black Caucus." *Journal of Black Studies*. 7: 29-45.

Mayhew, David R. 1974. *Congress: The Electoral Connection*. New Haven, CT: Yale University Press.

Menifield, Charles E. and Frank Julian. 1998. "Changing the Face of Congress: African-Americans in the Twenty-First Century. *Western Journal of Black Studies* 22, p. 18-30

Pianin, Eric. 1987. "Black Caucus Members Face Dilemma of Hill Loyalties: Tensions Grow as Group Comes of Age." *The Washington Post* September 23:A1, A16.

Politics in America. (various issues) Congressional Quarterly: Washington, D.C.

Shaw v. Reno, 509 U.S. 630 1992.

Singh, Robert. 1998. *The Congressional Black Caucus: Racial Politics in the U.S. Congress*. Sage: Thousand Oaks, CA.

Smith, Robert C. 1981a. "The Black Congressional Delegation." *Western Political Quarterly* 34: 203-221.

Smith, Robert C. 1981b. "Black Power and the Transformation From Protest to Politics."
Political Science Quarterly 96:431-443.

Statistical Abstract of the United States: U.S. Bureau of the Census: Washington, D.C. (various issues).

Steel, James. 1993. "Congressional Black Caucus at a Turning Point." *Crossroads* 28:22-25.

Stevens, Arthur G., Daniel P. Mulhollan, and Paul S. Rundquist. 1981. "U. S.

Congressional Structure and Representation: The Role of Informal Groups." *Legislative Studies Quarterly* 6: 415-437.

Swain, Carol M. 1992. "Changing Patterns of African-American Representation in Congress." In *The Atomistic Congress.* (eds) Allen D. Hertzke and Ronald Peters Jr.. Armonk, NY: M. E. Sharpe.

Swain, Carol. 1993. *Black Faces, Black Interests.* Harvard University Press: Cambridge, MA.

Thornburg v. Gingles. 478 U.S. 30 1986.

Whicker, Marcia L. and Lois Duke Whitaker. 1999. "Women in Congress." In *Women in Politics: Outsiders or Insiders.* (ed) Lois Duke Whitaker. Upper Saddle River, NJ.

Whitby, Kenneth. 1997. *The Color of Representation: Congressional Behavior and Black Interests.* University of Michigan Press: Ann Arbor, MI.

CHAPTER 3

The Institutional Roles of Women Serving in Congress: 1960-2000

Karen M. McCurdy

The representation of women in American politics is a difficult issue to study. One problem associated with the issue is the multiple meanings contained in the idea of representation as evidenced with the plethora of current research on the subject. The second problem lies in the paradox surrounding women in politics. Women make up slightly more than 51% of the population and exhibit the highest voting levels for any group in the U.S. With this in mind, it is quite clear that women are the most underrepresented group in Congress, state legislatures and other elected institutions in the country.

In addition to providing descriptive data on women in Congress, this chapter will also evaluate the role of women elected to serve in the United States Congress. Research shows that women have served in the United States Congress since 1917. The patterns of service, whether elective or appointive are however different over time, as well as the types of careers that women have pursued in Congress. A similar difference can be discerned between the chambers both in terms of service and careers. The chapter proceeds by first describing the pattern of representation left by women in Congress, and then moves on to the roles that women have played in the House and Senate. For the most part, the analysis centers on the 1960-2000 time period. However, in some instances, the research goes back a bit further to clearly show the progress/lack of progress made by women. In addition to the above, the chapter also considers women in the electorate as voters.

Women and Representation

Hanna Pitkin (1967) provides a template for evaluating styles of representation that have been used frequently by congressional scholars (Davidson 1969; Eulau and Karps 1984). Interestingly, several of the styles, which she herself discounted forty years ago, have become important recently in the discussion of women and minority representation in Congress. While *formal* representation may not be that important, except for a constitutional analysis, when considering the role of women in the political system, formal representation does affect women's' basic participation in American politics.

Pitkin's second category, *descriptive* representation was initially dismissed as unimportant to congressional research (Eulau and Karps 1977), but has recently been examined closely by scholars interested in increasing women and minority numbers in the elective fields of politics, both in state and national legislatures. The style of representation depends on the demographic characteristics of the constituency being reflected in the elected official. Thus, a Catholic legislator representing a predominantly Catholic district would be capable of providing descriptive representation to his or her constituents. This type of representation is a basic demographic feature of both the elected official and the constituency that is being reflected. As research has concentrated on finding mechanisms to increase the numbers of women, African-American, and Hispanic legislators, the importance for policy outcomes of these particular demographic categories has been examined (see Chapter 8 in this text; Thomas 1998).

The third of Pitkin's representative types, *substantive*, is the one which has achieved the most esteemed position in the congressional research (Swain 1993; Whitby 1997). Numerous studies have examined the role of representatives as they pursue public policy positions on behalf of their districts. Categorizing substantive representation into trustee and delegate roles has provided a theoretical basis for several empirical investigations of members of Congress at work, beginning with Davidson (1969) and continuing through to Fenno (1978) and Whitby (1997). The notion of representation being either working in the best interests of constituents as with a trustee, or reflecting the policy position of the constituents precisely as would a delegate is an unstated theme running throughout congressional research, whether it be behavioral or formal. Most of the time when congressional research is concerned with representation it is with this style of activity.

Pitkin's fourth type, *symbolic* representation retains a minor role in this chapter. Although when public policy decisions affecting women is the subject, the role of introducing bills which are perennially stalled in the committee system, or delivering floor speeches bringing to light the affect that particular policy positions will have on women in general or special subsets of the class of women, becomes more important.

Suffrage

The nineteenth amendment to the U.S. Constitution was ratified in August 1920, bringing the franchise to women citizens. Interestingly, Jeanette Rankin, the first woman to be elected to the U.S. Congress, served her first term in the House of Representatives prior to the point when women throughout the country became entitled to cast a vote for any candidate to the national legislature (Josephson 1974). The women's suffrage movement grew out of the abolitionist movement in the mid-nineteenth century, and was a part of the call for women's rights at the Seneca Falls Convention in 1848. By the latter decades of the nineteenth century, women's suffrage was accepted in several of the western territories[1], and became a heated topic of congressional debate when applications for statehood included provisions to retain women's voting rights. Wyoming in 1890, was the first state to contain the "bizarre electoral provision" which allowed women the vote, followed by other western rural states Colorado, Idaho, and Utah. In 1905, Carrie Chapman Catt set the National American Woman Suffrage Association on the path to universal women's suffrage by setting out a strategy for simultaneous state and federal campaigns. The first predominantly urban state to accept women's suffrage was Washington in 1910. Jeannette Rankin had worked for suffrage in Washington state and Montana, and in early 1911 she moved to New York state to be involved in the suffrage campaign there. By the fall of that year, she was in California pushing for the adoption of the suffrage amendment to the state constitution. As field secretary for the National American Woman Suffrage Association, Rankin traveled throughout the country, honing her political campaigning skills over the next two years. Following the successful Montana women's suffrage campaign, the next logical step for Rankin was to break the legislative barrier, which she accomplished in the 1916 congressional elections.

Table 3-1 contains a breakdown of women's service in Congress, by House and Senate membership from 1960 – 2000, with a complete listing of women' service since 1917 appearing in Appendix 3-1. Once women gained suffrage, or were recognized as having formal representation, women have served continuously in Congress, and their total numbers have increased gradually, but consistently in the 83 years that women have served in Congress. Examining the separate legislative chambers, it is clear that women have made more inroads in the House than in the Senate. The first woman to serve in the U.S. Senate, Rebecca Felton of Georgia, was appointed to the body in 1922, serving a single day before resigning her seat to the elected candidate for the vacancy. After this inauspicious beginning though, Hattie Caraway of Arkansas, who was appointed to fill a vacancy caused by the death of her husband. She was subsequently elected to the seat in 1932 and served for 14 years, becoming the first of several women who established long careers in the Senate.

Table 3-1: Numbers of Women Serving in the United States Congress 1960-2000

Congress	Years	# of Senate Women	% of Senate	# of House Women	% of House	Total Congress	% of Total
86th	1959-1961	2 (1D, 1R)	2/98	17 (9D, 8R)	.039	19 (10D, 9R)	.04
87th	1961-1963	2 (1D, 1R)	.02	18 (11D, 7R)	.041	20 (12D, 8R)	.04
88th	1963-1965	2 (1D, 1R)	.02	12 (6D, 6R)	.028	14 (7D, 7R)	.03
89th	1965-1967	2 (1D, 1R)	.02	11 (7D, 4R)	.025	13 (8D, 5R)	.02
90th	1967-1969	1 (0D, 1R)	.01	11 (6D, 5R)	.025	12 (6D, 6R)	.02
91st	1969-1971	1 (0D, 1R)	.01	10 (6D, 4R)	.023	11 (6D, 5R)	.02
92nd	1971-1973	2 (1D, 1R)	.01	13 (10D, 3R)	.030	15 (11D, 4R)	.03
93rd	1973-1975	0	.00	16 (14D, 2R)	.037	16 (14D, 2R)	.03
94th	1975-1977	0	.00	19 (14D, 5R)	.044	19 (14D, 5R)	.04
95th	1977-1979	2 (2D, 0R)	.02	18 (13D, 5R)	.041	20 (15D, 5R)	.04
96th	1979-1981	1 (0D, 1R)	.01	16 (11D, 5R)	.037	17 (11D, 6R)	.03
97th	1981-1983	2 (0D, 2R)	.02	21 (11D, 10R)	.048	23 (11D, 12R)	.04
98th	1983-1985	2 (0D, 2R)	.02	22 (13D, 9R)	.051	24 (13D, 11R)	.04
99th	1985-1987	2 (0D, 2R)	.02	23 (12D, 11R)	.053	25 (12D, 13R)	.05
100th	1987-1989	2 (1D, 1R)	.02	23 (12D, 11R)	.053	25 (13D, 12R)	.05
101st	1989-1991	2 (1D, 1R)	.02	29 (16D, 13R)	.067	31 (17D, 14R)	.06
102nd	1991-1993	4 (3D, 1R)[++]	.04	28 (19D, 9R)[+]	.064	32 (22D, 10R)[+]	.06
103rd	1993-1995	7 (5D, 2R)[+++]	.07	46 (34D, 12R)[+]	.106	53 (39D, 14R)[+]	.10
104th	1995-1997	9 (5D, 4R)[R]	.09	47 (30D, 17R)[+]	.108	56 (34D, 21R)[+]	.10
105th	1997-1999	9 (6D, 3R)	.09	54 (37D, 17R)[RR]	.124	63 (43D, 20R)[RR]	.12
106th	1999-2001	9 (6D, 3R)	.09	56 (39D, 17R)[RRR]	.129	65 (45D, 20R)[RRR]	.12

Note: The table shows the maximum number of women elected or appointed to serve in that Congress at one time. Some filled out unexpired terms and some were never sworn in.

+Does not include a Democratic Delegate to the House of Representatives, Eleanor Holmes Norton, from Washington, D.C.

++On election day 1992, three women served in the Senate, two were elected and one was appointed. On November 3rd, Dianne Feinstein won a special election to complete two years of a term, she was sworn in on November 10, 1992.

+++Includes Kay Bailey Hutchison (R-TX), who won a special election on June 5, 1993 to serve out the remaining year and one half of a term.

R Includes Sheila Frahm (R-KS), who was appointed on June 11, 1996 to fill a vacancy caused by resignation. She was defeated in her primary race to complete the full term.

RR Does not include two Democratic Delegates to the House of Representatives, Eleanor Holmes Norton from Washington D.C., and Donna M. Christian-Green from the Virgin Islands. Also does not include Susan Molinari (R-NY) who resigned August 1, 1997. Includes 4 women (2 Democrats and 2 Republicans) who won special elections in March, April, and June 1998.

RRR Does not include two Democratic Delegates, Eleanor Holmes Norton from the District of Columbia, and Donna M. Christian-Green from the Virgin Islands.

Sources: Center for American Women and Politics. 2000. "National Information Bank on Women in Public Office," Eagleton Institute of Politics, Rutgers University, http://www.rci.rutgers.edu/~cawp/facts/cawpfs.html; United States Congress, 1989, *Biographical Directory of Congress 1776-1989*, Senate Document 100-34 (Washington DC: U.S. Government Printing Office; *Congressional Quarterly*, 1991, Guide to Congress, 4th ed. Washington, D.C.: Congressional Quarterly Press; Michael Barone and Grant Ujifusa. 1999. *The Almanac of American Politics. 2000.* Washington, D.C.: National Journal. Percentages calculated by the author.

Gender and the Institutionalization of Congressional Service

One measure of the level of representation that women have achieved in Congress is to examine women legislators' penetration into the institutional leadership structures. Using Polsby's (1968) measures of the institutionalization of the House of Representatives, we can make some observations about women's service in Congress, and infer how influential women have become in the business of policy making within Congress. In particular, the cumulative years of service accrued by women (Table 3-2), and the average years served by decade (Table 3-3) give us an image of the potential magnitude of women's influence on policy making within the Senate and House.

By focusing on the percentage of women serving in Congress, as was the case in the previous discussion of representation, it is easy to ignore the fact that women once elected have been able to remain in the House of Representatives for very long periods of time, and even a few women have been able to serve as Senators for a long time. Having said that however, the pattern of cumulative service in the Senate is overwhelmingly that of filling in temporarily for a better candidate, often a male candidate. As shown in Table 3-2, thirteen of the twenty-seven women serving in the U.S. Senate served for less than a single two year Congress. Many served for merely a small number of days, weeks, or months until their states could elect a "proper" senator. Breaking this pattern of "place holding" though have been women elected to the Senate in the latter half of the twentieth century. Margaret Chase Smith (R, ME), the first woman elected directly to the Senate without completing an unexpired term, retains the record for cumulative service in the Senate for a woman at 24 years, leaving the Senate in 1973. Nancy Landon Kassebaum (R, KS) served for 18 years before retiring in 1997. The dean of Senate women currently serving is Barbara Mikulski (D, MD), who is in her 14th year as Senator.

The House of Representatives provides a more encouraging image of women in the national legislature. Many women were never re-elected, and many were defeated after their sophomore terms. Well over half of the 175 women who have served in the House since 1917, accumulated between 5 and 35 years of service. Table 3-3 allows us to examine whether the pattern of service in Congress is getting better or worse by looking at the average length of career by the decade of first service. The Senate shows a striking increase in the number of years that women averaged, particularly after 1949, when the average number of years

Table 3-2 **Women Representatives, Cumulative Years of Service (1917-2000)**

Years of Service	Number of Senators	Number of Representatives
less than 2	13	50
3-4	2	34
5-6	3	21
7-8	5	24
9-10	0	10
11-12	0	6
13-14	2	9
15-16	0	5
17-18	1	4
19-20	0	5
21-22	0	1
23-24	1	3
25-26	0	1
27-28	0	0
29-30	0	1
35	0	1
Total	27	175

Sources: Center for American Woman and Politics. 2000. "National Information Bank on Women in Public Office," Eagleton Institute of Politics, Rutgers University, http://www.rci.rutgers.edu/~cawp/facts/cawpfs.html; United States Congress, 1989, *Biographical Directory of Congress 1776-1989*, Senate Document 100-34 Washington, D.C: U.S. Government Printing Office); Congressional Quarterly. 1991. *Guide to Congress*, 4th ed. Washington, D.C.: Congressional Quarterly Press; Michael Barone and Grant Ujifusa. 1999. *The Almanac of American Politics*. 2000. Washington, D.C.: National Journal. Percentages calculated by the author.

served for those women elected to the 81st through 85th Congresses (1949-1959) was 8.67 years. The 96th through 100th Congresses (1979-1989) had average service of 9.5 years. It is interesting here that although women were not directly affected by the Voting Rights Act of 1965, the number of women elected to Congress has not only kept pace with other ethnic minority groups, but has clearly surpassed them relative to election rates. As we should expect, the women first elected during the final decade of the twentieth century have not had an opportunity to accumulate much service, and the dramatic increase in the number of women in the Senate to ten in that decade brought the average length of career down to 4.8 years.

**Table 3-3 Average Length of Career by Decade of First Service
in the U.S. Congress, 1917-199**

Decade of First Service	Average Length of Career		Number of Women Serving	
	Senate	*House*	*Senate*	*House*
1917-1929* 65th-70ᵗʰ Congress	1 day	10.75 yrs	1	8
1929-1939 71st-75th Congress	5 yrs	3.15 yrs	4	13
1939-1949 76th-80th Congress	1 yr	4.94 yrs	1	17
1949-1959 81st-85th Congress	8.67 yrs	11.87 yrs	3	15
1959-1969 86th-90th Congress	7 yrs	7.08 yrs	1	12
1969-1979 91st-95th Congress	5.5 yrs	10.19 yrs	4	21
1979-1989 96th-100th Congress	9.5 yrs	10.26 yrs	2	23
1989-1999 101st-105th Congress	4.8 yrs	4.82 yrs	10	60
Total Women Serving 65th-105th Congresses			26	169

Sources: Center for American Women and Politics. 2000. "National Information Bank on Women in Public Office." Eagleton Institute of Politics, Rutgers University, http://www.rci.rutgers.edu/~cawp/facts/cawpfs.html; United States Congress. 1989. *Biographical Directory of Congress 1776-1989*. Senate Document 100-34 Washington, D.C.: U.S. Government Printing Office; Congressional Quarterly. 1991. *Guide to Congress*. 4th ed. Washington, D.C.: Congressional Quarterly Press; Michael Barone and Grant Ujifusa. 1999. *The Almanac of American Politics* 2000. Washington, D.C.: National Journal. Percentages calculated by the author.

On the House side, the eight women elected in the 1920s served an average of 10.75 years. The next decades prior to World War II did not result in long congressional careers for women, but after the war, women's average length of career returned to double digits, only dipping to 7.08 years in the 1960s during the Civil Rights movement when there was a slight dip in the number of women in the House. Again, in the House the final decade of the 1900s was a very productive one for electing women to the national legislature. Although the average number of years of service declined to 4.82 years, this occurred as the number of women who were first elected in the 1990s more than doubled to sixty individuals, so we would expect the average service figure to dip quite a bit.

Somewhat surprisingly, given the attention in the feminist literature to the low numbers of women in Congress, once a woman gets over the hump of winning that first election, she seems to be able to rely on the advantage that accrues to all incumbents (Jacobson 1997). Having established that women can get re-elected, and that the pattern of long service has been present since the 1920s in the House, and the 1950s in the Senate, we can turn to another indicator of institutionalization, the development of a leadership hierarchy. In this case, we can examine the penetration that women have made into the well-established leadership hierarchy in each political party, and on congressional committees.

Leadership Advancement

Table 3-4 indicates the leadership positions held by women on congressional committees since the Legislative Reorganization of 1946 produced the modern committee system. There have been very few women committee chairs indeed, only one in the Senate, and five in the House of Representatives. The Republican party has a slight edge over the Democratic party in elevating more women to congressional chairmanships (3 to 2). Overall however, women do not seem to be making inroads in breaking through the committee leadership ceiling. Committee leadership positions are nearly completely dependent on lengthy congressional careers, and as we saw earlier, women in great numbers do not have long careers. We may, however, witness a change in this trend with the women elected since 1992. In the Senate, Nancy Kassebaum (R, KS) was the first woman to chair a full committee under the reorganized committee system, taking her Chair (Labor and Human Resources) when the Republicans regained the majority in 1995 at the beginning of the 104th Congress. Hattie Wyath Caraway (D, AR) was the first woman to chair a committee in the Senate, taking her gavel in the 1930s. Margaret Chase Smith (R, ME) was the first woman to advance to the Ranking Member position in the Senate, doing so on two separate Senate standing committees in the 1960s, Aeronautical and Space Sciences and Armed Services. The House committee seniority system has been more difficult for women to penetrate in the latter portion of

Table 3-4 Congressional Committee Leadership Posts Held by Women Since 1947

Leadership Position	Party	Congress & Year	Committee and Member
House of Representatives			
Committee Chair	GOP	80, 83-86 (1947-49, 1953-61) 104 (1993-95)	Veteran's Affairs (Rogers, MA) Small Business (Meyers, KS), and Standards of Official Conduct (Johnson, CT)
	Dem	81 (1949-51) 93-94 (1973-77)	House Administration (Norton, NJ) Merchant Marine & Fisheries (Sullivan, MO)
Ranking Minority Member	GOP	89-92 (1965-73) 81-82 (1949-53) 103 (1991-93)	Government Operations (Dwyer, NJ) Veteran's Affairs (Rogers (MA) Small Business (Meyers, KS)
	Dem	80 (1947-49) 104 (1993-95) 106 (1999-2001)	House Administration (Norton, NJ) Government Reform and Oversight (Collins, IL) Small Business (Velazquez, NY)
Senate			
Committee Chair	GOP	104 (1993-95)	Labor and Human Resources (Kassebaum, KS)
Ranking Minority Member	GOP	88 –91 (1963-71) 90-92 (1967-73) 103 (1991-93)	Aeronautical and Space Sciences; Armed Services (Smith, ME) Labor and Human Resources (Kassebaum, KS)

Sources: Garrison Nelson, 1993, *Committees in the U.S. Congress 1947-1992, Volume 1: Committee Jurisdictions and Member Rosters*, Washington DC: Congressional Quarterly Press; Congressional Quarterly. 1993. "Committee Guide: Players, Politics and Turf of the 103rd Congress," Vol 51, Supplement to No. 18; Congressional Quarterly, 1995, "Committee Guide: Players, Politics and Turf of the 104th Congress," Vol 53, Supplement to No. 12; *Congressional Quarterly*, 1997, "Committee Guide: Players, Politics and Turf of the 105th Congress," Vol 55, Supplement to No. 12; *Congressional Quarterly*, 1999, "Committee Guide: Players, Politics and Turf of the 106th Congress," Vol 57, Supplement to No. 2.

the 20th century, in part because while they are amassing impressive cumulative years of service, those numbers pale in comparison to their male colleagues. In the House, the 80th Congress in 1947 brought the first woman committee Chair and Ranking Members. Edith Nourse Rogers (R, MA) assumed leadership of the Veteran's Affairs committee in that Congress, while Mary Norton (D, NJ) rose to the Ranking Member position on House Administration. In the following Congress, these two women retained their leadership roles, while reversing majority and minority positions. Rogers ended her thirty-five year congressional career like many men had before her, dying while in office after 14 years serving as either Chair or Ranking Member of her committee. So the evidence suggests that there are not structural impediments to committee leadership spots for women members that differ much from those before their male colleagues, to be continue being returned to office by their constituents for a very long time.

Party Leadership

Positions in the party leadership are shown in Table 3-5. As noted in the table, women have been included in the leadership hierarchy only recently. In the Senate, women have held party leadership positions only since 1993. On the House side, women held the position of Secretary of the Caucus in the Democratic party as early as 1949, with six women holding this position since then. Rosa DeLauro (D, CT) is the Assistant to the Democratic Leader in the 106th Congress, and there are several women in the whip system for the Democrats. Republican women joined the leadership hierarchy in the 99th Congress (1985). Four Republican women hold leadership positions in the 106th Congress.

The effect of women on the institutional structure of Congress cannot be said to be great despite the number of years of service that will allow them to compete with their male colleagues for positions that have traditionally been associated with seniority. The incidence of term limits for House Republican committee chairmen may open the way for more women to hold the committee gavels. At this point though only one woman, Marge Roukema (R, NJ) has been mentioned as potentially ascending to the soon to be vacated chairs (CQWR 2000, p 630). She is the next person in line for Banking and Financial Services, but appears to have competition for that position. The other twenty committees are likely to be led by men, albeit different men than are currently leading them. Chairmanship swapping, or musical chairs for leaders appears to be the likely pattern for the 107th Congress should the Republicans retain the majority after the 2000 elections.

Table 3-5 Congressional Party Leadership Posts Held by Women

Leadership Position	Party	Congress & Year	Number of Women
House of Representatives			
Secretary of the Caucus	Dem	81 (1949-51); 83 (1953-55), 84 (1955-57) , 88(1963-65) ; 86-93 (1959-75); 97 (1981-83); 98 (1983-85); 99 (1985-87)	6: Woodhouse, Kelly, Sullivan, Chisholm, Ferraro, Oakar
Vice Chair of the Caucus	Dem	100 (1987-89); 104-105 (1995-99)	2: Oakar, Kennelly
Deputy Whip	Dem	106 (1999-2001)	1: Johnson
Minority Whip at Large	Dem	104-105 (1995-99); 106 (1999-2001)	2: Lowey, Slaughter
Chief Deputy Whip	Dem	102-103 (1991-95)	1: Kennelly
Deputy Minority Whip	Dem	104 (1995-97); 106 (1999-2001)	3: DeLauro, Woolsey, DeGette
Co-chair Policy Committee	Dem	104-105 (1995-99)	1: Clayton
Assistant to the Democratic Leader	Dem	106 (1999-2001)	1: Rosa DeLauro
Secretary of the Conference	GOP	103 (1993-95); 104 (1995-97); 106 (1999-2001)	3: Johnson, Vucanovich, Pryce
Vice Chair of the Conference	GOP	99-100 (1985-89); 104-105 (1995-99); 106 (1999-2001)	4: Martin, Molinari, Dunn, Fowler
Assistant Majority Whip	GOP	105-106 (1997-2001)	1: Granger
Deputy Majority Whip	GOP	104 (1995-97); 106 (1999-2001)	2: Fowler, Cubin
Senate			
Deputy Majority Whip	Dem	103 (1993-95)	1: Boxer
Assistant Floor Leader	Dem	103 (1993-95)	1: Mikulski
Secretary of the Conference	Dem	104-106 (1995-2001)	1: Mikulski
Deputy Majority Whip	GOP	104-106 (1995-2001)	1: Hutchison
Secretary of the Conference	GOP	105-106 (1997-2001)	1: Snowe

Source: Center for American Women and Politics. 1999. "Women in Congressional Leadership Roles," Fact Sheet 3/99.

Table 3-6 Number of Women Serving in the U.S. Congress from Individual States

Number of Women	Number of States	State
25	1	California
18	1	New York
12	1	Illinois
7	3	Florida, Maryland, Washington
6	3	Michigan, Ohio, Texas
5	10	Arkansas, Connecticut, Georgia, Indiana, Kansas, Louisiana, Missouri, New Jersey, Oregon, South Carolina
4	2	Pennsylvania, Tennessee
3	6	Alabama, Maine, Massachusetts, Nebraska, North Carolina, Utah
2	9	Arizona, Colorado, Hawaii, Idaho, Kentucky, Minnesota, Nevada, New Mexico, South Dakota
1	8	Montana, North Dakota, Oklahoma, Rhode Island, Virginia, West Virginia, Wisconsin, and Wyoming
0	6	Alaska, Delaware, Iowa, Mississippi, New Hampshire, Vermont

Note: Does not include non-voting Delegates from United States Territories and the District of Columbia.

Sources: Center for American Women and Politics. 2000. "National Information Bank on Women in Public Office," Eagleton Institute of Politics, Rutgers University, http://www.rci.rutgers.edu/~cawp/facts/cawpfs.html; United States Congress. 1989. *Biographical Directory of Congress 1776-1989*, Senate Document 100-34 Washington, D.C.: U.S. Government Printing Office; *Congressional Quarterly Guide to Congress*. 1991. 4th ed. Washington, D.C.: Congressional Quarterly Press; Michael Barone and Grant Ujifusa. 1999. *The Almanac of American Politics. 2000*. Washington, D.C.: National Journal.

Geographic Representation

What is apparent from the 175 women who have been elected to the House of Representatives as members, the 3 delegates, and the 27 women serving in the Senate, is that there is great variation in the geographic representation for women. A complete listing of women who have served in Congress since 1960 by name and state appears in Appendix 3-2. Rural states elected women first, both western and southern states. Many northeastern liberal states elected women to Congress only recently. California, Illinois, and New York have been good places for women pursuing office during all time periods. These states began electing women to national office in the 1920s, and continued sending women to Washington D.C. to represent them. As we can see in Table 3-6, six states, Alaska, Delaware, Iowa, Mississippi, New Hampshire, and Vermont, have yet to elect a woman to Congress. Some other states have only sent one woman to Congress, and some have not elected a woman in quite some time; Oklahoma since 1923, South Dakota since 1948, and West Virginia since 1965. Montana elected Jeannette Rankin twice, in 1917 and in 1941, but no other woman has been elected to Congress from there since then.

Table 3-7 considers the same data over the last forty years. The data shows that there is quite a bit or regional variety in the number of women elected. For example, California currently has the largest number of women in Congress at 15, while New York has 6, Florida has 5 and Texas has 4. Although these states have the largest number of women in Congress, the number of women is still quite low as a percentage of the states' total number of legislators in Congress. The table quite clearly shows that for the most part, the southern states appear to have the smallest number of women serving in Congress. This is somewhat expected given the traditionalistic culture that epitomizes the south. Krane and Shaffer (1992) indicate that the number of women candidates, at all levels, in the Deep South is less than the rest of the country in general. With the exception of Florida, no Deep South State currently has more than one woman in Congress.

Table 3-7 Women in Congress by Year and State

	1960	1965	1970	1975	1980	1985	1990	1995	2000
Arizona	0	0	0	0	0	0	0	1	0
Arkansas	0	0	0	0	0	0	0	1	1
California	0	0	0	2	1	2	2	10	15
Colorado	0	0	0	1	1	1	1	1	1
Connecticut	0	0	0	1	0	2	2	2	1
District of Columbia	0	0	0	0	0	0	1	1	1
Florida	0	0	0	0	0	1	1	5	5
Georgia	1	0	0	0	0	0	0	1	1
Hawaii	0	1	1	1	0	0	2	1	1
Idaho	1	0	0	0	0	0	0	1	1
Illinois	2	1	1	1	1	2	2	2	2
Indiana	0	0	0	0	0	1	1	1	1
Kansas	0	0	0	1	1	2	2	2	0
Kentucky	0	0	0	0	0	0	0	0	1
Louisiana	0	0	0	1	1	2	1	1	1

Table 3-7 (continued)

	1960	1965	1970	1975	1980	1985	1990	1995	2000
Maryland	0	0	0	2	4	4	4	3	2
Massachusetts	1	0	1	1	1	0	0	0	0
Michigan	1	1	1	0	0	0	0	1	3
Minnesota	0	0	0	0	0	0	0	0	0
Missouri	1	1	1	1	0	0	0	2	3
Nebraska	0	0	0	1	1	1	1	0	0
Nevada	0	0	0	0	0	1	1	1	1
New Jersey	1	1	1	2	1	1	1	1	1
New Mexico	0	0	0	0	0	0	0	0	1
New York	3	2	1	3	3	1	3	6	6
North Carolina	0	0	0	0	0	0	0	2	2
Ohio	1	1	0	0	1	2	2	2	3
Oregon	2	2	1	1	0	0	0	1	1
Pennsylvania	1	0	0	0	0	0	0	1	0
Rhode Island	0	0	0	0	0	1	1	0	0
South Carolina	0	1	1	0	0	0	1	0	0
Tennessee	0	1	0	1	1	1	1	1	0
Texas	0	0	0	1	0	0	0	3	4
Utah	0	0	0	0	0	0	0	2	0
Virginia	0	0	0	0	0	0	0	1	0
Washington	2	2	2	0	0	0	1	5	2
West Virginia	1	1	0	0	0	0	0	0	0
Wisconsin	0	0	0	0	0	0	0	0	1
Wyoming	0	0	0	0	0	0	0	1	1
Total	20	15	11	21	18	25	31	63	64

Source: Center for American Women and Politics. 2000. "National Information Bank on Women in Public Office," Eagleton Institute of Politics, Rutgers University, http://www.rci.rutgers.edu/~cawp/facts/cawpfs.html; United States Congress. 1989. *Biographical Directory of Congress 1776-1989*, Senate Document 100-34 Washington, D.C.: U.S. Government Printing Office; Congressional Quarterly. 1991. *Guide to Congress*, 4th ed. Washington, D.C.: Congressional Quarterly Press; Michael Barone and Grant Ujifusa. 1999. *The Almanac of American Politics. 2000.* Washington, D.C.: National Journal.

Women's Participation in Elections

There is quite a bit written on the role of women in elections. This paper will not belabor points that are made more fully elsewhere. However, some discussion is needed because the role of women as voters becomes an important factor for women legislators. If women do not

Table 3-8 Voter Registration Among United States Men and Women, 1966-1996

	1966	1970	1974	1978	1982	1986	1990	1994	1996
Women	68.6	66.8	61.7	62.5	64.4	65.0	63.1	63.7	67.3
Men	72.2	69.6	62.8	62.6	63.7	63.4	61.2	61.2	64.4
U.S. Total	70.3	68.1	62.2	62.6	64.1	64.3	62.2	62.5	65.9

Source: http://www.census.gov/population/socdemo/voting/history/vot01.txt

Table 3-9 Voter Turnout Among United States Men and Women, 1966-1996

	1966	1970	1974	1978	1982	1986	1990	1994	1996
Women	67.0	62.7	43.4	45.3	48.4	46.1	45.4	45.3	55.5
Men	71.9	56.8	46.2	46.6	48.7	45.8	44.6	44.7	52.8
U.S. Total	69.3	54.6	44.7	45.9	48.5	46.0	45.0	45.0	54.2

Source: http://www.census.gov/population/socdemo/voting/history/vot01.txt

vote then it will be difficult to build majority coalitions in support of women's policy proposals. Table 3-8 shows the percent of women registered to vote while Table 3-9 shows the voting turnout level in national elections since 1964. The pattern has been with men, fewer women were voting at the end of the twentieth century than were in the 1960s, and consistently lower percentages of women turned out to vote than were registered. These national trends are well known and widely discussed in journalistic as well as academic circles. There is cause for hope for women's issues in the policy process however, because women appear to have voted in larger percentages than men since the mid 1980s, although the differences are quite small. Whether this higher turnout for women voters is a trend that will continue remains to be seen. More importantly though it remains to be seen how many legislators will take note of women voter turnout rates.

Women's Policy Issues

Evidence from studies of state legislators indicates mixed results on the impact of women's styles as legislators. While on the one hand, women show more open styles and an interest in women centered policy themes (Thomas 1994; Rosenthal 1998), there is less evidence of representational styles that differ from male legislators (Reingold 1996). What we may in fact be seeing is that men are adapting more women gendered leadership styles (Duerst-Lahti and Kelly 1995). The women elected in the "year of the woman" have been studied quite a bit by research looking for any evidence of the policy effects of this large group of women who added two-thirds again as many women to the 103rd Congress as had served in the 102nd. There is evidence that these women brought with them a strong commitment to women's issues, and were responsible for keeping the attention high on a wide variety of policy issues of importance to women and families (Bingham 1997). In congressional time, seven years is really too short to tell what impact these women will have on the policy agendas of their respective committees. What is clear is that they are building seniority, and are assuming leadership roles on sub-committees where they will have greater access to the critical stages of policy making, and therefore should be able to make noticeable influence on public policy.

Implications and Conclusions

It is difficult to conclude that women are equally situated to men in the contemporary Congress given the evidence gathered in this chapter, and related research. However, it is equally difficult to conclude that women have made no difference to the institution. On the contrary, women have clearly been successful "congressmen" since at least the 1930s, amassing cumulative years of service and committee seniority similar to their male colleagues. In addition, the number of women in Congress has grown immeasurably since 1960. Further, since the 1970s, and the rise of the modern women's movement, women in Congress have gone beyond the stereotypic image of a congresswoman as a widow's legacy, perhaps charting her own political course in time, but more likely continuing on in the steps of her deceased husband. Congressional women in the last quarter of the twentieth century have a multitude of paths to the chamber, much like their male counterparts. This expansion of the images of women legislators will eventually have an impact on all aspects of women in political life, leaving ample room to redefine once again what representation means.

References

Barone, Michael and Grant Ujifusa. 1999. *The Almanac of American Politics 2000*. Washington DC: National Journal.
Bingham, Clara. 1997. *Women on the Hill: Challenging the Culture of Congress*. New York: Random House.

Center for the American Woman and Politics. 1999. "Women in Congressional Leadership Roles," *Fact Sheet* 3/99.

Center for the American Women and Politics. 2000. National Information Bank on Women in Public Office, Eagleton Institute of Politics, Rutgers University.

Congressional Quarterly. 1991. *Guide to Congress, 4th ed*, Washington DC: Congressional Quarterly, Inc.

Congressional Quarterly. 1993. "Committee Guide: Players, Politics and Turf of the 103rd Congress." Vol 51, Supplement to No. 18.

Congressional Quarterly. 1995. "Committee Guide: Players, Politics and Turf of the 104th Congress." Vol 53, Supplement to No. 12.

Congressional Quarterly. 1997. "Committee Guide: Players, Politics and Turf of the 105th Congress." Vol 55, Supplement to No. 12.

Congressional Quarterly. 1999. "Committee Guide: Players, Politics and Turf of the 106th Congress." Vol 57, Supplement to No. .

Darcy, R., Susan Welch, and Janet Clark. 1994. *Women, Elections and Representation*, 2nd ed. Lincoln: University of Nebraska Press.

Davidson, Roger. 1969. *The Role of the Congressman*. New York:Pegasus.

Dodson, Debra L. 1998. "Representing Women's Interests in the U.S. House of Representatives." In *Women and Elective Office: Past, Present, and Future*, eds. Sue Thomas and Clyde Wilcox, New York: Oxford University Press. pp 130-149.

Duerst-Lahti, Georgia, and Rita Mae Kelly. 1995. *Gender, Power, Leadership, and Governance*. Ann Arbor: University of Michigan Press.

Eulau, Heinz and Paul Karps.1977. "The Puzzle of Representation." *Legislative Studies Quarterly* 233-254.

Fenno, Richard F. 1978. *Home Style: House Members in Their Districts*. Boston: Little, Brown and Company.

Foerstel, Karen. 2000. "Chairmen's Term Limits Already Shaking Up House." *CQ Weekly* pp 628-634.

Gertzog, Irwin N. 1995. *Congressional Women: Their Recruitment, Integration, and Behavior, 2nd ed, revised and updated*. Westport, CT: Praeger.

Jacobson, Gary. 1997. *The Politics of Congressional Elections, 4th ed*, New York: Longman.

Josephson, Hannah. 1974. *Jeannette Rankin: First Lady in Congress*. New York: Bobbs-Merrill Co. Inc.

Krane, Dale and Stephen D. Shaffer. 1992. Culture and Politics in Mississippi: It's Not Just Black and White." In *Mississippi Government and Politics: Modernizers Versus Traditionalists*. eds. Dale Krane and Stephen D.

Shaffer, Lincoln: University of Nebraska Press.

Nelson, Garrison. 1993. *Committees in the U.S. Congress 1947-1992, Volume 1: Committee Jurisdictions and Member Rosters.* Washington DC: Congressional Quarterly Press.

Pitkin, Hanna. 1967. *The Concept of Representation.* Berkeley: University of California Press.

Rosenthal, Cindy Simon. 1998. *When Women Lead: Integrative Leadership in State Legislatures.* New York: Oxford University Press.

Swain, Carol. 1993. *Black Face, Black Interests.* Cambridge, MA: Harvard University Press.

Thomas, Sue. 1998. "Women and Elective Office: Past, Present, and Future," In *Women and Elective Office: Past, Present, and Future*, eds. Sue Thomas and Clyde Wilcox, New York: Oxford University Press. pp 1-14.

Thomas, Sue. 1994. *How Women Legislate.* New York: Oxford University Press.

United States Congress. 1989. *Biographical Directory of Congress 1776-1989.* Senate Document 100-34 Washington DC: U.S. Government Printing Office.

Whitby, Kenneth. 1997. *The Color of Representation.* Ann Arbor: University of Michigan Press.

Notes

1 Note that women had exercised the right to vote as property owners in local elections during colonial time. During the revolutionary war period and immediately after, new state constitutions provided for relaxed property standards for voting which in effect resulted in a new standard of wholly male suffrage. Women continued voting in some jurisdictions up until 1807 (See chapter 1, Darcy, Welch,, and Clark 1994).

CHAPTER 4

An Analysis of Descriptive and Substantive Latino Representation in Congress

Adolfo Santos and Carlos Huerta

The Latino population is one of the fastest growing minority groups in the United States, and early in this century they are expected to become the single largest minority group in the United States.[1] The growth of the Latino population has been the driving force behind the population changes that many states have experienced in recent years. With the changes that are occurring in the population, the issue of adequate representation has come to the forefront. Minority populations, and certainly Latino populations, will continue to call for greater representation. If the trend persists, this will mean a continued increase in electing minority and Latino representatives to legislative bodies. However, does the election of Latino representatives make a difference? This is the question that we address in this project. We determine whether electing Latinos to Congress improves the substantive representation of the Latino population. In the process, we delve into the role that Latino populations play in influencing the substantive representation of the Latino population.

In particular we concentrate our efforts around the following two questions. After which, we develop and test several hypothesis based on these questions.

> 1.) Have minority congressmen, in particular Latino members of Congress, been able to represent the interest of Latinos as Congress has become more conservative since 1994?

2.) What are the factors that affect legislative support
for Latino issues?

We begin by conceptualizing representation and take the position that
representation occurs when representatives sponsor and support issues that
are of interest to their constituents. We then evaluate the literature that looks
at minority, and in particular, Latino representation. Using several sets of
data, we first compare the legislative activity of Latino members in
Congress and compare them to non-Latino members in Congress. Secondly,
we use a variety of factors to explain support for issues that impact Latinos.

Concept of Representation

The concept of representation has a variety of meanings, but for
the purpose of this project we rely on two definitions – descriptive and
substantive representation (Pitkin 1967; Welch and Hibbing 1984; Hero
and Tolbert 1997). The former relies on the physical characteristics of
the representative to determine representation, while the later relies on
the behavior or "activity" of the representatives to determine the extent
to which representation has been achieved (Pitkin 1967, 143).
Descriptive representation can be said to have been achieved when representative bodies "look" like the society they purport to represent. If
50% of the population is female, then 50% of the members of the legislative body should also be female. If 11% of the population is African
American, then 11% of the members of the legislative body should also
consist of African American representatives. Similarly, if 12% of the
population is Latino, then 12% of the members of the representative
body should also be Latino. It is descriptive representation that John
Adams envisioned when he wrote that the legislature "should be an
exact portrait, in miniature, of the people at large, as it should think, feel,
reason and act like them" (Adams 1852-1865, 195). It is this type of representation that many in the minority community clamor for.
From this point of view it could hardly be said that the United
States Congress is a representative body. Currently only 10% of the
members of the House of Representatives are female, 9% are African
American and 4% are Latino. Evaluating representation on a descriptive
basis we could conclude that the United States Congress has not yet
achieved representative parity based on Adam's ideas. One of the reasons descriptive representation is preferred by many minority groups is

because of the implicit understanding that representatives who look like the people they represent will know best the policy preferences of those people. It is simply understood that representatives who look like their constituents will support policies that benefit their constituents. In a sense, this is what we hope to evaluate – the extent to which descriptive representation contributes to substantive representation. Does it matter if a member of Congress is Latino?

Substantive representation ignores the physical characteristics of members of Congress, and does not take for granted that members who look like their constituents will *act for* their constituents. Hanna Pitkin writes, "The activity of representing as acting for others must be defined in terms of what the representative does and how he does it, or in some combination of the two" (1967, 143). From this perspective, it can not simply be left to the physical characteristics of the representatives to insure that "action" is taken on behalf of the Latino population. Latino substantive representation is achieved when representatives "act for" the Latino community in the legislative arena.[2]

Minority Representation in Congress

Since the Voting Rights Act of 1965, the United States has witnessed the number of minority members in the House of Representatives increase dramatically (see De La Garza and DeSipio (1993) for an excellent discussion on the impact of Latinos on the Voting Rights Act.). In 1999, there were a total of 39 African Americans serving in the House – a major improvement from the first half of the twentieth century. Latino members of Congress have also seen their numbers improve. In Figure 4-1, we show the number of Latinos by Congress. The figure shows that by the 89th Congress, just after the signing of the Voting Rights Act of 1965, the number of Latino members of Congress began to increase. In the 89th Congress, three Latino members occupied congressional seats. This was the largest number of Latino members of Congress to occupy congressional seats up to that time. In Table 4-1, we see that only eight states have elected Latino members of Congress, with some of the earliest Latino representatives coming from states like New Mexico, California and Texas. Since the Voting Rights Act of 1965, the number of Latino members serving in Congress has gradually increased to nineteen in the 106th Congress.[3]

Figure 4.1 Hispanic Members of

the House of Representatives

1900-2000

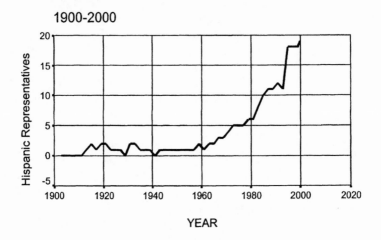

Table 4-1 Latino Members of Congress by State, 1960-2000

	1960	1965	1970	1975	1980	1985	1990	1995	2000
Arizona	0	0	0	0	0	0	0	1	1
California	0	1	1	1	1	3	3	4	6
Florida	0	0	0	0	0	0	1	2	2
Illinois	0	0	0	0	0	0	0	1	1
New Jersey	0	0	0	0	0	0	0	1	1
New Mexico	1	0	1	1	1	2	1	1	0
New York	0	0	0	1	1	1	1	2	2
Texas	0	2	2	2	2	4	4	5	6
Total	1	3	4	5	5	10	10	17	19

Source: http://lcweb.loc.gov/rr/hispanic/congress/contents.html

While the growth of Latinos has improved dramatically, there is still a significant gap between the number of Latino representatives and the percentage of the U.S. population that is Latino. The Latino population is estimated at 12%, while the number of Latino members in Congress is 4%. It is generally this type of data that researchers point to when suggesting that Latinos have not received adequate representation in Congress (Vigil 1984; Vigil 1994; Hibbing and Welch 1984; Swain 1993; Menifield 1998). Although there are a host of reasons for this discrepancy, the gap indicates that if representation is to be measured by the demographic characteristic of the members of Congress, then certainly the House of Representatives is not a portrait in miniature of the American people, as John Adams envisioned.

To what extent are the concerns of Latinos being fulfilled in Congress? The evidence appears to be mixed. One of the unintended consequences of the Voting Rights Act has been that as Congressional districts are drawn to insure that minority representatives will be elected, surrounding congressional districts have become more conservative and more Anglo (Overby and Cosgrove 1996, 541).[4] This strategy of packing minorities into districts has been used by Republican administrations to ensure that minority candidates get elected to office, while at the same time insuring that Republican candidates are elected to office (Brace, Grofman, and Handley 1987; and Davidson and Oleszek 1994, 56). While minority groups have pushed for the election of minority candidates, pursuing this strategy has contributed to the creation of a more conservative Congress that has less concern for minority interests. In other words, as descriptive representation has increased, substantive representation has decreased.

Research that examines the factors that affect support for Latino issues have produced conflicting findings (Hero and Tolbert 1995; Kerr and Miller 1997). Differences in the extent to which substantive representation exists may result from several conceptualization issues that need to be addressed. Of particular concern is that measures of Latino substantive representation rely on the interest group score-cards that measure liberal or ideological positions that may be better indicators of partisanship rather than of support for Latino issues (see Welch and Hibbing 1984; Hero and Tolbert 1995). We might even suggest that the reason Latino members of Congress do not seem to have an impact on support for Latino policy (as Welch and Hibbing 1984 and Hero and Tolbert 1995 have concluded) is because "Latino policy" is not being measured. Rather, what these studies seem to be measuring is support for the Democratic Party's position. If the party identification of the member of Congress accounts for the differences in support for Latino issues and overshadows the impact of Latino representatives (Kerr and Miller 1997), then perhaps it would make more sense to examine differences between Latino representatives and non-Latino

Democratic representatives (see Canon 1999 for similar discussion of African American representation). If there are differences between Latino and non-Latino Democrats, then this would be strong evidence that Latino representation does matter.

In order to further refine the concept of Latino representation, it is important to look at the particular Latino bills and amendments that members of Congress vote on. The Hero and Tolbert research uses a support score based on votes that are thought to be important for Latinos, for the 100th Congress developed by the Southwest Voter Research Institute, Inc. (SWVRI). A similar and more recent support score for the 105th Congress has been created by the National Hispanic Leadership Agenda (NHLA).[5] Many of these votes, while important for the Latino community, do not have an exclusive impact on Latinos. Kerr and Miller (1997) have found that the support scores are strongly related to the party identification of the members of Congress, and that most of the variance is explained by the members' party affiliation. We propose to examine the NHLA support score and check to see if there are any issues that do exhibit differences between Latino and non-Latino Democratic representatives.

Measurement and Methodology

In this study, we focus on the 105th Congress. The 105th Congress has a total of 18 Latino members in the House of Representatives. Fifteen of these members are Democrats and three are Republicans (see Table 4-2).[6] Texas has the largest Latino delegation, with six Latino members of Congress. California has the second largest Latino delegation with five members of the House. Florida and New York each have two Latino members while Arizona, Illinois and New Jersey each have one. The two Latino representatives from Florida and one of the six from Texas are members of the Republican Party. The 105th Congress has a total of 228 Republicans, 206 Democrats, and one Independent. This Congress has also been somewhat inactive, enacting only 394 public laws – a sizable portion of which has been introduced by Senators.[7]

Table 4-2 Latino Members of Congress by Party Identification, 1960-2000

	1960		1965		1970		1975		1980		1985		1990		1995		2000	
	D	R	D	R	D	R	D	R	D	R	D	R	D	R	D	R	D	R
Arizona	0	0	0	0	0	0	0	0	0	0	0	0	0	0	1	0	1	0
California	0	0	1	0	1	0	1	0	1	0	3	0	3	0	4	0	6	0
Florida	0	0	0	0	0	0	0	0	0	0	0	0	0	1	1	1	1	1
Illinois	0	0	0	0	0	0	0	0	0	0	0	0	0	0	1	0	1	0
New Jersey	0	0	0	0	0	0	0	0	0	0	0	0	0	0	1	0	1	0
New Mexico	0	1	0	0	0	1	0	1	0	1	1	1	1	0	1	0	0	0
New York	0	0	0	0	0	0	1	0	1	0	1	0	1	0	2	0	2	0
Texas	0	0	0	2	1	1	2	0	2	0	4	0	4	0	4	1	5	1
Total	0	1	1	2	2	2	4	1	4	1	9	1	9	1	15	2	17	2

Source: http://lcweb.loc.gov/rr/hispanic/congress/contents.html

To measure substantive representation, we use four different measures of legislative action. The first three measures simply allow us to compare the mean legislative activities of Latino and non-Latino members of Congress. Once this is done, a more rigorous model is tested in which we explain support for Latino issues using a multivariate model. In the first three measures of substantive representation, we count the number of bills, and the number of laws introduced by Latino and non-Latino members of Congress, and evaluate the impact that Latino introduced legislation has on Latinos. In the multivariate model, we rely on roll call votes on four issues that impact Latinos most directly. All of these measures of substantive representation capture elements of legislative *action*.

Comparison of Legislative Activity of Latino and Non-Latino Members of Congress

Our first hypothesis states: To improve their ability to substantively represent their Latino constituents, Latino members of Congress should sponsor bills at a higher rate than their fellow members of Congress. This should be particularly the case, for their fellow partisans.[8] In a slightly more stringent test of substantive representation, we hypothesize that Latino members of Congress provide greater substantive representation when their bills become laws at a higher rate than those of their colleagues. But, if the number of bills that actually becomes law is smaller for Latino members of Congress than for non-Latino members of Congress, then we would conclude that Latinos are receiving less substantive representation. More stringently still, we hypothesize that for Latino members of Congress to improve the substantive representation of Latinos, then they must introduce legislation that impacts Latinos directly.[9] Critical to each of these hypotheses is the extent and nature of legislative activity. These hypotheses allow us to test for substantive representation as an activity – as *acting for* Latinos.

Legislative Support for Latino Issues

After comparing the legislative activity of Latino and non-Latino members of the House of Representatives, we identify the factors that explain support for issues that impact Latinos most directly. Because we know that Democrats tend to support Latino issues and Republicans tend to oppose them, we focus our attention on Democrats (see Welch and Hibbing 1984; and Hero and Tolbert 1995). In this part of the paper, we want to know whether support for Latino issues can be explained by the ethnicity of the 18 Latino members and all of the non-Latino *Democrats*, while controlling for other factors. Using multivariate regression, we test a model in which we have hypothesized that support for Latino issues is a function of the members of Congress' ethnicity, the size of the Latino population in the congressional districts, and the ideological position of the respective members of Congress.

Using the National Hispanic Leadership Agenda (NHLA) scorecards for the 105th Congress, we identify four issues that Latino members of Congress support to a significantly greater extent than non-Latino Democrats (see Table 4-3). These four items are: allowing a nuclear waste dump in Sierra Blanca, Texas, allowing the military on the U.S.- Mexico border, restricting funding for standardized education testing, and the prohibition of campaign contributions by legal immigrants. These four items may represent issues where Latino representatives provide direct substantive representation. We calculate this measure of substantive representation as the percent of the time a representative votes in favor of these four items.

Table 4-3 Means Analysis of Latino Issues-Latino and Democratic Representativeness

Variable	Latino	Non-Latino	Difference
Military troops on the border	.81	.55	.26*
Ban on contributions by legal permanent immigrants	.88	.55	.33**
Texas radioactive waste	.89	.43	.45**
Restrict national standardized testing	1.00	.35	.65**

* = .05; ** = .01

Source: http://lcweb.loc.gov/rr/hispanic/congress/contents.html

We expect that the level of support of Latino issues is a function of the ethnicity of the Democratic members of Congress. And by ethnicity of course, we are simply referring to whether the member is Latino or not. Latinos are coded 1, and non-Latinos are coded 0. Although previous studies have found that Latino members of Congress do not seem to explain support for Latino issues, we nevertheless argue that Latino representatives do make a difference (Welch and Hibbing 1984; Hero and Tolbert 1995). Previous studies have found no relationship between the Latino ethnicity of the members of Congress and their support for Latino issues because many of the issues used to measure Latino substantive representation are issues that impact a broad segment of society – not simply Latinos. Thus, one might suggest that previous studies that attempt to explain support for Latino substantive representation may in actuality be explaining *Democratic* substantive representation.

Research of this type ordinarily uses percent Latino in the district as one of the independent variables. This variable usually overshadows the effect of the dummy variable used to distinguish between Latino and non-Latino representatives (Kerr and Miller 1997). For example, all eighteen of the Latino representatives in the 105th Congress are from districts with a high percentage of Latinos. It may therefore make more sense to examine the percent Latino in the district only for non-Latino Democratic representatives. A modified percent Latino variable is developed by creating a dummy variable (1–non-Latino, 0–Latino) and multiplying it by the percent Latino variable. This new variable assesses the impact of the non-Latino Democratic representatives with the percent Latino of the district. We expect that as the percent Latino of the district increases, so will support for Latino issues. Also, this should enhance the impact of the item measuring Latino representative. This variable is coded so that a district with 59% Latino has a value of .59. Furthermore, the Latino dummy variable will also be included in the model. A significant and negative effect will indicate that Latino members of Congress are more supportive of Latino issues than non-Latinos.

The ideology of the member of Congress is another factor to consider (Menifield 1998). The ideology of the members of Congress is measured using their American Conservative Union (ACU) score averages for the 105th Congress (average of 1997 and 1998 scores). The ACU scores range from 0 (very liberal) to 100 (very conservative). The ACU scores are subtracted from 100 yielding a score with the higher values representing liberalism and lower values conservatism[10]. The expectation is that the more liberal the member of Congress, the more supportive they will be of Latino issues. Thus, the model for testing support of Latino issues is represented by Equations 1 (EQ 1) and 2 (EQ 2). EQ 1 includes whether the member of Congress is Latino, the percent Latino of the district, and ideology. In EQ 2, the percent Latino of the district is replaced with the modified percent Latino of the district. Additionally, the models include all Latino representatives and non-Latino Democrats.

> *EQ 1: Latino support = Latino Representative + percent*
> *Latino of district + ideology*
> *EQ 2: Latino support = Latino Representative + modified*
> *percent Latino of district + ideology*

Findings

-Bill Sponsorship

In Figure 4-2, we show the average number of bills that Latino members of Congress have introduced and compare them to the number that non-Latino members have introduced. Our findings show that non-

Figure 4.2 Average Number of Bills

Introduced By Representatives

105th Congress (House only)

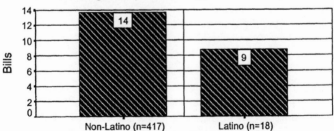

Note: Number of bills excludes amendments

Significance of F = .11

Latino members of Congress have introduced an average of 14 bills, compared to Latino members of Congress who have averaged 9 bills during the 105th Congress. This difference of 5 bills between Latino and non-Latino House members might suggest that Latinos are on average less active than their colleagues, but this may not necessarily be the case. This difference fails to demonstrate statistical significance in a two-tailed test.[11] The implication of this is that Latino members of Congress are not statistically different from their non-Latino colleagues. Even though this difference is statistically insignificant, the difference may even be smaller if we compare Democrats to Democrats.

In Figure 4-3, we show that on average, the 191 non-Latino Democratic House members of Congress sponsored 11.5 bills compared to Latino Democrats who, on average, introduced 8 bills during the 105th Congress.[12] This difference of 3.5 bills is considerably smaller than that found when comparing all non-Latinos to Latino House members. The implication of this is that because Republicans are in control of Congress, Democrats are slightly less inclined to submit bills for consideration. As before, this difference fails to pass the test of significance, suggesting that there is no meaningful difference between Latino and non-Latino Democratic House members. In using bill sponsorship as a

Figure 4.3 Average Number of Bills
Introduced by Democratic Reps

105th Congress (House only)

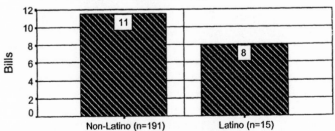

Democratic Representatives

Note: Number of bills excludes amendments

Significance of F = .2

Figure 4.4 Average Number of Laws

Introduced by Representatives

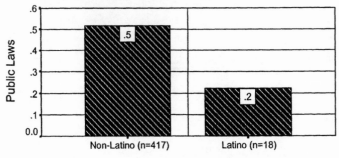

105th Congress (House only)

Representative

Significance of F = .25

measure of substantive representation, Latinos, while not receiving greater amounts of representation, are certainly not lagging far behind their colleagues.

-Public Laws

Our second measure of substantive representation compares the number of public laws that were introduced by Latino and non-Latino House members. Here, we are testing substantive representation a bit more stringently. While it is relatively easy to sponsor bills, it is considerably more difficult to convince other members to vote for passage of the legislation. Of the 4,874 bills that were introduced by the members of the House of Representatives during the 105th Congress, only 228 would actually become public laws.[13] In Figure 4-4, we note that non-Latino House members have on the average introduced .52 bills that become laws. Latino House members on the other hand, average .22 bills that become laws. As before, our test of significance suggests there is no real difference between the two groups. The evidence indicates that Latinos are not significantly more or less successful than their non-Latino colleagues at insuring that their bills become laws.

In Figure 4-5, we show the average number of bills introduced by

Figure 4.5 Average Number of Laws Introduced by Democrats

105th Congress (House only)

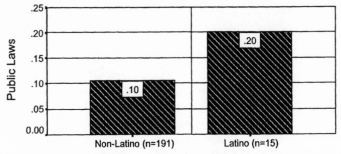

Representative

Significance of F = .28

Latino and non-Latino Democrats. The findings suggest that there is even less of a difference in the number of bills that become laws when we look only at the Democrats. As before, because the Republican Party did control the 105th Congress, it is safe to assume that Democrats would be less successful in seeing that their bills become laws. To ensure that we are comparing comparable groups, we only look at Democrats in Figure 5.[14] In Figure 4-5, we see that Latino Democrats are twice as successful in getting their bills enacted into laws than their fellow Democrats. As before, however, these differences are not statistically significant. There appears to be no statistically significant difference between the success of Latino Democrats and non-Latino Democrats in getting their bills enacted into laws.

The evidence thus far suggests that there are no significant differences between Latino and non-Latino members of the House of Representatives. The implication is that Latino members of Congress, while certainly not being more active than their non-Latino colleagues, are also, not less active than their colleagues. This is the case when we look at the number of bills and laws that are sponsored by the members of Congress. Perhaps a more stringent test still, is to see whether the laws that are introduced by Latino members of Congress actually intend to impact the Latino population in a positive manner.

-Sponsorship of Legislation which Directly Impacts Latinos

A more stringent test of substantive representation must take into account the actual substance of the legislation that is sponsored. For this we turn to the actual laws that Latinos sponsored during the 105th Congress. Although there are 18 Latino members of Congress, only four have been successful at getting their bills enacted into laws[15] – each sponsoring one successful public law.[16] None of these laws, however, have a direct or positive impact on Latinos in general. Of the four laws sponsored by Latinos, two established names for U.S. Post Offices.[17] One authorized the Secretary of the Treasury to develop a strategy to combat money laundering,[18] and one gave two school districts authority over public land.[19] It appears from reviewing the contents of the laws, that the Latino members of Congress are successful at enacting laws that have a more direct bearing on their individual districts, rather than impacting Latinos in general.

It is conceivable that the Republican Congress has circumvented the interests of Latinos because Latinos generally do not vote for Republicans. If Latinos do not vote for Republicans, then Republicans may not feel compelled to sponsor or support legislation that benefits Latinos. In fact, when we look at the number of bills that were identified by the National Hispanic Leadership Agenda (NHLA) as legislative issues that were of importance to Latinos few had a positive impact on Latinos. NHLA identified 24 measures that impacted Latinos, 17 (71%) of these had a negative impact on Latinos. Voting in favor of those 17 measures constituted voting against the Latino position taken by the NHLA. The implication of this is that while there are bills introduced that impact Latinos, the impact of the majority of those bills – at least in the 105th Congress, is adverse to the interests of Latinos. What then are the factors that affect legislative support for Latino issues?

-Legislative Support for Latino Issues

Equation 1 (Table 4-4) indicates that the impact of Latino representatives is insignificant. Had there been a substantial difference in support for Latino issues based on ethnicity, Latino Representatives would have had a significant effect. The percent Latino of the district variable had a positive and significant effect indicating that as the percentage of Latinos in the district increased the representative became more responsive to Latino issues. The suspicion is that the percent Latino of the district is overwhelming the ethnicity variable. Furthermore, the ideology of the member does impact support. The more

Table 4-4 Coefficient Estimates for Latino Support

Variable	b	beta
Non-Latino representative	-.14	-.12
Percent Latino in district	.59**	.33**
Liberalism	.66**	.35**
Constant	.02	
Number of cases	207	
Adjusted R-square	.28	
Standard error	.28	

* = .05; ** = .01

liberal the members of Congress, the more supportive they are. Additionally, it must be noted that these findings represent differences among Democratic and Latino House members. Thus, party is not affecting these findings.

The second model (Table 4-5) has the modified percent Latino of district variable. How does this affect the non-Latino representative variable? As expected, ethnicity now makes a difference. Latino representatives are more likely than non-Latino representatives to support Latino issues. Also, the modified percent Latino of district is having a significant and positive effect. This more precise measure tells us that as the percent Latino of a district increases (for non-Latino representatives), Latino support increases. This finding also suggests that Kerr and Miller (1997) were correct when they suspected that the percent Latino of the district was overpowering the impact of Latino representatives. Additionally, liberalism continues to have a positive effect – the more liberal, the more supportive.

Table 4-5 Coefficient Estimates for Latino Support, Modified Percent Latino in District

Variable	b	beta
Non-Latino representative	-.51**	-.43**
Percent Latino in district	.58**	.19**
Liberalism	.65**	.34**
Constant	.40**	
Number of cases	207	
Adjusted R-square	.28	
Standard error	.28	

* = .05; ** = .01

Implications and Conclusions

Representation has been and still is a contentious issue in our nation. The purpose of this project was to analyze Latino representation. More specifically we wished to address whether direct representation led to improved substantive representation and to examine the factors that enhance Latino substantive representation. The analysis found that Latino representatives provide comparable representation as that of non-Latino representatives. Latino representatives are as active as non-Latino representatives in bill sponsorship and in having their sponsored bills become laws. This evidence suggests that Latino representatives do not differ significantly from their non-Latino colleagues in the legislative arena. While Latino congressmen are not significantly less active than their non-Latino colleagues, they do not appear to be more active than their colleagues are. One can hardly conclude that Latinos are not in need of federal support to improve their standard of living given the economic and social plight of the Latino community. Given their poor economic standing, one might expect that Latino representatives have a major task before them if they are to improve the quality of life for Latinos in general. One might, therefore expect that Latino members of Congress, if they are to improve the substantive representation of Latinos, should be more active than their colleagues are in pursuing legislation that will benefit Latinos directly. And while one certainly recognizes that Latino members of Congress are in the minority, they can certainly use their power to introduce bills as a way of forcing a recalcitrant Congress to deal with the concerns of a population in much need of governmental support.

Latino members are not only not sending signals, but they are also not sponsoring legislation that benefits the Latino community. The analysis revealed that the laws sponsored by Latino representatives do not specifically address Latino issues. When the few laws introduced by the Latino members of the House of Representatives are considered, none of them comes close to resembling policy issues that impacted the Latino community in a positive sense. Furthermore, of the bills and amendments that the NHLA identified as issues that were of interest to Latinos, the vast majority had a negative impact on Latinos. One implication of this behavior is that Latino members of Congress are relegated to a position of *reactionaries* – reacting to the actions of the majority party rather than acting first, and forcing the

Majority party to react to their concerns.

Where we do see Latino representation matter is in a very narrow focus of policy positions. If we measure substantive representation narrowly – e.g. based on how Democratic members of Congress vote on four issues – our evidence suggests that Latino representatives appear to support Latino interests. The multivariate analysis provides evidence that on issues with a specific Latino interest, Latino representatives are more likely to support Latino issues than are non-Latino Democratic representatives. Latino members of Congress tend to vote strongly in favor of Latino issues, even more than other non-Latino Democrats; but this only on a narrow range of issues. Overall, our evidence suggests that Latino representation matters only modestly in explaining the substantive representation of Latinos, but Latino representation certainly does not appear to improve representation in some extraordinary manner that can not be attributed to partisanship.

References

Adams, John. 1852-1865. "Letters to John Penn, January 1776." *Works*. IV, 205. Boston: Little, Brown and Co.

Brace, Kimball, Bernard Grofman, and Lisa Handley. 1987. "Does Redistricting Aimed to Help Blacks Necessarily Help Republicans?" *The Journal of Politics* 49:169-85.

Canon, David T. 1999. *Race, Redistricting, and Representation: The Unintended Consequences of Black Majority Districts*. Chicago: The University of Chicago Press.

Davidson, Roger H. and Walter J. Oleszek. 1994. *Congress and Its Members.* 4th ed. Washington: CQ Press.

De La Garza, Rodolfo O. and Louis DeSipio. 1993. "Save the Baby, Change the Bathwater, and Scrub the Tub: Latino Electoral Participation after Twenty Years of Voting Rights Act Coverage." *Texas Law Review* 71:1479-1539.

Hero, Rodney E. and Caroline J. Tolbert. 1995. "Latinos and Substantive Representation in the U.S. House of Representatives: Direct, Indirect, or Nonexistent?" *American Journal of Political Science* 39:640-652.

Kerr, Brinck and Will Miller. 1997. "Latino Representation, It's Direct and Indirect." *American Journal of Political Science* 41:1066-1071.

Menifield, Charles E. 1998. "A Loose Coalition or a United Front: Voting Behavior within the Congressional Hispanic Caucus." *Latino Studies Journal*. 9:26-44.

Overby, Marvin, L. and Kenneth M. Cosgrove. 1996. "Unintended Consequences? Racial Redistricting and the Representation of Minority Interests." *Journal of Politics* 58:540-550.

Pitkin, Hanna F. 1967. *The Concept of Representation.* Berkeley: University of California Press.

Swain, Carol M. 1993. *Black Faces, Black Interests: The Representation of African Americans in Congress.* Cambridge: Harvard University Press.

U.S. Bureau of the Census. 1996. "Population Projections of the United States by Age, Sex, Race and Hispanic Origin: 1995-2050." *U.S. Bureau of the Census, Current Population Reports, Series P25-1130.*

Vigil, Maurilio E. 1984. "Hispanics Gain Seats in the 98th Congress after Reapportionment." *International Social Science Review* 59:20-30.

Vigil, Maurilio E. 1994. "Hispanics in the 103rd Congress: The 1990 Census, Reapportionment, Redistricting, and the 1992 Elections." *Latino Studies Journal* 5:40-76.

Welch, Susan and John R. Hibbing. 1984. "Hispanic Representation in the U.S. Congress." *Social Science Quarterly* 65:328-335.

Notes

1 We prefer to use the term Latino instead of Hispanic when referring to people of Latin-America origin who are currently living in the United States.

2 While we recognize that there is a certain symbolic utility achieved when electing minority public officials, we have chosen to focus only on the substantive outcomes achieved when electing Latinos.

3 In the fall of 1999, Congressman Joe Bacca was elected to California's 42nd congressional district, brining the total to nineteen.

4 Anglo refers to non-Hispanic white.

5 A more thorough discussion of the NHLA score is provided later in this section.

6 It should be noted that in this study we exclude representatives from Puerto Rico and Guam.

7 Because our focus is on the House of Representatives, legislation introduced by Senators is excluded from this analysis.

8 The second part of this first hypothesis assumes the same as the first, only now we are only looking at fellow Democrats.

9 The National Hispanic Leadership Agenda has identified a series of bills that are said to impact the Latino community. While we do not expect the Latino leadership to introduce legislation that negatively impact Latinos, we do expect

the Latino leadership to introduce legislation that impacts Latinos positively.

10 The scores are divided by 100 so that a 75 is coded as .75.

11 Note that our hypothesis does not assume that Latino members of Congress will introduce more or less bills than non-Latino members of Congress. We are not assuming a unidirectional relationship, thus the two-tailed test.

12 In figure 3, we only report the average bill sponsorship of Democrats, thus we exclude the three Republican Latino House members.

13 We rely on 219 of the 228 public laws to conduct our analysis. The reason for the discrepancy is that we have excluded the laws sponsored by the Representatives of the territories and the District of Columbia.

14 Note that we do not conduct a separate test for Republicans because of the small number of Latino Republicans.

15 We do not consider amendments/riders to other bills in this research.

16 Henry Bonilla of Texas sponsored Public Law 105-4, Silvestre Reyes of Texas sponsored 105-169, Jose Serrano of New York sponsored 105-87, and, Nydia Velázquez of New York sponsored 105-310.

17 Public laws 105-4 and 105-87.

18 Public Law 105-310.

19 Public Law 105-169.

CHAPTER 5

The Representation of Asian Americans in the U.S. Political System

Okiyoshi Takeda

Asian Americans are one of the fastest growing racial groups in the United States, yet political scientists have paid little attention to them. Studies of "race" are often analyses of black-white relations; research on "minorities" usually covers African Americans and Latinos, but not Asian Americans and Native Americans. In fact, Asian Americans are the racial group in America that is least studied by political scientists (Takeda 1999). Existing work on Asian American politics is heavily concentrated in the area of voting behavior (Uhlaner, Cain, and Kieweit 1989; Cain, Kieweit, and Uhlaner 1991; Lien 1994, 1997; Tam 1995; but see Tien and Levy 1998).

Of course, the lack of research does not necessarily represent a lack of political activity among Asian Americans themselves. In places like Southern California, where the Asian American population has been rapidly growing, Asian Americans have cooperated and competed with other racial minority groups for political representation, producing a unique dynamic that has caught the attention of many researchers (Fong 1994; Horton 1995; Saito 1998).[1] Asian Americans, however, have not been successful in sending their own representatives to Congress and state legislatures that match their population growth and socio-economic achievement. To what extent are Asian Americans represented in the U.S. political system, and what accounts for the lack of Asian faces in legislatures that match their population level? If Asian Americans cannot count on their own representatives, who represents their substantial interests in Congress?

This chapter provides one of the first systematic, political science accounts of Asian American political representation in the United States. It draws on literature relevant to the representation of other minority groups, and uses demographic and legislative data that have particular relevance to Asian Americans. It pays particular attention to their representation in Congress, both in its descriptive and substantial sense. That is, it examines why there are so few Asian American members in Congress (descriptive representation), and whether the interests of Asian Americans are represented in Congress without many Asian American members (substantive representation). Although the main focus of this chapter is on the national level, I also make a few references to state and local politics in locations where a large number of Asian Americans reside.

Due to the scarcity of political science research on Asian Americans, scholars in the discipline sometimes treat Asian Americans with conventional stereotypes rather than with systematic data and relevant studies produced in fields other than political science (Takeda 1999). This chapter therefore begins with a short discussion of who Asian Americans are and what demographic characteristics they have. It then moves on to a discussion of who represents them in U.S. Congress, followed by an overview of past and present Asian American members of Congress. Next it provides an analysis of Asian American substantive representation by examining which members cosponsored a House resolution that condemns stereotypes against Asian Americans. It concludes with a discussion of the evidence of descriptive and substantive representation provided in this chapter.

Who are Asian Americans?

Asian Americans are a diverse group of people. They include not only Japanese, Korean, and Chinese Americans, but also Filipinos, Southeast Asians (such as Vietnamese, Thai, Laotians, Cambodians, Hmong) and South Asians (who are from, or whose ancestors are from, India, Pakistan, Bangladesh, Sri Lanka, Nepal, Bhutan, and Maldives).[2] Some of them, in particular Chinese and Japanese, came to the United States in the nineteenth century, and their descendants are now reaching the fourth and fifth generations. The majority of Asian Americans (63.1 percent in 1990), however, are foreign-born (Shinagawa and Jang 1998, 73). This is because unlike European Americans and Latinos, Asian Americans were not allowed to immigrate to the United States freely before the 1965 immigration law abolished the national quota that virtually prohibited their immigration.

By the count of the 1990 census, there were about 7.2 million Asian Americans, comprising three percent of the national population. Their population, however, is rapidly growing; measured by the growth rate rather than by the sheer number of growth, Asian Americans are the fastest growing racial group (3.8% in 1994), even faster than Latinos (3.5%) (Shinagawa and Jang 1998, 136-37).[3] The number of Asian Americans is estimated to have reached 10.8 million in 1999, comprising approximately four percent of the U.S. population (U.S. Bureau of Census 2000). Among Asian Americans, Chinese (including those who originate from mainland China, Taiwan, and Hong Kong) are the largest group (23% in 1990), followed by Filipino (19%), Japanese (12%), Asian Indians (11%), Koreans (11%) and Vietnamese (8%) (Shinagawa and Jang 1998, 70). It is speculated that Filipinos may have exceeded Chinese in number in 2000; already in 1990, they were the largest Asian American ethnic group in California, greater in number than Chinese (Shinagawa and Jang 1998, 46).

Having origins in diverse places from Japan to Pakistan, Asian Americans are heterogeneous in terms of language, culture, social belief, religion, and political orientation. Unlike Latinos, who are by and large connected by their common Hispanic heritage (Spanish language and Catholic beliefs), Asian Americans are not unified by cultural or ethnic ties. Some even wonder whether such diverse people can be classified into one group.

Two forces, however, have contributed to the development of "Asian American" identity among Asian people of different ethnic origins (Espiritu 1992).[4] The first is a tendency of the mainstream society to lump together various Asian ethnic groups and disregard the differences among them. Non-Asian people often cannot distinguish Japanese Americans from Chinese Americans and Vietnamese Americans (or for that matter, from Japanese nationals). Asian Americans of one ethnic group are sometimes mistaken for another Asian ethnic group and become the target of discrimination and racial hatred. Somewhat echoing this tendency, the U.S. Census Bureau frequently reports population statistics on the level of "Asian Americans," although it collects data from individuals on the level of national level such as Japanese, Filipinos, and Asian Indians. Asian Americans are often forced to accept the "Asian" label because that is the sign with which non-Asian people recognize them in society.

In contrast, the second force that has helped unite Asians of different ethnic groups has risen from Asian Americans themselves. Although they vary in the countries of birth and the number of years they have lived in the United States, they become subject to the same anti-Asian discrimination and stereotypes, which still prevail in today's society (Umemoto 2000). This shared experience leads them to think that they have the same position and future in the race relations of the United States. In responding to outside forces, Asian Americans begin to create a common, pan-Asian identity that does not necessarily conflict with the ethnic identities that they already have. In particular, beginning with their participation in the anti-war, anti-white establishment movement in the late 1960s, activist Asian Americans have chosen to act at the pan-Asian level, partly because they gain more power if several ethnic groups are united into one force. Their pan-Asian activities have spread to other realms of society such as community organizing, college curriculum reform, and creative writing (Espiritu 1992; Wei 1993), although social and political activities at the ethnic level have not died down.

There is a tendency in society and in the academia alike not to regard Asian Americans as a disadvantaged minority group. Those who hold this view refers to the socio-economic "success" that Asian Americans have achieved in the postwar America. For example, one American government textbook writes:

> In general, however, the Asian American population has rapidly moved up the economic scale, with a higher-than-average median family income, and a rapid increase in the number of engineers, scientists, doctors, and other professionals, as well as independent businesspeople.
>
> Most extraordinary has been the increase in Asian Americans in higher education. Their average SAT score of 562 is 50 points above the national average, 34 percent above the average of white students . . . (Freedman 2000, 358)

Whether we can generalize this view all entire Asian Americans is questionable. Asian Americans in the activist rank and scholars in Asian American studies have objected to this view, critically calling it a "model minority" view (Suzuki 1977; Hurh and Kim 1989; Tuan 1998). Their arguments range from normative to empirical; here, I take up only two empirical claims. First, critics argue that the "success" image of Asian Americans does not account for many Asian immigrants who are well below the national average in socio-economic indices. The poverty rates are high among Southeast Asian refugee communities; 63.6% of Hmongs, 42.6% of Cambodians, and 34.7% of Laotians lived under the poverty line in 1990. These groups make a sharp contrast with other Asian groups; only 6.4% of Filipinos and 7.0 percent of Japanese Americans lived in poverty in 1990 (Shinagawa an Jung 1998, 71).[5]

Second, the critics of the "model minority" view maintain that the median family or household income, although frequently used (as in the textbook above), does not tell the entire story about the economic status of Asian Americans. They argue that, because Asian American families have more individuals in a family (3.8) than non-Hispanic whites do (3.1), the larger median family income for Asian Americans ($44,640 in 1993) than non-Hispanic whites ($41,110) does not translate into a richer status for the former. When calculated as per capita income, the median is lower for Asian Americans ($13,420 in 1990) than for non-Hispanic whites ($15,265) (Shinagawa and Jung 1998, 50). Furthermore, the criticism goes, because Asian Americans concentrate in states where cost of living is also high (such as California, New York, and Hawaii), their seemingly high income does not translate into as high spending power (Tuan 1998, 45).

The quick overview of the demography above suggests that it is not appropriate to treat Asian Americans with a certain, fixed image widely available in society. In fact, little of the basic statistics about Asian Americans presented here—the diversity in country of origin and the wide gap in socio-economic status among different ethnic groups—are known to political scientists. A discussion of Asian American politics, however, must be sensitive to the diverse nature of Asian Americans. Although I use the generic term "Asian Americans" and "Asians" in my foregoing discussion unless I specify otherwise, the reader is cautioned not to associate them with their image of a particular Asian ethnic group.

Where Do Asian Americans Live, and Who Represents Them?

At first glance, Asian Americans seem to live in concentrated areas. As many as 64% of all Asian Americans live in five states—California (3.9 million in 1998), New York (995,000), Hawaii (757,000), Texas (556,000), and Illinois (453,000) (U.S. Bureau of Census 2000). Although the top three states are well known to be the states in which many Asian Americans reside, Texas and Illinois as the fourth and fifth states may be a fresh finding to some people. This can be explained by the tendency of Asian Americans to live in metropolitan areas (95%, compared to 75% for non-Hispanic whites in 1990) (Shinagawa and Jang 1998, 45). Houston and Chicago are among the top ten cities with the largest Asian American population (Shinagawa 1996, 97).

Who represents Asian Americans in Congress? If Asian Americans had a descriptive representation in proportion to their share of population in the nation (three to four percent), there should be thirteen to seventeen House members and three to four Senators who are Asian Americans. Like other racial minority groups and women, however, Asian Americans have not achieved descriptive representation, especially in the House. Currently, in the 106th Congress (1999-2000), only three voting members in the House[6] and two Senators are Asian Americans. All of these current members are Democrats.

Given that Asian Americans are the majority in Hawaii in terms of population, it is not surprising that both Senators and one of the two House members from the state are Asian Americans. They include: Senator Daniel Inouye (Japanese American), Senator Daniel Akaka (Chinese and Native Hawaiian), and Representative Patsy Mink (Japanese American). The remaining two current House members are Robert Matsui from California (Japanese American) and David Wu from Oregon (Chinese American). Given the large Asian American population in California, one may wonder why more Asian Americans are not elected from the state? Indeed, Asian Americans comprise as much as 10% of the California population. Why aren't there more Asian Americans elected from California (and other states in which many Asian Americans live, such as New York and Illinois)?

In order to answer this question, population statistics at the House district level rather than at the state level should be examined. If a large number of Asian Americans live in a state, but are scattered among different House districts, their voting power is not sufficient to send their own representatives to the House because of the lack of concentration. This is true even if they register to vote and go to the voting booth in the same frequency as other racial groups.[7] The statistics shown in Table 5-1 suggests that this is the case. The table lists all House districts with 10% or more Asian Americans: there are 28 of these districts in the nation (the table also lists David Wu's district, which is not among the 28).[8] It also lists the percentage of white, African American, and Hispanic population in the district, the current member elected from the district (with indication of whether they belong to the Congressional Asian Pacific Caucus, which will be discussed below), and the unofficial estimate of Asian American population in the district in 2000.[9]

Looking at Table 5-1, a very different picture if presented from the population statistics at the state level. Except for the two districts in Hawaii, Asian Americans are not a majority in any district in the nation—the largest proportion of Asian Americans in the U.S. mainland is just 27.8% (California District 8, which includes San Francisco Chinatown). Unlike African Americans and Latinos, Asian Americans do not have any district other than in Hawaii in which they can expect to elect a member of their own race simply by relying on their voting power. Even in districts in which they account for ten or more percent of the population, whites or Latinos are usually the majority. It is then no coincidence that most of the districts in Table 5-1 are represented by white or Latino members.

Table 5-1 House Districts with 10 Percent or More Asian Americans in 1990

Rank 1990	House District	Major City in District[1]	Asian Am. in District %(1990)	White, African Am. &Hispanic % (1990)			Member,[3] 106th Congress (1999-2000), Party, Race	Asian Am. in District %(2000),Rank[4]
1	Hawaii-1	Honolulu	66.7%	29	2	5	**Abercrombie** (D, White)	69.93% [1]
2	Hawaii-2	Hilo	57.1%	38	2	9	**Mink** (D, Asian)	61.27% [2]
3	Calif.-8	San Francisco	27.8%	52	13	15	**Pelosi** (D, White)	33.10% [4]
4	Calif.-12	Daly City	25.7%	65	4	14	**Lantos** (D, White)	33.23% [3]
5	Calif.-31	El Monte	22.9%	48	2	58	**Martinez** (D, Latino)	25.13% [7]
6	Calif.-30	Los Angeles	21.4%	44	3	60	**Becerra** (D, Latino)	23.77% [8]
7	Calif.-16	San Jose	21.1%	55	5	36	**Lofgren** (D, White)	30.53% [5]
8	N.Y.-12	New York City	19.5%	34	14	57	**Velazquez** (D, Latino)	19.02% [12]
9	Calif.-13	Fremont	19.4%	64	7	18	**Stark** (D, White)	27.54% [6]
10	Calif.-09	Oakland	15.8%	45	32	11	Lee (D, African)	21.74% [9]
11	Calif.-50	San Diego	14.9%	47	14	40	**Filner** (D, White)	17.30% [19]
12	Calif.-7	Vallejo	14.4%	63	17	13	Miller, George (D, White)	21.14% [10]
13	Calif.-39	Fullerton	13.8%	73	3	22	Royce (R, White)	18.52% [15]
14	Calif.-5	Sacramento	13.2%	66	13	14	**Matsui** (D, Asian)	18.61% [14]
15	Calif.-28	West Covina	13.1%	71	6	24	Dreier (R, White)	15.82% [21]
16	Calif.-36	Torrance	12.5%	78	3	15	Kuykendall (R, White)	15.41% [25]
17	Calif.-46	Santa Ana	12.4%	67	2	49	Sanchez (D, Latino)	18.15% [16]
18	Calif.-14	Mountain View	12.2%	78	5	13	**Eshoo** (D, White)	18.99% [13]
19	Wash.-7	Seattle	11.7%	76	10	3	McDermott (D, White)	15.81% [22]
20	N.Y.-7	New York City	11.6%	70	10	21	Crowley (D, White)	19.22% [11]

Table 5-1 (continued)

Rank 1990	House District	Major City in District [1]	Asian Am. in District %(1990)	White, African Am. &Hispanic % (1990)			Member,[3] 106th Congress (1999-2000), Party, Race	Asian Am. in District %(2000),Rank [4]
21	Calif.-11	Stockton	11.5%	75	6	20	Pombo (R, White)	17.76% [18]
22	Calif.-15	Santa Clara	11.4%	82	2	10	Campbell (R, White)	17.86% [17]
23	Calif.-45	Huntington Beach	11.0%	82	1	15	Rohrabacher (R, White)	16.86% [20]
24	Calif.-37	Compton	10.8%	26	34	44	Millender-McDonald (D, African)	12.35% [29]
25	N.Y.-5	New York City	10.53%	84	3	7	Gary Ackerman (D, White)	15.50% [24]
26	Calif.-27	Glendale	10.50%	71	8	20	Rogan (R, White)	12.96% [28]
27	Calif.-41	Pomona	10.1%	68	7	31	**Miller, Gary** (R, White)	13.80% [26]
28	Illinois-9	Chicago	10.0%	73	12	9	Schakowsky (D, White)	10.50% [40]
...	...	...	...				...	
98	Oregon-1	Portland	3.2%	93	1	4	**Wu** (D, Asian)	
	Mean		2.9%					
	Median		1.2%					

Source: U.S. Bureau of Census (1990); National Committee for an Effective Congress (NCEC) (1999).

1) In some districts, only part of the listed city belongs to the districts.
2) From left to right, white, African American, and Hispanic % in district. Due to the census classification in which Hispanic can be any race, the total percentage of these three groups plus Asian Americans exceeds 100.
3) Members belonging to the Asian Pacific American Caucus are shown in bold letters.
4) Population statistics in 2000 are unofficial estimates by NCEC and not from the US Census.

Why are Asian Americans not able to have their own majority-minority districts like African Americans and Latinos? One reason is that Asian Americans are not only smaller in number, but also more scattered in residential pattern than African Americans and Latinos.[10] The diversity of Asian Americans in ethnicity and socio-economic status discussed in the previous section explains this pattern. In particular, Asian Americans in the professional ranks tend to live in the suburbs, making it difficult to create an Asian majority district in urban areas.

Yet, even in places where Asian Americans do make a cohesive residential segment, they are not large enough to create their own majority-minority district. Quite often, areas that have an increasingly significant Asian-American population are also heavily populated by Latinos. It is worth noting in Table 5-1 that as many as three districts out of the top ten Asian districts have a Latino majority with a Latino representative. The three Latino-dominated districts—California District 31, California District 30, and New York District 12—have approximately a 20% Asian American population.

A good example to illustrate this point is the case of San Gabriel Valley in Southern California (Saito 1998, Ch. 6). This suburban area saw a rapid influx of Asian immigrants in the 1980s and 1990s. In particular, Monterey Park has become the first city outside Hawaii that had a majority Asian population (57.5 percent of 60,000 in 1990), and it has come to be called the "first suburban Chinatown" (Saito 1998, 160; Horton 1995; Fong 1994). Three adjacent cities (Alhambra, Rosemead, and San Gabriel) also had at least a 30% Asian population in 1990; with the four cities combined, 43.1 percent of the 231,000 citizens were Asians. Yet, these four cities were not large enough to create a House district of their own; they would need 570,000 to do so. Their population was even smaller than the number needed to create a single state assembly district (372,000) (Saito 1998, 169). Therefore Asian Americans had to work with Latinos, who were populous in the entire San Gabriel Valley, during the redistricting process following the 1990 census. The two groups had the common interest to secure a district for themselves from white incumbent members, and Asian American and Latino political leaders worked together to that effect. The result, however, is the consistent election of a Latino member to the U.S. House (Matthew Martinez in District 31) as well as to the California Assembly. Dominated in number, Asian Americans have not yet achieved descriptive representation in this area beyond the city council level.[11] Judy Chu (Chinese American), former city council member and mayor of Monterey Park, ran for the State Assembly in 1998, but was defeated in the Democratic primary by a Latino opponent.

Asian Americans in Congress and California Legislature: Why Are There So Few?

Research on Asian American political representation is very scarce. Various editions of *National Asian Pacific American Political Almanac*, edited by Nakanishi and Lai and published by UCLA's Asian American Studies Center (1995, 1996, 1998-99) is virtually the only comprehensive informational source, listing Asian American elected and appointed officials at the national, state, and local level.[12] Even a list of Asian Americans who have served Congress is not readily available (and some existing lists either miss some members or include wrong members). Probably due to their small numbers, no one has published books similar to *Black Americans in Congress, 1870-1989* (Ragsdale and Treese 1990) and *Hispanic Americans in Congress, 1822-1995* (Enciso, North, and the Hispanic Division, Library of Congress, 1995) on Asian American members of Congress. A report prepared by the Congressional Research Service (CRS) is the only official document that lists all Asian Americans who have served in Congress (Tong 2000).

Although this CRS report identifies 38 Asian American individuals who have served Congress, many of them are Resident Commissioners from the Philippines before the islands became independent in 1946 and non-voting members from Guam and American Samoa. Removing these members, Table 5-2 lists all of the thirteen past and current full voting members of Congress who are Asian Americans.[13] Several observations are in order. First, many of the members are Japanese Americans, Democrats, and from Hawaii. This reflects the tendency of Japanese Americans to affiliate with the Democratic party and the structure of the politics in Hawaii that has been dominated by white and Japanese American Democrats. Second, despite theses tendencies, the first Asian American ever elected to Congress was a South Indian American (Dalip Singh Saund), and not a Japanese American. Born in India in 1899, and became a citizen in 1949, he was elected to represent Riverside and Imperial Counties in California, fending off his opponents' allegations that he was not really an American (Saund 1960; Schultz et al 2000, 333). After Saund served for three terms, no South Asian has served the U.S. Congress, however. Third, no Filipino has ever been elected to Congress, even though they are the second largest ethnic group among Asian Americans. Even in Hawaii, in which Filipinos accounted for 17.3% of the population in 1990 (second largest to Japanese Americans, who are 27.7% (Shinagawa 1996, 95)), no Filipinos have been elected to Congress there. It was only in 1994 when Hawaii first elected its Filipino American governor (Benjamin Cayatano). The underrepresentation of Filipinos in government and among activist Asian Americans poses a serious question to those building an interethnic coalition among Asian American groups (Okamura 1998, 33; Saito 1998, 163).

Table 5-2 Asian Americans Who Served in the United States Congress [1]

Year Served	Member	Ethnicity	Party	District
House				
1957-1963	Dalip Singh Saund	South Indian American	Democrat	California 29th District
1959-1963	Daniel K. Inouye	Japanese American	Democrat	Hawaii At-Large
1963-1977	Spark M. Matsunaga	Japanese American	Democrat	Hawaii At-Large,[2] then 1st District
1965-1977	Patsy T. Mink	Japanese American	Democrat	Hawaii At-Large,[2] then 2nd District
1975-1995[3]	Norman Y. Mineta	Japanese American	Democrat	California 13th, then 15th District
1977-1990[4]	Daniel K. Akaka	Chinese & Native Hawaiian	Democrat	Hawaii 2nd District
1979-present	Robert T. Matsui	Japanese American	Democrat	California 3rd, then 5th District
1987-1991	Patricia F. Saiki	Japanese American	Republican	Hawaii 1st District
1990[5]-present	Patsy T. Mink	Japanese American	Democrat	D-Hawaii 2nd District
1993-1999	Jay C. Kim	Korean American	Republican	California 41st District
1999-present	David Wu	Chinese American	Democrat	Oregon 1st District
Senate				
1959-1977	Hiram L. Fong	Chinese American	Republican	Hawaii
1963-present	Daniel K. Inouye	Japanese American	Democrat	Hawaii
1977-1983	S. I. Hayakawa	Japanese American	Republican	California
1977-1990[6]	Spark M. Matsunaga	Japanese American	Democrat	Hawaii
1990[4]-present	Daniel K. Akaka	Chinese & Native Hawaiian	Democrat	Hawaii

1) Full voting members only.
2) Until 1968, Hawaii elected two House members from an at-large, statewide district, which was split in 1970.
3) Resigned from office to accept a position at Lockheed Martin Company.
4) Appointed to late Senator Matsunaga's seat; elected to the seat by special election in the same year.
5) Elected by special election to the seat held by Representative Akaka, who was appointed to the Senate.
6) Died in office on April 15, 1990.

Source: Complied by the author from Congressional Quarterly (1998) and Tong (2000).

At the state level Asian Americans have not achieved descriptive representation in winning state elected offices. Outside of Hawaii, Gary Locke of the state of Washington (in office 1997- present) is the only Asian American who has been elected to the governor's office. California, whose population is now more than 10% Asian Americans, has elected only eight Asian Americans to its 80-member state House and only one to its 40-member state Senate (Table 5-3).[14] This grim pic-

Table 5-3 Asian Americans Who Served in the California State Legislature

Year Served	Member	Ethnicity	Party	District
House				
1963-1966	Alfred H. Song	Korean American	Democrat	45th (Los Angeles County)
1967-1974	March Fong Eu	Chinese American	Democrat	15th (Alameda County)
1969-1970	Tom Hom	Chinese American	Republican	79th (San Diego County)
1973 [1]-1980	Paul T. Bannai	Japanese American	Republican	53rd (Los Angeles County)
1975 [2]-1980	S. Floyd Mori	Japanese American	Democrat	15th (Alameda County)
1993-1998	Nao Takasugi	Japanese American	Republican	37th (Ventura County)
1997- present	Mike Honda	Japanese American	Democrat	23rd (Santa Clara County)
1999- present	George Nakano	Japanese American	Democrat	53rd (Los Angeles County)
Senate				
1967-1978	Alfred H. Song	Korean American	Democrat	26th (Los Angeles County)

1) Elected by special election on June 26, 1973 to a seat vacated by a deceased member.

2) Elected by special election on March 4, 1975 to a seat vacated by a deceased member.

Source: Complied by the author using Saito (1998, 217), State of California (1975), Secretary of the State of California (various years), and Nakanishi and Lai (1995, 1996, 1998-99).

ture, however, should be counterbalanced by several Asian Americans who have held other statewide offices. In California, Marge Fong Eu served as Secretary of State for nearly twenty years from 1975 through 1994; her adopted son, Matt Fong, served as State Treasurer from 1995 through 1998 (as a Republican, although his mother Marge was a Democrat). In Delaware, S.B. Woo was the Lieutenant Governor from 1985 to 1989 (Ng 1995, 1677).

Why have Asian Americans not been more successful in electing themselves to key offices in government? This is an intriguing question in light of the relative "success" of Asian Americans in other sectors of society such as economics and education. Certainly, as we have seen, we should be careful not to overstate the level of success of Asian Americans in society. After surveying the existing studies on glass ceiling, Woo (2000, Ch. 2) concludes that Asian Americans are less likely to move into administrative and managerial positions and have lower returns on their education than white counterparts are (see also Tang 1997). Nevertheless, the gap of Asian American achievement between political and non-political sectors is noteworthy, because socio-economic status is one of the key variables that usually explain the political success of an ethnic group (Ong and Nakanishi 1996, 288).

A popular explanation for this phenomenon is cultural. According to this line of argument, Asian Americans have not advanced themselves in politics because of their unique cultural values. The argument goes: Asian parents stress hard work and academic success, and therefore Asian students strive to become doctors, engineers, and lawyers instead of politicians; moreover, Asians place an emphasis on modesty and self-restraints, therefore, running for elections, which involves advertising one's own name and strength, is antithetical to the values they grow up with (Schaefer 1998, 318).[15]

We can make at least three arguments against this popular explanation (Hing 1993, 153-68). First, there are a number of instances of political activism of Asian people, both in old times and in recent years and both in their home countries in Asia and in the United States. In the first half of the twentieth century, many Korean and Chinese activists, whose independence movement was suppressed by the Japanese colonial rule, moved to the United States and continued their cause (Chan 1991, 98-100). In more recent years, Asian Americans have conducted political activities of various kinds to make themselves heard within the U.S. political system, from voter registration drives to campaign against anti-Asian violence (Wei 1993).

Second, although few Asian Americans have won high-level elected offices, this does not necessarily mean that few ever ran for these offices. Indeed, there is a long list of Asian Americans who took the challenge of running for high-level offices and lost. In the 1998 election, Matt Fong won the Republican primary for the U.S. Senate from California but lost to Democratic incumbent Barbara Boxer; John Lim, a naturalized Korean American, also won the Republican primary for the U.S. Senate from Oregon but was defeated by Democratic incumbent Ron Wyden. In 1993, Los Angeles city council member Michael Woo lost his race for mayor of the city against Richard Riordan (Brackman and Erie 1998). In Nevada, Cheryl Lau ran for governor in 1994 and for U.S. House in 1996 but lost in Republican primary in both times (Schultz et al 2000, 298). Certainly, some of the Asian American women politicians interviewed by Chu (1989) report conflicts between their traditional values and the assertiveness required to win an election. But the fact that a number of Asian Americans run for school district, city, and county-level, if not state-level offices (and many win, as Chu (1989) records) suggests that such internal conflicts can be overcome by the efforts and political socialization on the part of Asian American candidates.

Third, political participation is not limited to voting and running in elections (Nakanishi 1998). Asian Americans have contributed substantial amount of money to political candidates, at least until the Clinton-Gore campaign finance "scandal" (see below) occurred. Contributions from Chinese and Japanese Americans accounted for 10% of the late Los Angeles Mayor Tom Bradley's campaign funds (Brackman and Erie 1998, 79).

We must therefore explain the lack of descriptive representation of Asian Americans, not by cultural terms, but by historical, political and structural conditions. As mentioned above, the dispersed residential pattern of Asian Americans makes it difficult to create Asian American majority districts. Yet, the immigrant status and ethnic diversity of Asian Americans present particular problems in achieving their descriptive representation, and the past history of discrimination against Asians also adds negative effects.

First, immigrants (naturalized citizens) are generally less likely than native born citizens to vote in election. Language barriers, unfamiliarity with the U.S. political system, and social and economic hardships all have had a negative impact on Asian American electoral participation. In this regard, it is important to recall that as many as two-thirds of Asian Americans are foreign born, although some of them have undergone political socialization within the United States as they immigrated with their parents in their childhood.[16] In order for non-citizen immigrants to vote, they have to go through three steps: naturalization, voter registration, and actual voting. Records indicate that Asian American voter registration is low and this is exacerbated with low voter turnout levels. As many as 74% of registered Asian American immigrants actually voted in 1994, but only 49% of naturalized citizens registered to vote (and this registration rate is four percent lower than that for Latinos, according to Ong and Nakanishi (1996)).[17] As a result, the rapid increase in the Asian American population does not translate into the same level of increase as the number of Asian American voters, and Asian Americans do not have a large ethnic-voting base as they could. Although not all Asian Americans will vote just because of candidates' ethnicity, a report issued by the Asian American Legal Defense and Education Fund (published in Nakanishi and Lai 1998-99, 36) notes that the entry of a (eventually unsuccessful) Chinese American candidate into a race for the New York State Assembly in a Queens, New York district boosted the turnout of Asian American voters for both parties. This episode suggests that the barrier for election of Asian American legislators is not purely cultural but can be overcome by such activities as voter registration drive.

Second, for Asian Americans, another aspect of their demographic characteristics, diversity in ethnic background, adds further complication to the prospect of ethnic voting and representation. When only one Asian American candidate is running from a district with a large number of Asian voters of the same ethnicity, he or she may have a good chance of soliciting ethnic votes. Reality is not always as simple as that. To begin with, if multiple Asian candidates of different ethnic backgrounds pursue the office, they may end up splitting the Asian American vote that could elect one Asian candidate if they were not divided. For example, when a special election for the California State Assembly was held in Los Angeles in 1991, a Japanese American, a Korean American, and a Filipino American candidates ran. Not only did these candidates split the Asian votes, the latter two candidates received votes for the most part from their own ethnic groups (Lai 1994). Moreover, even if only one Asian American candidate runs, Asian voters may not associate with the candidate if they belong to an ethnic group different from the candidate.[18] For example, Japanese Americans may not feel close to a South Asian candidate. The case of a half-Japanese, half-South Asian candidate for the U.S. House of Representative, Ram Yoshino Uppuluri, is very suggestive in this regard. Because Uppuluri ran from a district with few Asian voters (Tennessee's fourth district), he could not expect to receive ethnic votes, so he solicited publicity and campaign contributions from the Asian American community outside the district. Partly because of his South Asian last name, and partly because of the desire of South Asians to elect their own representative, Uppuluri received wide support from South Asian communities all over the nation. He received very little interest from Japanese American communities. Nonetheless, Uppuluri was defeated in a Democratic primary in 1994 (Srikanth 1998).

The third factor against descriptive representation of Asian Americans is the negative impact of historical discrimination and ostracization against the group. A series of federal laws, such as the Chinese Exclusion Act of 1882, the Immigration Act of 1917 (which created the "Asiatic barred zone" to stop Korean and Indian immigration) and the Tydings-McDuffie Act of 1934 (which limited immigration visa from

Philippines to only 50), kept Asians from growing in number like other immigrant groups, in particular those from Europe (Chan 1991; Hing 1993).[19] Moreover, two Supreme Court decisions, *Takeo_Ozawa v. United States* (1922) and *United States v. Bhagat Singh Thind* (1923), ruled that Asian immigrants could not naturalize (and therefore shut down the possibility to vote).[20] This trajectory in history "delayed the development of electoral participation and representation by Asian Americans in California and elsewhere until the second and subsequent generations during the post-World War II period" (Nakanishi 1998, 9).

The past discrimination also created an image of Asian Americans as perpetual foreigners. Although the legal restrictions against their immigration and naturalization were removed by a series of laws from the 1940s through the 1960s, the tendency of society to regard Asian Americans as foreigners continued (Kim 1999). This tendency manifested itself in two events in the late 1990s: Clinton-Gore campaign finance "scandal" and the Chinese "espionage" of nuclear arms secret (which will be discussed later in this chapter). In the former case, John Hwang, a naturalized Chinese American, was suspected (and later indicted) for his bundling of illegal campaign contributions from Asian non-citizens. The media, which seldom reports Asian American political activities, largely characterized this incident as the improper influence of foreign money, casting doubt on the political participation of Asian Americans in general (Wu and Nicholson 1997; Wang 1998). Moreover, the Democratic National Committee contacted many legal Asian American campaign contributors to verify their citizenship status. The DNC only called individuals who had "Asian-sounding" surnames. Asian Americans who happened to spell their names Young instead of Yang, for example, were not contacted (ABC Nightline 1999). The entire incident has had a negative impact on subsequent Asian American political participation, in particular running for offices and contributing money.

Substantive Representation of Asian Americans in Congress

Since, few Asian Americans have been elected to U.S. Congress and other elected offices, how are their interests represented in government? With structural obstacles to the election of Asian Americans, full descriptive representation (having Asian faces in Congress in proportion to their population) may be difficult. Substantial representation, in which the interests of Asian Americans are represented by members who are not necessarily Asian, is therefore all the more important for Asian Americans. To what extent are Asian American interests represented in U.S. Congress?

The past decade has produced a number of studies on substantive representation of African Americans and Latinos (Swain 1993; Hero and Tolbert 1995; Lublin 1997; Tien and Levy 1998). Substantive representation is concerned with whether the interests of a demographic group are represented in the beliefs and behaviors of members of a legislature. Unlike descriptive representation, substantive representation does not require election of members who share demographic characteristics with the group in question. Rather, it is concerned with whether members "act for" the group in the form of legislating and voting (Pitkin 1967).

At least two problems make it difficult to conduct research on substantive representation of Asian Americans in the same manner as on African Americans and Latinos. First, what are "Asian American interests?" Whether there are such interests, is not clear. Unlike African Americans and Latinos, who are heavily Democratic and liberal, Asian Americans are more divided in terms of party affiliation, although their voting behavior is more leaned toward the liberal side (Lien 1999). The activist rank of Asian Americans tend to share the same policy goals with African Americans and Latinos and cooperate with them, but we cannot generalize their opinions to the entire Asian American population for sure. Although we do not yet see the rise of conservative Asian American policy organizations, with the lack of national-level public opinion data of Asian Americans, it is best not too assume the policy orientation of Asian Americans in one direction.

Second, even if "Asian American interests" are defined, it is still difficult to identify the actions of members of Congress that are conducted clearly in favor of Asian Americans and not for some other groups. On the one hand, some legislative actions are too inclusive. For example, hate crime legislation will benefit Asian Americans because crimes targeted at Asian Americans have not ceased in society. Yet such legislation will also benefit other racial minority groups, and it is difficult to ascertain whether members support the legislation because they want to help Asian Americans or minorities in general. On the other hand, some legislative actions are too narrow to gauge Asian American interests. Several bills were introduced in Congress in the 1980s and 1990s that would have benefited a particular Asian American ethnic group. Some of them were enacted into law; the most notable of these is the Civil Liberties Act of 1988, which authorized reparation money for the people of Japanese decent who were interned in camps during World War II (Hatamiya 1993). Other bills were more modest and targeted at other Asian groups. For example a bill was introduced to authorize equal benefits for Filipino veterans from World War II (Vergara 1997).[21] A bill sought to recognize Hmong veterans who joined the United States intelligence activities during the U.S. combat in Southeast Asia. Although these bills were strongly supported by Asian American civil rights groups, it is difficult to assume that Asian Americans of all ethnic groups benefit from these bills.

There is one issue, however, which Asian Americans of almost all ethnic and political orientations agree—distaste for being regarded as foreigners (Tuan 1998). Although some Asian Americans are third, fourth, and even fifth generations and do not speak any Asian language, non-Asian Americans often praise them for speaking fluent English, or ask them "where are you really from?" when they insist they are American born. Even conservative Asian Americans do not like being treated this way. Yet the tendency of mainstream society to couple Asian nationals and Asian Americans still continues, and may have even become stronger in the wake of the Clinton-Gore campaign finance "scandal" and the nuclear secret "espionage" case at Los Alamos National Laboratory.

On March 6, 1999, the *New York Times* broke a story that People's Republic of China stole nuclear secrets from the United States and developed sophisticated nuclear warheads that it could not produce before (Risen and Gerth 1999). On May 25, Congress's Select Committee headed by Representative Christopher Cox (R-CA) released a detailed report that confirms the suspicion (U.S. House 1999). The individual who emerged as a suspect was Dr. Wen Ho Lee, a naturalized Taiwanese American scientist at Los Alamos. On December 10, 1999 Lee was indicted by a federal grand jury and arrested on 59 counts of charges such as mishandling of classified information. Yet, the federal government could not find direct evidence that Lee passed nuclear secrets to the Chinese government, and the charge against Lee did not include espionage.

The whole event made newspaper and television headlines. The media emphasized a fear that China might have caught up with the U.S. in nuclear technology. For example, the cover of the *Time* magazine that analyzed the Cox report had a picture of an Asian eye peeping through a five-star shape window with a caption "The Next Cold War? It is not that simple. And the Chinese Spy Scandal shows why." (*Time* 1999). The media frequently mentioned that Lee is a Chinese American and has made a trip to China. However, many Asian Americans, especially those working in the nuclear science field, feared that they may become suspect of spying the U.S. just because they have an Asian face (Butterfield and Kahn 1999). Having learned a lesson from the campaign finance "scandal" case, Asian Americans quickly responded and formed a broad coalition to condemn anti-Asian bias in the case (Sterngold 1999). Dr. Lee himself filed a counter lawsuit against the federal government, saying that the government violated his privacy by leaking personal information to the media and wrongfully portrayed him as a spy (Lewis 1999).

Asian American members of Congress responded, too. On May 24, 1999, the day before the scheduled release of the Cox report, Congressional Asian Pacific Caucus members took the floor during the special speech session and addressed the issue. On May 27, David Wu, the only Chinese American member of the House and the vice president of the Caucus, introduced a concurrent resolution "expressing the sense of Congress relating to recent allegations of espionage and illegal campaign financing that have brought into question the loyalty and probity of Americans of Asian ancestry" (H.Con.Res. 124). The resolution was referred to the Judiciary Committee, which ordered it to be reported on September 22, 1999. On November 2, 1999, the House passed the resolution by voice vote and sent it to the Senate; by that date, 75 members (63 Democrats and 12 Republicans) cosponsored the resolution.

One way to analyze how Asian Americans' substantial interests are represented in Congress is to examine which members cosponsored this resolution. Cosponsorship has been studied by congressional scholars as an action to express or signal members' policy preferences (Krehbiel 1995; Kessler and Krehbiel 1996; Wilson and Young 1997). It is also used in a study to examine which members are more likely to deal with legislation that has racial content (Canon 1999). Although cosponsorship may not be the strongest form of legislative activity that a member can engage in, members' signing on this resolution indicates that they care about Asian Americans (or at least they want to take such a position on paper).

Explaining which members cosponsored this resolution and why will therefore help us reveal the mechanism of substantive representation of Asian Americans. In particular, in light of the past literature cited above that examined the impact of minority population over policies and member activities, we are particularly interested in whether the percentage of Asian Americans in member districts has an impact on whether members signed on the resolution. The former is the key independent variable of this analysis and the latter is the dependent variable.[22] Hatamiya (1993) argues that members with high percentage of Asian Americans in districts were more likely to vote for the redress for Japanese American camp internees, although she acknowledges that this factor cannot explain why members with virtually no Asian Americans in districts voted for it.

As an alternative key independent variable, we also examine whether a representative's membership in Congressional Asian Pacific Caucus makes a difference in cosponsoring this resolution. The caucus was founded on May 16, 1994, by the then-House member Norman Mineta (D-CA). The caucus aims to establish policies "relating to person of Asian and/or Pacific Islands ancestry who are citizens or nationals of, residents of, or immigrants to, the United States, its territories and possessions," and to "ensure that legislation passed by the United States Congress, to the greatest extent possible, provides for the full participation of Asian Pacific Americans and reflects the concerns and needs of the Asian Pacific American communities" (Congressional Asian Pacific Caucus 2000). Currently, all five Asian American members of Congress as well as fourteen House members and one Senator (Patty Murray (D-WA)) are members of the caucus; the caucus chair is Robert Underwood (D-Guam), a non-voting member. As Table 1 shows, many members of the caucus represent districts with a large number of Asian Americans. Nine of the representatives from the ten districts with largest percentage of Asian Americans are members of the caucus. Except for Gary Miller (R-CA), all current caucus members are Democrats.

In addition to these explanations, we have three competing hypotheses on member's cosponsorship. Hypothesis one: liberal members are more likely to sign on the resolution because the resolution deals with an issue that liberals care about discrimination against minorities. To account for this possibility, I include members' ideological scores in my model, as expressed by Poole and Rosenthal's (1997) W-NOMINATE scores.[23] The second, related hypothesis is that racial minority members are more likely to sign on the resolution because they are sensitive to issues of discrimination. To account for this possibility, I include a dummy variable for racial minority members (Asian Americans, African Americans, and Latinos) in my model.[24] The third alternative explanation is that some members cosponsor a larger number of bills than others, and that the signing on this particular resolution can simply be explained by members' general tendency to cosponsor bills. To account for this possibility, I include in my model a variable for the number of bills and resolutions that members cosponsored in the 106th Congress (1999-2000).[25] The model also includes the following control variables: mean per capita income of district; membership in the Judicial Committee (which ordered the resolution to be reported); gender variable; percentage of member's votes in the 1998 general election; and member's seniority in the House.

Because the dependent variable takes only two values (1 for cosponsoring the resolution, and 0 for not cosponsoring), I used a logit model to estimate this multivariate model. Table 5-4 reports the results of the analysis. Model 1 tests the hypothesis that members from a district with a larger percentage of Asian Americans are more likely to cosponsor the resolution. Model 2 tests the hypothesis that members belonging to the Congressional Asian Pacific Caucus are more likely to cosponsor the resolution.

The results suggest that both hypotheses are strongly supported. The percentage of Asian Americans in member districts (in Model 1) and membership in the Congressional Asian Pacific Caucus (in Model 2) are both found to have a clear, positive impact on cosponsorship, with coefficients significant at the 0.01 level or at the 0.05 level. Two of the three alternative hypotheses are also supported. Liberal members are found to be more likely to cosponsor the resolution (because conservative members have larger NOMINATE scores, the negative sign of the coefficient for member ideology supports the hypothesis), and members who cosponsor a larger number of bills and resolutions are found to be more likely to cosponsor the resolution. Racial minority members, however, are not found to have a clear impact on cosponsorship. Although 5 of the 18 Latino members (27.8 percent) and 13 of the 37 African American members (35.1 percent) signed on the resolution (which are larger than the percentage of cosponsorship among all members, 16.5 percent), the impact of members' race seems to be accounted for by other variables in the model.

Table 5-4 Prediction of House Members' Cosponsorship of H.Con.Res. 124, Resolution to Condemn Stereotypes against Asian Americans (Logit Model)

Variables	Prediction	Model 1 Coefficient	Model 1 Z-score	Model 2 Coefficient	Model 2 Z-score
Key Variables					
Percentage of Asian Americans in District	Positive	0.129	(z=3.405)***	(Not Included)	
Membership in Asian Pacific American Caucus	Positive	(Not Included)		1.511	(z=2.575)**
Alternative Hypo. Variables					
Member Ideology	Negative	-1.703	(z=-4.227)***	-1.773	(z=-4.452)***
Racial Minority Member	Positive	0.650	(z=1.438)	0.710	(z=1.594)
Number of Bills Cosponsored by Member	Positive	0.003	(z=1.906)*	0.003	(z=2.048)*
Control Variables					
Mean Per Capita Income of District	?	0.605	(z=1.666)*	0.992	(z=2.806)***
Membership in Judicial Committee	Positive	0.129	(z=0.247)	0.185	(z=0.358)
Women Member	Positive	-0.734	(z=-1.650)*	-0.654	(z=-1.518)
Percentage of Votes in 1998 General Election	?	-0.010	(z=0.896)	-0.008	(z=-0.705)
Member Seniority	?	-0.014	(z=0.037)	-0.008	(z=-0.218)
Constant	(N.A.)	-3.053	(z=-2.935)***	-3.554	(z=-3.491)***
Number of Observations		435		435	
Log Likelihood		-144.49		-149.48	
Pseudo R-square		0.2598		0.2341	
Correctly predicted obs.		85.5%		84.1%	

Note: The dependent variable is whether House members cosponsored H.Con.Res. 124, a resolution to condemn stereotypes against Asian Americans. $p<.01$***, $p<0.05$**, $p<0.1$*

The logit model assumes a non-linear relationship between the dependent and independent variables, and as a result, the coefficients like those reported in Table 5-4 are difficult to interpret. To follow King's

(1989) advice, I have therefore calculated how the likelihood of cosponsorship changes as the key independent variables change.[26] Table 5-5 reports the change of the likelihood of cosponsorship as the percentage of Asian Americans in member districts changes from 0 to 50 percent, when other variables are set to their mean values. The impact of the Asian American population is far from negligible. Although, the probability of signing the resolution is only 7.4% if no Asian Americans live in members' districts, it increases to 22.7% when Asian Americans account for 10% of the district population. When the percentage of Asian Americans reaches 20%, the probability of signing the resolution is over 50%; if Asian Americans are the majority of members' district, the probability exceeds 90%.[27] As far as the population statistics are concerned, members seem to respond to the "power of numbers" of Asian Americans, and substantive representation seems to be working to that extent.

This result, if taken at face value, suggests that House members are indeed responding to the power of their constituencies as measured by the percentage of Asian Americans in their districts. This is at least not a bad news to Asian Americans. It means that they can increase their substantive representation by having more Asian Americans in a district. It then becomes all the more important for Asian Americans to participate in the redistricting process so that their communities are not divided into multiple districts. It would also become important for Asian Americans to have more naturalized immigrants register to vote, because, as we have seen, this is the step of the immigrants' process toward voting that Asian Americans lag behind other minorities.

We have to add two qualifications to this simple conclusion, however. First, the result is based on a single resolution and difficult to generalize. In particular, cosponsorship is not the strongest form of supporting legislation available for members, and the resolution, if passed by the Senate, does not have legal effects unlike regular legislative bills. Moreover, joining the effort to condemn stereotypes against Asian

Table 5-5 Probability of House Members' Cosponsorship of the Concurrent Resolution to Condemn Stereotypes against Asian Americans (H.Con.Res.124)

Percentage of Asian Americans in District	0%	2.9% (Mean)	5%	10%	15%	20%	25%	50%
Probability of Members' Signing on the Resolution	7.4%	10.4%	13.2%	22.7%	36.0%	50.9%	64.4%	93.8%

Americans is not so controversial that it may offend somebody. A real test of substantive representation of Asian American interests will be when support for a particular bill means a loss of benefits for some other groups, say whites or Latinos. Members who signed on the resolution above may not support such a drastic bill.

Second, the result that substantive representation seems to be working should not de-emphasize the importance of descriptive representation. Even Swain (1993, 217), an opponent of the creation of majority-minority districts, admits that "Descriptive representation has its own value." Certainly, not all Asian American members of Congress may work for the interests of Asian Americans. Senator S.I. Hayakawa (R-CA) opposed the redress for Japanese American camp internees during World War II (Hatamiya 1993, 232; Saito 1998, 103), and Asian American civil rights activists denounced Representative Jay Kim (R-CA) for not working for the policy goals they espoused and for engaging in illegal financial transactions that led to his defeat in Republican primary in 1998 (Nash, Soo and Lee 1998). Yet the facts that the resolution above was introduced by an Asian American member and that the other two Asian American members were among the 21 original cosponsors of the resolution suggest that these members work for Asian Americans more strenuously than other members who merely signed on the resolution.

Implications and Conclusions

This chapter provided one of the first systematic accounts of Asian American representation in the U.S. political system, in particular in Congress. It analyzed their representation both in descriptive and substantial terms. With regards to descriptive representation, the research shows that except in Hawaii, Asian Americans are underrepresented in Congress, and to a lesser degree, at state legislatures. The main contributing factor is that Asian Americans are dispersed among various congressional districts; but the diversity in their ethnic backgrounds and the history of exclusion from the U.S. political process also account for the difficulty in electing Asian American legislators. It is important, however, to recognize that, although these obstacles are formidable, they are not insurmountable. Asian Americans may be able to strengthen their voice by participating in the redistricting process following the 2000 census and ensuring that their communities, especially those in California and New York, are not divided into multiple districts. They may also be able to strengthen ties among different Asian ethnic groups by identifying the issues that affect all the groups. In any case, the argument that Asian Americans are politically weak because of their cultural characteristics is not supported in light of the historical, political, and structural evidence examined in this chapter.

In terms of substantive representation, the chapter finds that members from districts with a larger percentage of Asian Americans are more likely to sign on the resolution condemning stereotypes against Asian Americans. This result, along with the fact that such a resolution has never passed the House—a phenomenon not seen in the case of campaign finance "scandal"—is encouraging to Asian Americans. Certainly, whether and how Asian Americans can have their interests represented in the American political system beyond this case remains to be seen. Yet, descriptive and substantive representation are not mutually exclusive terms to Asian Americans, for whom representation is still at a low level in both terms and for whom the discussion of drawing majority-minority districts is far from reality unlike African Americans and Latinos. Asian Americans still need to pursue further political representation through both venues—by electing more of Asian Americans and by pressuring non-Asian legislators.

References

ABC Nightline. 1999. *Asian-American.* Aired on June 28.

Brackman, Harold, and Steven P. Erie. 1998. "At Rainbow's End: Empowerment Prospects for Latinos and Asian Pacific Americans in Los Angeles." In *Racial and Ethnic Politics in California.* eds. Michael B. Preston, Bruce E. Cain, and Sandra Bass. 2: 73-107. Berkeley, Calif.: Institute of Governmental Studies Press.

Butterfield, Fox and Joseph Kahn. 1999. "Chinese Intellectuals in U.S. Say Spying Case Unfairly Casts Doubts on Their Loyalties." *New York Times.* May 16. A32.

Cain, Bruce E., D. Roderick Kiewiet, and Carole J. Uhlaner. 1991. "The Acquisition of Partisanship by Latinos and Asian Americans." *American Journal of Political Science* 35: 390-422.

Canon, David T. 1999. *Race, Redistricting, and Representation: The Unintended Consequences of Black Majority Districts.* Chicago: The University of Chicago Press.

Chan, Sucheng. 1991. *Asian Americans: An Interpretive History.* New York:

Twayne.

Cho, Wendy K. Tam. n.d. *Expanding the Logic Behind Campaign Contributions: Lessons from Asian American Campaign Contributors.* Typescript. University of Illinois, Urbana-Champaign.

Chu, Judy. 1989. *Asian Pacific American Women in Mainstream Politics. In Making Waves: An Anthology of Writings by and about Asian American Women.* ed. Asian Women United of California, 405-21. Boston: Beacon Press.

Congressional Asian Pacific Caucus. 2000. Congressional Asian Pacific Caucus homepage <http://www.house.gov/underwood/capc>.

Congressional Quarterly. 1998. *Congressional Elections, 1946-1988.* Washington, D.C.: Congressional Quarterly.

Enciso, Carmen E., Tracy North, and the Hispanic Division, Library of Congress. 1995. *Hispanic Americans in Congress. 1822-1995.* Washington, D.C.: U.S. Government Printing Office.

Espiritu, Yen Le. 1992. *Asian American Panethnicity: Bridging Institutions and Identities.* Philadelphia: Temple University Press.

Fong, Timothy P. 1994. *The First Suburban Chinatown: The Remaking of Monterey Park, California.* Philadelphia: Temple University Press.

Freedman, Leonard. 2000. *Power and Politics in America.* 7th ed. Fort Worth, TX: Harcourt Brace.

Hatamiya, Leslie T. 1993. *Righting a Wrong: Japanese Americans and the Passage of the Civil Liberties Act of 1988.* Stanford, CA.: Stanford University Press.

Hero, Rodney E. and Caroline J. Tolbert. 1995. "Latinos and Substantive Representation in the U.S. House of Representatives: Direct, Indirect, or Nonexistent?" *American Journal of Political Science* 39: 640-52.

Hing, Bill Ong. 1993. *Making and Remaking Asian America Through Immigration Policy, 1850-1990.* Stanford: Stanford University Press.

Horton, John. 1995. *The Politics of Diversity: Immigration, Resistance, and Change in Monterey Park, California.* Philadelphia: Temple University Press.

Hurh, Woo Moo and Kwang Chung Kim. 1989. "The 'Success' Image of Asian Americans: Its Validity, and Its Practical and Theoretical Implications." *Ethnic and Racial Studies* 12: 512-38.

Kessler, Daniel and Keith Krehbiel. 1996. "Dynamics of Cosponsorship." *American Political Science Review* 90: 555-66.

Kim, Claire Jean. 1999. The Racial Triangulation of Asian Americans. *Politics and Society* 27: 105-38.

King, Gary. 1989. *Unifying Political Methodology: The Likelihood Theory of*

Statistical Inference. New York: Cambridge University Press.

Krehbiel, Keith. 1995. "Cosponsors and Wafflers from A to Z." *American Journal of Political Science* 39: 906-23.

Lai, James S. 1994. *At the Threshold of the Golden Door—Ethnic Politics and Pan Asian Pacific American Coalition Building: A Case Study of the Special 1991 California 46th Assembly District Primary Election.* Unpublished Master's Thesis. UCLA.

Lewis, Neil A. 1999. "Imprisoned Scientist Sues U.S. Agencies." *New York Times.* December 21. A28.

Lien, Pei-te. 1994. "Ethnicity and Political Participation: A Comparison Between Asian and Mexican Americans." *Political Behavior* 16: 237-264.

_____. 1997. *The Political Participation of Asian Americans: Voting Behavior in Southern California.* New York: Garland.

_____. 1999. "What Ties That Bind? Comparing Patterns of Political Opinion Across Major Asian American Groups." Paper presented at the annual meeting of the American Political Science Association, Atlanta, GA.

Lublin, David. 1997. *The Paradox of Representation: Racial Gerrymandering and Minority Interests in Congress.* Princeton, NJ: Princeton University Press.

Macchiarola, Frank J. and Joseph G. Diaz. 1993. "Minority Political Empowerment in New York City: Beyond the Voting Rights Act." *Political Science Quarterly* 108: 37-57.

Nakanishi, Don T. and James S. Lai. 1995 [1996, 1998-99]. *National Asian Pacific American Political Almanac.* 6th ed. [7th ed., 8th ed.]. Los Angeles: UCLA Asian American Studies Center.

Nakanishi, Don T. 1998. "When Numbers Do Not Add Up: Asian Pacific Americans and California Politics." In *Racial and Ethnic Politics in California.* eds. Michael B. Preston, Bruce E. Cain and Sandra Bass. Vol. 2, eds., 3-43. Berkeley, CA: Institute of Governmental Studies.

Nash, Phil Tajitsu. 1999. "Winning a Say—District by District." *Asian Week: The Voice of Asian America* November 4, 10.

Nash, Phil Tajitsu, Julie D. Soo and Richard Lee. 1998. "Impeachment's Irony: The Unsettling Parallels of Jay Kim and Bill Clinton." *Asian Week: The Voice of Asian America.* December 24, 15-17.

National Committee for an Effective Congress (NCEC). 1999. *Congressional Districts with Asian Pacific American Population of 5% or More.* Mimeo.

Ng, Franklin. 1995. *The Asian American Encyclopedia.* Vol. 6, U.S. Immigration

Commission-ZuZu Ben. New York: Marshall Cavendish.

Okamura, Jonathan, Y. 1998. *Imagining the Filipino American Diaspora: Transnational Relations, Identities, and Communities*. New York: Garland.

Ong, Paul, and Don T. Nakanishi. 1996. "Becoming Citizens, Becoming Voters: The Naturalization and Political Participation of Asian American Immigrants." In *The State of Asian Pacific America: Reframing the Immigration Debate: A Public Policy Report*. eds. Bill Ong Hing and Ronald Lee. 275-305. Los Angeles: LEAP Asian Pacific American Public Policy Institute and UCLA Asian American Studies Center.

Pitkin, Hanna Fenichel. 1967. *The Concept of Representation*. Berkeley, Calif.: University of California Press.

Poole, Keith T. and Howard Rosenthal. 1997. *Congress: A Political-Economic History of Roll Call Voting*. New York: Oxford University Press.

Ragsdale, Bruce A. and Joel D. Treese. 1990. *Black Americans in Congress, 1870-1989*. Washington, D.C.: U.S. Government Printing Office.

Reed, Judith. 1992. "Of Boroughs, Boundaries and Bullwinkles: The Limitations of Single-Member Districts in a Multiracial Context." *Fordham Urban Law Review* 19: 759-80.

Risen, James and Jeff Gerth. 1999. "China Stole Nuclear Secrets for Bombs, U.S. Aides Say." *New York Times* March 6. A1, A6.

Saito, Leland T. 1998. *Race and Politics: Asian Americans, Latinos, and Whites in a Los Angeles Suburb*. Urbana, IL: University of Illinois Press.

Saund, D.S. 1960. *Congressman from India*. New York: E. P. Dutton.

Schaefer, Richard T. 1998. *Racial and Ethnic Groups*. 7th ed. New York: Longman.

Schultz, Jefferey, Andrew Aoki, Kerry L. Haynie, and Anne M. McCulloch. 2000. *Encyclopedia of Minorities in American Politics*. Vol. 1. African Americans and Asian Americans. Phoenix, AZ: Oryx Press.

Secretary of the State of California. Various Years. Roster: California State, County, City and Township Officials, State Officials of the United States. Sacramento, CA: California Office of State Printing.

Shinagawa, Larry Hajime. 1996. "The Impact of Immigration on the Demography of Asian Pacific Americans." In *The State of Asian Pacific America: Reframing the Immigration Debate: A Public Policy Report*. eds. Bill Ong Hing and Ronald Lee. 59-126. Los Angeles: LEAP Asian Pacific American Public Policy Institute and UCLA Asian American Studies Center.

Shinagawa, Larry Hajime and Michael Jang. 1998. *Atlas of American Diversity*.

Walnut Creek, CA: Alta Mira Press.

Srikanth, Rajini. 1998. "Ram Yoshino Uppuluri's Campaign: The Implications for Panethnicity in Asian America." In *A Part, Yet Apart: South Asians in Asian America*, eds. Lavina Dhingra Shankar and Rajini Srikanth. 186-214. Philadelphia: Temple University Press.

State of California. 1975. *California Blue Book.* Sacramento, CA: California Office of State Printing.

Sterngold, James. 1999. "Coalition Fears An Asian Bias in Nuclear Bias." *New York Times* December 13. A1, A30.

Suzuki, Bob H. 1977. "Education and the Socialization of Asian Americans: A Revisionist Analysis of the "Model Minority Thesis." *Amerasia Journal* 4: 23-51.

Swain, Carol M. 1993. *Black Faces, Black Interests: The Representation of African Americans in Congress.* Cambridge, MA: Harvard University Press.

Takeda, Okiyoshi. 1999. "Why Political Scientists Don't Study Asian American Politics, But Historians and Sociologists Do: A Reality Check on the Discipline and Search for Remedies." Paper presented at the annual meeting of the Midwest Political Science Association, Chicago.

Tam, Wendy. 1995. "Asians—A Monolithic Voting Bloc?" *Political Behavior* 17: 223-49.

Tang, Joyce. 1997. "The Model Minority Thesis Revisited: (Counter) Evidence from the

Science and Engineering Fields." *Journal of Applied Behavioral Science* 33: 291-315.

Tien, Charles and Dena Levy. 1998. "Asian-American and Hispanic Representation in the U.S. House of Representatives." Paper presented at the Midwest Political Science Association, Chicago: IL.

Time. 1999. June 7th Issue.

Tong, Lorraine H. 2000. "Asian Pacific Americans in the United States Congress." *Congressional Research Service Report for Congress*, 97-398 GOV.

Tuan, Mia. 1998. "Forever Foreigners or Honorary Whites?: The Asian Ethnic Experience Today." New Brunswick, NJ: Rutgers University Press.

Uhlaner, Carole J., Bruce E. Cain, and D. Roderick Kieweit. 1989. "Political Participation of Ethnic Minorities in the 1980s." *Political Behavior* 11: 195-231.

Umemoto, Karen. 2000. "From Vincent Chin to Joseph Illeto: Asian Pacific Americans and Hate Crime Policy." In *The State of Asian Pacific*

America: Transforming Race Relations: A Public Policy Report, ed. Paul M. Ong, 243-78. Los Angeles: LEAP Asian Pacific American Public Policy Institute and UCLA Asian American Studies Center. U.S. Bureau of Census. 1990. *Summary Tape File 3*. Obtained from Census CD: Complete U.S. Block Data and Maps (CD-ROM). East Brunswick, N.J.: GeoLytics, 1998.

_____. 2000. *Census Bureau Facts for Features: Asian Pacific American Heritage Month*: May 1-31. Downloaded from internet. Available at <http://www.census.gov/Press-Release/www/2000/cb00ff05. html>.

U.S. House. 1999. *Report of the Select Committee on U.S. National Security and Military/Commercial Concerns with the People's Republic of China*. 105th Cong., 2d Sess. H. Rpt. 105-851.

Vergara, Vanessa B.M. 1997. "Broken Promises and Aging Patriots: An Assessment of US Veteran Benefits for Filipino World War II Veterans." *Asian American Policy Review* 7: 163-82.

Wang, Ling-chi. 1998. "Race, Class, Citizenship, and Extraterritoriality: Asian Americans and the 1996 Campaign Finance Scandal." *Amerasia Journal* 24: 1-21.

Wei, William. 1993. *The Asian American Movement*. Philadelphia: Temple University Press.

Wilson, Rick K. and Cheryl D. Young. 1997. "Cosponsorship in the U.S. Congress." *Legislative Studies Quarterly* 22: 25-43.

Woo, Deborah. 2000. *Glass Ceilings and Asian Americans: The New Faces of Workplace Barriers*. Walnut Creek, CA: AltaMira.

Wu, Frank and May Nicholson. 1997. "Have You No Decency? Racial Aspects of Media   Coverage on the John Huang Matter." *Asian American Policy Review* 7:1-37.

Notes

1 All of these studies were conducted by sociologists and historians. Elsewhere I have discussed why sociologists and historians, rather than political scientists, have taken up Asian American politics as their research agenda (Takeda 1999).

2 Pacific Islanders (Native Hawaiians, Samoans, Guamanians, Tongans etc.) were included in the Asian American category in the 1990 census but were given a separate category from Asian Americans in 2000.

3 Of course, measured by the actual number of increased people, Latinos (897,000 in 1994) surpass Asian Americans (336,000) (Shinagawa and Jang 1998, 137).

4 An incident that illustrates both these two moments is the killing of Vincent Chin in Detroit in 1982. Chin, a Chinese American, was mistaken by a Japanese national and beaten to death by two white men, one of whom had recently been laid off by an automobile company in the city suffering from recession. Asian Americans of various ethnic groups all over the nation formed a coalition to call for justice; the fact that a Chinese American was mistaken for a Japanese prompted the formation of Asian American political groups at the interethnic, rather than ethnic, level (Espiritu 1992, Ch. 6).

5 The Asian average of the proportion of those below poverty line is 14.0 percent. This is approximately the same, and not lower than, the average for all Americans (Shinagawa and Jang 1998, 71, 143).

6 Additionally, two non-voting members, Faleomagaeva (D-American Samoa) and Underwood (D-Guam) are Pacific Islanders. Some statistics of minority representation merely note the number of Asian American House members as five, without mentioning that they do not have full voting power. It is not well known, however, that they can introduce bills and resolutions just as full voting members do.

7 The issue of registration and turnout rates will be discussed in the next section.

8 There are 63 House districts in which Asian Americans account for 5 percent or more of the population as measured by the 1990 census; that number increased to 96 in the 2000 estimate (NCEC 1999).

9 Racial breakdown of district-level population estimate in 2000 is not available from the U.S. Bureau of Census at the time of this writing. The estimate in the table, calculated by the National Committee for an Effective Congress and released by the Democratic National Committee (summarized in Nash (1999) in *Asian Week*, a weekly magazine for Asian Americans), is provided only for informational purpose.

10 For a case in New York City council redistricting showing this point, see Reed (1992, 772-76). Although Asian Americans accounted for seven percent of the city's population (and is estimated to be ten percent in 2000), a single Asian member has yet been elected to the 51-member city council (Macciarola and Diaz 1993, 53).

11 This, of course, is so far as descriptive representation is concerned. Latino elected officials such as state senator Art Torres advocated for Asian American interests as well as financially supported by Asian Americans (Saito 1998, 164, 172).

12 The almanac was also published five times during the 1978-1984 period.

13 The biography of these members are available in Schultz et al (2000) and on the "Biographical Directory of the United States Congress, 1774-Present" webpage <http://bioguide.congress.gov>.

14 Again, no Filipino has been elected to the California legislature, although Filipinos are the largest Asian American ethnic group in California. It is noteworthy, however, that Filipinos are elected to the legislatures of Maryland (David Valderrama), Washington (Velma Veloria), and West Virginia (John Amores) in the 1990s (Nakanishi and Lai 1995, 1996, 1998-99).

15 Some speculate that Asian American candidates who run in a predominantly white district can benefit from a positive stereotype of Asians as diligent and hardworking and also from an image that they are less "threatening" and more conservative than African Americans and whites (Saito 1998, 167). Some even go further and argue that Asian women particularly have the characteristics that are favored by the U.S. mainstream society (Chu 1989, 413). Although these arguments are often "talked about" among Asian Americans, we do not yet have data to test these hypotheses.

16 Furthermore, we have to discount these statistics, because this and most other census statistics include non-citizen immigrants, temporal workers and international students (Ong and Nakanishi 1996, 277).

17 Another reason that Asian American voting power is discounted is that the proportion of its age group under 18 is larger than that of other racial groups. Because of the population structure of immigrants, the median age of native-born Asian Americans is only 15.8 (Shinagawa 1996, 73).

18 Cho's (n.d.) analysis of campaign contributions to Asian American candidates underscores this observation.

19 The Japanese immigration was suspended by the so-called Gentlemen's Agreement between the two countries in 1907 and officially banned by the Immigration Act of 1924 together with immigration from other areas in Asia except for the Philippines.

20 260 U.S. 178 (1922); 261 U.S. 204 (1923).

21 The veteran benefits for Filipinos who fought for the United States are kept at the level of 50 percent of other veterans. An alternative provision to allow Filipino veterans to receive 75 percent of their Supplemental Security Income (SSI) if they go back to the Philippines was enacted during the 106th Congress.

22 Ideally, we may qualify the percentage of Asian Americans in House districts by their voter registration and turnout rates. Although such data are available for House districts in California, to my knowledge they are not available at the district level for all districts in the nation.

23 At the time of this writing, the available NOMINATE scores are computed out of the floor votes up to the end of October 1999 (just before the resolution passed the House).

24 I have one dummy for all minority members because if separate dummies for Asian American, African American, and Latino members are included, the Asian dummy is dropped from the model (all three Asian American House members cosponsored the resolution). In the latter model, African American and Latino member dummies do not have a statistically significant coefficient, and the remaining coefficients do not differ substantially from those reported in Table 4.

25 Since the 106th Congress has not adjourned at the time of this writing, the data used here are the number of bills and resolutions members cosponsored up to May 5, 2000.

26 In the case of Model 2, non-caucus members are predicted to sign the resolution by 9.9 percent, whereas caucus members are expected to do so by 33.4 percent.

27 One may wonder if this result was driven by the two outlier districts of Hawaii. The regression coefficients change very little when these two observations are dropped.

CHAPTER 6

American Indian Representation in the 20th and 21st Centuries

Geoff Peterson and Robert Duncan

American Indians are often the forgotten minority when discussing American politics. This may be due to their concentration in remote reservations, their lack of participation in the political process, their concentration in a few states, or a variety of other reasons. Whatever the cause, scholars, politicians, and government bureaucrats often ignore American Indians as a group when discussing minority political behavior and representation[1]. While it is true that American Indians have, as a group, been less involved in the national political milieu than any other minority group, that does not imply that the group can or should be overlooked.

This lack of involvement, combined with the relatively small numbers of American Indians in most states, has also made it easier to ignore them. While American Indians only make up 0.8% of the total population of the United States[2], they are concentrated in a few states, giving them the potential to exert real political power in those areas. In fact, American Indians make up more than five percent of the population in seven states: Alaska, Arizona, Colorado, Montana, New Mexico, Oklahoma, and South Dakota. It is this concentration of potential voting power that makes American Indians a political force that must be considered.

Emboldened by the new potential economic power of casino gambling and other economic interests, the American Indian population of the United States is becoming increasingly politically active. While their representation in government continues to be limited primarily to local and state offices, this new level of activity has opened many doors for American Indians in the political realm.

This chapter begins by providing a brief history of American Indian forced transition to a European style of governance, followed by a thorough analysis of the federal institutions that were created to "manage" the American Indian population. Further, we examine issues of measurement prior to our discussion of American Indians pursuing office at each level of government and the issues that are of importance to them.

History of American Indian Voting and Representation

To understand the American Indian voting patterns and how they are represented in elected offices, one must first understand the historical complexities and the unique "nation to nation" relationships between the tribes and the federal government. From a historical perspective, the arrival and subsequent colonization of the New World spelled doom for the traditional ways of American Indians. Unlike the perceptions of most non-Indians, most American Indian tribes were village dwelling, agrarian societies with political authority, laws, and spiritual beliefs. Their cultures were very imbued with nature and the environment. It has been estimated that anywhere from 1 million to 4 million American Indians inhabited the continent. American Indians views of life, earth, individuality, and community all merged in their approach to land ownership. This issue is at the heart of all confrontations, legal and violent, between the tribes and federal government.

The official United States government policy for American Indians has been assimilation and acculturation. Assimilation and acculturation both focus on subsuming American Indian culture into the dominant European paradigm and was greatly opposed by a majority of American Indians. Evidence shows that the federal government wanted to totally destroy the American Indian cultures whenever and wherever possible. To speed up the assimilation process, the national government imposed European-style educational systems, particularly boarding schools that removed children from the rest of the tribe, to indoctrinate European values into the younger generations. Efforts were also made to convert American Indians to Christianity, but were largely unsuccessful. When assimilation and acculturation failed to work, eradication was seen as the only other viable option.

The first settlers coveted the rich, fertile Indian lands. Some attempted to live peacefully with the Indians and share in the abundance of natural resources available. Most, however, wanted to relocate the Indians to the West. As the population of the United States grew, the Indians were pushed farther and farther west. President Andrew Jackson, convinced the "Great American Desert" was useless, passed The Indian Removal Act of 1830. This legitimized the United States policy of relocation of the American Indians. The forced "Trail of Tears" by the Five Civilized Tribes to present-day Oklahoma is one of the bleakest chapters of American Indian and United States history. Even after the Supreme Court ruled in favor of American Indian land rights and their sovereign status as independent nations[3], removals continued. The thirst for land continued with the coming of the railroads and the discovery of mineral deposits in territories previously ceded to Indian tribes.

The Indian Removal Act of 1830 was followed by numerous other successful attempts to forcibly acquire Indian land. The Dawes Severalty Act of 1887, the Curtis Act of 1898 (written by a Kaw tribal member himself), the Dead Indian Land Act of 1902, and the Burke Act of 1906, all added to the Federal government land coffers. Although there were generally formal agreements in place between the tribes and the government for these lands, these agreements were often coerced and rarely were the conditions of the treaties carried out in good faith.

The Federal government may have negotiated these treaties in good faith with tribal officials, who they believed spoke for the entire tribe, but that was not always the case. Many times these officials were actually the minority of the tribes. These treaties caused tremendous division and resentment within the tribes already weakened by inner tribal rivalry and disputes. These divisions aided the BIA in not fulfilling the provisions, as corrupt officials and members diverted many of the funds and provisions intended for the tribes. As a result, a majority of Indians did not receive their benefits.

Although the federal government generally ignored most treaties, they often extended citizenship to American Indians. By 1917, more than two-thirds (2/3) of all American Indians were citizens of the United States. It was not until the passage of the Snyder Act of 1924 that suffrage was granted to all Indians, although the granting of the franchise still did not guarantee the right to vote. Arizona did not allow tribal members to vote until 1948 and New Mexico did not offer the franchise until 1962.

The Reorganization Act of 1934 and the "Indian New Deal" were attempts to continue the assimilation process. Although successful to some degree in aiding tribal economic and political progress, American Indians continued to push for the terms of treaties to be met. This continued through the 1950's as additional attempts were made to terminate Indian policies. The new policies encouraged Indians to move off the reservations and relocate to urban areas with more economic opportunities. Although many did, they found their plight no better than other minorities facing racism and discrimination.

States began to balk at termination policies realizing they would have to assume the responsibility for their new citizens. The Kennedy administration gave American Indians new hope by creating policies designed to encourage economic development on reservations with Indian participation. A new concept, supertribalism, gained emphasis among American Indians. Supertribalism allowed American Indians to foster and maintain their tribal and cultural identities while still joining mainstream America.

Extra-Tribal Organizations

Many attempts have been made to organize American Indians beyond tribal divisions in order to push for greater political power and representation. The great Shawnee leader, Tecumseh, attempted to organize the eastern tribes in the early 1800's. He was unsuccessful because of deep divisions both between and within the individual tribes. Even with the threat of extinction, American Indians were unable to ban together for their common good.

In the 20th century, many movements have attempted to unite American Indians into a cohesive political, economic, and cultural group. The goals of these groups have traditionally been focused on achieving the complete enforcement and compliance of the numerous treaties between the tribes and the federal government. Although the Bureau of Indian Affairs is delegated by Congress to administer the provisions of these treaties, American Indian groups have alleged numerous instances of mismanagement, corruption and incompetence by the Bureau. The list of groups that have tried to organize American Indians at the national level includes: The Society of American Indians (SAI), National Congress of American Indians (NCAI), United American Indians (UNA), National Traditionalist Movement (NTM), Confederation of American Indian Nations (CAIN), National Tribal Chairman's Association (NTCA) and the most active recently, the American Indian Movement (AIM).

The American Indian Movement began in Minneapolis, Minnesota in 1968 as a response to the mistreatment of Indians by "European-American" local police. Members of the Chippewa tribe formed "Indian Patrols" to police the reservation and shadow local law enforcement while on the reservations. These patrols were successful in diminishing the amount of harassment and brutality in American Indian neighborhoods. George Mitchell and Dennis Banks, who had emerged as leaders of the patrol, decided to organize formally to protect migrating American Indians from ethnically selective law enforcement policies. (Olson p.167). AIM, along with other groups began to monitor activities of the federal government and states, particularly any discussion of termination of treaties, tribes and tribal rights.

Motivated by threats of termination, these groups turned to militancy to press their cases. The occupation of Alcatraz, the Trial of Broken Treaties, and the occupation of the Bureau of Indian Affairs headquarters in Washington, D.C. were all examples of American Indian attempts to dramatize their demands for self-determination, tribal lands, and tribal identities. The movement came to national attention in 1973 at Wounded Knee on the Pine Ridge Reservation in South Dakota. The occupation of Wounded Knee by AIM activists culminated in the death of two FBI agents in 1973. The conviction of Leonard Peltier and others of these crimes galvanized public opinion over the American Indian issues. Peltier is considered a political prisoner by many and his personal plight has garnered worldwide attention.

One of the many positive contributions of the AIM movement was the gradual adaptation of the "Twenty Points Platform." It is one of the first Indian proposals generated by Indians addressing their concerns. Starting with the Nixon Administration, a number of laws have been enacted to guarantee tribal sovereignty and rights. These attitudes have continued through the Clinton years. A restoration of sovereignty, examination of land rights and claims and a revitalization of culture dominate tribal concerns today.

Sovereignty and Dual Citizenship

When the Europeans arrived, American Indian communities were comprised of individual sovereign nations. The federal government treated these communities as individual states, and signed numerous treaties with them. This unique relationship continues today. By accepting the treaties and land allotments, American Indians became American citizens. But, like formerly freed slaves, Indians suffered from the same "Jim Crow" laws that denied them access to the voting booth. Since the repeal of these disenfranchising laws in the 1950s and 1960s, American Indians have been allowed to participate in tribal, local, state, and federal elections. Although all American Indians have access to this "dual citizenship" by law, most have decided not to engage in federal politics.

The acknowledgment of the various tribes as independent sovereign nations has been the cornerstone of Indian policy. As more and more treaties were signed, administration of the treaties came under the purview of the Bureau of Indian Affairs. The Bureau of Indian Affairs works on an individual tribe by tribe basis, implementing the treaties and national Indian policy. American Indians enjoy dual, actually triple citizenship. They are members of their tribe, the United States and their individual states. This "triple citizenship" has caused a number of problems concerning jurisdictions and allegiances. State legislatures have found it necessary and advantageous to cooperate with the tribes, particularly in states with a substantial population or large land area.

While tribes participate in programs along with federal and state agencies, the programs do not fall completely under federal jurisdiction while on Indian land. It is this special relationship that has caused a "white backlash" in some areas. Some members of the white population who live near American Indian reservations feel that the special status of tribes gives reservation governments an unfair advantage. While it is true that the sovereign status of the tribes gives them certain economic advantages over other communities[4], it is clear that American Indians have not been given the financial, educational and political support insured by the original treaties. Although eligible to pursue state and federal offices as dictated by the Constitution, most American Indians do not want to be assimilated into American culture and prefer to work politically within their tribe and seek tribal rights. An appreciation and support for tribal cultures and ways have replaced the days of assimilation and acculturation.

But Where Are They? Issues Of Measurement

One of the largest barriers to the study of American Indian representation in government is the problem of measurement. Throughout the 19th and 20th centuries, accurate measures of the indigenous peoples of North America were unavailable. For decades the United States Census Bureau did not differentiate between American Indians, Asians, or any of the other races included in the "other" category, and the Current Population Survey conducted by the Department of Labor did not recognize American Indians as a separate category until 1990. To compound this problem, American Indians are less likely to participate in governmental attempts to measure their population, often resulting in significant underestimates of the American Indian population.

The measurement problem is further compounded by the difficulty in defining who is an American Indian and who is not. Although most tribes require that members be at least one-quarter American Indian to join, some tribes use a standard of one-half or one-eighth tribal heritage as the criterion for membership. The attempts by the federal government to move American Indian children into white homes to "civilize" them in the 19th and early 20th centuries further complicated this issue, as many of these "deported" children married into white bloodlines and never knew their true lineage. The result is that there is no clear measure of the percentage of the population that is American Indian.

Another problem in measuring representation is that many American Indians denied their heritage for the purposes of gaining access to white society. Many of the Jim Crow laws in the South treated American Indians as if they were African-Americans, and white society generally treated American Indians as ignorant brutes. While there is no clear evidence of elected officials denying their heritage to be elected, the history of American popular culture is replete with entertainers and sports figures who downplayed or denied their Indian lineage in order to be accepted by white audiences.

This measurement problem is also evident when looking at elected officials in government. When Ben Nighthorse Campbell was elected as a representative (and later a senator) from Colorado in 1986, most of the major press outlets called him the first American Indian ever elected to Congress. While it was true that it had been several decades since an American Indian had served in Congress, he was by no means the first. For example, Benjamin Reifel served as a representative from South Dakota from 1960 to 1970, and Charles Curtis from Kansas served as a representative, senator and vice-president from the late 19th and early 20th centuries.

Measuring Representation: The Issues

There are a variety of factors that impact the degree of representation garnered by American Indians in the United States. Some of the issues are similar to those faced by other minorities, while others are factors are unique to the American Indian population. American Indian tribes, like most other minority groups, have lost representation through legislative gerrymandering and Jim Crow laws. Similar to most other minorities, low voter turnout in state and national elections has also decreased the level of representation for most American Indians (Peterson 1998).

There are, however, several issues that affect American Indian representation that are unique. The long and often contentious relationship between the federal government (particularly the Bureau of Indian Affairs) and the American Indian population has been very influential in creating a culture of distrust among American Indians. The numerous wars, relocations, broken treaties, and "civilization" attempts during the 19th and early 20th centuries bred a strong belief among most American Indians that the state and federal governments could not be trusted. This situation was further exacerbated by the apathy, corruption, and appalling treatment most American Indians suffered at the hands of the Bureau of Indian Affairs throughout most of the 20th century.

Since the emergence of the American Indian Movement in the 1960s, many American Indians have focused their efforts on tribal government rather than on state and federal representation. The revitalization of the tribal governments and the new movement towards tribal sovereignty has breathed life into many dormant reservation governments, and many American Indians feel that the issues that affect them directly are best addressed at the tribal level.

This move towards increased tribal involvement has been aided by the rapid expansion of legalized gambling and other forms of economic development on American Indian reservations. Gambling has poured billions of dollars into the coffers of many tribes, and controlling how those funds are spent has become the primary political concern for many American Indians in the United States. The tribal policy issues surrounding American Indian gambling money are numerous and complicated, but these issues also represent a clear opportunity for American Indians to control their own financial and political agendas, rather than depending on the largess of the federal and state authorities.

In many tribes, the combination of distrust towards the federal government and the re-emergence of tribal governance has altered the representation calculus. While American Indians may not focus their efforts on gaining representation in state and national governments, they may well be satisfied with their level of representation through their control of their tribal destinies[5].

Representation At The National Level

In general, American Indians have achieved very little representation at the national level. Only a handful of American Indians have ever served in either house of Congress, and few American Indians have ever served in the Cabinet or in the upper levels of the judiciary system. Measurement issues clearly come into play here, as there may well be some members of Congress or the Cabinet that were American Indians and did not acknowledge their heritage.

Historically, Charles Curtis, a Kaw tribal member from Kansas, held the highest office ever by an American Indian, eventually serving as vice-president under President Herbert Hoover. Other American Indians have served in either the House or Senate, but the numbers were always very small. Since 1960, a total of two American Indians have served in either chamber of the national legislature, Representative Reifel from South Dakota and Senator Nighthorse Campbell from Colorado. For these officials, it is clear that they were elected *despite* being an American Indian, rather than *because* they were American Indians. Reifel and Curtis often downplayed their tribal ties in their campaigns, and Nighthorse Campbell does not make his American Indian heritage the centerpiece of his campaigns[6].

Table 6-1 shows a breakdown of the American Indian representation at the national level. Clearly, American Indians are significantly underrepresented. This, of course, is typical of the lack of minority representation of any sort at the national level.

In terms of non-elected (judicial and bureaucratic) appointments, the numbers are also extremely small. With the exception of the Bureau of Indian Affairs, which has moved to include more American Indian

Table 6-1 Number of American Indian Members in the US Congress, 1960-2000.

	American Indian Members Members	Total Members in Congress	Percentage Of Seats Held by American Indians	American Indian Population Percentage
1960-70	1	535	0.19%	1.6%
1970-80	0	535	0.00%	1.4%
1980-90	0	535	0.00%	0.8%
1990-2000	1	535	0.19%	0.6%

Source: Reddy, Marlita A. 1993. *Statistical Record of Native North Americans.* 1998 Detroit: Gale Research.

staff members over the past thirty years, American Indian representation at the higher echelons of the federal government has been minuscule.

Representation At The State Level

While representation of American Indians at the national level has been extremely weak, their level of representation at the state and local levels of government has been significantly higher. This is driven by a variety of factors, but the most obvious one is the localization of American Indian populations. The reservation system created by Congress and the Bureau of Indian Affairs concentrated American Indian populations in small geographic areas. While these concentrations are often too small to affect the results of state-wide races for the national legislature, they are large enough to give American Indians an effective voice in state and local government. Many reservations completely encompass one or more counties, making the tribal population the majority for county-level elections. In addition, most state legislative districts are small enough that any individual reservation may be included in several districts. When this occurs, it allows the reservation population to have a significant impact on the results of state legislative elections.

Not surprisingly, the states with the highest percentage of American Indians in state and local offices are also the states with the highest percentage of American Indians in the population. The eight states with the highest percentage of American Indians account for 90% of all American Indian state legislators, as shown in Table 6-2.

Table 6-2 American Indian Representation In State Legislatures, 1992[7]

	Total Number of Legislators	*Number of American Indian Legislators*	*Percentage of American Indian Legislators*
Alaska	58	11	19.0%
Arizona	91	5	5.5%
Montana	150	4	2.7%
New Mexico	112	6	5.4%
North Carolina	170	1	0.6%
North Dakota	147	1	0.7%
Oklahoma	149	5	3.4%
South Dakota	105	3	2.9%
Colorado	100	1	1.0%
All States	7424	41	0.6%

Source: Reddy, Marlita A. 1993. *Statistical Record of Native North Americans.* 1998 Detroit: Gale Research.

What is interesting about these results is that the percentage of legislators (0.6%) is actually quite close to the overall American Indian population percentage (0.8%). This seems to indicate that when American Indian populations are in a position to have a clear and positive impact on election outcomes, they take advantage of the opportunity.

It is also worth noting that the level of representation in state legislatures does not vary significantly between the upper and lower chambers. In 1992, American Indians accounted for 0.5% of all state house members and 0.6% of all state senators. Tables 6-3 and 6-4 provide a more detailed breakdown of American Indian representation in the state houses and state senates.

Table 6-3 American Indians in the State Houses, 1992

	House Members	American Indian Members	Percentage of American Indian House Members	American Indian Population Percentage
Alaska	38	6	15.8%	15.6%
Arizona	61	4	6.6%	5.6%
Montana	100	4	4.0%	6.0%
New Mexico	70	4	5.7%	8.9%
North Carolina	120	1	0.8%	1.2%
North Dakota	98	0	0.0%	4.1%
Oklahoma	101	3	3.0%	8.0%
South Dakota	70	2	2.9%	7.3%
Colorado	65	1	1.5%	8.3%
All States	5440	29	0.5%	0.8%

Source: Reddy, Marlita A. 1993. *Statistical Record of Native North Americans*. 1998 Detroit: Gale Research.

Table 6-4 American Indians in State Senates, 1992

	Number of Senators	American Indian Senators	Percentage of American Indian Senators	American Indian Percentage
Alaska	20	5	25.0%	15.6%
Arizona	30	1	3.3%	5.6%
Montana	50	0	0.0%	6.0%
New Mexico	42	2	4.8%	8.9%
North Carolina	50	0	0.0%	1.2%
North Dakota	49	1	2.0%	4.1%
Oklahoma	48	2	4.2%	8.0%
South Dakota	35	1	2.9%	7.3%
Colorado	35	0	0.0%	8.3%
All States	1984	12	0.6%	0.8%

Source: Reddy, Marlita A. 1993. *Statistical Record of Native North Americans*. 1998 Detroit: Gale Research.

The evidence certainly indicates that American Indians can and do participate in the political process at the state level. By representing the needs of the tribal communities in the state legislatures, American Indian representatives and senators are able to move their agendas forward. It is also possible, if not likely, that the gambling issue plays a significant role in American Indian involvement at the state level. Since decisions on tribal gambling agreements are made between the tribal governments and the states, having tribal members within the legislature would be a logical method by which to encourage open discussion and dispute resolution.

Representation At The Local Level

Like American Indian representation at the state level, it is clear that tribal members are far more involved in local politics when compared to national politics. Local elected officials are generally defined as city and county offices[8], and thus the geographic size of the electoral districts are even smaller than those for the state legislatures. In many cases, these offices represent counties or portions of counties. Given that most reservations often include entire counties and reach into several, it should come as no surprise that the smaller district size affords American Indians even more opportunities to be represented. Table 6-5 shows the breakdown of representation of American Indians in local governments in the ten states in which they have the most elected officials.

Table 6-5 American Indian Representation In Local Government, 1992

	Elected Local Officials	American Indian Elected Local Officials	Percentage of American Indian Elected Local Officials	American Indian Population Percentage
Alaska	1,674	603	36.0%	15.6%
Arizona	3,050	83	2.7%	5.6%
Montana	4,905	78	1.6%	6.0%
New Mexico	1,981	30	1.5%	8.9%
North Carolina	5,227	23	0.4%	1.2%
North Dakota	15,277	38	0.2%	4.1%
Oklahoma	8,627	371	4.3%	8.0%
South Dakota	9,529	55	0.6%	7.3%
Colorado	8,325	8	0.1%	8.3%
California	18,699	54	0.3%	0.8%
All States	493,830	1,800	0.4%	0.8%

Source: Reddy, Marlita A. 1993. *Statistical Record of Native North Americans.* 1998 Detroit: Gale Research.

Again, the evidence clearly shows that American Indians are willing to participate in the process when they believe they have an opportunity to influence the electoral outcomes. Although most of the states in question have a lower percentage of local American Indian officials compared to the overall American Indian population, the state of Alaska stands out. In Alaska, American Indians are actually significantly overrepresented at the local level compared to the size of the population. Although there are no clear explanations for this discrepancy, much of it may be driven by the relatively friendly relations between the Alaskan Indians and the non-Indian populations.

Implications and Conclusions

In general, American Indians are still underrepresented in the political realm. While their levels of representation are improving at the state and local levels, American Indians have had little success gaining national representation. This lack of national representation is likely a consequence of localized populations, dispersed interests and a lack of interest in national policy. For most American Indians, the decisions made by the state and local governments are as important, if not more so, than those decisions made by the federal government. As tribal economic development continues to rely more and more heavily on casino gambling, the decisions made by state legislatures become the decisions most carefully monitored.

Although American Indians are underrepresented at all levels of government in elected positions, they are not politically inactive, rather they often choose not to be active in popularly elected positions. American Indians are very active in tribal governments and in causes that directly affect their individual tribes, reservations and interests. Since most of the top officials at the Bureau of Indian Affairs are American Indians, tribal members have been successful in refocusing the Bureau's mission to protect the interests of all American Indians. After years of charges of incompetence, inefficiencies and actual corruption, the Bureau today has been very successful and continues to improve on its mission.

American Indians are also active as a political party constituency especially through lobbying and campaign contributions[9]. However, the most politically active American Indians are flexing their political muscle right at home in their individual tribes and reservations. Since the inception of the Indian Gaming Regulatory Act, tribes have begun to benefit from this lucrative business. Through gambling and other forms of tribal economic development, American Indians are becoming a force in politics. With the control of these interests, along with the federal government's increased commitment to restoring tribal treaties, local tribal leaders are becoming more powerful both within their tribes and within all levels of government.

We would be remiss if we did not briefly point out that the lack of representation for American Indians is driven, at least in part, by the low voter turnout among American Indian populations. Although the reasons for low turnout among tribal members are still unclear, there are literally dozens of studies tracking the exceptionally low American Indian turnout in elections (Peterson 1997 & Peterson 1998). Whether the new spark of gambling revenue will encourage tribal members to participate in the political process has yet to be demonstrated (Peterson 1999). Given that the revenue from gambling and other business interests are improving both the educational systems and the economic status of many American Indians, it seems likely that may well improve political participation among American Indians. If that occurs, it will be a substantial step forward for American Indian representation.

References

Cornell, Stephen. 1988. *The Return of the Native, American Indian Political Resurgence.* New York: Oxford University Press. 1988.

Corntassel, Jeff J and Witmer II, Richard C. 1997. "American Indian Tribal Government Support of Office-Seekers: Findings From the 1994 Election." *The Social Science Journal* 34, p. 511.

Deloria, Vine Jr. 1998. *The Nations Within.* University of Texas Press: Austin, TX.

Hero, Rodney E. 1998. *Faces of Inequality, Social Diversity in American Politics.* New York: Oxford University.

Johansen, Bruce E. 1982. *Forgotten Founders, How the American Indian Helped Shape Democracy.* Boston: Harvard Common Press.

Johnson, Susan. 1998. "From Wounded Knee to Capitol Hill". *State Legislatures* 24, p.14.

Lowry, Rich. 1997. "Racing for dollars." *National Review* 49, p.20.

National Conference of State Legislatures: National Council of American Indian Legislators, 1999.

Olson James S. and Raymond Wilson. 1986. *American Indian, In the Twentieth Century.* Chicago: University of Illinois.

Peterson, Geoff. 1997. "American Indian Voting in Presidential Elections: 1952-1988." Working Paper.

Peterson, Geoff. 1998. "American Indian Turnout in the 1990 and 1992 Elections." *American Indian Quarterly* Spring.

Peterson, Geoff. 1999. "Bets and Ballots: How the Introduction of Gambling Altered Native American Voting Behavior." Working Paper.

Prucha, Francis Paul. 1995. *The Indians in American Society, from the Revolutionary War to the Present.* Berkley: University of California Press.

Reddy, Marlita A., 1993. *Statistical Record of Native North Americans.* Detroit: Gale Research.

Thompson, William N. 1996. *American Indian Issue, A Reference Handbook.* Santa Barbara: ABC-CLIO Inc.

United States Census, Estimates of Demographics of States, 1994.

Wunder, John R. 1996. *Constitutionalism and American Indians, 1903-1968.* New York: Garland Publishing.

Notes

1 For example, the federal government did not recognize American Indians as a separate category in the Current Population Study (the largest labor survey in the nation) until 1990.

2 Virtually all demographic experts on minority populations agree that American Indians are consistently under counted by the census, although the level of error is most likely no greater than for most other minority groups in the United States.

3 In Cherokee v. Georgia, Marshall spoke of Indians as in a "state of pupilage" and declared their relation to the United States " resembles that of a ward to his guardian" and "look to our government for protection" (Prucha p. 14).

4 Most reservation businesses are exempt from state and federal taxes, allowing them to sell cigarettes, for example, at much lower prices than the non-reservation businesses. The issues surrounding legalized reservation gambling also continue to be a source of substantial controversy in many states.

5 The lack of empirical research on American Indian political beliefs and tendencies is no more evident than when we try to judge how American Indians view their relationships with their tribal and other governmental institutions. While these explanations appear to fit the current patterns of American Indian political activity, there is no concrete evidence to support or disprove these conjectures at this point in time.

6 It is interesting to note that all three American Indian elected to Congress in this century were Republicans (Nighthorse Campbell was first elected as a Democrat and re-elected as a Republican) when most American Indian identify themselves as members of the Democratic party (Peterson 1998).

7 For all states with at least one American Indian legislator. Several states with large American Indian populations had no representation in the state legislature.

8 Local officials counted in this section include county governing commissions, school boards, city councils, mayors, and most other elected officers at the county/city level.

9 In 1996, several tribal organizations, including Cheyenne-Arapaho Tribe of Oklahoma and the Pequot Tribe of Connecticut, donated large sums of money to both state and national party election funds, and it seems likely many more will do so in future elections.

CHAPTER 7

Voters, Non-voters and Minority Representation

Patrick Ellcessor and Jan E. Leighley1

One of the least contested conclusions in the study of political behavior is that voters' political attitudes and policy positions are fairly representative of non-voters. Wolfinger and Rosenstone (1980) offer some of the earliest evidence on this point, concluding that the demographic differences between voters and non-voters do not translate into substantial differences in their opinions on various policy issues, party identification or self-reported ideology (see also Gant and Lyons 1988; Shaffer 1982; Studlar and Welch 1986). Most recently, Bennett and Resnick (1990) consider the implications of non-voting more broadly, reporting that non-voters are not necessarily less egalitarian or more anti-civil rights than voters. Largely echoing Wolfinger and Rosenstone's findings, Bennett and Resnick also conclude that there are few significant differences in the policy attitudes of voters and non-voters.

All of these findings, however, rely on national survey samples that are comprised almost entirely of non-Hispanic whites. It is simply impossible to assess whether minority individuals are similarly represented, with extremely small numbers of African American and Latino (or any other minority) respondents. At the same time, studies of African American and Latino electoral politics provide little insight on this question as they typically consider questions of representation with respect to the racial/ethnic composition of (elected) governing bodies, or the ability to successfully elect a Black or Latino candidate (see, for example, de la Garza and DeSipio 1992; de la Garza, Menchaca and DeSipio 1994; Dawson 1994;

Hero 1992; Pinderhughes 1987; Swain 1995; Tate 1993). The question of whether or not minority voters are representative of minority non-voters is all the more important when one considers the lower levels of aggregate turnout among minorities such as Latinos and Asian-Americans (Rosenstone and Hansen 1993, Chapter 8; U.S. Census Bureau 1998).

We propose below a theoretical framework for analyzing the representativeness of voters and non-voters, positing that electoral representativeness is a function of both race and class, and that the nature of this relationship is likely to vary across levels of panethnicity. We focus separately on whites, African Americans, Latinos and Asian Americans, using data from the 1995 *Washington Poll on Race Relations*, a national survey with minority oversamples.[2] We compare attitudes of voters and non-voters on the openness and fairness of the American political system, domestic policy issues, governmental spending and governmental responsibility for racial equality using correlational and chi-square analyses. We find that there are some important differences and other similarities between voters and non-voters across different racial and ethnic groups. We also find that Anglo, African American, Latino and Asian American voters and non-voters overwhelmingly support the American political and economic system.

Voters vs. Non-voters

Bennett and Resnick (1990) offer the definitive statement on policy differences between voters and non-voters. Using data from the National Election Studies, as well as the General Social Survey, they consider two broad questions: whether or not non-voters hold values or attitudes that are inimical to democracy and whether or not non-voters hold policy positions that differ from voters. They find little evidence that non-voters are more alienated from our democratic political system, less trustful of government, or more likely to have anti-civil libertarian or bigoted attitudes; non-voters are, however, slightly less patriotic and tend to be less informed about politics.

Aside from non-voters being slightly more isolationistic than voters, Bennett and Resnick find that most policy differences between voters and non-voters relate to domestic policies other than abortion or government assistance to minorities. Bennett and Resnick report that non-voters are slightly more likely than voters to support an expanded government role in domestic issues, being more opposed to curtailing government spending for health and education services and more supportive of the government guaranteeing jobs to everyone. The biggest differences, however, emerge on spending preferences:

> "Nonvoters would have federal spending increased for social security, food stamps, and, to a lesser degree, to improve blacks' conditions. Although voters would also support more money for Social Security, they are less supportive than nonvoters" (Bennett and Resnick 1990: 793).

These policy differences, however, are not corroborated by differences in ideology, partisanship or vote intention. Ideological differences between voters and non-voters in the 1980s varied by year—sometimes non-voters were more liberal, sometimes not—but were always quite small. Consistent with this, Bennett and Resnick speculate that had non-voters actually showed up at the polls, none of the electoral outcomes would have changed.

Finally, Bennett and Resnick consider whether non-voters are more egalitarian in their political values than are voters. Using a battery of questions regarding equality (i.e., equal opportunity) in the U.S. today, they find that non-voters differ significantly from voters in two out of three years, but that the relationship is very weak. Consistent with this, Bennett and Resnick report that non-voters and voters differ with regard to believing "it should or should not be the government's responsibility to reduce income differences between the rich and poor," (p. 798), with non-voters being slightly more likely to believe that it is the government's responsibility. Since this relationship, too, is quite weak, they conclude that it is of marginal importance, and claim more broadly:

> *Nonvoters do not always, or even usually, differ from voters in their policy opinions, views on socialism, or their egalitarianism.* Therefore, elected officials, even if they have finely tuned antennas, may not always be able to discriminate between their voting and nonvoting constituents' policy opinions." (1990: 799; italics in the original)

On Class and Self-Interest in Public Policies

As with previous research on the policy representativeness of voters and non-voters, Bennett and Resnick (1990) are silent regarding the theoretical significance of these empirical findings. The underlying assumptions motivating the expectation that voters' and non-voters' policy positions *should* differ are two-fold: first, the decision to vote is determined largely by individuals' socioeconomic status, and, second, individuals' preferred policy positions reflect their socioeconomic self-interest.

One can hardly dispute the first assumption. Brady, Verba and Schlozman (1995), for example, argue that high-status individuals are more likely to participate than low-status individuals because they are more likely to have the opportunity to develop the skills (or otherwise gather the resources, i.e., time, money, etc.) necessary to participate (see also Leighley and Nagler 1992; Wolfinger and Rosenstone 1980).[3] Moreover, this class bias has been documented as a strong and relatively stable feature of voter turnout in national elections since the 1960s (Leighley and Nagler 1992).

The problem with the second assumption (that socioeconomic status structures individuals' policy positions), is that previous research on socioeconomic status and self-interest/policy positions provides only mixed evidence. Erikson and Tedin (1995), for example, note that the relationship between individuals' (subjective) class and opinions on government spending are "quite modest." While they find dramatic differences in support for federal government program spending between recipients and non-recipients, there is a moderate relationship between family income and individuals' opinions on government spending and the responsibility of the government to guarantee jobs for everyone.

A modest relationship between class and policy preferences might plausibly explain Bennett and Resnick's (1990) findings. To the extent that lower-SES individuals believe that more government spending on programs; government efforts to reduce inequality and provide jobs to everyone; and maintaining (or increasing) health and education spending is in their economic self-interest, Bennett and Resnick should have observed significant differences between voters and non-voters on these issues—which they did. On the other hand, if such differences are motivated by abstract ideological principles of limited government, individualism, etc., then Bennett and Resnick should have observed significant differences in the political ideology (and perhaps partisanship) between voters and non-voters—which they did not. Trivial or non-significant differences on other matters (e.g., foreign affairs, patriotism) likewise are consistent with this assumption of policy positions reflecting individuals' economic self-interest. Thus, Bennett and Resnick's findings are broadly consistent with the assumption that class has a significant effect on individuals' policy preferences. But because this is a relatively weak relationship, the actual differences observed between voters and non-voters are not staggering.[4]

Class, Race, Ethnicity and Self-Interest

The assumption that individuals' political attitudes and electoral choices reflect their economic interests is stated more explicitly in numerous discussions of the future of Black electoral politics. With a significantly larger (and growing) Black middle-class today than thirty years ago, both scholars and activists are engaged in discussions regarding how such economic diversity might change the nature of Black electoral politics (see, for example, Hochschild 1995; Huckfeldt and Kohfeld 1989). Dawson (1994: 5) succinctly summarizes the debate: "The central question, simply stated, is whether race or class is more important in shaping African American politics."

Dawson (1994) contends that socioeconomic status is critical in determining African Americans' attitudes towards redistributing wealth because individual economic well-being functions as a prerequisite for helping other individuals within one's racial group. Nevertheless, African Americans' perceptions of linked fates (i.e., the belief that what happens to the group will substantially affect individuals within the group) tend to mediate the impact of individual economic self-interest on their attitudes toward economic redistribution. More affluent African Americans tend to have stronger perceptions of linked fate, which acts as a counterbalance to self-interest and thus increases high-status African Americans' support of redistributive policies. Less affluent African Americans, on the other hand, hold weaker perceptions of linked fate and tend to place greater emphasis on their own self-interest in determining their positions on redistributive policies.

More specifically, Dawson claims that African Americans with higher levels of education are more, not less, likely to view their fate as linked to other African Americans, thus contradicting the claim that higher socioeconomic status "weaken(s) the attachment to race" (Dawson 1994: 80-82). In two issue domains, however, individual socioeconomic status is critically important, according to Dawson: attitudes toward redistributing wealth and toward African American political and cultural autonomy.[5]

Dawson's argument, then, suggests that the class-interest assumption motivating research on the differences between voters and non-voters should hold in terms of redistribution of wealth but not in other substantive areas. That is, we expect that African American voters and non-voters are likely to be similar with respect to issues regarding racial equality and federal government spending (which is oriented toward helping African Americans as a group), but are likely to be significantly dissimilar with regard to fundamental beliefs about redistributing wealth. Thus, our findings on the representativeness of voters vs. non-voters for African Americans should be similar to our findings for Anglos on issues regarding redistribution of wealth (i.e., class interests should dominate), but be notably different on issues regarding racial equality and federal government spending (i.e., the interests of the racial or ethnic group will dominate).

What, then, should we expect as we consider the representativeness of Latino and Asian American voters? Following Dawson's (1994) logic, we believe the answer to this question rests in part on the extent to which Latinos and Asian Americans rely on the notion of a "linked fate" in politics. To the extent that more highly educated, high income Latinos and Asian Americans believe in their economic and political fates being tied to how Latinos and Asian Americans fare as groups, then the underlying relationships between class, policy self-interest and voting should be weakened. Also, instead of observing class-related differences between voters and non-voters (as we expect in the case of Anglos), we should observe Latino and Asian American voters adopting more group-defined, rather than self-defined, notions of self-interest in expressed policy preferences.

Since, we have no direct way to test this proposition regarding the relative importance of "linked fate" across racial and ethnic groups, our argument thus far merely pushes the question back another level to asking *why* some racial/ethnic groups will be more likely to rely on a notion of linked fate in formulating their policy preferences. We argue that the likelihood of minority individuals adopting a "linked fate" approach to assessing self-interest in politics develops concurrently with the group's level of panethnicity, "the development of bridging organizations and the generalization of solidarity among ethnic subgroups of ethnic collectivities" (Lopez and Espiritu 1990: 198). At the micro-level, panethnicity refers to the likelihood that racial/ethnic individuals identify with the larger, panethnic collectivity most commonly identified by mainstream society (such as Asian Americans, Latinos or Hispanics) rather than, or in addition to, their identification with their native origin groups (e.g., Japanese-Americans, Chinese-Americans, Mexican-Americans or Cubans) (see Jones-Correa and Leal 1996).

Although many scholars (see Lien 1997, Jones-Correa and Leal 1996, Lopez and Espiritu 1990) agree that Latinos and Asian Americans confront barriers to panethnic identification and that the Black identity is stronger than both the Asian American and Latino identity, scholars and activists are not in agreement over which group, Latinos or Asian Americans, has been more successful in overcoming obstacles to their panethnic identification. Many scholars and political activists (see Aguilar-San Juan 1994) hold that Asian Americans and Latinos confront several of the same formidable obstacles to their sense of panethnic identification. For instance, both the Asian American and Latino communities are comprised of a significant number of individuals who are not American citizens and thus do not enjoy many of the rights and privileges American citizenship affords. Many of these individuals may also view their residency in the United States as temporary and thus may not have many opportunities or desires to interact with individuals outside of their own specific nationality. Clearly, this would inhibit the formation of a strong sense of a panethnic identity.

In their case studies of Latinos, Asian Americans, Native Indians and Indo Americans in the United States, Lopez and Espiritu find that Latinos are "clearly the least panethnic." They argue that "Latino subgroups see no compelling material reason to merge their efforts; moreover they believe that they have cogent reasons to pursue their own paths, developing political and economic power in their regional arenas" (Lopez and Espiritu 1990: 219). Drawing on Lopez and Espiritu's (1990) analysis to extend Dawson's argument, we hypothesize that Asian American voters and non-voters will be significantly *different* with respect to fundamental beliefs about redistributing wealth, with non-voters being more likely than voters to support such policies. Second, we hypothesize that Asian American and Latino voters and non-voters are likely to be *similar* with respect to issues regarding racial equality and federal government spending. Testing these hypotheses thus allows us to determine whether or not Dawson's argument extends to Latinos and Asian Americans.

In the analysis below we use data from the 1995 *Washington Poll on Race Relations*, a national survey with oversamples of African

Americans, Asian Americans and Latinos. We rely primarily on the use of tabular analysis, where the chi-squared statistic is used to assess whether or not observed attitudinal differences between voters and non-voters are large enough that they cannot be attributed to mere sampling error.

Table 7-1 Respondents' Attitudes on General Political Issues (Voters and Non-voters)

	Anglo			African American		
Variable	*Voters*	*Non-V*	χ^2	*Voters*	*Non-V*	χ^2
Limit Business Tax	63.1	64.9	0.33	62.1	57.7	6.93*
Balanced Budget	93.7	93.6	0.46	93.0	93.7	1.97
Cut Income Tax	71.5	62.8	7.48*	93.0	57.6	1.72
Reform Welfare	94.8	90.6	7.95**	85.3	89.8	2.42
Reform Medicare	74.4	76.2	0.44	67.8	76.2	6.05*
Limit Abortion	39.7	44.4	1.49	37.8	41.2	3.44
Limit AA	9.1	67.2	2.96	36.3	42.5	2.86
	Hispanic			Asian Americans		
Variable	*Voters*	*Non-V*	χ^2	*Voters*	*Non-V*	χ^2
Limit Business Tax	62.4	64.1	0.71	65.0	61.9	0.93
Balanced Budget	91.7	91.8	1.35	96.2	93.3	2.56
Cut Income Tax	69.8	68.1	6.37*	66.4	68.2	4.11
Reform Welfare	89.9	85.7	2.22	92.4	86.5	10.79**
Reform Medicare	78.2	73.5	4.17	81.7	80.3	1.92
Limit Abortion	45.9	64.0	9.47**	35.0	34.9	4.13
Limit AA	50.0	49.5	1.68	57.4	60.4	4.78

*p<0.10; **p<0.05.

Source: Washington Post Poll on Race Relations conducted on July 20-August 9; September 18-28, 1995. The exact wording of the question is as follows: *I'm going to read you a list of issues being considered in Congress. For Each one, please tell me if you think it is something Congress should or should not do. (Read item) (Get answer, then ask) Is that something you feel strongly that Congress should/shouldn't do, or don't you feel very strongly about it?).* The figures reported in the table reflect the percentage of individuals who responded that they feel Congress should do something about a given issue. The following is a list of abbreviations we use in this table: Non-V is an abbreviation for Non-Voters, Limit Business Tax is an abbreviated phrase that stands for limiting business tax breaks, and AA is an abbreviation for Affirmative Action.

Domestic Policy Attitudes

Table 7-1 presents data on voters' and non-voters' opinions regarding their substantive preferences on what Congress should do, presented separately by racial/ethnic group.[6] Consistent with Bennett and Resnick's (1990) findings, Anglo voters and non-voters differ in only two instances: voters are significantly more likely to believe that Congress should cut personal income taxes and that Congress should reform the welfare system. Both of these differences are consistent with class differences between Anglo voters and non-voters.

Fewer, and less systematic, differences emerge for African Americans, Hispanics and Asian Americans. African American voters are slightly more likely than non-voters to believe that Congress should limit tax breaks for business, and are significantly less likely than non-voters to believe that Congress should reform Medicare. Similar to Anglos, Hispanic voters are more likely than non-voters to believe that Congress should cut personal income taxes, which is consistent with an economic self-interest argument. The only other difference between Hispanic voters and non-voters is that the latter are significantly more likely to believe that Congress should put more limits on abortion.

The only issue on which Asian American voters and non-voters differ significantly is on reforming the welfare system: approximately 92% of Asian American voters, compared to approximately 86% of Asian American non-voters, believe strongly that this is something Congress should do. On two issues, balancing the budget and limiting affirmative action, there are no significant differences between voters and non-voters within any of the four groups. Thus, our findings are generally consistent with Bennett and Resnick (1990): we find few differences between voters and non-voters, and most of the differences we observe are consistent with the assumed economic self-interests of voters and non-voters.

Tables 7-2 and 7-3 present data on a different type of public policy question, whether the individual prefers reducing federal spending on particular programs "in order to balance the federal budget and avoid raising taxes." Consistent with the economic self-interest argument, we expect here that individuals will be most likely to favor spending reductions in programs that benefit others, or, alternatively, will not prefer spending reductions that are perceived to benefit themselves. We present in Table 7-2 those policies that provide more universalistic benefits in terms of eligibility and enrollment, while we present in Table 7-3 those policies that are oriented more directly toward low-income individuals.

Table 7-2 Respondents' Attitudes towards Reductions in Federal Spending
          (Voter and Non-voters)

Variable	Anglo			African American		
	Voters	Non-V	χ^2	Voters	Non-V	χ^2
Social Security	37.5	40.0	0.21	27.6	50.8	10.26**
Student Loans	48.2	47.7	0.01	30.3	44.3	3.69*
Medicare	39.9	43.1	0.37	26.2*	44.3	6.48**
Defense	52.7	54.1	0.06	58.0	65.6	1.02

Variable	Hispanic			Asian Americans		
	Voters	Non-V	χ^2	Voters	Non-V	χ^2
Social Security	29.4	35.5	0.47	36.3	48.1	2.34
Student Loans	35.3	34.9	0.00	31.3	39.3	1.16
Medicare	30.0	31.7	0.04	43.8	47.6	0.24
Defense	51.0	66.1	2.52*	74.0	62.7	2.38

*p<0.10; **p<0.05.

Source: Washington Post Poll on Race Relations conducted on July 20-August 9; September 18-28, 1995. The exact wording of the question is as follows: *A number of spending reductions have been proposed in order to balance the federal budget and avoid raising taxes. Would you favor or oppose making major spending reductions in each of the following federal programs?).* The figures reported in the table reflect the percentage of individuals who responded that they favor major spending reductions in certain federal programs. Please note that the column heading "Non-V" is an abbreviation for Non-Voters.

In Table 7-2 we find no statistically significant differences between either Anglo voters or non-voters, or Asian American voters and non-voters. For Anglos, differences between voters and non-voters are typically within two percentage points. For Asian Americans, the differences are substantially larger (though still insignificant), with non-voters typically more in favor of spending reductions than voters are. Similar to the findings for Anglos, we find only one case where Hispanic voters differ significantly from Hispanic non-voters: non-voters are more likely than voters to prefer spending reductions in defense.

In striking contrast to these findings, however, Table 7-2 documents systematic differences between African American voters and non-voters, with non-voters being significantly *more* likely to support spending reductions on social security, student loans and Medicare. Hence, the general conclusion drawn from Table 7-2 is that (with one exception) voters are representative of non-voters for Anglos, Asian Americans and

Table 7-3 Respondents' Attitudes towards Reductions in Federal Spending (Voters and Non-voters)

Variable	Anglo			African American		
	Voters	Non-V	χ^2	Voters	Non-V	χ^2
Medicaid	43.8	43.8	0.00	30.0	45.9	4.73**
Welfare	67.2	59.3	1.42	47.1	51.7	0.35
Public Housing	56.9	41.8	7.23**	31.0	44.3	3.31*
Aid for Cities	61.4	53.2	2.22	39.4	41.3	0.41
Head Start	40.1	40.4	0.00	30.1	41.4	2.38
Food Stamps	55.1	51.4	0.44	37.2	48.3	2.13
Job Training	48.2	51.8	0.43	40.6	41.9	0.03
Tax Credit	50.2	50.9	0.02	36.1	48.4	2.73*
Child Health	33.2	39.4	1.36	27.1	39.3	3.03*
Legal Aid	49.7	46.9	0.18	29.6	45.9	5.03**

Variable	Hispanic			Asian Americans		
	Voters	Non-V	χ^2	Voters	Non-V	χ^2
Medicaid	37.5	37.7	0.00	39.7	40.2	0.00
Welfare	56.0	48.4	0.64	47.1	59.8	0.38
Public Housing	54.0	42.9	1.39	38.0	49.4	2.15
Aid for Cities	50.0	47.5	0.07	48.7	57.0	1.07
Head Start	40.4	32.7	0.64	34.7	55.0	5.46**
Food Stamps	49.0	38.7	1.21	51.3	52.5	0.02
Job Training	38.0	45.3	0.62	37.0	44.6	0.97
Tax Credit	47.1	46.9	0.00	56.6	36.1	6.67**
Child Health	34.0	31.7	0.06	34.2	34.5	0.00
Legal Aid	34.0	34.9	0.01	41.3	36.6	0.37

*p<0.10; **p<0.05.

Source: Washington Post Poll on Race Relations conducted on July 20-August 9; September 18-28, 1995. The exact wording of the question is as follows: *A number of spending reductions have been proposed in order to balance the federal budget and avoid raising taxes. Would you favor or oppose making major spending reductions in each of the following federal programs?* The figures reported in the table reflect the percentage of individuals who responded that they favor major spending reductions in certain federal programs. The following is a list of abbreviations we use in this table: Non-V is an abbreviation for Non-Voters, Tax Credit is an abbreviated form for policies that grant tax credits to the poor, and Legal Aid is an abbreviated form for policies that grant legal aid to the poor.

Hispanics; but that voters are typically less supportive of spending reductions than are non-voters within the African American community. These findings suggest that, at minimum, African American non-voters tend to be more conservative with regard to spending on universalistic programs than are African American voters.

The results in Table 7-3—for policies oriented more toward the poor—are similar to those reported in Table 7-2. The basic question is whether the individual prefers spending reductions in these redistributive programs in order to avoid raising taxes or to balance the budget. Anglo voters and non-voters differ with respect to preferences on federal spending reductions on only one of these programs: public housing. Specifically, Anglo voters are significantly more likely than non-voters to prefer spending cuts for this program. This is mostly consistent with our expectations, in that these are programs they may benefit from the least.

Asian American voters and non-voters also differ with respect to their support for federal spending cuts in two programs, Head Start and tax credits for low-income families. Asian American non-voters are significantly more likely than voters to support spending reductions for Head Start, while Asian American voters are more likely than non-voters to support spending reductions for tax credits for low income families. The latter finding, in particular, is consistent with the class differences between Asian American voters and non-voters, with voters being less likely to benefit from tax credits for low-income families.

The findings for African Americans and Hispanics in Table 7-3 are broadly consistent with those presented in Table 7-2. Without exception, Hispanic voters are representative of Hispanic non-voters, with no significant differences reported for any of the programs. Also, similar to Table 7-2, in all cases where African American voters differ significantly from non-voters, non-voters are more likely to prefer spending reductions. Even where these differences are not statistically significant—on aid to cities and Head Start—non-voters tend to favor spending reductions more than voters do. This finding is in stark contrast to an economic self-interest argument.

Hence, with the exception of African Americans, the findings in Tables 7-2 and 7-3 again suggest that voters are typically representative of non-voters, and that this is fairly consistent across issues and ethnic groups. Moreover, exceptions to these findings of representativeness are typically consistent with a class-based notion of self-interest in public policies. The most striking result and the consistency with which these arguments fail to hold for African Americans thus support Dawson's argument regarding the importance of a "linked fate" for African Americans. We now turn to examine the representativeness of voters versus non-voters issues of racial equality.

Issues of Equality

Table 7-4 presents voters and non-voters opinions on whether it is the responsibility of the federal government to ensure that "minorities have equality with whites" in several areas. As noted above, we expect that, African American voters as well as Latino and Asian American voters will be more similar to non-voters in their beliefs regarding the government's responsibility to ensure equality. Anglo non-voters, on the other hand, will be more likely than voters to believe that it is the government's responsibility to ensure equality, owing to their lower economic status.

Table 7-4 Respondents' Attitudes towards Governmental Responsibility for Promoting Equality in Domestic Policy Areas (Voters and Non-voters)

| Policy Area | Anglo | | | African American | | |
	Voters	Non-V	χ^2	Voters	Non-V	χ^2
Income	26.2	48.2	17.85**	70.9	67.7	0.21
Employment	31.6	55.9	20.05**	80.3	67.3	7.34**
Housing	28.6	43.2	7.86**	77.8	59.0	7.51**
Education	62.6	71.6	5.33*	92.9	90.1	2.15**
Health Care	58.5	66.7	2.24	90.7	86.3	1.09
Criminal Justice	74.6	73.9	0.02	90.2	91.3	0.07

| Policy Area | Hispanic | | | Asian Americans | | |
	Voters	Non-V	χ^2	Voters	Non-V	χ^2
Income	55.1	71.4	3.20*	40.7	39.0	0.05
Employment	67.2	59.3	1.42	58.0	63.1	0.44
Housing	56.9	41.8	7.23**	53.1	48.8	0.30
Education	61.4	53.2	2.22	82.9	87.1	0.62
Health Care	40.1	40.4	0.00	77.6	80.4	0.20
Criminal Justice	55.1	51.4	0.44	86.8	83.3	0.42

*p<0.10; **p<0.05.

Source: Washington Post Poll on Race Relations conducted on July 20-August 9; September 18-28, 1995. The exact wording of the question is as follows: *Do you believe it is the responsibility or isn't the responsibility of the federal government to make sure minorities have equality with whites in each of the following areas, even if it means you will have to pay more in taxes? Making sure minorities have (READ LIST).* The figures reported in the table reflect the percentage of individuals who responded that they believe it is the federal government's responsibility to promote equality in the respective policy areas. Please note that the column heading "Non-V" is an abbreviation for Non-Voters. The "Criminal Justice" policy area specifically refers to how individuals are treated by the judicial system and by law enforcement agencies.

This latter expectation is handsomely met in Table 7-4. In four out of the six areas of equality, Anglo non-voters are significantly more likely to believe that it is the government's responsibility to ensure equality with whites. And for equality of health care services, though the relationship is not significant, it is in the right direction: non-voters are *more* likely to believe in government responsibility. In dramatic contrast to this systematic difference between Anglo voters and non-voters, in not one instance do Asian American voters differ significantly from non-voters with respect to their beliefs in government responsibility for equality. Hence, Asian American voters are fairly representative of Asian American non-voters with regard to beliefs in equality, while Anglo voters are systematically non-representative of non-voters.

The results for African Americans and Hispanics are mixed. As shown in Table 4, African American voters are significantly more likely than non-voters to believe that it is the government's responsibility to ensure equality in three of the six areas: employment, housing and education. Hispanic voters likewise fail to represent non-voters' views in three areas—income, housing and health care—though in exactly the opposite direction: Hispanic non-voters are significantly more likely than voters to believe in the government's responsibility to ensure equality. This suggests that class interests may dominate racial/ethnic interests for Hispanics, while group interests may dominate class interests for African Americans.

We thus find general support for our claims that, class interests will be reflected in Anglo opinions on equality and that African Americans voters will be more likely to support government responsibility for equality and hence display a pattern opposite that for Anglos. Hispanic non-voters are more supportive of the government's role in guaranteeing equality than are Hispanic voters, which suggests that class is a more important influence on Hispanics' policy preferences than ethnicity.

Engagement in the Political System

Finally, we consider the differences between voters and non-voters across ethnic/racial groups on several different attitudinal measures indicating some level of involvement or engagement with the political system. Table 7-5 presents comparisons between individuals' self-reported party identification and political ideology of voters and non-voters across our four ethnic and racial groups. For both Anglos and Hispanics, there are statistically significant differences between voters

Table 7-5 Respondents' Attitudes towards the Political System (Voters and Non-voters)

Variable	Anglo Voters	Non-V	χ^2	African American Voters	Non-V	χ^2
American Dream	82.4	81.0	0.21	67.9	72.7	1.03
Party ID						
%Democrat	39.7	42.5	32.78**	87.0	71.3	16.80**
%Republican	51.3	35.0		5.4	9.1	
%Independent	8.9	22.6		7.7	19.6	
Ideology						
%Liberal	19.8	34.8	19.04**	37.8	38.2	2.87
%Moderate	42.2	34.8		37.5	32.4	
%Conservative	37.9	30.8		24.8	29.5	
Political Awareness						
%Unaware	7.6	14.9		5.0	12.5	
%Not too aware	28.6	32.5	14.08**	20.3	24.3	16.98**
%Fairly aware	47.5	41.7		39.2	43.8	
%Very aware	16.3	11.0		32.5	19.4	

Variable	Hispanic Voters	Non-V	χ^2	Asian Americans Voters	Non-V	χ^2
American Dream	80.0	71.9	1.99	83.1	72.4	5.47**
Party ID						
%Democrat	58.8	53.8	2.76	43.9	45.3	094
%Republican	31.4	28.8		43.9	39.7	
%Independent	9.8	17.4		12.1	15.1	
Ideology						
%Liberal	21.7	34.8	11.73**	28.7	21.2	7.42

Table 7-5 (continued)

Variable	Hispanic Voters	Non-V	χ^2	Asian Americans Voters	Non-V	χ^2
%Moderate	44.3	23.7		47.7	41.9	
%Conservative	34.0	41.5		23.5	36.8	
Political Awareness						
%Unaware	12.71	16.8		6.3	10.3	
%Not too aware	30.4	28.7	3.92	27.7	35.1	5.01
%Fairly aware	33.3	39.9		49.7	41.6	
%Very aware	23.5	14.7		16.4	13.0	

*p<0.10; **p<0.05.

Source: Washington Post Poll on Race Relations conducted on July 20-August 9; September 18-28, 1995. Please note that the column heading "Non-V" is an abbreviation for Non-Voters. The "American Dream" variable refers to whether or not individuals believe that the American Dream is achievable.

and non-voters. Anglo voters are more conservative than are Anglo non-voters, while Hispanic voters are more moderate than Hispanic non-voters are. Anglo voters, however, tend to be more Republican than non-voters are, while Hispanic voters tend to be more Democratic than Hispanic non-voters are.

African American voters are representative of non-voters with respect to political ideology, but not party identification: African American voters are significantly more likely to be Democrats than are non-voters. No significant differences emerge between Asian American voters and non-voters on either political ideology or party identification, suggesting that Asian American voters are representative of non-voters in this regard.

The final two aspects of political engagement focus more specifically on matters associated with race. The first is a question asking respondents how closely they have followed news about racial relations and affirmative action. For Anglos and African Americans there are significant differences between voters and non-voters: voters tend to pay more attention than non-voters to racial matters. However, whether this reflects a broader level of interest in politics, or instead indicates the salience of race across these groups is not clear.

The second measure of political engagement is a question about whether individuals believe in the American Dream, which we believe reflects the extent to which individuals feel that "the system" is open to them, and provides opportunities for success. In this respect it is an indicator of diffuse support for our political and economic systems. As shown in Table 5, there are no differences between voters and non-voters within any group in believing in the American Dream. Approximately 80% of Anglos, 70% of African Americans, 75% of Hispanics and 80% of Asian Americans believe in the American Dream. At this most abstract level, then, we find that voters are again representative of non-voters.

Implications and Conclusions

The overriding question motivating this research is whether the conclusion that voters are representative of non-voters is accurate while controlling for race and ethnicity. The previous claim, based on national surveys comprised almost entirely of Anglos, generally holds true for Hispanics and Asian Americans. However, there are substantial differences between African American voters and non-voters. The most systematic of these differences relates to preferences on spending reductions, and our findings are contrary to conventional wisdom: African American non-voters are substantially more likely to prefer federal spending reductions than are African American voters, and these differences are evident across a wide range of issues.

This finding, we believe, provides empirical support for Dawson's claim that the increasingly large African American middle class is particularly sensitive to group interests in making political choices or adopting policy preferences. And this is likely evidenced in their attitudes toward federal spending. An interesting aspect of this finding, of course, is the lack of self-interest displayed by African American non-voters' preferences for reduced spending on programs from which they benefit. Consistent with our finding, our analysis demonstrates that for African Americans, voters are typically more likely than non-voters to support government responsibility for equality. We interpret this finding as additional confirmation of Dawson's argument regarding the continuing significance of race, despite increasing class heterogeneity, in African American politics.

Finally, we have presented evidence that there are numerous similarities and differences between voters and non-voters within and across racial and ethnic groups in terms of political engagement. These similarities and differences have important implications for democratic representation, political participation and party competition. We have shown that there is overwhelming support for the American political and economic system among voters and non-voters in every racial and ethnic group. This suggests that most individuals believe that the system fairly rewards individuals for their efforts and guarantees and protects individual rights.

Although the prevalence of widely shared beliefs in abstract democratic principles among these groups is reassuring to our democratic ethos, our findings give us cause to re-examine the vitality and nature of our American democratic character. We have presented evidence of significant differences that exist between voters and non-voters and across racial and ethnic groups in terms of specific policy attitudes, ideology, party identity and political awareness. MacKuen, Erikson, and Stimson (1989) and Wlezien (1995) suggest that citizens transmit their general policy preferences to political elites through their vote decisions and that the political system automatically adjusts to changes in the political climate. Hence, the machinery of the political system is responsive and representative.

Yet, the political system can only serve its representative function if large majorities of citizens express their policy preferences by voting or, alternatively, if voters closely mirror non-voters in terms of ideology and party identification. Our data indicates that about 71% of Anglos who are eligible to vote actually choose to do so, compared to approximately 40% of Hispanics, approximately 45% of Asian Americans, and 67% of African Americans; lower levels of turnout by these minority groups are also documented in census data on registration and voting in presidential elections. Our findings suggest that although Latinos and Asian Americans vote at lower rates than Anglos and African Americans, non-voters in these groups appear to be more accurately represented by voters than are African American non-voters represented by African American voters.

These findings should also be considered in light of two broader implications regarding elite political behavior. First, we wonder how these attitudinal differences between voters and non-voters reflect elite mobilization strategies—and the extent to which the bias that we observe here might indeed be sustained by elites themselves as they seek to mobilize, or target, supporters. That is, those political elites who benefit from the current composition of the electorate hardly have an incentive to mobilize those who differ from their constituency (DeSipio 1996).

Second, political elites may correctly assume that voters signal their policy preferences through their vote choice during election campaigns. Yet African Americans' preferences are not representative of their groups' aggregated preferences and also ignore the differential turnout levels across racial/ethnic groups with respect to federal spending, to the extent that this occurs and political elites faithfully represent *voters'* preferences, political elites may produce public policies that operate counter to the interests of large segments of the *non-voting* African American population. Although voter participation does not guarantee policy satisfaction, it does provide most racial and ethnic groups in America with a voice in their own political self-determination.

References

Bennett, Stephen Earl and David Resnick. 1990. "The Implications of Nonvoting for Democracy in the United States." *American Journal of Political Science* 34: 771-802.

Brady, Henry E., Sidney Verba, and Kay Lehman Schlozman. 1995. "Beyond SES: A Resource Model of Political Participation." *American Political Science Review* 89: 271-94.

de la Garza, Rodolfo O. and Louis DeSipio. 1992. *From Rhetoric to Reality: Latino Politics in the 1988 Elections.* Boulder, Colorado: Westview.

de la Garza, Rodolfo O., Martha Menchaca and Louis DeSipio. 1994. *Barrio Ballots: Latino Politics in the 1990 Elections.* Boulder, Colorado: Westview.

Dawson, Michael C. 1994. *Behind the Mule: Race and Class in African American Politics.* Princeton, New Jersey: Princeton University Press.

DeSipio, Louis. 1996. *Counting on the Latino Vote.* Charlottesville, Virginia: University of Virginia Press.

Erikson, Robert S. and Kent L. Tedin. 1995. *American Public Opinion*, 5th ed. New York: Allyn and Bacon.

Espiritu, Yen Le. 1992. *Asian American Panethnicity: Bridging Institutions and Identities.* Philadelphia: Temple University Press.

Gant, Michael M. and William Lyons. 1988. "The Implications of Non-Voting for Democratic Theory." Presented at the annual meeting of the Midwest Political Science Association. Chicago.

Hero, Rodney E. 1992. *Latinos and the U.S. Political System: Two-Tiered Pluralism.* Philadelphia, Pennsylvania: Temple University Press.

Hochschild, Jennifer L. 1995. *Facing Up to the American Dream: Race, Class, and the Soul of the Nation.* Princeton, New Jersey: Princeton University Press.

Huckfeldt, Robert and Carol Weitzel Kohfeld. 1989. *Race and the Decline of Class in American Politics.* Urbana, Illinois: University of Illinois Press.

Jones-Correa, Michael and David L. Leal. 1996. "Becoming "Hispanic": Secondary Panethnic Identification Among Latin American-Origin Populations in the United States." *Hispanic Journal of Behavioral Sciences* 18: 214-254.

Kiewet, D. Roderick. 1983. *Macroeconomics and Micropolitics: The Electoral Effects of Economic Issues.* Chicago: University of Chicago Press.

Leighley, Jan E. and Jonathan Nagler. 1992. "Socioeconomic Class Bias in Turnout, 1972-1988: The Voters Remain the Same." *American Political Science Review* 86: 725-36.

Lien, Pei-te. 1997. *The Political Participation of Asian Americans: Voting Behavior in Southern California.* New York: Garland.

Lopez, David and Yen Espiritu. 1990. "Panethnicity in the United States: A Theoretical Framework." *Ethnic and Racial Studies* 13: 198-224.

MacKuen, Michael B., Robert S. Erikson, and James A. Stimson. 1989. Macropartisanship. *American Political Science Review* 83: 1125-1142.

McClain, Paula D. and Joseph Stewart, Jr. 1999. *"'Can't We All Get Along?' Race and Ethnic Minorities in American Politics* (2nd edition, updated). Boulder, Colorado: Westview Press.

Omatsu, Glenn. 1994. "The 'Four Prisons' and the Movements of Liberation: Asian American Activism from the 1960s to the 1990s." In Karin Aguilar-San Juan, ed., *The State of Asian America: Activism and Resistance in the 1990s*, pp. 19-70, Boston: South End Press.

Pinderhughes, Dianne M. 1987. *Race and Ethnicity in Chicago Politics: A Reexamination of Pluralist Theory.* Urbana: University of Illinois Press.

Rosenstone, Steven J. and John Mark Hansen. 1993. *Mobilization, Participation, and Democracy in America.* New York: Macmillan.

Shaffer, Stephen D. 1982. "Policy Differences between Voters and Non-voters in American Elections." *Western Political Quarterly* 35: 496-510.

Studlar, Donley T. and Susan Welch. 1986. "The Policy Opinions of British Nonvoters: A Research Note." *European Journal of Political Research* 14: 139-48.

Swain, Carol M. 1995. *Black Faces, Black Interests: The Representation of African Americans in Congress.* Cambridge: Harvard University Press.

Tam, Wendy K. 1995. "Asians—A Monolithic Voting Bloc?" *Political Behavior* 17: 223-249.

Tate, Katherine. 1993. *From Protest to Politics: The New Black Voters in American Elections.* Cambridge: Harvard University Press.

U.S. Census Bureau. 1998. Voting and Registration in the Election of November 1996. *Current Population Reports: Population Characteristics.* P20-504.

Verba, Sidney, Kay Lehman Schlozman, Henry Brady, and Norman H. Nie. 1993. "Citizen Activity: Who Participates? What Do They Say?" *American Political Science Review* 87: 303-318.

Wlezien, Christopher. 1995. "The Public as Thermostat: Dynamics of Preferences for Spending." *American Journal of Political Science* 39: 981-1000.

Wolfinger, Raymond E. and Steven J. Rosenstone. 1980. *Who Votes?* New Haven: Yale University Press.

Notes

1 This research was supported by a Faculty Mini-Grant from the Race and Ethnic Studies Institute of Texas A&M University.

2 The *Washington Post Poll on Race Relations* contains over-samples of 380 African-Americans, 197 Hispanics and 345 Asian Americans. These data were purchased through the Roper Center with funds provided by the Program in American Politics, The Center for Presidential Studies of the Bush School of Government and Public Service. We use the terms "Hispanic" and "Latino" interchangeably and also refer to non-Hispanic whites as "Anglos." We recognize, of course, that these labels are not universally accepted.

3 Rosenstone and Hansen (1993) argue that the strong association between socioeconomic status and political participation reflects the mobilizing activities of political elites.

4 Analysis of our data for the entire sample reveals that individuals' policy preferences (see Tables 7-2, 7-3, 7-4 and 7-5 for a listing of the policy items used in this study) are not consistently correlated with socioeconomic status, as measured separately by education and income.

5 Contrary to Dawson, Erikson and Tedin (1995) claim that for African-Americans there is no relationship between class and opinions on social welfare issues.

6 Factor analysis revealed that all of the issues in Table 7-1 loaded on one factor for all groups except for "Limiting Tax Breaks for Business" and "Limiting Abortion." Both of these items loaded on different factors. Limiting abortion probably belongs on a religious or libertarian dimension, while limiting tax breaks for business appears to belong on a populist dimension. Each of the remaining issues loaded at 0.50 or higher, which suggests that all of these items are measuring issues that share a common dimension.

CHAPTER 8

The Effects of Redistricting on the Underrepresented

Charles E. Menifield and Frank Julian

One of the most politically complex legislative processes in our government today is the construction of legislative districts. Legislative redistricting is the process of redrawing the lines of a voting district for the purpose of electing a candidate to represent a group of citizens. These lines are redrawn every ten years following the census. Under normal circumstances, the political party that has a numerical advantage in each state legislature at the time the lines are drawn draws the district lines to benefit their party in the subsequent elections. However, this apparent advantage evaporates if there is significant movement of the population in ensuing years.

The purpose of this chapter is to document the effects of legislative redistricting on minority candidates (particularly, racial minorities) from an institutional and behavioral perspective. In order to accomplish this purpose, we examine redistricting cases and legislation beginning with the original gerrymander in 1812 up to the most recent redistricting and related cases, *Hunt v. Cromartie* (526 U.S. 541 1999), *Reno v. Bossier Parish School Board* (120 S.Ct. 866 2000), and *Rice v. Cayetano* (120 S.Ct. 1044 2000). Our research considers case law and legislation in view of the population growth and voting behavior among members of minority groups. Lastly, we assess the ramification of these findings on the future of minority participation and representation in the political process.

Redistricting Yesterday

Legal maneuvering over legislative districts is not a recent occurrence. The original gerrymander by Governor Gerry Elbridge, a member of the Constitutional Convention, a former congressman, Governor of Massachusetts, and Vice President under James Madison, was drawn in 1812 in order to give his party an advantage in the upcoming election. Benjamin Russell, an opponent of Elbridge and publisher of the Federalist-leaning newspaper, the *Massachusetts Centinel,* coined the term gerrymander. Apparently, the shape of the district resembled a salamander (*Congressional Quarterly's Guide to Congress* 1982).

The recent debate surrounding legislative redistricting can be traced to the 1950s and 1960s when several states, having created voting districts with unequal population, found their mal-apportionment challenged in court. In *Colgrove v. Green* (328 U.S. 549 1946) the Supreme Court had ruled that challenges to mal-apportioned districts were political questions and relief should be sought through the political process. However, the federal courts became the final arbiter of this issue in 1962, when the Supreme Court overturned *Colgrove,* ruling by a 6-2 vote in *Baker v. Carr* (369 U.S. 186 1962) that reapportionment is a judicially reviewable question, because no state can deny any citizen the equal protection of the law under the Fourteenth Amendment. In a subsequent decision in *Reynolds v. Sims* (377 U.S. 533 1964), the court ruled that members of both houses of a state legislature must be elected from voting districts of equal populations. This principle was applied directly in *Wesberry v. Sanders* (376 U.S. 1 1964) when the court established the one person-one vote rule.

During this period, Congress also passed the Civil Rights Act of 1964 (CRA) requiring public accommodations to be open to all citizens and prohibiting discrimination in employment on the basis of gender and race. President Johnson also issued Executive Order 11246 in 1965 to add further strength to the CRA. The CRA was followed quickly by the Voting Rights Act of 1965 (VRA) and the subsequent amendments of 1970, 1975, and 1982, which sought to enfranchise African Americans, particularly in the Deep South. Southern white citizens had used tools such as literacy and property requirements to disenfranchise minority voters since shortly after the Civil War. Section 2 of the VRA, as amended, states that

no voting qualification or prerequisite to voting or standard,

practice or procedure shall be imposed or applied by any
State or political subdivision in a manner which will result
in a denial or abridgement of the right of any citizen of the
United States to vote on account of race (42 U.S.C.
Sec.1973).

As Davidson and Grofman (1994) indicate, this act, along with
other efforts to increase minority voting, had a dramatic affect on the
election of African Americans to state legislatures throughout the south.
In fact, states such as Mississippi and South Carolina, two of the more
conservative states, which had no African Americans in office at the
time the Voting Rights Act was passed, each had 20 state representatives
by 1985. In the Deep South as a whole, the number of African
Americans in state legislatures increased from 2 in 1965 to 232 in 1993
(Menifield and Julian 1998).

Although there is very little literature that argues that Hispanics
benefited from the VRA and the CRA, we also note that there was a similar increase in their representation in state legislatures during this period in states where there are large numbers of Hispanic citizens. (*see also*
DeSipio 1996). The number of Hispanics elected to the state legislature
and other state executive offices more than doubled in California,
Florida, Texas and New Mexico from 1983 to 1994 (*Statistical Abstract
of the U.S.* various issues). The number of Hispanic state legislators
increased from 113 in 1984 to 172 in 1994. Although this chapter does
not consider women directly, they likewise increased their numbers in
state legislatures from 387 in 1984 to 2,524 in 1994 (*Statistical Abstract
of the U.S.* various issues).

The increase in African American and Hispanic legislators can be
correlated directly to an increase in voter registration and voter turnout.
As Table 8-1 shows, African Americans and women registered to vote in
relatively large numbers in 1966. It is also clear that the percentage of
these groups registering to vote has been fairly stable with a small
decline over the 28-year study. In 1956, prior to the passage of the VRA
of 1965, 24.9% of the African American population was registered to
vote in eleven southern states.[1] By 1964, this average had grown to
43.1% in these southern states. However, states such as Mississippi witnessed little growth over that period, registering only 6.7% of the
African American population in 1964, an increase of 1.7% from the
1956 rate (Alt 1994).

Table 8-1 Voter Registration Among Members of Minority Groups

	1966	1970	1974	1978	1982	1986	1990	1994	1996
African American	60%	61%	55%	57%	59%	64%	59%	59%	63.5%
Hispanic	NA	NA	35	33	35	36	32	31	35.7
Women	69	67	62	63	64	65	63	64	67.3
White	72	70	64	64	66	65	64	65	67.7
U.S. Total	70%	68%	62%	63%	64%	64%	62%	63%	65.9%

Source: Http://www.census.gov/population/socdemo/voting/history/htable01.txt

As Table 8-2 shows, registration and voter turnout does not necessarily correlate positively. On the contrary, the gradual decrease occurring in registration had a much more significant impact on turnout. The most significant decline in voter turnout has been among the Hispanic population. Their turnout rate is less than half that of women and white citizens in general. African Americans are also following the same downward trend as that of Hispanics, while women on the other hand have fairly consistent rates of turnout.

Redistricting Today

Minority candidates saw electoral success a lot sooner at the state and local level than at the federal level. African Americans and Hispanics did not see significant gains in at the federal level via congressional representation until 1992. This change was not a coincidence. In the early 1990s, the U.S. bureau of the Census evaluated the population and determined that there were numerous populations of African Americans and Hispanics capable of electing a member of their racial group to office, if the district lines were drawn to maximize those populations.

Furthermore, in *Thornburg v. Gingles* (478 U.S. 30 1986), the Supreme Court had ruled that purposely diluting minority voting

Table 8-2 Voter Turnout Among Members of Minority Groups

	1966	1970	1974	1978	1982	1986	1990	1994	1996
African American	42%	44%	34%	37%	43%	43%	39%	37%	51%
Hispanic	NA	NA	23	24	25	24	21	20	27
Women	53	53	43	45	48	46	45	45	56
White	57	56	46	47	50	47	47	47	56
U.S. Total	55%	55%	45%	46%	49%	46%	45%	45%	54.2%

Source: Http://www.census.gov/population/socdemo/voting/history/htable01.txt

strength was unconstitutional. Finally, Section 5 of the Voting Rights Act required counties with a history of racial discrimination to submit all election law changes, including redistricting, to the United States Department of Justice for "pre-clearance." Under pre-clearance, state governments must create majority-black districts when possible without abridging the voting rights of other citizens.

As a result, congressional districts were redrawn in every state in the Deep South, except Arkansas, to elect at least one African American. The results of redrawing the districts led to a record election for African Americans and Hispanics going to Congress in 1992. Both groups doubled their congressional representation.

However, everyone was not pleased with these newly created districts. In North Carolina, which had its original redistricting plan rejected by the Department of Justice because the federal agency believed the Tarheel State could create not one, but two minority-majority districts, members of the state's Republican Party filed a suit, *Pope v. Blue* (809 F.Supp. 392 E.D.N.C. 1992). Suits by private individuals who believed their voting rights had been negatively affected by government action had been authorized by revisions to the Voting Rights Act. In this suit the plaintiffs argued that their rights had been impinged by some of the new minority-majority districts, which were oddly shaped in order to "capture" as many African-Americans as possible. The 1st District looked like a "bug splatter" on a windshield, and the 12th District stretched 185 miles along Interstate-85 through ten counties. Seven of the counties had a history of racial discrimination in elections and fell under the Voting Rights Act's pre-clearance requirement (Sellers, Cannon and Schousen 1998).

The U.S. District Court dismissed the case and the Supreme Court upheld the dismissal. *Pope v. Blue* (506 U.S. 81 1992). However, several white North Carolina residents from the Durham area, who had been included in a redrawn minority-majority district, also decided that they had been denied their right to elect a person of their choice due to the oddly-shaped districts, so they also filed suit. After the lower court ruled against the white plaintiffs on the ground that the state had a long history of racial discrimination in elections, and the plaintiffs suffered no personal injury or abridgement of their constitutional rights, the plaintiffs appealed to the Supreme Court.

In *Shaw v. Reno* (509 U.S. 630 1993) the Supreme Court, by a 5-4 vote, held that the drawing of legislative districts to increase minority representation may infringe upon the rights of the white voters. Justice

Sandra Day O'Connor, writing for the majority, noted that the minority-majority districts had shapes which closely resembled some of the more egregious forms of gerrymandering which southern whites had previously used to dilute black voting strength. The majority concluded that the plan was an effort to segregate voters by race, an unconstitutional outcome of the redistricting effort. The case was remanded to the lower court with instructions that the new district lines must reflect a "compelling state interest" and must be "narrowly tailored" (Gronke and Wilson 1996). Any redistricting plan, because it can result in voter disenfranchisement or in the dilution of voting strength, must meet the "strict scrutiny" standard of the federal courts.

This decision paved the way for residents of other states to file similar lawsuits. In fact, suits were filed in Florida, Georgia, Louisiana, and Texas, as well as a new challenge to North Carolina's third attempt to meet both the demands of the Voting Rights Act and the restrictions placed on the state by the Supreme Court. The Supreme Court resolved two of these cases in 1996, the Texas case of *Bush v. Vera* (517 U.S. 952 1996) and the North Carolina case of *Shaw v. Hunt* (517 U.S. 899 1996). In separate 5-4 decisions, the Court ruled that the creation of minority-majority districts is unconstitutional. Writing for the Court's conservative majority, Justice Sandra Day O'Connor indicated that state legislators had improperly focused on race while ignoring traditional redistricting principles, thereby violating the Equal Protection Clause of the Fourteenth Amendment. Districts drawn for the sole purpose of maintaining or enhancing the voting power of minorities violate the rights of white, majority citizens, the Court concluded.

The recent change of attitude toward minority issues on the part of the Supreme Court can be attributed to a single fact: changes in the composition of the Court. Presidents Reagan and Bush appointed five justices to the High Court in their collective twelve years in office. In addition, the conservative William Rehnquist replaced centrist Warren Burger as Chief Justice. As a result, the Court became increasingly conservative and hostile toward legislative redistricting aimed at helping minorities gain representation in Congress. Four of the five Reagan/Bush appointees voted against the concept of majority-minority districts. These same justices have voted against affirmative action in recent years (*see, e.g., City of Richmond v. J.A. Croson Co.* (488 U.S. 469 1989); *Adarand Constructors, Inc. v. Pena* (515 U.S. 200 1995).

As a result of these two decisions, the North Carolina legislature went back to the drawing board and attempted to draw district lines, which could pass the Court's standards. The 12th District is represented by Mel Watt, one of two-minority House members elected in 1992 from a state, which had not sent an African American to Congress since 1901. The redrawn 12th District looked a little different from the one which the Court had rejected, but perhaps not enough. The original 12th District was 185 miles long, largely following I-85, connecting pockets of African American voters. The district was comprised of 57% African American voters. The new 12th District is 71 miles long, still follows I-85, and African American voters represent 47% of the electorate.

The redrawn 12th District was challenged before a three-judge federal district court. The judges ruled via summary judgement (prior to trial) that the new district was flawed on its face, that the lines had still been drawn to assure the election of an African American representative. *Hunt v. Cromartie* (34 F.Supp.2d 1030 E.D.N.C. 1999). However, in 1999, a unanimous Supreme Court decided that the three-judge court had erred by using summary judgement to throw out the new district without holding a trial on the issues. *Hunt v. Cromartie* (526 U.S. 541 1999).

In this case, the State of North Carolina used a new approach to argue on behalf of the constitutionality of the 12th District. It argued that the state had created a suspicious-looking district to assure that a Democrat would be elected from the district, rather than a Republican. Since African Americans are far more likely to vote for a Democratic candidate, the state continued, it only made sense to draw the district lines to include as many African Americans as possible in the district. Hence, race was not an unconstitutional "predominant factor" in drawing district lines; rather it was a natural outcome of gerrymandering the district lines on behalf of Democratic candidates. The state noted that the Supreme Court had traditionally upheld the right of a state legislature to gerrymander districts for the purpose of aiding the party which controlled the state legislature at the time. *See also Karcher v. Daggett* (462 U.S. 723 1983); *Gomillion v. Lightfoot* (364 U.S. 339 1960) (gerrymandering may result in "uncouth" shapes). *But see Davis v. Bandemer* (478 U.S. 109 1986) (Political gerrymandering is a justiciable issue under the Fourteenth Amendment when election results prove discriminatory intent and outcome.).

It does not appear that this most recent case congressional redistricting case represents any change of heart by any member of the Court. The five most conservative members once again voted as a block. The four centrist justices, who had dissented in the earlier decisions, all joined the majority in voting to return the case to the three-judge federal district court for a trial on the merits of the case. However, the centrists joined Justice Stevens' concurring opinion, employing different grounds in deciding to return the case for trial than Justice Thomas stated in his majority opinion.

Justice Thomas and his four conservative colleagues decided the case on a pure procedural technicality, the improper use of summary judgement to decide the case. Thomas was clearly skeptical of North Carolina's argument. "Evidence tends to support an inference that the state drew its district lines to support an impermissible racial motive... Summary judgement, however, is only appropriate where there is no genuine issue of material fact." Obviously, here there was such an issue; thus a trial on the merits was warranted" (*Hunt v. Cromartie* 526 U.S. 549 1999).

In comparison, Justice Stevens noted that the Court has permitted some rather strange looking districts in the past. Gerrymandering for political advantage sometimes results in odd-looking districts. An odd shape, like the snake-like North Carolina 12th District, may "provide strong evidence that either political or racial factors motivated its architects, but sheds no light on the question of which factor was more responsible for subordinating any of the state's 'traditional' districting principles" (*Hunt v. Cromartie* 526 U.S. 555 1999).

Justice Stevens made one additional point in his concurring opinion. He noted that white North Carolinians had a habit of registering Democrat and voting Republican. This was especially true in districts in which African Americans comprised more than one-third of the voters. Therefore, he reasoned, it would be understandable that the North Carolina legislature, controlled by the Democratic Party, would want to put as many faithful Democrats in a district as possible. After all, who has voted more faithfully Democratic than African Americans?

Table 8-3 Key Redistricting Cases

Supreme Court Case	Year	Supreme Court Case	Year
Baker v. Carr	1962	Miller v. Johnson	1995
Beer v. U.S.	1976	Pope v. Blue	1992
Bush v. Vera	1996	Reynolds v. Sims	1964
Colgrove v. Green	1946	Shaw v. Hunt	1996
Davis v. Bandemer	1986	Shaw v. Reno	1992
Fortson v. Dorsey	1965	U.S. v. Hayes	1995
Gomillion v. Lightfoot	1960	Thornburg v. Gingles	1986
Hunt v. Cromartie	1999	Wesberry v. Sanders	1964
Karcher v. Daggett	1983		

Not surprisingly, the court in *Rice v. Cayetano* (120 S.Ct. 1044 2000) came down strongly (7-2 vote) against allowing race to be a factor in granting voting rights. A Hawaiian law granted a unique right to native Hawaiians: the right to vote for trustees of the Office of Hawaiian Affairs, managers of a trust fund for native Hawaiians. The Supreme Court ruled that non-native Hawaiians should also have the right to vote for trustees on the ground that it violated the Fifteenth Amendment to use ancestry as a proxy for race in defining voter eligibility. To allow the state to screen out potential voters based on ancestry, would mean the state would be permitted to abridge voting rights based on race, a clear constitutional violation. Even the Voting Rights Act could not save this form of state-sanctioned voter discrimination.

The new millennium opened with another challenge to the pre-clearance requirement of the Voting Rights Act. Bossier Parish in Louisiana, a county which is required to attain federal pre-clearance of its voting regulations due to historic *de jure* discrimination, set out to redraw its electoral districts as a result of the 1990 census. The county had a 20% African American population, and due to historic housing patterns, two of the twelve districts could have been minority-majority districts. The local NAACP chapter protested a plan adopted by the school board which would spread black voters across several districts, thereby virtually assuring the continued election of an all-white school board. Section 5 of the Voting Rights Act authorizes pre-clearance if a proposed voting change "does not have the purpose and will not have the effect of denying or abridging the right to vote on account of color."

Nonetheless, Attorney General Janet Reno turned down the school board's voting plan, noting there are sufficient pockets of African American population to create two minority-majority districts. The Supreme Court granted pre-clearance by a 6-3 vote. Justice Scalia, writing for the majority, noted that "(P)reclearance...does not represent approval of the voting change; it is nothing more than a determination that the voting change is no more dilutive (of minority voting power) than what it replaces...." (*Reno v. Bossier Parish School Board* 120 S.Ct. 875 2000). Scalia concluded that Section 5 was designed merely to prevent "backsliding," and since the proposed voting plan left black citizens no worse off than they were before, it was not prohibited by the Voting Rights Act.

The political problems of African Americans and Hispanics over the course of the past decade were not solely wrapped up in Supreme Court decisions, however. After the 1994 congressional elections, Republicans assumed command of both the House and Senate for the first time in decades. Led by Newt Gingrich, the new Speaker of the House, the Republicans began to set their new agenda for the 104th Congress (Cloud 1994). On January 4, 1995, the Republican's agenda began to take shape with a proposal to change several rules, one of which would eliminate public funding for Legislative Service Organizations (LSOs) and other committees and subcommittees. The rule failed on a roll call vote, 201-227, but passed on the subsequent voice vote (H. Res. 6. Rules of the House/Commit With Instructions). Hence, the Congressional Black and Hispanic Caucuses, along with other LSOs lost funding, staff, and office space needed to maintain caucus activity. This vote to eliminate these groups set the tone and made clear the intentions of majority congressmen.

Redistricting Tomorrow

If current institutional and voter trends continue, the year 2000 will no doubt bring about more problems for African American and Hispanic citizens. President Clinton is a lame duck President. Should a Republican succeed Clinton, this will possibly affect African Americans and Hispanics negatively in two different ways.

First, the Supreme Court has split its last five congressional redistricting cases by votes of 5-4 with a conservative majority. If Chief Justice Rehnquist resigns or other justices resign in the next four years, a Republican President would undoubtedly replace retirees with conservative justices. Hence, the current conservative advantage on the Court likely would be maintained or expanded and all new minority-majority congressional districts would be endangered.

Second, Democrat Presidents have consistently been an asset for African American Congressmen. However, if a Republican President wins, all three branches of government would be dominated by Republican values, assuming Republicans maintain control of Congress. Since Republicans have made their stance clear, African Americans and Hispanics cannot look for their overt and direct support in the maintenance of minority-majority districts. If Swain (1993) and Bullock (1996) are correct, African Americans will need these super minority-majority districts to win, because they do not vote in sufficiently large numbers to elect African American candidates without them.

In addition, African Americans and Hispanics may not be able to look to other Democrats for assistance. Research by Hill (1995) and

Patterson (1996) has shown that the creation of these minority-majority districts was one factor in the success of the Republican party in the 1992 and 1994 elections. Essentially, Democrats were moved into a few larger, safe majority-minority districts. The remainder of the southern districts were dominated by white conservatives, prime Republican ground.

The best national strategy for the Democrats would be to disburse Democratic voters across more districts, unpacking the minority-majority districts and creating more districts in which the party has a fair chance of electing its candidates. If the Democrats followed this strategy, the percentage of African American and Hispanic voters would decline in these districts and the number of Republicans would grow. Hence, whether Republicans or Democrats control the White House and Congress in the new millennium, African Americans and Hispanics run the risk of losing ground.

Of course, redistricting is driven by census data and the U.S. Bureau of the Census is conducting the next census during the year 2000. This census will no doubt reveal several large concentrations of African Americans and Hispanics throughout the South and other regions of the country. However, given recent history, there is no reason to presuppose that any new majority-minority districts will be created. As Table 8-4 shows, it is projected that Hispanics will outnumber African Americans and thus become the largest minority groups in the U.S. by the year 2010. In parts of the Southwest, California, and Florida the sheer overwhelming numbers of Hispanics in concentrated geographic areas may bode well for their representation.

Implications and Conclusions

This research has revealed several important points with regard to the descriptive representation of minorities in the United States. First, the

Table 8-4 Population Data (000)

	1996	2000	2005	2010
White	219,641	225,522	232,463	239,588
Black	33,611	35,454	37,734	40,109
Hispanic	27,804	31,366	36,057	41,139
American Indian, Aluet, and Eskimo	2,273	2,402	2,572	2,754
Asian and Pacific Isl.	9,728	11,245	13,212	15,265
Total	265,253	272,330	274,634	297,716

Source: http://www.census.gov/population/www/projections/popproj.html

passage of the 1965 Voting Rights Act was the first crucial step in the process of African Americans and Hispanics achieving some sort of parity in the election process. Although there have been other institutional problems, both groups for the most part have enjoyed some electoral success. However, the behavioral analysis clearly shows a long term problem centered around a continual decrease in African American and Hispanic voter registration and turnout. The problem is most pronounced in the South, where both groups make up a larger percentage of the population, but are not proportionally represented in Congress. Therefore, legislative redistricting is not the sole key to solving the problem.

African Americans and Hispanics may not be able to look to the courts or to Congress for assistance in increasing their ability to descriptively and arguably substantively represent members of their race in Congress. The court system, which once defended the rights of African American and Hispanic citizens to actively participate in government, is now reversing previous decisions by discouraging the creation of majority-minority districts, even in areas that have large black and Hispanic populations. Although the conservative Republican Party has not directly stated that African American and Hispanic citizens should not be in Congress, their actions suggest that they will not provide extraordinary services to any non-Republican members or potential members of Congress. This attitude, no doubt, is facilitated by poor voter registration and turnout among the black population in the South and other regions of the country.

References

Alt, James. 1994. "The Impact of the Voting Rights Act on Black and White Voter Registration in the South." In *Quiet Revolution in the South: The Impact of the Voting Rights Act of 1965-1990*, eds. Chandler Davidson and Bernard Grofman, Princeton, NJ: Princeton University Press.

Bullock III, Charles S. 1996. "Racial Composition of District Population and The Election of African-American Legislators." *Southeastern Journal of Political Science* 24:611-628.

Cloud, David, 1995. "GOP, to Its Own Great Delight, Enacts House Rules Changes." *CQ Weekly Report* January 7:13-15.

Davidson, Chandler and Bernard Grofman. Eds.1994. *Quiet Revolution in the South: The Impact of the Voting Rights Act 1965-1990*. Princeton, NJ: Princeton University Press.

Hill, Kevin A, 1995. "Does the Creation of Majority Black Districts Aid Republicans? An Analysis of the 1992 Congressional Elections in Eight Southern States." *The Journal of Politics* 57: 384-401.

Menifield, Charles E. 1998. "A Loose Coalition or a United Front: Voting Behavior Within the Congressional Hispanic Caucus." *Latino Studies Journal* 9: 27-44.

Menifield, Charles E. and Frank Julian. 1998. "Changing the Face of Congress: African-Americans in the Twenty-First Century." *The Western Journal of Black Studies* 22: 18-30.

Patterson, Benjamin W. 1996. "Does the Creation of Majority-Minority Districts Benefit the Republican Party?" Paper presented at the 1995 Southern Political Science Association Conference, Tampa, FL.

Sellers, Patrick J., Cannon, David t., and Matthew M. Schousen. 1998. "Congressional Redistricting in North Carolina." In *Race and Redistricting in the 1990s*. ed. Bernard Grofman. New York: Agathon Press.

Swain, Carol. 1993. *Black Faces, Black Interests The Representation of African Americans in Congress*. Cambridge, MA: Harvard University Press.

Statistical Abstract of the United States: (various editions) Washington, D.C.: U.S. Bureau of the Census.

Vega, Arturo. 1993. "Variations and Sources of Group Cohesiveness in the Black and Hispanic Congressional Caucuses." *Latino Studies Journal* 14: 79-92.

Case Law

Adarand Constructors, Inc. v. Pena, 515 U.S. 200 (1995)

Baker v. Carr, 369 U.S. 186 (1962)

Beer v. U.S., 425 U.S. 130 (1976)

Bush v. Vera, 517 U.S. 952 (1996)

City of Richmond v. J.A. Croson Company, 488 U.S. 469 (1989)

Colegrove v. Green, 328 U.S. 549 (1946)

Davis v. Bandemer, 478 U.S. 109 (1986)

Fortson v. Dorsey, 379 U.S. 433 (1965)

Gomillion v. Lightfoot, 364 U.S. 339 (1960)

Hunt v. Cromartie, 526 U.S. 541 (1999)

Karcher v. Daggett, 462 U.S. 725 (1983)

Miller v. Johnson, 515 U.S. 900(1995)

Pope v. Blue, 809 F.Supp. 392 (E.D.N.C. 1992), *aff'd.* 506 U.S. 801 (1993)

Reno v. Bossier Parish School District, 120 S.Ct. 866 (2000)

Reynolds v. Sims, 377 U.S. 533 (1964)
Rice v. Cayetano, 120 S.Ct. 1044 (2000)
Shaw v. Hunt, 517 U.S. 899 (1996)
Shaw v. Reno, 509 U.S. 630 (1992)
Thornburg v. Gingles, 478 U.S. 30 (1986)
U.S. v. Hayes, 515 U.S. 737 (1995)
Wesberry v. Sanders, 376 U.S.1 (1964)

Notes

1 The eleven southern states included in this group are Alabama, Arkansas, Florida, Georgia, Louisiana, Mississippi, North Carolina, South Carolina, Tennessee, Texas and Virginia.

CHAPTER 9

Black State Legislators: A Case Study of North Carolina and Maryland

Tyson D. King-Meadows and Thomas F. Schaller

Four decades ago, there were too few black state legislators in the United States to conduct any significant study of their impact. Today, with more than five hundred black legislators nationwide,[1] including sizeable formalized caucuses in twenty American states, students of legislative politics are in a far better position to assess the significance of black representation in state legislatures. The key empirical issue raised by the increased number of black state legislators is the relationship between descriptive representation and substantive representation.[2] Questions abound regarding how much of an impact a legislator's race has on the coalition building process, and whether black legislators are more likely to propose and support particular policies (Bositis 1994; Bratton and Haynie 1999; King-Meadows and Schaller 1999; Singh 1998). Other scholarly inquiries address at what district percentage black constituents (whether residents, registrants, voting-age population or likely voters) optimize the substantive policy representation they receive from legislators (Cameron, Epstein and O'Halloran 1996; Epstein and O'Halloran 1999; Hill 1995; Lublin 1997). However couched, any examination of the collective impact black representatives have on legislative processes and outcomes requires an investigation of the voting behavior of legislators.

In this chapter, we examine voting cohesion among black state legislators. As preface to analysis, in the first half of the chapter we discuss the remarkable growth of black state legislators in recent decades, and then review the relevant scholarly literature on race and representation. In the second half of the chapter, we provide a case study analysis of the voting cohesion of black legislators in two states, Maryland and North Carolina, on contested roll call votes over a two-year period. We compare the voting behavior of the two state black caucuses against each other, as well as against the respective set of white legislators from each state that represent districts with significant minority populations. Are these two black caucuses — similar in some respects, but so different in other ways — similarly cohesive? Are black legislators in each state more cohesive than their respective white counterparts? The answers to these and related questions speak directly to the questions of whether the rise in the number of black faces in state legislators over the past three decades has altered the quality and degree of substantive representation for African Americans.[3]

State Black Legislative Representation: History and Theory

In order to address the descriptive-substantive representation question, in this section we briefly chronicle the growth in recent decades of the number of black state legislators, and review the theoretical and empirical literature related to the participation and influence of these legislators.

-Black State Legislators

Table 9-1 chronicles the growth of black state legislators over the past two decades. As the table indicates, black candidates have yet to capture state legislative seats in either Hawaii, Idaho, and Montana, and have won only a few, seats in New Mexico, New Hampshire, Nebraska, Wyoming, Utah, West Virginia, and Vermont. The limited degree of black legislative representation in these states is understandable, given the small number and geographic concentration of African American citizens within these states. Clearly, most black state legislators have come from, and continue to represent, states east of the Mississippi River, especially Southern states.

legislators, Button, Hedge and Spear (1996a, 1996b) discovered that black legislators tend to report greater frustration with their legislative experiences, and also view racial progress in their states less optimistically, than white legislators do. Similarly, Bratton and Haynie (1999) concluded that black state legislators were less successful than women state legislators in getting minority-sponsored legislation passed. Nevertheless, it is clear that the increase in the number of black state legislators has brought not merely symbolic, but material benefits to African American communities by virtue of their increased presence in the legislative environment — regardless of what happens when votes are cast at roll call.

Still, legislative voting (on the floor, or in committees and sub-committees) is a power of undeniable consequence, and the descriptive-substantive representation tradeoff issue cannot be dismissed. Common to studies that suggest a tradeoff are two underlying assumptions. The first is that white legislators who represent districts with significant African American populations provide their black constituents substantive representation that these constituents would otherwise forego if they were instead packed into perversely majority-minority districts (Lublin 1997; Swain 1993); that is, African American constituents would be advantaged by having a presence in a greater number of minority-influenced districts, even if this meant electing fewer black legislators. The second assumption, related to the first and often more contentious, is that support for African American black interests will be a function, to some degree, of the racial composition of the districts. Though there are several competing conjectures about the relationship between composition of the district and support for African American interests (for a good summary, see Cameron, Epstein and O'Halloran 1996), the unifying sense is that support is more constituency-driven than legislator-driven. Put another way, the voting behavior of legislators will be better explained by a continuous variable (the percent of African American, or perhaps more broadly, minority voters in the district) rather than a discrete and dichotomous variable (racial identity of the legislators themselves).

We think these two assumptions potentially mislead students of legislative behavior, because they ignore the importance of racial group identity on black legislative voting. Moreover, we believe that the description-substantive tradeoff is too often rooted in a myopic focus on the *number* rather than the *value* of votes cast by black legislators and white legislators representing districts with sizeable black constituencies. A vote is a vote is a vote, of course. But a vote's value is also a function of its reliability, and so too the value of a voting bloc is a function of its reliability or cohesiveness. For instance, voting block cohesiveness is fundamental to the ability of legislators, minorities particularly, to bargain with chief executives (Singh 1998; Sullivan 1990). Much as the expected value of a lottery with a smaller prize and a larger probability often exceeds that of one with a larger payoff but a smaller probability, a small but cohesive black legislative contingent may exercise greater influence than a larger but more fractured one.[6] This is especially true when the larger "contingent" depends upon support and allegiance for African American policy initiatives from white legislators who represent districts with significant African American sub-constituencies. The fact is that all votes are *not* the same if racial group identity and solidarity (Johnson and Secret 1996) compels black legislators to support issues or take positions that white legislators from similarly composed racial districts do not (Gerber, Morton and Rietz 1998). Simply put, the *quantitative* value of a legislator's vote is a function in large part of its *qualitative* reliability.

Accordingly, we contend that voting cohesion is key to understanding and assessing the qualitative value of black legislative representation. But cohesiveness is coincidental, and therefore less meaningful, if it is merely the byproduct of voting by legislators from similar districts. Cohesion matters most when constituent interests diverge, and when the race of the legislators differs. Does the degree of district heterogeneity among caucus members affect cohesion? How cohesive are white and black legislators from districts with significant minority populations? The answers to these questions speak directly to the issue of the qualitative value of black state legislators' votes.

Roll Call Voting in Maryland and North Carolina:
A Natural Experiment

For racial representation to have meaning, black legislators must vote in a concerted, cohesive fashion on important legislation. The Maryland and North Carolina state legislative black caucuses provide a compelling natural experiment for studying voting cohesion. Because the members of the Maryland Legislative Black Caucus (MDLBC) represent a much more homogeneous set of constituencies than do their counterparts in the North Carolina Legislative Black Caucus (NCLBC), cohesion among caucus members may be more elusive for the latter. Our

Table 9-3 Comparing the Maryland and the North Carolina Black Caucuses

Maryland	House	Senate	Caucus
Members	28	9	37
Ran Unopposed in 1998, number (pct.)	22 (84.6)	7 (77.8)	29 (82.9)
Mean Vote Percentage, 1998	96.5	98.2	96.91
Mean Years Seniority	6.30	6.44	6.33
Unique Counties Represented	4	2	4
District Minority Voting Age Pct., mean (s)	75.7 (14.1)	77.4 (9.7)	76.1 (12.9)
Seats with ≥ 20% MVAP, number (pct.)	69 (48.9)	23 (48.9)	92 (48.9)
Seats with ≥ 40% MVAP, number (pct.)	36 (25.5)	12 (25.5)	48 (25.5)

North Carolina	House	Senate	Caucus
Members	17	7	24
Ran Unopposed in 1998, number (pct.)	14 (82.4)	4 (57.1)	18 (75.0)
Mean Vote Percentage, 1998	96.7	83.3	92.8
Mean Years Seniority	8.24	8.86	8.42
Unique Counties Represented	30	24	40
District MVAP Percent., mean (s)	54.5 (6.7)	44.2 (14.8)	51.5 (10.3)
Seats with ≥ 20% MVAP, number (pct.)	56 (46.7)	29 (58.0)	85 (50.0)
Seats with ≥ 40% MVAP, number (pct.)	19 (15.8)	7 (14.0)	26 (15.3)

Source: Data for this table were taken from a variety of sources, including the official Maryland and North Carolina legislative websites, as well as an internal state document, "1992 State Legislative Districts," prepared by the Maryland Office of Planning (April, 1992).

study relies on roll call data for the two-year legislative period 1997-98, in both states and for each chamber, for all contested third-reading votes, defined as floor roll calls for which there were a minimum of 10% nay votes. Before proceeding to the roll call vote analyses, we explain why the similarities and differences of the Maryland and North Carolina legislative black caucuses present an interesting, natural experiment.

-Legislative Design Similarities

The Maryland and North Carolina state legislatures are similar with respect to several key aspects of design (see Table 9-3). First, both states feature bicameral legislatures and use multi-member districts (MMDs) to elect some (but not all) of its members.[7] Second, district sizes are roughly equivalent. The approximate size of Maryland's senate districts in 1990 was 101,730 persons; North Carolina senate districts had roughly 132,570 residents each.

Although Maryland elects more than two-thirds of its lower house "delegates" from three-member districts, the lower house single-member district population for Maryland is 33,910, compared to 55,240-person lower house districts in North Carolina.[8] Against the national backdrop, where district size ranges from California's senate (744,000) to New Hampshire's house (2,770), the difference in district sizes between the two states is small.

-Black Legislative Caucus Similarities

The MDLBC and NCLBC experienced similar electoral histories. In the 1950s, a few pioneer legislators in each state broke the color barrier. With the passage of the Voting Rights Act in 1965 and the subsequent end of malapportionment, the number of black legislators began to increase as it did in other states (Bullock, 1992; Grofman and Handley, 1991). Formal caucuses in each state emerged soon thereafter. Presently, and in stark contrast to the state of affairs just forty years ago, caucus members from both states enjoy a high degree of electoral security, with most legislators running unopposed for re-election and, sometimes, first election.

The first three black legislators elected in Maryland this century won seats in 1954. The black legislative contingent did not exceed four until the first election following reapportionment in the wake of the Supreme Court's decisions in *Baker v. Carr* (1962) and *Reynolds v. Simms* (1964). With the 1966 election, the number of Maryland black state legislators jumped from four to twelve, then rose to eighteen following the 1970 elections, and has continued to grow steadily to its current size of thirty-seven members. Caucus growth in North Carolina was a bit slower. There was only one black state legislator at the beginning of the 1970s, and the number of black legislators did not exceed six (four in the assembly, two in the senate) until the 1982 election. Then, the incorporation in 1982 of procedural protections into the Voting Rights Act with Section 2 amendments, coupled with redistricting following the 1980 census, triggered a rise in the number of black legislators in North Carolina to twelve and then sixteen following the 1982 and 1984 elections, respectively (Bullock 1992). Since the mid-1980s, the NCLBC has increased steadily to reach its current size of twenty-four members.

Today, members of both caucuses also enjoy a high degree of electoral security. As Table 9-3 shows, the mean vote share in the 1998 elections for the thirty-seven current MDLBC members was 98.1%, in large part attributable to the fact that thirty-one members ran unopposed.

Though not quite as high, NCLBC members were elected to office with a mean vote share of 92.8%. This figure reflects the fact that eighteen of North Carolina's twenty-four members ran unopposed for their seats. Most members are elected from majority-minority districts. But as we will see, the racial composition of the districts in the two states differs in important ways.

In sum, the Maryland and North Carolina legislatures are bicameral, similar in district size, and feature some use of multiple-member districting. The statewide African American populations are similar, although African American constituents in North Carolina are slightly more under-represented (descriptively) in their legislature. Lastly, the electoral histories of the two black legislative caucuses bear some similarities, although procedural impediments likely kept North Carolina's caucus from growing as quickly as Maryland's.

-Legislative Design Differences

The electoral features of the Maryland and North Carolina legislatures are disparate in ways that may influence the cohesiveness of the state black caucuses. For starters, North Carolina's legislators, in both chambers, serve two-year terms, whereas Maryland legislators serve four-year terms. In this regard, both states are outliers. Of the forty-nine bicameral state legislatures, the modal format (employed by fully thirty-four states) is two-year lower house terms and four-year upper house terms. The term-length difference gives North Carolina legislators shorter electoral leashes, perhaps making constituent demands more immediate and pressing for them. On the other hand, two factors probably neutralize this electoral difference. First, current members of the North Carolina caucus have an average of two more years legislative experience and seniority than Maryland's black legislators. Second, as noted above, North Carolina legislators enjoy a very high degree of electoral security.

A more important electoral difference pertains to district magnitude and nesting. Although both states use some form of multi-member districting, as stated above, there are important differences. Maryland uses MMDs only in the lower house. There are forty-seven legislative districts, each of which elects one senator and three lower house members. In thirty-five of these districts, three lower house members — known in Maryland as "delegates" — are chosen at-large from the identical senate district. Three of the remaining twelve districts feature three, single-member delegate districts; the final nine districts feature one single-member and one two-member delegate district (with twice the population, of course).[9] Though multi-member districts elect some members of both chambers of the North Carolina legislature, they are used in a much more limited (and complicated) way. The fifty state senators are elected from thirty-four single-member districts and eight two-member districts; the one hundred and twenty house members, meanwhile, are chosen from eighty-one single-member districts, twelve two-member districts, and five three-member districts. A final, crucial difference is that the one hundred and twenty North Carolina house districts are not necessarily nested within senate districts as they are in Maryland.

Because district magnitude affects both the racial composition (Gerber, Morton and Rietz 1998; Moncrief and Thompson 1992) and ideological diversity (Adams 1996) of state legislatures, these structural-electoral differences alter the nature and quality of representation for every citizen, but minorities especially. District magnitude and nesting affect constituency heterogeneity, both between and within the two caucuses. In the case of Maryland, the nesting of districts creates *identical* constituencies for many caucus members. Moreover, the nesting of districts creates an artifactual inter-chamber homogeneity in Maryland that does not exist in North Carolina. Currently, for example, in seven legislative districts the senator and all three delegates are MDLBC members. In two other districts, two of the three delegates and the senator are black.[10] All told, then, thirty-four of the thirty-seven members[11] of the MDLBC represent constituencies shared by at least two other caucus members, and twenty-eight of these thirty-four legislators represent districts shared by three other caucus members. For these sets of caucus members, districts are homogeneous in the strictest sense: Their constituencies not only have the same *percentage* of African American residents, but literally the same *residents*. By comparison, and despite the use of MMDs in both chambers, only two members of the NCLBC hail from the same multi-member district.[12]

-Caucus Differences

As of the 1998 elections, there are thirty-seven black legislators in the 188-seat Maryland legislature (twenty-eight, or 19.9%, of House seats; nine, or 19.1%, of Senate seats), and twenty-four in North Carolina's 170-seat legislature (seventeen, or 14.2%, of House seats; seven, or 14.0%, of

Senate seats). In both states, the seat shares are lower than the population shares (24.9% and 22.1%, respectively), but in North Carolina descriptive under-representation is greater; African American voters in Maryland enjoy a better seats/voters ratio than black North Carolinians.

NCLBC members also represent a geographically more heterogeneous set of districts. This is in part attributable to district magnitude, as discussed above. But it is also a consequence of the more dispersed African American population in North Carolina. In Maryland, with but four exceptions in the past four decades black legislators have come from one of two areas in the state: The Baltimore City-Baltimore County metropolitan area, and Prince Georges County, bordering Washington, D.C.[13] Black legislators in North Carolina, by contrast, have been elected from various areas across the state, including districts that include parts of various medium-to-large cities such as Charlotte, Durham, Fayetteville, Greensboro, Raleigh, Wilmington and Winston-Salem, as well as districts anchored in small-city communities like Conway, Enfield, Goldsboro, Jamestown, Rocky Mount and Wilson. As Table 9-3 shows, the seventeen current North Carolina house members represent at least some part of thirty different counties, and the seven senators represent twenty-four different counties — with no two senators sharing even a single, mutual county. Taken as a whole, the 24-member caucus represents some part of forty different counties, reflecting the more rural dispersion of blacks in North Carolina relative to Maryland. Maryland has only twenty-four counties,[14] to North Carolina's one hundred. But the respective percentage of total counties represented by the two caucuses (16.6% and 40.0%) is not comparable. In short, the NCLBC represents a geographically more diverse and diffuse set of constituencies than the historically two-county MDLBC.

These differences in the geographic diversity between the two caucuses are further manifested in the mean percentage of the minority voting age populations (MVAP). Looking again at Table 9-3, NCLBC members represent districts that are, on average, lower and much more variable in the percentage of minorities. The mean percentages (based on 1990 Census baselines) are lower caucus-wide in North Carolina (51%, compared to 75% in Maryland), as well as for the respective chambers. The racial composition is much more varied in North Carolina as well, as reflected by the smaller standard deviations. Again, the lower variance is somewhat artifactual, a consequence of the fact that almost every member of the MDLBC, by virtue of the near-univer-

FIGURE 9-1

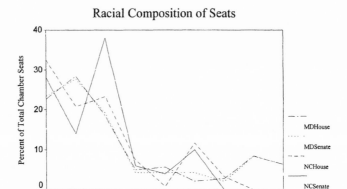

Racial Composition of Seats

Percent Minority Age Voting Population (MVAP)

sal use of nested, multiple-member districts, represents the identical constituency that at least one, and sometimes as many as three other members of the caucus does. But this is precisely the point: The electoral design of the Maryland legislature, coupled with racial geography, combine to make Maryland's black caucus more homogeneous than North Carolina's black caucus.

Figure 9-1 further depicts the differences in the racial composition of districts. In both states, there is a roughly bi-modal distribution of seats[15] based on their minority age voting populations (MVAP). First, of course, a significant portion of seats in both state lower chambers contain less than 20% minorities. However, the seat distributions beyond 20% vary considerably. Notice that the chart is anchored, so to speak, in the quintile between 30-49% MVAP; with the minor exception of North Carolina's lower house seats between 40-49%, all four legislative chambers have the same, small percentage of seats in this range. Below this, North Carolina has a higher percentage of seats with smaller, but still significant MVAPs, i.e., those between 20-29%. White legislators, including some Republicans, often capture these seats.

But the important differences occur above the anchor, among the majority-minority seats. Here we see that Maryland has a cluster of perversely majority-minority (MVAP ≥ 70%) seats, almost all of which currently are represented by black legislators, whereas there are just a few seats in the North Carolina house and none in the senate so drawn. Instead, in North Carolina there is a greater share of seats that scholars (Cameron, Epstein and O'Halloran 1998; Lublin 1997) would deem preferable for maximizing substantive black representation, i.e., majority-minority seats that are not wastefully over-packed with minority voters. Whatever the strategic implications of these differences, given the fact that the entire MDLBC caucus is elected from the extremely majority-minority districts, whereas NCLBC members are elected from a more racially diverse set, the MVAP distribution across legislative seats again distinguishes the two caucuses.

Summarizing this section, it is clear that the MDBLC and NCLBC are similar in many ways, but different in important respects. Most notably, members of the NCLBC represent a more heterogeneous set of districts, both in terms of geography and racial composition. These differences suggest that, ceteris paribus, cohesion might be easier to achieve for the more homogeneous set of black legislators in Maryland.

-Contested Roll Call Voting Cohesion

To compare levels of internal cohesiveness between the MDLBC and NCLBC, and between white and black legislators within each state, we used roll call voting data for the 1997-98 legislative period. Specifically, we collected floor roll call votes for all caucus members and non-caucus members representing districts with minority populations equal to or greater than 20%.[16] In an approach similar to that of Harmel, Hamm and Thompson (1983), for the above sets of legislators we recorded the last vote on all contested, third-reading actions on binding legislation. That is, we excluded the following: (a) any vote where the percentage of nays, divided by the sum of ayes and nays, did not exceed 10 percent; (b) all but the final vote[17] taken on bills that came before the chamber more than once during the same legislative session;[18] and, (c) votes on non-binding resolutions, floor amendments, adoption of favorable/unfavorable committee reports, procedural motions, motions to re-commit, and other, miscellaneous floor actions. Together, these delimiters pair down the number of votes per session from between 1,200 and 1,600 to several dozen litmus votes.

For each vote, we computed a cohesion score, again based on the number of ayes divided by the sum of ayes and nays.[19] We collected data on two discrete sets of legislators: black caucus members (LBC), and white legislators with minority voting-age district population shares equal to or greater than 20 percent (MVAP20). In addition, to control for party effects, we also created a subset of the latter category that excludes Republicans (DEM20). On each measure, the majority position of the LBC was used as the baseline. Thus, LBC cohesion scores were by definition bounded by .500 and 1, and cohesion scores for the MVAP20 and DEM20 subgroups could only exceed LBC scores if the votes were in the same direction.[20] Computed for each vote in each session, cohesion percentages for black and white legislators were then analyzed four ways:

- First, we computed session *means* for each chamber;
- Second, we differenced the cohesion scores for MVAP20 and DEM20 from LBC cohesion scores for each vote to create *head-to-head* scorecard comparisons of the degree of cohesiveness across the series of votes during the legislative session;
- Third, we generated *paired correlation coefficients* between these same two pairs for the session-wide series of cohesion scores; and,
- Finally, we generated *paired difference* t-tests to test the significance of the differences in cross-session cohesion scores.

Tables 9-4a and 9-4b thus report on the voting behavior of black legislators and white legislators with significant minority constituencies on the subset of substantive votes for which these two legislatures were most divided. Before looking at the results, it is necessary to digress momentarily to discuss expectations for the relationship between the statistics reported in Tables 9-4a and 9-4b, specifically the significance of the paired correlation coefficients, r, relative to the paired t-statistics, t. Three possible permutations exist, as depicted in the matrix of Figure 9-2, below.

FIGURE 9-2

Is t significant?

		yes	no
Is r	yes	consistent, wide gap	consistent, small or no gap
significant?	no	variable, wide gaps	n/a

Basically, if LBC cohesion exceeds that of the compared group on a consistent basis, and that consistent gap is large enough, both statistics will be significant. If the gap is consistent, but small or non-existent, only *r* will be significant. And if there are large, but variably sized gaps, *t* should be significant, though to a degree dependent on the variability in the cohesion score gaps.

Table 9-4a Voting Cohesion in MD, by Session and Chamber

Maryland	Senate (46 Votes)			House (75 votes)		
1998	LBC	MVAP20	DEM20	LBC	MVAP20	DEM20
N	8[a]	14	10	27[a]	43	33
Mean	.839	.668	.717	.857	.785	.832
LBC Head-to-Head	---	34-9-3	27-12-7	---	56-12-7	32-16-27
Correlation w/LBC (r)	---	.271	.302	---	.593***	.622***
Paired Diff. w/LBC (t)	---	3.94***	2.95**	---	4.93***	1.57
	Senate (52 votes)			House (83 votes)		
1997	LBC	MVAP20	DEM20	LBC	MVAP20	DEM20
N	9	14	10	26	43	33
Mean	.860	.686	.734	.853	.792	.854
LBC Head-to-Head	---	44-7-1	33-10-9	---	63-18-2	41-28-14
Correlation w/LBC (r)	---	.591***	.614***	---	.546***	.627***
Paired Diff. w/LBC (t)	---	7.06***	4.65***	---	3.32**	0.541

sig.: *=.01; **=.005; ***=.001

[a]MDLBC member Larry Young was forced to resign his Senate seat at the start of the 1998 session, and cast no votes on contested roll calls; MDLBC Delegate Carmena Watson was appointed to fill a vacated seat for part of the 1998 session.

Table 9-4b Voting Cohesion in NC, by Session and Chamber

North Carolina	Senate (23 Votes)			House (60 votes)		
1997-98	LBC	MVAP20	DEM20	LBC	MVAP20	DEM20
N	7	23	19	17	41	30
Mean	.988	.797	.872	.817	.631	.657
LBC Head-to-						
Head	---	19-1-3	14-2-7	---	43-15-2	42-18-0
Correlation						
w/LBC (r)	---	.148	-.249	---	.097	.200
Paired Diff.						
w/LBC (t)	---	6.52***	3.94**	---	5.19***	4.61***

sig.: *=.01; **=.005; ***=.001

Looking first at Maryland, it is clear from Table 9-4a that the MDLBC senators are more internally cohesive than either the group of white legislators representing districts with significant minority constituencies (MVAP20), or even the subgroup of white Democrats (DEM20). In the House, MDLBC delegates are only significantly more cohesive than the combined set of Republicans and Democratic counterparts from districts with significant minority constituencies. When the Republicans are removed, however, there is no difference between MDLBC members and white Democrats. But it is perhaps the most rudimentary measure of all those reported throughout Table 9-4a and Table 9-4b — the session-wide, head-to-head cohesion "scorecards" — that is most telling. It shows that on the most contentious issues during a legislative session. Maryland's black legislators are, at the very least, the most cohesive group on two of every three votes (v. DEM20, House98), and often as frequently as eight of every ten votes (v. MVAP20, Senate97).

Turning next to Table 9-4b and North Carolina, it is obvious that the NCLBC is extremely cohesive, with defections from the majority caucus position rare. This is especially true in the Senate, where the dramatic head-to-head scores and the high mean cohesion score reflect the fact that black senators were perfectly unified on all but two of the twenty-three contested votes taken during the 1997-98 legislative session. Meanwhile, House caucus members exhibit only slightly lower levels of cohesion. Compared to the MVAP20 group and its DEM20 subgroup, LBC cohesion differences are highly significant in every case. Another interesting feature of the North Carolina data is that the voting cohesion scores swing wildly, with insignificant *r*'s resulting from several legislative measures for which the votes of white and black legislators were almost diametrically opposed. Finally, although the low number of contested votes in the Senate makes it difficult to generalize, the head-to-head scorecards in the House show black legislators exhibiting greater cohesiveness than their white counterparts on roughly three of every four votes.

Looking at Tables 9-4a and 9-4b together, two general conclusions can be made. First, and of greatest relevance to the present inquiry, the fact that members of the North Carolina caucus represent a more heterogeneous set of constituencies in no way undermines their internal cohesion. Indeed, NCLBC members are *more* cohesive than their MDLBC counterparts in both chambers. This fact is magnified by the significant differences in cohesion between black and white legislators in North Carolina on contested issues. Black cohesiveness is not simply a function of universally high levels of cooperation within chambers.

Second, and not surprisingly, partisanship plays an important role in the cohesion differences between black and white legislators. When Republicans are eliminated from the analysis, the cohesion differences diminish in all six instances, though sometimes only slightly. On the one hand, this affirms the conventional wisdom that minorities are ill served by creating situations that enhance the electoral chances of Republicans, who will clearly support their policy positions at lower rates than Democrats. On the other hand, the partisan differences accentuate the fact that constituency composition by itself fails to compel Republicans to support black policy positions many white Democrats do.

Implications and Conclusions

The rapid growth in recent decades of the share of seats held by state black legislators has changed the face of American state legislatures. In our case study of the Maryland and North Carolina legislative black caucuses, we found cohesiveness to be strong. As a group, black legislators in both states were more internally cohesive than their white counterparts who represent districts with significant African American constituencies. Moreover, the greater constituency heterogeneity among members of the North Carolina caucus, relative to Maryland, did not undermine cohesiveness for black legislators in North Carolina. This suggests that racial group identity, quite possibly motivated and reinforced by the operations and behavior of the respective black caucuses, acts to unite black legislators in ways they otherwise might not.

Scholars of interest group politics have documented the ability of racial identity to solve the collective action problem and motivate individuals to pursue those "participatory and expressive benefits" derived from concerted, directed behavior (Tate 1993; Chong 1991). Within the legislative environment, policy benefits are awarded to those groups most capable of such collective and direct action (Hammond 1997). Legislative black caucuses provide legislators with a formalized structure for directing those energies towards the collective good, however defined. Achieving the collective good, however, is only obtained by the enforcement of an internal cohesion that would surpass anything that constituent- or electoral-based forces might impose. Given the level of constituency heterogeneity among members of the North Carolina caucus, it is futile to assume that a natural-flowing level of cohesion could deliver the type of substantive benefits desired by African American North Carolinians.

Whether motivated by race or necessity, caucus cohesion affects not only outcomes, but the coalition building *process*. Cohesiveness facilitates the effective and strategic allocation of resources dedicated toward building biracial coalitions. Unification of purpose and action maximizes the likelihood of passing Democratic policies, while lowering the premium needed for converting potential coalition partners into MDLBC- or NCLBC-supported (or led) coalitions. In a three-group coalition/bargaining game, incentive structures are created that encourage two of the groups to conspire against the third. A sizeable and cohesive black caucus is an attractive as a potential coalition partner. By extension, desire to have the caucus' reliable block of votes as part of a coalition compels potential partners to act early in the legislative process.

Cohesion also endows caucus members with the added value of "reputational capital" (Hinich and Munger 1994). Reputation serves three functions. First, it acts as a proxy for information about how caucuses conceptualize policies. Second, legislators use the reputation of colleagues to determine the likelihood that they keep commitments to stated or implicit policy stances. Third, and finally, reputation is used to assess the ability of a caucus to deliver a unified group of supporters. Cohesive, loyal, and active groups are therefore more likely to accumulate "deposits" with the majority party (Hammond 1997; Cox and McCubbins 1993) for future "withdrawal" on contentious policies. Akin to presidential bargaining, the reputational resources available to black caucuses can diminish through the ineffective or fraudulent use of the advantages afforded by such capital. The *qualitative* use of block voting in legislative environments therefore creates additional baselines and criteria through which potential coalition members can evaluate caucus members, activities, and proposals. We suggest that cohesion among black and other minority legislators (whether in opposition or support of the position of the white Democratic majority) represents the most explicit intention to create opportunities for bargaining with white legislators. We believe future exploration into this process-oriented approach to understanding the dilemmas inherent to building biracial coalitions will provide a better understanding of how state legislators achieve racial representation beyond parochialism.

The number of black state legislatures has grown dramatically in recent decades, especially in eastern and southern states where for years African American communities were appallingly underrepresented. Rising seat shares held by black legislators do not guarantee proportionate gains in influence over the legislative process or its outcomes, however. For this growth to translate into significant policy change for African American constituencies, the contemporary generation of black legislators will need to fully exercise its cooperative and collective powers. This is not to suggest that black legislators must parrot one another, or that disagreements among caucus members are unhealthy. Rather, what matters is the qualitative value of black state legislators' behavior, especially voting. Indeed, the level of voting cohesion exhibited by black legislators may prove to be the most important indicator of how (and how much) black faces translate into black interests, for cohesiveness is what distinguishes a caucus in name from a coalition in practice.

References

Adams, Greg D. 1996. "Legislative Effects of Single-Member v. Multi-Member Districts," *American Journal of Political Science* 40: 129-44.

Bositis, David. 1998. "Introduction." In *Redistricting and Minority Representation,* (ed) David Bositis,. Washington, D.C.: Joint Center for Political and Economic Studies.

Bratton, Kathleen A., and Kerry L. Haynie. 1999. "Agenda Setting and Legislative Success in State Legislatures: The Effects of Gender and Race," *Journal of Politics* 61: 658-79.

Bullock, Charles S. 1992. "Minorities in State Legislatures," In *Changing Patterns in State Legislative Careers,* (eds) Gary F. Moncrief and Joel A.

Thompson, Ann Arbor, MI: University of Michigan Press.

Button, James, and David Hedge. 1996. "Legislative Life in the 1990s: A Comparison of Black and White State Legislators," *Legislative Studies Quarterly* 21: 199-218.

Cameron, Charles, David Epstein, and Sharyn O'Halloran. 1996. "Do Majority-Minority Districts Maximize Substantive Black Representation in Congress?" *American Political Science Review* 90: 794-12.

Canon, David T. 1995. "Redistricting and the Congressional Black Caucus," *American Politics Quarterly* 23: 159-89.

Chong, Dennis. 1991. *Collective Action and the Civil Rights Movement.* Chicago: University of Chicago Press.

Cox, Gary, and Mathew McCubbins. 1993. *Legislative Leviathan.* Los Angeles: University of California Press.

Engstrom, Richard L. 1995 "Voting Rights Districts: Debunking the Myths," *Campaigns and Elections* 16: 24-46.

Engstrom, Richard L., and Michael D. McDonald. 1981. The Election of Blacks to City Councils: Clarifying the Impact of Electoral Arrangements on the Seats/Population Relationship," *American Political Science Review* 75: 344-34.

Epstein, David, and Sharyn O'Halloran. 1999. "Measuring the Electoral and Policy Impact of Majority-Minority Voting Districts: Candidates of Choice, Equal Opportunity, and Representation," *American Journal of Political Science* 43: 367-95.

Gerber, Elizabeth, Rebecca B. Morton, and Thomas A. Rietz. 1998. "Minority Representation in Multimember Districts," *American Political Science Review* 92: 127-44.

Grofman, Bernard, and Lisa Handley. 1991. "The Impact of the Voting Rights Act on Black Representation in Southern State Legislatures," *Legislative Studies Quarterly* 16: 111-28.

Guinier, Lani. 1994 *The Tyranny of the Majority.* New York: Free Press.

Hamm, Keith E., Robert Harmel, and Robert Thompson. (1983) "Ethnic and Partisan Minorities in Two Southern State Legislatures," *Legislative Studies Quarterly* 8: 177-89.

Hammond, Susan. 1997. "Congressional Caucuses in the 104th Congress," In *Congress Reconsidered*, 6th edition. (eds) Lawrence Dodd and Bruce Oppenheimer, Washington: CQ Press.

Harmel, Robert, Keith Hamm, and Robert Thompson. 1983. "Black Voting Cohesion and Distinctiveness in Three Southern Legislatures," *Social Science Quarterly* 64: 183-92.

Hedge, David, James Button and Mary Spear. 1996. "Accounting for the Quality of Black Legislative Life: The View From the States," *American Journal of Political Science* 40: 129-44.

Hill, Kevin. 1995. "Does the Creation of Majority Black Districts Aid Republicans?" *Journal of Politics* 57: 384-401.

Hinich, Melvin, and Michael C. Munger. 1994. *Ideology and the Theory of Political Choice*. Ann Arbor, MI: University of Michigan Press.

Johnson, James B., and Philip E. Secret. 1996. "Focus and Style: Representational Roles of Congressional Black and Hispanic Caucus Members," *Journal of Black Studies* 26: 245-73.

Johnson, Nicole E. 2000. "Resources and the Representation of African Americans in the State Legislature," *Southeastern Political Review* 28: 151-63.

Kerr, Brinck, and Will Miller. 1997. "Latino Representation, It's Direct and Indirect," *American Journal of Political Science* 41: 1066-1071.

King-Meadows, Tyson, and Thomas F. Schaller. 2000. "Racial Segregation and Gerrymandering: The Effects of Size and Diffusion of Minority Populations on Gerrymandering Outcomes in 30 American States," forthcoming, *American Review of Politics*, Fall 2000.

Lublin, David. 1997. *The Paradox of Representation: Racial Gerrymandering and Minority Interests in Congress*, Princeton, NJ: Princeton University Press.

Massey, Douglas S., and Nancy A. Denton. 1988. "The Dimensions of Residential Segregation," *Social Forces* 67: 281-315.

Miller, Cheryl M. 1990. "Agenda-setting by State Legislative Black Caucuses: Policy Priorities and Factors of Success," *Policy Studies Review* 9: 339-54.

Moncrief, Gary F., and Joel A. Thompson. 1992. "Electoral Structure and State Legislative Representation: A Research Note," *Journal of Politics* 54: 246-56.

Petrocik, John R., and Scott W. Desposato. 1998 "The Partisan Consequences of Majority-Minority Redistricting in the South, 1992 and 1994," *Journal of Politics* 60: 613-33.

Pitkin, Hanna Fenichel. 1967 *The Concept of Representation*. Berkeley, CA: University of California Press.

Riffe, Daniel. 1992. "Comparison of Sources of Information for Black State Legislators," *Western Journal of Black Studies* 16: 199-204.

Rosenthal, Alan. 1998. *The Decline of Representative Democracy*. Washington, D.C.: CQ Press.

Shingles, Richard D. 1981. "Black Consciousness and Political Participation: The Missing Link," *American Political Science Review* 75: 76-91.

Singh, Robert. 1998. *The Congressional Black Caucus*. Thousand Oaks, CA: Sage Publications.

Sullivan, Terry O. 1990. "Bargaining with the President: A Simple Game with New Evidence," *American Political Science Review* 84: 1167-96.

Swain, Carol. 1993. *Black Faces, Black Interests: The Representation of African Americans in Congress*. Cambridge, MA: Harvard University Press.

Tate, Katherine. 1993. *From Protest to Politics*. New York: Russell Sage Foundation.

Tschoepe, Gary. 1997. "The Influence of African American Representation on State AFDC Policy," *State & Local Government Review* 29: 156-65.

Tversky, Amos, and Daniel Kahneman. 1996. "The Framing of Decisions and the Psychology of Choice," In *Rational Choice*, ed. Jon Elster, New York: NYU Press, Pp. 123-41.

Vedlitz, Arnold, and Charles A. Johnson. 1982. "Community Racial Segregation, Electoral Structure, and Minority Representation," *Social Science Quarterly* 63: 729-36.

Walton, Hanes, ed. 1994. *Black Politics and Black Political Behavior*. Westport, CT: Praeger.

Whitby, Kenny J. 1997. *The Color of Representation: Congressional Behavior and Black Interests*. Ann Arbor: University of Michigan Press.

Notes

1 *Black Elected Officials, Statistical Summary 1993-1997*, David A. Bositis (1998).

2 The growth in the number of black state legislators in some ways mirrors the overall growth in black elected and appointed officials in the United States over the past three decades. Data available from the Joint Center for Political and Economic Studies demonstrates that the number of black public officials has grown dramatically since the 1970s and at every level of government, but especially in state and local governments.

3 We use "African Americans" to refer to communities or constituencies, and "black" to refer to legislators, if only because the formal title of most state caucuses uses the latter.

4 Based on 1990 U.S. Census Bureau data, we calculated the racial dissimilarity index (c.f., Massey and Denton, 1988) for North Carolina and Maryland, using counties as the unit of aggregation analysis. Indices are

bounded by 0 and 1, with lower values meaning less racially dissimilar, although scores about .500 are rare. Maryland's .464 score is dramatically higher than North Carolina's .278.

5 Many of these studies focus on Congress. Although the national and state legislative environments and electoral dynamic differ in important ways, the findings in the congressional literature have general relevance for the present study.

6 Although we are not concerned here with issues of voter efficacy, it is interesting to note that many studies indicate that people tend toward risk aversion — even to the point of "irrationally" preferring lotteries with smaller, more certain payoffs over longshot lotteries with greater expected values (Tversky and Kahneman, 1986). Accordingly, there is reason to suspect black voters may view smaller, more reliable contingents of black legislators more favorably than larger, less reliable ones — even if the latter promise better long-run payoffs. Similarly, potential coalition partners within the legislature will rate caucus members as more preferable when caucus members exhibit reliability.

7 Maryland uses multiple-member districts to elect most of its lower, House of Delegates. North Carolina uses multiple-member districts in a limited fashion, but for elections to both chambers.

8 Figures are for single-member districts, based on 1990 Census data, as tabulated and reported by Rosenthal (1998, Table 1.1).

9 In all twelve cases, the districts are nested. That is, the three house seats, whether chosen in single- or double-member districts, are wholly contained within the geographic borders of the larger, senate district.

10 The seven districts with one black senator and three black delegates are 10, 24, 25, 40, 41, 44 and 45; the two districts with one senator and two delegates are 26 and 43.

11 Delegates Rushern Baker, of Prince George's County, and Rudolph Cane, of Wicomico County, are the exceptions; both represent single-member districts. Delegate Frank Turner, of Howard County, represents a two-member district along with a white legislator.

12 Theodore J. McKinney and Mary E. McAllister, from two-member House District 17.

13 According to documents on file in the Maryland state legislative library, only Aris T. Allen (Anne Arundel County, 1967-1982), Richard N. Dixon (Carroll County, 1983-1996), and current legislators Frank Turner (Howard County) and Rudolph Cane (Wicomico County) are the only black legislators ever elected from other than Baltimore County, Baltimore City or

Prince Georges County.

14 Actually, Maryland has twenty-three counties; Baltimore City is the twenty-fourth political jurisdiction.

15 The table reports seats, not districts, with multi-member districts simply multiplied by the district magnitude.

16 We chose to use minority voting-age population, the more inclusive measure than black voting age population, for several reasons. First, it eliminates the minor problem of black-white racial populations failing to sum to 100 percent. Second, as Lublin (1997) and others have suggested, non-black minority populations often provide natural political allies for black voters, so their inclusion is relevant. Third, the non-black minority percentages (5.26 and 2.23 in MD and NC, respectively) are small enough that they do not complicate this study as might be the case for states with significant Asian and Latino populations.

17 Often, legislation passes a chamber more than once because it has been altered, usually in response to actions in the other chamber. Though the multiple actions taken may well represent votes on starkly different pieces of legislation, to avoid the possibility of assigning additional weight to essentially similar measures, we counted only the vote occurring latest during the legislative session.

18 Here, legislative design differences interfere. North Carolina conducts biennial sessions, akin to the U.S. Congress, whereas Maryland has annual sessions. Accordingly, there is only one set of results for North Carolina, but two for Maryland, for the 1997-98 period.

19 In Maryland, the exhaustive list of possible votes for a member is as follows: "aye," "nay," "not voting," "absent," and "absent (excused)." The problematic category, of course, is "not voting"; these non-action actions are equivalent to abstaining, but connote dissent. However, because of the ambiguity associated with casting a "not voting" vote, we chose to exclude them from the calculations along with absentee votes of both varieties.

20 There were, of course, a few rare cases when MVAP20 and DEM20 groups were more cohesive in the *opposite* direction. But these were few, and occurred only in Maryland. More to the point, in a study focusing on the influence of minority constituencies on legislative voting, using the caucus' majority position as the baseline is warranted.

CHAPTER 10

A Wave of Change: Women in State and Local Governments

Charles E. Menifield and Regina C. Gray1

The strides made by women at all levels of government over the last fifty years have not gone unnoticed by voters, politicians or researchers. In the year 2000, sixty-five women held seats in Congress and 1,669 occupied seats in state legislatures around the country. Women account for 12% of congressional seats and 23% of the state legislatures (Center for American Women and Politics 2000). It is the dual purpose of this chapter to document the growth of women in state and local governments over the latter part of last century and to compare bill sponsorship in the Mississippi and Vermont legislatures. In so doing, we provide a descriptive analysis of the women in each of the fifty state legislatures as characterized by House and Senate membership and party identification since 1975. In addition, we examine women governors since 1974, women mayors since 1981, and women in other state elected positions since 1969. With regards to leadership, we examine the number of women committee chairs and party leaders in the House and Senate in each of the 50 states in 1999. Lastly, we conduct a comparative case study analysis of women in the Mississippi and Vermont legislatures. Specifically, we examine bill sponsorship data in the 1999-2000 legislative session to determine the number of bills proposed by women, the nature of those bills, passage rate, and bill co-sponsorship. We also compare committee chairs, vice-chairs, and seniority status of the women in each of these General Assemblies.

Although we consider many questions in our research, a few clearly come to the fore. *General Descriptive Analysis*: Has the number of women in state and local governments grown consistently over the last thirty years? Are women making advances into leadership positions in state legislatures at the committee and party level? Do women tend to identify with the Democratic or Republican Party? *Case Study Analysis*: Does bill co-sponsorship affect the success or demise of legislation sponsored by women? Do women tend to introduce more social policy legislation relative to other types of legislation? Does committee chair assignments affect bill passage rates?

Brief Overview of the Literature

Studies of women in politics at all levels of government have proliferated in the last twenty years. In fact, the number of studies escalate as the number of women in political offices increase. In addition, the creation of women's organizations, both inside and outside of government, such as the Center for American Women and Politics (CAWP) at Rutgers University and Women's Caucuses, aid in the dissemination of information about the goals and pursuits of women at all levels.

Rather than spend an exorbitant amount of time and space discussing the literature, we provide the reader with a plethora of scholarly publications on women in politics classified by areas of interest. The following, however, is not an exhaustive list of resources. This list merely provides the reader with a foundation from which to begin a literature review.

A.) *Women in Congress*: Paxton 1945; Block 1978; Gertzog 1984; Darcy, Welch and Clark 1984; Carpini, et al. 1993; Fowler 1993; Vega et al. 1995; Burrell 1996; Menifield 1996; Dolan 1997; Swain 1997; Whicker and Whitaker 1999.

B.) *Women in State Legislatures*: Havens et al. 1991; Kolb 1991; Thomas 1991; Moncrief 1992; Jewell et al. 1993: Thomas 1994; Barrett 1995; Whistler 1999; Ford and Dolan 1999; Hawks and Staton 1999; Rule 1999.

C.) *Women in the Law and the Courts*: Cook 1978, 1980a, 1980b, 1984; Goldstein 1979; Gryski et al. 1986; Allen and Wall 1987; Prestage 1987; Binion 1993: Martin 1993; Allen and Wall 1993; Martin 1999; O'Connor and Clark 1999; Reid 2000; Wall 2000.

D.) *Women and the Executive Branch*: Grimes 1990; Caroli

1995; O'Connor 1996; Borelli 1997; Burrell 1997; Reynolds 1999; Burrell 1999; Weir 1999; Whicker and Issacs 1999.

E.) Women in State and Local Governments: Welch and Karnig 1979; Ambrosius 1984; Antolini 1984; Boles 1984; Gruberg 1984; Uhlaner et al. 1986; Darcy, Welch and Clark 1987; Bullock et al. 1991; MacManus et al. 1999; Mettler 2000; Reid 2000.

F.) Women in Campaigns: Barber and Kellerman 1986; Wilhite 1986; Kahn et al. 1991; Kahn 1994a; Kahn 1994b; Seligman 1961; Mandel 1981; Carroll 1984; Carroll 1994; Tien, et al. 1999; Rausch et al. 1999; Scharrer et al. 2000.

G.) Women and Public Policy: Sapiro 1981; Boles 1982; Gelb and Palley 1982; Gelb and Palley 1987; Jones and Jonasdottir 1988; Dodson 1991; Murphy 1997; Bamberger 1999; Blair 1999; Conway et al. 1999; Johnson 1999; Thompson 1999; Palley and Palley 2000.

H.) Feminist Theory: Freidan 1963; Mezey 1978; Jaggar 1983; Conway et al. 1987; Fraser 1987; Connover 1988; Gelb 1989; Freeman 1989; Wilcox, 1989; Sylvester 1994; Hirschmann and Di Stefano 1996; Caraway 1999; Iannello 1999; James 1999; Kelly 1999; Lewis 1999; Ring 1999; Rudy 1999.

I.) Comparative Studies: Newland 1975; Giele et al. 1977; Liston 1978; Welch et al. 1986; Norris 1987; Welch and Studlar 1990; Brill 1995; Herrick 1997; Scharrat and Kaschak 1999; and Tripp 1999.

J.) Women, Public Opinion and Participation: Poole and Zeigler 1985; Beckwith 1986; Christy 1987; Hewitt 2000.

K.) Gender and Ethnicity: Baker et al. 1984; Darcy et al. 1988; Overby et al. 1994; Barrett 1995; Rosenthal 1995; Prindeville et al. 1999; and Mansbridge 1999.

L.) The Gender Gap: Wright 1989; Cook 1991; Kahn et al. 1991; Kahn 1994; Norrander 1997; Sapiro 1997; Verba et al. 1997; Mattei 1998; Rozell et al. 1998; Anderson 1999; Carroll 1999; Frankovic 1999; Kaufman et al. 1999; Sainsbury 1999; Sigel 1999.

M.) Women and Political Parties: Baer 1993; Paddock 1997; Niven 1998.

Research Design

The majority of the descriptive data in the tables is almost exclusively from the Center for American Women and Politics (CAWP) (http://www.rci.rutgers.edu/~cawp/). In some cases, the CAWP data was compared with data contained in the *Statistical Abstract of the U.S.*

The bill sponsorship data used in the comparative case study is from the official web sites for the state of Vermont (http://www.state.vt.us/) and Mississippi (http://www.ls.state.ms.us/). In conducting the study, the first item on our agenda was to evaluate the seniority system and committee chair and vice-chair assignment process in each house relative to the number of committees. Next, we examine the number of bills proposed, type of bill, and the passage rate of legislation. Lastly, we examine the rate of co-sponsored legislation (with male members only). The votes for Mississippi are split into two separate data sets, one set for 1999 and a second set for 2000. The votes for Vermont are all in one data set.

Data Analysis

Since 1969, the number of women holding public office at the state level has more than quadrupled. As Table 10-1 shows, women held a mere 6.6% of the total number of state wide elective offices in 1969. In 2000, women hold almost one-third of all statewide elective offices. Similar growth was experienced in state legislatures. In fact, the number of women holding seats in the state legislatures from 1973 to 1977 has almost doubled. In 2000, women hold nearly one quarter of all these positions.

-Women in State Legislatures

In 1894, history was made when three women, Carrie C. Holly, Frances S. Clock and Clara Cressingham, all Republicans, were elected to the Colorado State House of Delegates. Minnie Buckingham Parker (R), the first African American woman to serve in a state legislature, was

Table 10-1 Percentage of Women in State Elective Offices

	1969	1973	1977	1981	1985	1989	1993	1997	2000
State Wide Elective	6.6%	7.6	9.9	10.5	13.3	14.3	22.2	26.0	28.5
State Legislatures	4.0%	5.6	9.1	12.1	14.8	17.0	20.5	21.6	23.0

Source: Center for American Women and Politics. 1999. *National Information Bank on Women in Public Office*, Eagleton Institute of Politics, Rutgers University.

appointed to succeed her husband who died in office in 1929. Parker was a member of the West Virginia House. Crystal Dreda Bird Fauset (D) was the first African American woman elected to a state legislature in 1938. She served in the Pennsylvania State Assembly.

A glance at Table 10-2 shows that women who aspired to an office in state legislatures from 1975 to 2000 has the greatest numerical growth in the Deep South. In fact, when converted to percentages of the entire Assembly, the Deep South states experience the largest percentage increase since 1975. For example, the number of women legislators serving in the Alabama Assembly in 2000 has increased substantially since 1975 (over a one thousand percent increase). Despite this growth, all of the Deep South states, with the exception of Florida and Georgia, still have the smallest number of women state legislators between 1975 and 2000.

Numerically, the Northeast and West appear to be the best locations for women seeking legislative seats. New Hampshire, in particular, has the largest number of women serving in their state legislature when compared to all other states. The state ranks in the top 5% of states with the largest percentage of women in the legislature at 32%. Additionally, New Hampshire has the largest legislature in the U.S. Currently Washington has the largest percentage of women in the legislature at 40.8%. Nevada and Arizona round out the top three positions at 36.5% and 35.6%, respectively. In 2000, Alabama, Oklahoma, South Carolina, Kentucky and Mississippi have the smallest percentage of women legislators at 7.9%, 10.1%, 11.2%, 11.6% and 12.1%, respectively.

Table 10-2 Women State Legislators, by State

	1975	1980	1985	1990	1995	2000	Rank	Total # in Leg.
Alabama	1	6	9	8	5	11	50	140
Alaska	9	6	11	12	14	11	33	60
Arizona	18	17	18	27	27	32	3	90
Arkansas	3	5	10	10	17	20	43	135
California	3	12	15	19	25	31	15	120
Colorado	16	23	24	29	31	34	4	100
Connecticut	26	44	41	41	50	55	9	187
Delaware	10	9	10	10	13	15	22	62
Florida	13	17	31	26	31	38	23	160
Georgia	10	17	23	24	43	45	32	236
Hawaii	10	14	14	18	15	17	25	76
Idaho	10	10	24	31	29	26	18	105
Illinois	14	32	30	33	41	45	16	177
Indiana	9	12	19	21	33	27	35	150

Table 10-2 Women State Legislators, by State (continued)

	1975	1980	1985	1990	1995	2000	Rank	Total # in Leg.
Iowa	14	18	22	25	27	32	27	150
Kansas	9	22	30	42	46	55	5	165
Kentucky	5	10	9	8	11	16	47	138
Louisiana	2	2	5	3	14	23	41	144
Maine	24	42	44	58	48	52	12	186
Maryland	19	28	36	43	54	55	10	188
Massachusetts	16	19	33	34	48	52	14	200
Michigan	9	16	16	22	33	36	21	148
Minnesota	8	24	29	37	50	57	11	201
Mississippi	6	2	4	10	20	21	46	174
Missouri	12	22	26	29	39	43	26	197
Montana	14	17	22	27	36	37	19	150
Nebraska	1	5	8	10	12	12	20	49
Nevada	7	7	10	14	22	23	2	63
New Hampshire	104	124	140	136	126	135	6	424
New Jersey	9	8	12	13	16	19	42	120
New Mexico	5	7	13	15	23	31	13	112
New York	9	18	24	23	38	44	30	211
North Carolina	15	22	20	24	28	31	34	170
North Dakota	16	18	18	24	22	26	37	147
Ohio	8	10	12	17	32	28	28	132
Oklahoma	6	12	13	13	16	15	49	149
Oregon	11	20	18	18	26	27	8	90
Pennsylvania	9	12	13	17	30	32	45	253
Rhode Island	9	15	23	23	36	38	17	150
South Carolina	7	11	10	15	21	19	48	170
South Dakota	11	11	15	20	19	14	44	105
Tennessee	5	6	11	13	18	22	39	132
Texas	8	12	16	19	33	32	38	181
Utah	8	8	7	12	15	22	29	104
Vermont	22	39	47	60	54	57	7	180
Virginia	6	9	11	15	16	23	40	140
Washington	18	35	35	43	58	60	1	147
West Virginia	9	16	23	26	20	24	36	134
Wisconsin	10	20	25	34	32	31	24	132
Wyoming	7	17	24	22	19	18	31	90
Total	610	908	1107	1273	1532	1669	7424	

Source: U.S. Bureau of the Census. *Statistical Abstract of the United States*: Washington, D.C. (Various issues). Center for American Women and Politics. 2000. *National Information Bank on Women in Public Office*, Eagleton Institute of Politics, Rutgers University.

Table 10-3 provides the distribution of women legislators in the House and Senate for each state. Due to the large number of members in state houses in general, it is not surprising that the number of women in the House is correspondingly higher than in the Senate. In fact, since 1975 the percentage gap between the House and Senate has widened considerably. However, there is an aberration to this phenomenon. Women in Washington have been quite successful in winning Senate seats. In 1975, the ratio of House to Senate seats was 4:1. By the year 2000, the ratio increased to 4:3. Another case that stands out is the 1990 legislative session in Indiana where women in the Senate outnumber those in the House 11 to 10.

Similar to the previous table, the regional differences are quite abundant. The South is quite striking in this regard. Generally speaking, southern states have a very small number of women in their senates. Currently, Arkansas is the only state with a Senate that has no women members. With the exception of Georgia and Florida, all Deep South states fall in the bottom quartile of states with a small number of women in the House and Senate. Women have the greatest success in the Northeast and West. When considered collectively, women in New Hampshire tend to do better in both chambers of the legislature than those in other states and regions of the country.

Table 10-3 Women State Legislators by House and Senate Memberships

	1975		1980		1985		1990		1995		2000	
	H	S	H	S	H	S	H	S	H	S	H	S
Alabama	1	0	6	0	7	2	7	1	4	1	8	3
Alaska	7	2	4	2	7	4	8	4	10	4	8	3
Arizona	13	5	12	5	14	4	22	5	19	8	25	7
Arkansas	3	0	4	1	9	1	8	2	16	1	20	0
California	3	0	10	2	11	4	14	5	20	5	21	10
Colorado	13	3	19	4	19	5	22	7	21	10	22	12
Connecticut	22	4	36	8	36	5	34	7	42	8	46	9
Delaware	8	2	7	2	7	3	6	4	7	6	9	6
Florida	12	1	13	4	22	9	16	10	25	6	31	7
Georgia	9	1	15	2	21	2	22	2	35	8	36	9
Hawaii	6	4	10	4	8	6	11	7	10	5	12	5
Idaho	9	1	8	2	21	7	22	9	22	7	20	6
Illinois	12	2	28	4	20	10	21	12	31	10	33	12
Indiana	6	3	8	4	13	6	10	11	19	14	14	13
Iowa	10	4	16	2	19	3	19	6	17	10	21	11

Table 10-3 (continued)

	1975		1980		1985		1990		1995		2000	
Kansas	8	1	18	4	25	5	33	9	32	14	41	14
Kentucky	3	2	8	2	7	2	6	2	9	2	12	4
Louisiana	2	0	2	0	5	0	3	0	12	2	21	2
Maine	23	1	36	6	35	9	48	10	37	11	36	16
Maryland	16	3	25	3	33	3	35	8	47	7	46	9
Massachusetts	14	2	14	5	28	5	29	5	40	8	42	10
Michigan	9	0	16	0	14	2	20	2	30	3	31	5
Minnesota	7	1	19	5	20	9	27	10	32	18	35	22
Mississippi	5	1	2	0	4	0	7	3	16	4	16	11
Missouri	11	1	20	2	24	2	27	2	36	3	38	5
Montana	10	4	13	4	17	5	21	6	27	9	29	8
Nebraska	1		5		8		10		12		12	
Nevada	4	3	5	2	7	3	10	4	17	5	18	5
New Hampshire	102	2	121	3	133	7	130	6	120	6	127	8
New Jersey	6	3	7	1	9	3	10	3	15	1	16	3
New Mexico	3	2	5	2	11	2	11	4	15	8	21	10
New York	6	3	14	4	19	5	17	6	29	9	36	8
North Carolina	13	2	19	3	16	4	20	4	22	6	24	7
North Dakota	13	3	15	3	15	3	19	5	13	9	20	6
Ohio	7	1	9	1	10	2	14	3	24	8	23	5
Oklahoma	5	1	11	1	10	3	7	6	9	7	9	6
Oregon	8	3	19	1	12	6	11	7	19	7	19	8
Pennsylvania	8	1	11	1	11	2	15	2	26	4	25	7
Rhode Island	7	2	10	5	15	8	14	9	26	10	27	11
South Carolina	7	0	9	2	8	2	13	2	18	3	16	3
South Dakota	7	4	8	3	11	4	13	7	14	5	9	5
Tennessee	4	1	5	1	10	1	11	2	15	3	17	5
Texas	7	1	11	1	15	1	16	3	29	4	28	4
Utah	8	0	6	2	6	1	11	1	14	1	18	4
Vermont	21	1	35	4	43	4	54	6	43	11	47	10
Virginia	6	0	8	1	11	0	12	3	12	4	15	8
Washington	14	4	27	8	28	7	33	10	38	20	37	23
West Virginia	8	1	14	2	20	3	19	7	15	5	20	4
Wisconsin	9	1	18	2	22	3	30	4	24	8	20	11
Wyoming	6	1	14	3	22	2	18	4	18	1	13	5
Total	522	88	775	133	918	189	1016	257	1203	328	1289	380

Source: Center for American Women and Politics. 2000. *National Information Bank on Women in Public Office*, Eagleton Institute of Politics, Rutgers University.

History teaches us that elections at the state and local levels tend to be dominated by candidates running under the Democratic Party banner. Although there are pockets around the country where Republican Party candidates are competitive, the edge overtime certainly leans heavily in favor of Democrats. Table 10-4 provides the results of trends in party identification from 1980 to the present. Overall the number of female elected state legislators who identify with the Democratic Party has consistently outnumbered Republicans. To be sure, over the last twenty years, the gap has continued to widen with each election. Given the ideological nature of the Democratic Party, it is not surprising that women gravitate toward the party. Research has shown that women legislators are more likely to pursue social policy legislation when compared to their male counterparts (Menifield 1996). Similarly, Democrats are much more likely to support liberal social policies than Republicans.

Table 10-4 Women State Legislators, by State and Party ID

	1980		1985		1990		1995		2000	
	D	R	D	R	D	R	D	R	D	R
Alabama	5	1	8	1	7	1	5	0	8	3
Alaska	4	2	5	6	5	7	6	7*	4	7
Arizona	7	10	6	12	11	16	10	17	13	19
Arkansas	3	2	9	1	9	1	14	3	16	4
California	6	6	9	6	10	9	19	5*	25	5*
Colorado	11	12	8	16	11	18	15	16	15	19
Connecticut	20	24	14	27	23	18	34	16	38	17
Delaware	5	4	5	5	4	6	2	11	5	10
Florida	11	6	18	13	15	11	23	8	23	15
Georgia	14	3	19	4	19	5	29	14	33	12
Hawaii	7	7	8	6	16	2	11	4	12	5
Idaho	3	7	9	15	11	20	9	20	7	19
Illinois	12	20	12	18	15	18	20	21	24	21
Indiana	5	7	10	9	10	11	13	20	14	13
Iowa	6	12	14	8	16	9	11	16	14	18
Kansas	11	11	13	17	21	21	15	31	21	34
Kentucky	9	1	7	2	5	3	5	6	10	6
Louisiana	2	0	5	0	3	0	12	2	18	5
Maine	22	20	23	21	34	24	29	18*	34	16**
Maryland	24	4	32	4	38	5	42	12	44	11
Massachusetts	13	6	24	9*	25	9	33	15	42	10
Michigan	10	6	10	6	13	9	19	14	20	16
Minnesota	16	8	17	12	23	14	30	20	34	23

Table 10-4 (continued)

	1980		1985		1990		1995		2000	
Mississippi	2	0	4	0	9	1	17	3	17	4
Missouri	18	4	18	8	20	9	18	21	23	20
Montana	9	8	17	5	21	6	18	18	26	11
Nebraska	N/A				N/A					
Nevada	4	3	4	6	10	4	11	11	16	7
New Hampshire	52	72	44	96	50	86	48	78	75	60
New Jersey	4	4	7	5	6	7	7	9	11	8
New Mexico	2	5	1	12	8	7	15	8	17	14
New York	12	6	21	3	19	4	29	9	31	13
North Carolina	18	4	13	7	14	10	10	18	17	14
North Dakota	3	15	9	9	13	11	9	13	13	13
Ohio	4	6	8	4	12	5	13	18	13	15
Oklahoma	7	5	8	5	11	2	11	5	9	6
Oregon	13	7	12	6	12	6	15	11	17	10
Pennsylvania	3	9	5	8	9	8	15	15	16	15
Rhode Island	12	3	14	9	16	7	28	8	31	7
South Carolina	9	2	9	1	11	4	10	11	8	11
South Dakota	4	7	3	12	12	8	8	11	5	9
Tennessee	3	3	5	6	5	8	13	5	16	6
Texas	10	2	10	6	13	6	20	13	18	14
Utah	4	4	2	5	6	6	5	10	11	11
Vermont	23	16	27	20	36	24	34	20	42	14
Virginia	8	1	9	2	10	5	12	4	15	8
Washington	21	14	20	15	27	16	34	24	40	20
West Virginia	14	2	18	5	22	4	13	7	16	8
Wisconsin	11	9	13	12	19	15	17	15	14	17
Wyoming	8	9	13	11	11	11	7	12	11	7
Total	504	399	599	496	746	517	843	673	1002	650

* 1 Independent   ** 2 Independents

Source: Center for American Women and Politics. 2000. *National Information Bank on Women in Public Office*, Eagleton Institute of Politics, Rutgers University.

The table also provide us with several other notable observations. First, states such as New Hampshire, Connecticut, Illinois, and New Mexico, which were once solid Republican strongholds for women, have lost seats to Democrats in each subsequent election. Today, female Democratic legislators outnumber their female Republican counterparts. Among these states, only Arizona, Idaho and

Kansas have consistently had more female Republicans than Democrats over the period of this study.

Overall, 1990 appears to have been the golden year for women Democratic candidates in the United States. They held the majority over their Republican counterparts in 30 of the 50 states and equaled the number of Republican women in 3 other states. Sixty-nine percent of all female state legislators were Democrats in 1990. In 2000, 61% of all female legislators were members of the Democratic Party.

-Women in the Governor's Office

Women in the Governor's Office is a recent phenomenon. The first female Governor was Nellie Taylor Ross (D) of Wyoming who won a special election in 1925 She replaced her husband who died in office and served until 1927. Miriam Ferguson (D) was the second female Governor. She was elected in Texas in 1925 and again in 1933 (CAWP 2000). No other woman would win a gubernatorial election until Lurleen Wallace (D) was elected in 1967 in Alabama and Ella Grasso (D) in Connecticut. There were no women governors, nor were there any women seeking gubernatorial positions in 1970 and 1972 (CAWP 2000).

By 1974, three women ran for governor. However, only 1 woman, Ella Grasso (D), was elected. She was reelected again in 1978. In 1982, Kay Orr of Nebraska became the first Republican female governor. In 1986, there were no women Governors. However, by 1990, the Decade of the Woman was especially evident by the success of 3 out of the 7 women gubernatorial candidates who won elections that year. Each woman was elected in states where no woman had previously served. In 2000, Jane Dee Hull (R) from Arizona, Jeanne Shaheen (D) from New Hampshire, and Christine Todd Whitman (R) currently serve as Governors of their respective states (see Table 10-5).

Five women ran for the Governor's Office in 2000 and three were successfully elected bringing the total number of women governors to five. Jeanne Shaheen (D) was the only female incumbent seeking a second term. Ruth Ann Milner (D) from Delaware and Republican Judy Martz, both former lieutenant governors, won the office in their first bid. Ruth Dwyer (R) of Vermont and Heidi Heitkamp (D), former Attorney General of North Dakota, lost their election bids. Hence, the old record high of three women in Governors' Office was shattered.

Representation of Minority Groups in the U.S.

Table 10-5 Women Governors 1974-1998

	1974		1978		1982		1986		1990		1994		1998		2000	
	R	W	R	W	R	W	R	W	R	W	R	W	R	W	R	W
Alabama	0	0	0	0	0	0	0	0	0	1	0	1	0	0	0	0
Arizona	0	0	0	0	0	0	1	0	0	0	0	0	1	1*	1	NE
California	0	0	0	0	0	0	0	0	1	0	1	0	0	0	0	0
Colorado	0	0	0	0	0	0	0	0	0	0	0	0	1	0	0	0
Connecticut	1	1	1	1	0	0	1	0	0	0	1	0	1	0	0	0
Delaware	0	0	0	0	0	0	0	0	0	0	0	0	0	0	1	1
Hawaii	0	0	0	0	0	0	0	0	0	0	1	0	1	0	0	0
Iowa	0	0	0	0	1	0	0	0	0	0	1	0	0	0	0	0
Illinois	0	0	0	0	0	0	0	0	0	0	1	0	0	0	0	0
Kansas	0	0	0	0	0	0	0	0	1	1	0	0	0	0	0	0
Maryland	1	0	0	0	0	0	0	0	0	0	1	0	1	0	0	0
Maine	0	0	0	0	0	0	0	0	0	0	1	0	0	0	0	0
Montana	0	0	0	0	0	0	0	0	0	0	0	0	0	0	1	1
Nebraska	0	0	0	0	2	1	1	0	0	0	0	0	0	0	0	0
New Hampshire	0	0	0	0	0	0	0	0	0	0	0	0	1	1	1	1
New Jersey	0	0	0	0	0	0	0	0	0	0	0	0	1	1	1	NE
Nevada	1	0	0	0	1	0	0	0	0	0	0	0	1	0	0	0
North Dakota	0	0	0	0	0	0	0	0	0	0	0	0	0	0	1	0
Oregon	0	0	0	0	0	0	1	0	1	1	0	0	0	0	0	0
Pennsylvania	0	0	0	0	0	0	0	0	1	0	0	0	0	0	0	0
Rhode Island	0	0	0	0	0	0	0	0	0	0	1	0	1	0	0	0
Texas	0	0	0	0	0	0	0	0	1	1	1	0	0	0	0	0
Vermont	0	0	0	0	1	0	0	0	0	0	0	0	1	0	1	0
Washington	0	0	0	0	0	0	0	0	0	0	0	0	0	0	0	0
Wyoming	0	0	0	0	0	0	0	0	1	0	1	0	0	0	0	0
Total	3	1	1	1	5	1	4	0	7	3	11	0	10	3	6	5

R=Ran in Election; W=Won the Election; NE=No election this period.

* Jane Dee Hull became Governor through constitutional succession in September 1997 upon resignation of the previous governor and subsequently won the election by a landslide in 1998.

Source: Center for American Women and Politics. 2000. *National Information Bank on Women in Public Office*, Eagleton Institute of Politics, Rutgers University.

-Women Mayors

The number of women mayors in cities with a population of 30,000 or more rose steadily until 1999 (see Table 10-6). In 1999 the number of women occupying the mayor's office only increased by 1.

Similar to other elected offices considered in this research, the greatest percentage and numerical growth occurs between 1989 and 1993, when the number of female mayors increases to 175 from a previous record high of 112. The vast majority of growth occurred in California. In 1989, there were 26 female mayors, and by 1993 there were 53. Illinois is the only other state that has had more than 10 female mayors (CAWP 2000).

Table 10-6 Women Mayors in Cities over 30,000

State	1981	1985	1989	1993	1997	1999
Alabama	0	0	1	1	2	2
Arizona	1	0	1	1	3	3
Arkansas	0	1	1	1	1	1
California	29	23	26	53	53	57
Colorado	2	3	4	7	9	10
Connecticut	3	3	6	7	6	8
Florida	3	6	6	11	9	9
Georgia	2	0	1	3	3	4
Hawaii	1	0	0	1	2	2
Idaho	0	0	0	0	1	1
Illinois	7	7	4	7	11	8
Indiana	1	1	1	1	2	3
Iowa	0	0	1	0	2	2
Kansas	1	1	0	2	5	4
Kentucky	0	0	1	1	1	1
Louisiana	0	0	0	1	1	1
Maine	1	0	2	0	0	0
Maryland	1	1	0	0	1	1
Massachusetts	3	3	5	5	7	7
Michigan	4	6	7	11	7	5
Minnesota	2	2	0	0	9	5
Missouri	0	2	4	5	1	3
Montana	0	0	1	0	1	1
Nebraska	1	0	0	1	1	1
New Hampshire	0	0	1	0	0	0
Nevada	1	0	1	2	1	1
New Jersey	4	4	3	4	8	8
New Mexico	0	1	0	0	1	1
New York	4	3	5	5	1	5
North Carolina	0	1	1	3	6	4
North Dakota	0	0	0	0	1	1
Ohio	1	1	3	3	8	5
Oklahoma	1	1	0	3	1	1

Table 10-6 (continued)

State	1981	1985	1989	1993	1997	1999
Oregon	0	1	0	4	3	3
Pennsylvania	2	1	5	4	3	3
Rhode Island	0	0	0	1	1	2
South Carolina	0	0	1	2	2	2
Tennessee	0	0	1	0	3	3
Texas	1	4	6	10	7	7
Utah	0	0	0	2	3	3
Virginia	0	0	8	4	3	4
Washington	1	0	3	5	5	5
West Virginia	0	1	0	1	1	1
Wisconsin	2	2	2	3	5	4
Wyoming	0	1	0	0	1	1
Total	79	80	112	175	202	203

Source: Center for American Women and Politics. 2000. *National Information Bank on Women in Public Office*, Eagleton Institute of Politics, Rutgers University. U.S. Bureau of the Census, *Statistical Abstract of the United States*: Washington, D.C. (Various issues). National Conference of Mayors, Washington, D.C.

Regional variations are not significant in this table. The southern region for instance have very few cities with populations above 30,000 during the period of this study. The same can be said for a number of Western and Midwestern states. Thus, the reader should expect to see a small number of mayors in this category regardless of the influence of gender. Nevertheless, Delaware, Mississippi, South Dakota and Vermont did not have a woman serve as mayor in a city with more than 30,000 from 1981-1999. With consideration to the period of this study and the population criterion, we find that twelve states have never had more than one female mayor at any given time (CAWP 2000).

-Committee Chair and Leadership Assignments

The number of women committee chairs is highly correlated with the total number of women in each legislature. However, committee assignments are a function of majority party control. As previously discussed, women Democrats far outnumber women Republicans in state legislatures. In 1999, Democrats controlled twenty-seven of the fifty state legislatures. Tables 10-7 through 10-10 provide the reader with the states that have the highest and lowest percentage of women committee

Table 10-7 States with the Highest Percentage of Women who Chair Committees, 1999 (House and Senate)

State	% Women	State	% Women	State	% Women
Washington	78.8	Vermont	37.0	Arizona	30.6
Colorado	42.9	California	34.4	Nevada	30.0
Maine	41.7	Connecticut	31.1	Kansas	27.4

Source: Center for American Women and Politics (CAWP). 2000. *National Information Bank on Women in Public Office.* Eagleton Institute of Politics, Rutgers University.

chairs and states with the highest and lowest percentage of women in leadership positions.

The data in Table 10-7 shows that Washington has the largest percentage of women chairing committees by far in state legislatures. Concomitantly, the state is ranked number one in the ratio of men to women in the House and Senate combined. Colorado and Maine follow at a distant second and third at 42.9% and 41.7%, respectively. Both states are also in the top quartile of states with large numbers of women legislators. On the one hand, Colorado has a Republican dominated legislature with 19 Republican women. In contrast, Maine has a Democrat-dominated legislature with 34 of the 50 women identifying as Democrats.

Given the results of the data analysis in Table 10-2, it is not surprising to find the south over-represented in states with the lowest percentage of women who chair committees (Table 10-8). The table shows the top nine states that have the smallest percentage of women in chair positions. Six out of the nine states in this category are southern states. Arizona leads the list of southern states with 2.6% of all committee chair assignments in 1999. Mississippi is second at 3.0%. A plausible explanation for why women are not selected/elected to chair positions in Arizona may be due to the partisan split among women. However, Republicans are the majority party in 1999 and the majority of the female legislators are Republican as well.

In 1999, women hold 11.2% of the 338 leadership positions available in state legislatures. They are represented in 9% of the Senate leadership positions (155) and 13.1% of the House leadership positions (183). These positions include majority and minority party leaders, floor leaders, and whips. Table 10-9 shows that Washington also has the

Table 10-8 States with the Lowest Percentage of Women who Chair Committees, 1999 (House and Senate)

State	% Women	State	% Women	State	% Women
Arizona	2.6	South Carolina	3.8	Alabama	8.5
Mississippi	3.0	Louisiana	5.9	Montana	8.6
Tennessee	3.7	Pennsylvania	6.4	Kentucky	9.4

Source: Center for American Women and Politics. 2000. *National Information Bank on Women in Public Office*, Eagleton Institute of Politics, Rutgers University.

highest percent of women in leadership positions followed closely by Connecticut at 42.9%. The difference between the highest ranked state in this category and the ninth ranked state is 27 percentage points. The percent of women in leadership positions drops rather sharply from Connecticut (42.9%) to New Hampshire (37.5%) and continues on a downward trend (Table 10-10).

In fact, twenty-five states have no women in leadership positions. Similar to the data collected on female mayors, we did not expect to find

Table 10-9 States with the Highest Percentage of Women in Leadership Positions, 1999 (House and Senate)

State	% Women	State	% Women	State	% Women
Washington	44.4	Maine	33.3	Wyoming	20.0
Connecticut	42.9	Nevada	28.6	South Carolina	16.7
New Hampshire	37.5	Arizona	25.0	Alaska	16.7

Source: Center for American Women and Politics. 2000. *National Information Bank on Women in Public Office*, Eagleton Institute of Politics, Rutgers University.

Table 10-10 States with the Lowest Percentage of Women in Leadership Positions, 1999 (House and Senate)*

State	% Women	State	% Women	State	% Women
Alabama	0	Connecticut	0	Indiana	0
Arkansas	0	Delaware	0	Kentucky	0
California	0	Georgia	0	Louisiana	0

Note: Maryland, Mississippi, Missouri, Nebraska, New Jersey, New Mexico, North Carolina, North Dakota, Oklahoma, Pennsylvania, South Dakota, Texas, Utah, Vermont, Virginia, and West Virginia have no women in leadership positions.

Source: Center for American Women and Politics. 2000. *National Information Bank on Women in Public Office*, Eagleton Institute of Politics, Rutgers University.

a large percentage of women leaders simply due to the small number of leadership positions. As the number of women in the House and Senate increases, so too does the number of female leaders.

Comparative Case Study Analysis

Mississippi and Vermont are two excellent states to conduct a comparative analysis of female legislative behavior. The most significant reason is the gross differences between the two states. In 2000, Mississippi is ranked 46th, having one of the smallest populations of women in the state legislature. By comparison, Vermont is ranked 7th with a fairly large contingency of women in its General Assembly. This particular disparity not only allows us to compare the legislative behavior of a small contingency of women relative to a larger coalition of women, but also allows us to uncover strategies that women use to succeed in getting legislation passed.

Mississippi is a rural state characterized by a very traditionalistic political culture that emphasizes a strong commitment to the existing social and political order. Vermont has a moralistic culture that stresses community involvement (Elazar 1972). In moralistic cultures, there is a belief that each citizen has an obligation to participate in activities that benefit the common good as a whole without regard to personal status or economic gain (Krane and Shaffer 1992).

The Mississippi legislature meets 125 days immediately following an election and three other periods for 90 days each. The House has a total of 122 members and the Senate has 52 members (4th largest in the U.S.) (Feig 1992). Democrats have more or less controlled the legislature since Reconstruction. Republicans have made some in-roads, but not enough to threaten the balance of power (Feig 1992). Although the number of women in the legislature is small, women and African Americans have made considerable advances into the General Assembly since the Voting Rights Act of 1965 became law (Menifield and Antwi-Bosiako 2000; Menifield and Rudd 2000).

Vermont's legislature has 30 members in its Senate and 150 in the House. The Assembly meets January through late April (16 or 17 weeks). Currently, there are 95 Democrats, 61 Republicans, and 4 Independents in the House. The Senate consists of 17 Democrats and 13 Republicans.

Table 10-11 shows that women make up 13% of the House membership in Mississippi and 31.3% in Vermont in 2000. There are 35 standing committees in the Mississippi House and 3 of those committees have women who serve as chair while 7 women served as vice-chair. The average years of service for women are 7.4 in the Mississippi House. Women Democrats outnumber Republican women by a 3 to 1 margin.

In Vermont, there are 15 standing committees. Four committees have women chairs and 7 had women vice-chairs. All women chairpersons in both houses are members of the Democratic majority. The average years of service in the House are 6.0 years for women. Women Democrats in Vermont also outnumber Republican women in the House 3 to 1 in 2000.

The latter part of the data in Table 10-11 reveals a few similarities and some differences between the two groups in the Senate. First, the percentage of women in the Vermont Senate (33%) is considerably higher than that of the women in the Mississippi General Assembly (11%). The average years of service shift in favor of the female legislative delegation in Vermont by more than two years. Similar to the House, Democrats prevail in both states. There is only one Republican female senator between the two states. Vermont has 6 female committee chairs and 2 vice-chairs, while Mississippi has 5 in each group.

-Bill Sponsorship

Table 10-12 shows the results of the bill sponsorship analysis. As this table illustrates, women in the House in the 1999-2000 legislative session introduced 420 bills with a passage rate of 21%. As mentioned previously, there are three female committee chairpersons among the standing committee chairs, one of which is Mary Ann Stevens who currently chairs the Insurance Committee. Chairman Stevens uses her position and influence to pass a number of insurance-related bills, legislation

Table 10-11 Women Committee Leaders in the Mississippi and Washington General Assemblies, 2000

	# in House	% of House	Av. Serv.	# of Dem.	# of Rep.	# of. Chairs	# of V-Chairs	Tot. # of Standing Comm.
Mississippi	16	13.1	7.4	12	4	3	7	35
Vermont	47	31.3	6.0	34	13	4	7	15

	# in Senate	% of Senate	Av. Serv.	# of Dem.	# of Rep.	# of. Chairs	# of V-Chairs	Tot. # of Standing Comm.
Mississippi	6	11.0	4.2	6	0	5	5	35
Vermont	10	33.0	6.5	9	1	6	2	12

Source. http://www.ls.state.ms.us/. http://www.state.vt.us/.

Table 10-12 Legislative Activity of Women House Members

	1999-2000 Mississippi	1999-2000 Vermont
Bills Introduced	420	274
Bills Passed	89	49
Co-sponsored Bills	55	35
Passage Rate	21%	18%
Number of Women	16 (12% of tot.)	47 (31.7% of tot.)

Source. http://www.state.vt.us/, http://www.ls.state.ms.us/.

strengthening law enforcement practices, and various types of other leg-islation with the support of her male colleagues. She has been quite instrumental in getting several laws that benefit women in general, including policies that enhanced the right of privacy for women. She also proposed a bill requiring liability insurance for all vehicle owners. Thirty-five pieces of legislation that she proposed were passed and signed by the governor, including the bill requiring liability insurance. Fifty-five of the 89 bills introduced by women and subsequently signed by the governor have at least one male co-sponsor. Bills that did not have male co-sponsors were much less likely to pass.

Relatively speaking, women House members in Vermont experi-ence a similar success rate to female legislators in Mississippi. About 18% of the 278 bills introduced were passed into law. However, it must be noted that women in the Vermont legislature make up a much larger proportion of the General Assembly (31.7%) than women in the Mississippi House (12%). A more important consideration was the num-ber of co-sponsored bills. Thirty-five of the 49 bills that were introduced by women had at least one male co-sponsor. These bills passed success-fully and subsequently became law.

When comparing aggregate-level data with data at the individual level, we find that the passage rate for women committee chairs in Mississippi is higher than for those who do not chair committees (Table 10-13). In Vermont, the passage rate is lower among committee chairs even when co-sponsored legislation is considered. However, there is one exception. Kathleen Keenan, who chairs the Committee on Commerce proposed the greatest number of bills among female committee chairs and has the greatest passage rate. It must also be noted that twelve or her fourteen bills that passed had male co-sponsors.

Previous research confirms that committees are not equal. For example, in Mississippi and Vermont, the Appropriations, Rules, and

Ways and Means committees are the most powerful in the House as they are in general. No woman chaired these powerful House committees in Mississippi. However, there are some secondary committees that exhibit quite a bit of influence. The Judiciary B, Banks and Banking, and the Insurance committees are the top second tier committees in the Mississippi House. As noted before, Mary Ann Stevens chairs the Insurance Committee and Diane Peranich serves as vice-chair of the Banks and Banking Committee in 2000. In Vermont, the Committee on Natural Resources and Energy, Judiciary, and Health and Welfare are second tier committees. The Committee on Health and Welfare currently has a women vice-chair (Ann Pugh), and Mary Sullivan chairs the Committee on Natural Resources and Energy. Although Sally Fox chairs the Appropriations Committee in Vermont, the results do not indicate a high success rate for the legislation that she proposed.

-Nature of Legislation Proposed

Mississippi: Given what is commonly known about the poor social and economic conditions that exist in Mississippi, the findings for this section of the analysis are not surprising. The data show that women legislators are mainly concerned with three main areas in 1999: education, law enforcement, and health and welfare (see Table 10-14). Collectively, these three areas are relevant in 37% of the bills proposed by female

Table 10-13 Women House Committee Chairs Bill Sponsorship Data

Mississippi	Bill Introduced	Co-Sponsored*	Passed **
Alyce Clark	30	4	4 (100%)
Eloise Scott	19	11	11 (100%)
Mary Ann Stevens#	95	6	32 (19%)
Vermont			
Sally Fox	6	1	2 (50%)
Mary Sullivan	7	0	0 (0%)
Val Vincent	13	2	4 (50%)
Kathleen Keenan	39	12	14 (86%)

* Co-sponsored with at least one male.
** Percent co-sponsored bills passed.
# Six of the thirty-two bills that passed had women co-sponsors who were chairs or vice-chairs on other committees.

Source. http://www.state.vt.us/, http://www.ls.state.ms.us/.

lawmakers. Although these areas are frequently addressed in most states, Mississippi tends to rank very low on a number of welfare and education-related issues. Most attention is devoted, but not limited to teacher salaries, the escalating number of single female-headed households, the rise in juvenile crime, teenage pregnancy, infant mortality rates, and the burgeoning epidemic of sexually transmitted diseases. Female legislators in Mississippi have proposed various legislative initiatives that seek to combat these social problems. Legislation was especially prominent in the areas that relate to the health and public welfare of children, parents, and retired persons.

In the area of law enforcement, women are mostly concerned with juveniles being housed with adult offenders, punitive drug use measures, and the increasing rise in juvenile delinquency. They proposed education programs both in the public school system and in the criminal justice system to rehabilitate youth and adult offenders. Lastly, there are a number of recognition bills that passed. Recognition bills honor an individual or group for some accomplishment or contribution that benefited the state. With rare exception, this type of legislation almost always passes with a large number of co-sponsors.

Vermont: Previous research suggests that women have traditionally been the champions of social and welfare policies in state legislatures and in Congress (Menifield 1996). Although there may be some validity to this widespread belief, the present research demonstrates that women in the Vermont legislature have very broad interests. However, there are four key areas that appear to be the most important for women: business regulation, education, health and welfare, and natural resources/conservation/environment (see Table 10-14). These four areas comprise 62% of the bills proposed by women in the 1999-2000 legislative session. The high volume of legislation in these areas is a function of two important factors: committee assignments and district location. Based on public opinion indicators, education and health issues top the list of the most important issues in every state. The chair of the Committee on Education (Representative Vincent) and the vice-chair on the Committee on Health and Welfare (Representative Pugh) are women. Representative Keenan and Bratleboro are chair and vice-chair of the Committee on Commerce, respectively. Rep. Sheltra is vice-chair of the Committee on Fish, Wildlife & Water Resources, and Rep.

Table 10-14 Nature of Legislation Proposed by Women House Members in Mississippi and Vermont, 1999-2000

Category	Mississippi	Vermont
Administrative	12	7
Agriculture	0	5
Appropriations	4	3
Boards and Commissions	8	0
Business Regulation	15	24
Child Care	6	2
Civil Rights	1	1
Communication	0	0
Courts/Legal	24	14
Economic and Community Dev.	7	6
Education	47	25
Ethics	2	1
Gambling/Alcohol	1	2
Health Care	23	25
Housing	0	1
Insurance	35	18
International	0	1
Labor	15	18
Law Enforcement	55	19
Licensing	23	9
Local Government	16	18
Nat. Resources/Conservation/Env.	6	29
Public Safety	12	4
Public Utility	1	3
Real Estate	6	1
Recognition	37	3
Suffrage	5	3
Taxation	19	19
Tourism	8	1
Welfare	32	12
Total	420	274

Source. http://www.state.vt.us/, http://www.ls.state.ms.us/.

Sullivan is chair of the Committee on Natural Resources & Energy. Their influential positions allow these women leaders to push their agendas and win important legislative battles.

The type of legislation proposed and passed varied and provides ample evidence that there is an array of interests among women in state legislatures. Among this assortment of legislation includes Representative Alfano of Calais's education bill that would "require the department of education and Vermont public schools to identify and remediate toxic material and indoor air quality problems in Vermont public schools" (H. 192). One controversial bill introduced by Rep. Sheltra would make it a crime to "take the life of a fetus through murder, manslaughter, negligence, battery or assault," (H.357). Rep. Keenan of St. Albans City introduced a number of bills affecting labor, business regulation and the environment. Lastly, bills that addressed women's health care needs and abortion issues are almost exclusively proposed by women (H. 104 and H. 345 respectively).

Following the first-tier issues that included education and health care, second-tier issues that appears to be important to women legislators in Vermont are taxation, local government issues, insurance issues, law enforcement and labor. Between the first- and second-tier, there were quite a few similarities in both states' governmental agendas. This finding suggests that women legislators across the country have similar interests.

Implications and Conclusions

This chapter presents some interesting findings. Overall, the number of women in state and local offices has steadily risen over the last thirty years. This is particularly true at the state level where women make up almost 25% of all state legislatures in 2000. We expect this growth to continue as the diversity in state government increases. In addition, the analysis demonstrates that women tend to identify more often with the Democratic Party than with the Republican Party. This trend predominates at the state level although the number of women who run under the Republican banner has increased in a few states that were historically dominated by Democrats. Not surprisingly, the growth of women legislators in the House of Representatives continues to exceed that of women in the Senate. Southern states consistently have the smallest number and percentage of women legislators in the country. This phenomenon is evident even when chair and vice-chair positions are considered. However, states such as Maine and Washington state legislatures have been very progressive in selecting women for leadership positions.

At the mayoral and gubernatorial levels, we find that the number of women is very small relative to the entire population. However, we admonish the reader to consider several additional limitations of this research before proceeding. First, there are only 50 governors and the number of women seeking this office has continued to decline. Moreover, our mayoral analysis primarily focused on cities that have populations larger than 30,000. Therefore, the total number of cases is drastically limited. Nevertheless, we note that the number of women mayors in California has nearly doubled in the last twenty years.

Our case study analysis also reveals some interesting results. First, we find bill co-sponsorship to be highly correlated with the success of legislation. Specifically, we find that women in both the Mississippi and Vermont legislature are more likely to pass legislation when there is at least one male co-sponsor. Second, we find that a large coalition of women does not necessarily correspond to higher bill passage rates among women. Despite having a much larger contingency of women in the House, Vermont's female legislators are no more successful in passing legislation than their counterparts in Mississippi. Thus, both partisanship and co-sponsorship predominates.

The key to understanding the success of women legislators in these two state legislatures requires an understanding of the committee assignment process. Some female chairs are able to use their position to influence legislation in all areas. This was abundantly true for women in the Mississippi General Assembly and a lot less true for women in the Vermont legislature. In fact, three of the four female chairs in Vermont proposed a total of 26 pieces of legislation and 6 of these bills passed. We find that the lack of a male co-sponsor contributed to this phenomenon. Lastly, we are not surprised to find that women in both state legislatures introduced a large number of bills related to social policy. Legislation that benefit women and children in general is a high priority.

This analysis merely skims the surface for research in the area of women in state legislatures. Without question, additional studies on the subject are needed as the population becomes more diverse. In simpler terms, as the number of women in state and local governments continues to increase, we should likewise expect the bureaucracy to become representative of the broader population. Nevertheless, the political gates are open and women can expect to command a greater presence at all levels of government in the future.

References

Allen, David W. and Diane E. Wall. 1987. "The Behavior of Women State Supreme Court Justices: Are They Tokens or Outsiders?" *The Justice System Journal* 12: 232-245.

Allen, David W. and Diane E. Wall. 1993. "Role Orientations and Women State Supreme Court Justices." *Judicature* 77: 156-165.

Ambrosius, Margery M. and Susan Welch. 1984. "Women and Politics at the Grassroots: Women Candidates for State Office in Three States, 1950-1978." *The Social Science Journal* 21: 29-42.

Anderson, Kristi. 1999. The Gender Gap and Experiences with the Welfare State. *PS: Political Science & Politics* 32: 17-19.

Antolini, Denise. 1984. "Women in Local Government: An Overview." In *Political Women*, ed. Janet Flammang . Beverly Hills, CA: Sage.

Baer, Denise L. 1993. "Political Parties: The Missing Variable in Women and Politics Research." *Political Research Quarterly* 46: 547-76.

Baker, Tod A., Robert P. Steed, and Laurence W. Moreland. 1984. "Gender and Race Among Democratic Party Activists in Two Southern States." *Social Science Quarterly* 65: 1088-1091.

Bamberger, Ruth. 1999. "Sex at Risk in Insurance Classifications? The Supreme Court as Shaper of Public Policy." In *Women in Politics: Outsiders or Insiders?* ed. Lois Duke Whitaker. Upper Saddle River, NJ: Prentice Hall.

Barber, James D. and Barbara Kellerman. 1986. *Women Leaders in American Elections.* Upper Saddle River, NJ: Prentice Hall.

Barrett, Edith J. 1995. "The Policy Priorites of African American Women in State Legislatures." *Legislative Studies Quarterly* 20: 223-48.

Beckwith, Karen. 1986. *American Women and Political Participation.* NY: Greenwood Press.

Binion, Gayle. 1993. "The Nature of Feminist Jurisprudence." *Judicature* 77: 140-43.

Blair, Diane. 1999. "The Handmaid's Tale and the Birth Dearth: Prophecy, Prescription, and Public Policy." In *Women in Politics: Outsiders or Insiders?* ed. Lois Duke Whitaker. Upper Saddle River, NJ: Prentice Hall.

Block, Judy R. 1978. *The First Woman in Congress: Jeanette Rankin.* New York: NY.

Boles, Janet K. 1982. "Building Support for the ERA: A Case of Too Little, Too Late." *PS: Political Science and Politics* 14: 572-77.

_____. 1984. "The Texas Woman in Politics: Role Model or Mirage?" *The Social Science Journal* 21: 79-89.

Borelli, Maryanne. 1997. "Gender, Credibility, and Politics: The Senate Nomination Hearing of Cabinet Secretaries-Designate, 1975 to 1993." *Political Research Quarterly* 50: 171-197.

Brill, Alida. 1995. *A Rising Public Voice: Women in Politics Worldwide.* New York: Feminist Press at the City University of New York.

Bullock, Charles S. and Susan A. MacManus. 1991. "Municipal Electoral Structure and the Election of Councilwomen." *The Journal of Politics* 91: 75-89.

Bullock III, Charles S. and Patricia Heys. 1992. "Recruitment of Women for Congress: A Research Note." *Western Political Quarterly* 25: 416-423.

Burrell, Barbara. 1996. *A Woman's Place is in the House.* Ann Arbor: University of Michigan Press.

_____. 1997. *Public Opinion, The First Ladyship, and Hillary Rodham Clinton.* New York: Garland Publishing.

_____. 1999. "The Governmental Status of the First Lady in Law and in Public Perception." In *Women in Politics: Outsiders or Insiders?* ed. Lois Duke Whitaker. Upper Saddle River, NJ: Prentice Hall.

Caraway, Nancie E. 1999. "The Riddle of Consciousness: Racism and Identity in Feminist Theory." In *Women in Politics: Outsiders or Insiders?* ed. Lois Duke Whitaker. Upper Saddle River, NJ: Prentice Hall.

Caroli, Betty B. 1995. *First Ladies.* New York: Oxford University Press.

Carpini, Michael D. and Ester Fuchs. 1993. "The Year of the Women? Candidates, Votes, and the 1992 Elections." *Political Science Quarterly* 108: 29-36.

Carroll, Susan. 1984. "Women Candidates and Support for Women's Issues: Closet Feminists." *Western Political Quarterly* 37: 307-23.

Carroll, Susan J. 1994. *Women as Candidates in American Politics.* Bloomington: Indiana University Press.

Center for American Women and Politics (CAWP). 2000. *National Information Bank on Women in Public Office*, Eagleton Institute of Politics, Rutgers University.

Christy, Carol A. 1987. *Sex Differences in Political Participation: Process of Change in Fourteen Nations.* New York: Prager.

Cook, Beverly. 1978. "Women Judges: The End of Tokenism." In *Women in the Courts.* eds. Winifred L. Hepperle and Laura Crites. Williamsburg: National Center for State Courts.

_____. 1980a. "Women Judges and Public Policy in Sex Integration." In *Women in Local Politics.* ed. D. Steward. Metuchen, N.J.: Scarecrow Press.

_____. 1980b. "Will Women Judges Make a Difference in Women's Legal Rights? A Prediction for Attitudes and Simulated Behavior." In *Women, Power and Political Systems*. eds. M. Rendel and G. Ainsworth. London: Croom Helm.

_____. 1984. "Women Judges: A Preface to Their History." *Golden Gate University Law Review* 14: 572-609.

Cook, Elizabeth A. and Clyde Wilcox. 1991. "Feminism and the Gender Gap— A Second Look." *The Journal of Politics* 53: 1111-1122.

Conway, Jill K., Susan C. Bourque and Joan W. Scott (eds). 1987. *Learning About Women: Gender, Politics and Power*. Ann Arbor: University of Michigan Press.

Conway, Ahern and Steuernagel 1999. "Rethinking Pink and Blue: Gender, Occupational Stratification and Political Attitudes." In *Women in Politics: Outsiders or Insiders?* ed. Lois Duke Whitaker. Upper Saddle River, NJ: Prentice Hall.

Conover, Pamela J. 1988. "Feminists and the Gender Gap." *The Journal of Politics* 50: 985-1010.

Darcy, R. Susan Welch and Janet Clark. 1987. *Women, Elections and Representation*. New York: Longman.

Darcy, R. and Charles D. Hadley. 1988. "Black Women in Politics: The Puzzle of Success." *Social Science Quarterly* 69: 629-45.

Dodson, Debra L. 1991. *Gender and Policymaking: Studies of Women in Office*. Rutgers University: Center for the American Woman and Politics.

Dodson, Debra L. and Susan J. Carroll. 1991. *Reshaping the Agenda: Women in State Legislatures*. Rutgers University: Center for the American Woman and Politics.

Dolan, Julie. 1997. "Support For Women's Interest in the 103rd Congress: The District Impact of Congressional Women." *Women and Politics* 18: 81-94.

Elazar, Daniel. 1972. *American Federalism: A View From the States*. 2d ed. New York: Thomas Y. Crowell Co.

Feig, Douglas G. 1992. "The State Legislature: Representatives of the People or the Powerful?" In *Mississippi Government and Politics*. eds. Dale Krane and Stephen D. Shaffer. Lincoln, University of Nebraska Press.

Ford, Lynn E. and Kathleen Dolan. 1999. "Women State Legislators: Three Decades of Gains in Representation and Diversity." In *Women in Politics: Outsiders or Insiders?* ed. Lois Duke Whitaker. Upper Saddle River, NJ: Prentice Hall.

Fowler, Linda L. 1993. *Candidates, Congress, and the American Democracy*. Ann Arbor: University of Michigan Press.

Frankovic, Kathleen A. 1999. "Why the Gender Gap Became News in 1996." *PS: Political Science & Politics* 32: 20-22.

Fraser, Nancy. 1987. "What's Critical about Critical Theory?" *In Feminism as Critique*, ed. Seyla Benhabib and Drucilla Cornell. Minneapolis: University of Minnesota Press.

Freidan, Betty. 1963. *The Feminine Mystique.* New York: Norton.

Freeman, Jo. 1989. "Feminist Activities at the 1988 Republican Convention." *PS: Political Science and Politics* 22: 39-47.

Gelb, Joyce. 1989. *Feminism and Politics.* Berkeley: University of California Press.

Gelb, Joyce and Marian L. Palley. 1982. *Women and Public Policies.* Princeton, NJ: Princeton University Press.

Gertzog, Irvin N. 1994. *Congressional Women: Their Recruitment, Treatment, and Behavior.* NY: Praeger Publishers.

Giele, Janet Z. and Audrey C. Smock. 1977. *Women: Roles and Status in Eight Countries.* New York: Wiley.

Goldstein, Leslie F. 1979. *The Constitutional Rights of Women: Cases in Law and Social Change.* New York: Longman.

Green, Joanne C. 1998. "The Role of Gender in Open-Seat Elections for the U.S. House of Representatives: A District Level Test For A Differential Value for Campaign Resources." *Women and Politics* 19: 33-55.

Grimes, Ann. 1990. *The Making of the First Ladies.* New York: Morrow Publishing.

Gruberg, Martin. 1984. "From Nowhere to Where? Women in State and Local Politics." *The Social Science Journal* 21: 29-42.

Gryski, Gerard S., Eleanor C. Main, and William J. Dixon. 1986. "Models of State High Court Decision Making in Sex Discrimination Cases." *The Journal of Politics* 48: 143-55.

Havens, Catherine M. and Lynne M. Healy 1991. "Do Women Make a Difference." *The Journal of State Government* 64: 63-67.

Hawks, Joanne V. and Carolyn Ellis Staton. 1999. "On the Eve of Transition: Women in Southern Legislatures, 1946-1968." In *Women in Politics: Outsiders or Insiders?* ed. Lois Duke Whitaker. Upper Saddle River, NJ: Prentice Hall.

Herrick, Rebeka and Almira Sapieva. 1997. "Perceptions of Women Politicians in Kazakhstan." *Women and Politics* 18: 27-40.

Hewitt, W.E. 2000. "The Political Dimensions of Women's Participation in Brazil's Base Christian Communities (CENs): A Longitudinal Case Study from Sao Paulo." *Women and Politics* 1: 1-26.

High-Pippert, and John Comer. 1998. "Angela Female Empowerment: The Influence of Women Representing Women." *Women & Politics* 19: 53-66.

Hirschmann, Nancy J. and Christine Di Stefano (eds). 1996. *Revisioning the Political: Feminist Reconstructions of Traditional Concepts in Western Political Theory.* Boulder, CO: Westview Press.

Iannello, Kathleen P. 1999. "Anarchist Feminism and Student Power: Is This Any Way to Run a Women's Studies Program?" In *Women in Politics: Outsiders or Insiders?* ed. Lois Duke Whitaker. Upper Saddle River, NJ: Prentice Hall.

Jaggar, Alison M. 1983. *Feminist Politics and Human Nature.* Totowa, N.J.: Rowman and Littlefield.

Jewell, Malcolm and Marcia L. Whicker. 1993. "The Feminization of Leadership in State Legislatures." *PS: Political Science and Politics* 26: 705-12.

Johnson, Roberta A. 1999. "Affirmative Action and Women. In *Women in Politics: Outsiders or Insiders?*" ed. Lois Duke Whitaker. Upper Saddle River, NJ: Prentice Hall.

Jones, Kathleen B. and Anna G. Jonasdottir (eds). 1988. *The Political Interest of Gender: Developing Theory and Research With a Feminist Face.* Newbury Park: Sage Publications.

Joy, James. 1999. "Radicalising Feminism." *Race and Class* 40: 15-31.

Kahn, Kim F. 1994. "Does Gender Make a Difference? An Experimental Examination of Sex Stereotypes and Press Patterns in Statewide Campaigns." *American Journal of Political Science* 38: 162-195.

_____. 1994. "The Distorted Mirror: Press Coverage of Women Candidates for Statewide Office." *The Journal of Politics* 56: 154-173.

Kahn, Kim F. and Edie N. Goldenberg. 1991. "Women Candidates in the News: An Examination of Gender Differences in U.S. Senate Campaign Coverage." *The Public Opinion Quarterly* 55: 180-199.

Kaufman, Karen M. and John R. Petrocik. 1999. "The Changing Politics of American Men: Understanding the Sources of the Gender Gap." *American Journal of Political Science* 43: 864-87.

Kelly, Elizabeth. 1999. "Grounds for Criticism: Coffee, Passion, and the Politics of Feminist Discourse." In *Women in Politics: Outsiders or Insiders?* ed. Lois Duke Whitaker. Upper Saddle River, NJ: Prentice Hall.

Kolb, Deborah M. and Gloria C. Coolidge. 1991. "Her Place at the Table." *The Journal of State Government* 64: 68-71.

Krane, Dale and Stephen D. Shaffer. 1992. "Culture and Politics in Mississippi: It's Not Just Black and White." In *Mississippi Government and Politics.*

eds. Dale Krane and Stephen D. Shaffer. Lincoln: University of Nebraska Press.

Lewis, Carolyn V. 1999. "Are Women For Women? Feminist and Traditional Values in the Female Electorate." *Women and Politics* 20: 1-28.

Liston, Robert A. 1978. *Women Who Ruled: Cleopatra to Elizabeth II*. New York: J. Messner.

MacManus, Susan A., Charles S. Bullock III., Frances E. Atkins, Laura J. Hoffman, and Adam Newmark. 1999. "'Winning in My Own Backyard': County Government, School Board Positions Steadily More Attractive to Women Candidates." In *Women in Politics: Outsiders or Insiders?* ed. Lois Duke Whitaker. Upper Saddle River, NJ: Prentice Hall.

Mandel, Ruth B. 1981. *In the Running: The New Woman Candidate*. NY: Ticknor & Fields.

Mansbridge, Jane. 1986. *Why We Lost the ERA?* IL: University of Chicago Press.

Mansbridge, Jane. 1999. "Should Blacks Represent Blacks and Women Represent Women? A Contingent" Yes." *The Journal of Politics* 61: 628-57.

Manza, Jeff., and Clem Brooks. 1998. "The Gender Gap in U.S. Presidential Elections: When? Why? Implications?" *American Journal of Sociology* 103: 1235-66.

Martin, Elaine. 1993. "The Representative Role of Women Judges." *Judicature* 77: 166-73.

_____. 1999. "Women Judges: The New Generation." In *Women in Politics: Outsiders or Insiders?* ed. Lois Duke Whitaker. Upper Saddle River, NJ: Prentice Hall.

Mattei, Laura R.W. 1998. "Gender and Power in American Legislative Discourse." *The Journal of Politics* 60: 440-61.

Matland, Richard E. and Deborah D. Brown. 1992. "District Magnitude's Effect on Female Representation in U.S. State Legislatures." *Legislative Studies Quarterly* 16: 469-92.

Menifield, Charles E. 1996. *Influence on Minority Groups in Congress: The Black, Women's Issues and Hispanic Caucuses*. Unpublished Doctoral Dissertation: University of Missouri.

Menifield, Charles E. and Kwame Badu Antwi-Bosiako. 2000. "African American Legislators in the Mississippi General Assembly: A Historical Analysis." In *MS Votes*. ed. Charles E. Menifield. John C. Stennis Institute of Government: Mississippi State University.

Menifield, Charles E. and Kiffany Rudd. 2000. "Women in the Mississippi

Legislature: A Historical Analysis." In *MS Votes*. ed. Charles E. Menifield. John C. Stennis Institute of Government: Mississippi State University.

Mettler, Suzzanne. 2000. "State's Rights, Women's Obligations: Contemporary Welfare Reform in Historical Perspective." *Women and Politics* 21: 1-34.

Mezey, Susan G. 1978. "Does Sex Make a Difference? A Case Study of Women in Politics." *Western Political Quarterly* 31: 492-501.

Moncrief, Gary F. and Joel A. Thompson. 1992. "Electoral Structure and State Legislative Representation: A Research Note." *The Journal of Politics* 54: 246-56.

Murphy, Patricia. 1997. "Domestic Violence Legislation and the Police: The Role of Socio-Economic Indicators, Political Factors and Women's Political Activism on State Policy Adoption." *Women and Politics* 18: 27-53.

Newland, Kathleen. 1975. *Women in Politics: A Global View*. Washington: World Watch.

Niven, David. 1998. "Party Elites and Women Candidates: The Shape of Bias." *Women and Politics* 19: 57-80.

Norrander, Barbara. 1997. "The Independence Gap and the Gender Gap." *The Public Opinion Quarterly* 61: 464-76.

Norris, Pippa. 1987. *Politics and Sexual Equality: The Comparative Position of Women in Western Democracies*. Boulder: Rienner.

O'Connor, Karen. 1996. "Wives in the White House: The Political Influence of First Ladies." *Presidential Studies Quarterly* 26: 835-53.

O'Connor, Karen and Patricia Clark. 1999. "Women's Rights and Legal Wrongs: The U.S. Supreme Court and Sex Discrimination." In *Women in Politics: Outsiders or Insiders?* ed. Lois Duke Whitaker. Upper Saddle River, NJ: Prentice Hall.

Overby, Marvin and Beth M. Henschen. 1994. "Race trumps Gender? Women, African Americans, and the Senate Confirmation of Justice Clarence Thomas." *American Politics Quarterly* 22: 62-73.

Paddock, Joel. and Elizabeth Paddock. 1997. "Differences in Partisan Style and Ideology Between Female and Male State Party Committee Members." *Women and Politics* 18: 41-56.

Palley, Marian L. and Howard A. Palley. 2000. "Rethinking a Women's Health Care Agenda." *Women and Politics* 21: 75-99.

Paxton, Annabel. 1945. *Women in Congress*. Richmond, VA: The Deitz Press.

Poole, Keith T. and L. Harmon Zeigler. 1985. *Women, Public Opinion, and Politics.: The Changing Political Attitudes of American Women*. NY:

Longman.

Prestage, Jewel L. 1987. "Black Women Judges: An Examination of Their Socio-economic, Educational and Political Backgrounds, and Judicial Placements." In *Readings in American Political Issues.* eds. Franklin D. Jones and Michael O. Adams. Dubuque, IA: Kendall Hunt.

Prindell, Diane-Michelle, and Teresa B. Gomez. 1999. "American Indian Women Leaders, Public Policy, and the Importance of Gender and Ethnic Identity." *Women and Politics* 20: 17-32.

Rausch, Jr. John D., Mark J. Rozell and Harry L. Wilson. 1999. "When Women Lose: A Study of Media Coverage of Two Gubernatorial Campaigns." *Women and Politics* 20: 1-21.

Reid, Magaret, Brinck Kerr and William H. Miller. 2000. "A Study of the Advancement of Women in Municipal Government Bureaucracies: Persistence of Glass Ceilings?" *Women and Politics* 21: 35-53.

Reid, Tracy. 2000. "The Role of Gender in Judicial Campaigns: North Carolina Trial Court Races." *Southeastern Political Review* 28: 551-76.

Reynolds, Andrew. 1999. "Women in the Legislatures and Executives of the World: Knocking at the Highest Glass Ceiling." *World Politics* 51: 547-72.

Rudy, Kathy. 1999. "Liberal Theory and Feminist Politics." *Women and Politics* 20: 33-57.

Rosenthal, Cindy S. 1995. "The Role of Gender in Descriptive Representation." *Political Research Quarterly* 48: 599-611.

Rozell, Mark J. and Clyde Wilcox. 1998. "A GOP Gender Gap? Motivations, Policy, and Candidate Choice." *Women and Politics* 19: 91-106.

Rule, Wilma. 1999. "Why Are More Women Legislators?" In *Women in Politics: Outsiders or Insiders?* ed. Lois Duke Whitaker. Upper Saddle River, NJ: Prentice Hall.

Sainsbury, Diane. 1999. "Beyond the "Great Divide: Women in Partisan Politics Before and After the Federal Suffrage Amendment." *Women and Politics* 20: 59-80.

Sapiro, Virginia. 1981. "Research Frontier Essay: When are Interests Interesting? The Problem of Political Representation of Women." *The American Political Science Review* 75: 701-716.

Sapiro, Virginia. Pamela J. Conover. 1997. "The Variable Gender Basis of Electoral Politics: Gender and Context in the 1992 U.S. Election." *British Journal of Political Science* 27: 497-523.

Scharrer, Erica and Kim Bissell. 2000. "Overcoming Traditional Boundaries: The Roles of Political Activity in Media Coverage of First Ladies."

Women and Politics 21: 55-83.

Seligman, Lester. 1961. "Political Recruitment and Party Structures: A Case Study." *American Political Science Review* 60: 77-86.

Sharratt, Sara and Ellyn Kaschak. 1999. *Women in the Former Yugoslavia*. Binghamton, NY: The Haworth Press.

Sigel, Roberta. 1999. "Gender and Voting Behavior I the 1996 Presidential Election: An Introduction." *PS: Political Science & Politics* 32: 4-6.

Swain, Carol M. 1997. "Women and Blacks in Congress: 1870-1996." In *Congress Reconsidered*. eds. Lawrence C. Dodd and Bruce I. Oppenheimer. Washington, D.C: CQ Press.

Sylvester, Christine. 1994. *Feminist Theory and International Relations in a Postmodern Era*. New York: Cambridge University Press.

Thomas, Sue. 1991. "The Impact of Women on State Legislative Policies." *Journal of Politics* 53: 958-976.

Thomas, Sue and Susan Welch. 1991. "The Impact of Gender on Activities and Priorities of State Legislators." *Western Political Quarterly* 44: 445-56.

Thomas, Sue. 1994. *How Women Legislate*. New York: Oxford University Press.

Thompson, Joan H. 1999. "The Family and Medical Leave Act: A Policy for Families. In *Women in Politics: Outsiders or Insiders?*" ed. Lois Duke Whitaker. Upper Saddle River, NJ: Prentice Hall.

Tien, Checchio, and Miller 1999. "The Impact of First Wives on Presidential Campaigns And Elections." In *Women in Politics: Outsiders or Insiders?* ed. Lois Duke Whitaker. Upper Saddle River, NJ: Prentice Hall.

Tripp, Aili Mari. 1999. *Women and politics in Uganda*. Aili Mari Tripp. Madison: University of Wisconsin Press.

Uhlaner, Carole J. and Kay L. Schlozman. 1986. "Candidate Gender and Congressional Campaign Receipts." *The Journal of Politics* 48: 30-50.

Vega, Arturo and Juanita Firestone. 1995. "The Effects of Gender on Congressional Behavior and the Substantive Representation of Women." *Legislative Studies Quarterly* 20: 213-22.

Verba, Sidney, Nancy Burns, Kay L. Schlozman. 1997. "Knowing and Caring About Politics: Gender and Political Engagement." *The Journal of Politics* 59: 1051-72.

Wall, Diane E. 2000. "A Woman of Many 'Firsts': The Honorable Lenore Prather." *Southeastern Political Review* 28: 531-50.

Weir, Sara J. 1999. "The Feminist Face of State Executive Leadership: Women as Governors." In *Women in Politics: Outsiders or Insiders?* ed. Lois Duke Whitaker. Upper Saddle River, NJ: Prentice Hall.

Welch, Susan and Albert Karnig. 1979. "Sex and Ethnic Differences in

Municipal Representation." *Social Science Quarterly* 60: 465-81.

Welch, Susan. and Donley T. Studlar. 1986. "British Public Opinion Toward Women in Politics: A Comparative Perspective." *Western Political Quarterly* 39: 138-54.

Welch, Susan and Donley T. Studlar. 1990. "Multi-member Districts and the Representation of Women: Evidence From Britain and the United States." *The Journal of Politics* 52: 391-412.

Whicker, Marcia L. and Hedy L. Issacs 1999. "The Maleness of the American Presidency. In *Women in Politics: Outsiders or Insiders?"* ed. Lois Duke Whitaker. Upper Saddle River, NJ: Prentice Hall.

Whicker, Marcia L. and Lois D. Whitaker 1999. "Women in Congress. In *Women in Politics: Outsiders or Insiders?"* ed. Lois Duke Whitaker. Upper Saddle River, NJ: Prentice Hall.

Whistler, Donald E. and Mark C. Ellickson. 1999. "The Incorporation of Women in State Legislatures: A Description." *Women and Politics* 20: 81-97.

Wilcox, Clyde. 1989. "Feminism and Anti-feminism Among Evangelical Women." *The Western Political Quarterly* 42: 147-60.

Wilhite, Allen and John Theilmann. 1986. "Women, Blacks and PAC Discrimination." *Social Science Quarterly* 67: 283-98.

Wright, Erik O. 1989. "Women in the Class Structure." *Politics and Society* 17: 35-66.

Notes

1 The authors wish to thank Demecher Ware and Leslie E. Taylor, former graduate students at Mississippi State University, and Kiffany Rudd, a former undergraduate political science major at Mississippi State University for their data entry skills.

CHAPTER 11

Hispanics Representation in State and Local Governments

Charles E. Menifield

According to the U.S. Bureau of the Census, in roughly ten years (2010), Hispanics[1] will become the largest minority group in the United States[2] (Pachon and DeSipio 1992; Affigne 2000). Hispanic growth is centered in the west and southwest (Moore and Pachon 1985). The implications of this growth pattern will have a tremendous affect on the political process at each level of government. The main purpose of this chapter is to document the growth and substantive ability of Hispanic representatives in state and local governments up to the close of the twentieth century and to evaluate how current behavioral patterns are likely to affect future representation issues.

Unlike African Americans, archival data for all Hispanic Elected Officials (HEOs) are not readily available prior to 1985. Past representation is important in this type of research, but it is not the central focus of this study. Although there are some similarities between the political behavior and ideology of Hispanics and African Americans, there are some significant differences. Namely, political participation. This difference takes a paramount position in this study because it will ultimately determine whether Hispanic citizens will be able to use their growth pattern to substantially benefit themselves in the future (Radelat 2000).

First, a review of the political participation literature is provided. This section first examines participation in general and then moves on to specific pieces of literature that examine Hispanic behavior. The ideas espoused in this literature serve as the foundation upon which the subsequent substantive arguments are based.

Second, the descriptive analysis begins by examining the political behavior of Hispanics since 1972. Next, descriptive data are provided for Hispanics at the state and local level. Hispanic leadership on committees and within political parties during the 1999-2000 legislative sessions in Arizona, California, Florida, New Mexico, New York and Texas are considered. These states currently have the largest Hispanic populations (as a percentage of the entire population) as well as the most Hispanic state legislators.

Lastly, the analysis considers the formation of legislative caucuses at the state level. According to Marquez and Jennings (2000), one of the major obstacles to Latino political activity is the lack of a mobilizing agent. This section examines the partisan makeup of these caucuses, organizational structure and mission. The objective of this section is to determine whether these groups seek to mobilize and represent Hispanic citizens.

Political Participation

Most political scholars would agree that political participation is one of the key elements of power. Studies have proliferated seeking to explain participation from a number of different angles: voter characteristics, political parties, mobilization and contextual factors. For the most part, previous scholarly studies showed that citizens who were in the highest economic strata were much more likely to participate in politics. When education, income or occupation were used to define social status, this generalization appears to consistently hold true (Campbell, Converse, Miller and Stokes 1960; Verba and Nie 1972; Cassel and Hill 1981; Leighley and Nagler 1992).

One of the best efforts to explain voter turnout was the socioeconomic model proposed by Verba and Nie (1972). As they described this model:

> ...the social status of an individual—his job, education, and income—determines to a large extent how much he participates. It does this through the intervening effects of a variety of civic attitudes conducive to participation: attitudes such as a sense of efficacy, of psychological involvement in politics, and a feeling of obligation to participate (13).

Those in the higher economic strata can be furthered separated by another set of variables: homeownership, marital status, and age (Lewis, McCracken and Hunt 1994). Leighley and Nagler (1992) found that demographic factors such as race and gender were important variables in voter turnout models, but education was the more reliable predictor of voter turnout in general (Montonya, Hardy-Fanta, and Garcia 2000). However, Wolfinger (1994) found that the role of income did not change dramatically when age and education were considered. Further, Wolfinger and Rosenstone (1980) posit that marital status influenced participation. Married women and men were much more likely to participate than single persons were. Again, age played a significant role in their model.

Arvizu and Garcia (1996) found in their study of Latino participation in 1988 that education did not appear to uniformly explain turnout rates when specific groups were analyzed. While the socioeconomic class variable was affected by a generation gap, "employment status, or the lack of employment for Mexican, Puerto Rican, and to a lesser degree, Cuban cohorts, was negatively correlated with turnout" (p. 115). Overall, they found that age was the most salient variable in explaining turnout in the 1988 election based on the data in the Latino National Political Survey (LNPS). This variable was followed by years in the U.S., home ownership and education in terms of explanatory power.

Bass and Casper (1999) argued that nativity and country of origin were important variables in models predicting voting behavior (Blank 1974; Conway 1991; Jewell and Olson 1988; Inglehart 1997). Using the most recent Census data, they found that income, education, employment status, home ownership, residential longevity, employment level (professional v. non-professional), gender, race and marital status to be the key determinants in assessing voter behavior. Specifically, they found that native born citizens were more likely to register and vote than naturalized citizens were. Citizens who were born in the U.S. were much more likely to register and vote than those who were born in Europe, Asia, and Latin America were. Age, education, income and residential longevity were key components in predicting naturalized residents registration and voting patterns (Sierrra, Carrillo, DeSipio, and Jones-Correa 2000). Interestingly, region of origin was not related to registration or voting patterns when length of time in the U.S. was placed in the model (Falcon 1988; Moreno and Warren 1992; Garcia 1997). Moore and Pachon (1985) argued that deprivation might impact political participation among immigrants. "Cuban Americans who escaped a repressive regime in Cuba may view the political world of the United States quite differently from a Mexican-American political activist born and reared in the barrio who can trace generations of his family caught in the same environment" (p. 174).

Squire, Wolfinger, and Glass (1987) considered residential mobility relative to registration and voting behavior patterns and found that movers resemble stayers on motivational factors related to voting and that this outcome remains apart from other socioeconomic and demographic factors. However, the requirement that they register to vote for a second time when they move was a key obstacle for future registration (Gilliam 1985; Paterson and Caldeira 1983). Residential longevity was a very important variable in voter turnout studies in the U.S. because 16% of all Americans move every year (Hansen 1997).

Pachon and DeSipio (1992) noted in their study of Hispanic citizens that age was an important variable. Most Hispanic citizens were not old enough to vote and among those who were left, a large percentage did not vote. As a result, policy makers were somewhat ambivalent and unresponsive to their needs. Browning, Marshall, and Tabb (1984) conducted a regional study validating this statement. In their analysis of ten Northern California cities, they found that Hispanics were not only underrepresented in government, but despite making up more than 10% of the overall population, the governments were unresponsive to their needs.

Hero (1989a; 1990) conducted a similar analysis in two Colorado cities, Pueblo and Denver, and found some correlations and additional findings to Browning, Marshall and Tabb (1984). First, the structure of the government affects the varying levels of political mobilization. Unlike the ten California cities and Pueblo, political mobilization appeared to be higher in Denver. One central factor affecting mobilization was the fact that the city had a Hispanic mayor that had been in office since 1983 (Hero 1989b; see also Vigil 1984; Mansbridge 1999). As a result, the city seemed to be more responsive to the needs of Hispanic residents.

Others suggested that the political experience of Latinos was not universal and that behavior can vary dramatically when different regions and states were examined (Blank 1974; Garcia and de la Garza 1977). Michelson's (2000) study of political efficacy among Chicago Latinos revealed that Latinos do not exhibit the same pattern of internal or external efficacy as Anglos. Latinos felt that their political reality was one of high empowerment and voting was more of a symbolic act. Hence, they had a lower score on the internal efficacy variable and a higher score on one of the external efficacy variables.

Using the LNPS data set, Diaz (1996) found that organization membership had a strong impact on Latino political participation. This was particularly true among Mexican and Puerto Rican Americans who generally display low rates of political participation (see Moore and Pachon 1985, chapter 10). Turnout and registration rates did not appear to increase during presidential election years when the rates increased for the entire population. Using data from California, Florida and Texas, Shaw, de la Garza, and Lee (2000) studied Latino turnout in the 1996 presidential election and found that mobilization efforts were a very important factor in eliminating the turnout gap among the Latino population (see also Wrinkle, Stewart, and Polinard 1996). In addition, other factors such as income and age appear to play significant roles in the lack of participation. Most interesting though was that they found that a large percentage of those claiming to have been registered were in fact not registered and subsequently did not participate in the election. Their perception was that this group will be the key constituency for future mobilization efforts. Once mobilized, the group will be an effective asset for potential candidates (see also Tostado 1985). Most recently, Hritzuk and Park (2000) found that social structural variables including integration into politically active social networks, exposure to mobilization, and organization affiliation increased the likelihood that Latinos will participate in government (see also Abalos 1986; Mejias 1999; Marquez and Jennings 2000).

According to Casper and Bass (1998), using data obtained from the Current Population Survey, 20.4% of the Hispanic population indicated that they did not vote in the 1996 elections because they were too busy or did not have the time, while 14.4% indicated that they were not interested (see also DeSipio 1996). These percentages were actually lower than both African and White Americans. The Other Reasons category appeared to make up the difference between the three groups.

Hero and Campbell (1996) found using the LNPS data that Latinos were much less likely than other groups to participate in non-election functions such as attending rallies, signing petitions and volunteering to assist a candidate. Mexican and Puerto Rican Americans are more likely than Cuban Americans to get involved in these type of activities. Garcia and de la Garza (1985) did however find that Latinos were twice as likely to be involved in protest activities when compared to others (see Hero, Garcia, Garcia and Pachon (2000) for an excellent exposition on Hispanic political participation).

Data Analysis

The first table (11-1) shows the states with the largest Hispanic populations and Hispanic representatives in their general assemblies in 1999. As seen, New Mexico had the largest Hispanic population at 40.7% followed by California and Texas respectively. The number of Hispanic representatives more or less followed the same trend. As the percentage of Hispanic citizens increased so did the percentage of Hispanic representatives in the general assembly. New Mexico's General Assembly was 37% Hispanic in 1999. Nevada had the smallest number in this category at .02%.

These numbers were a bit deceiving. According to Pachon and DeSipio (1992), in the early 1990s, approximately 35% of the Latino population was under the age of 18 and in 1980, only two in three Latinos was a U.S. citizen (see also Baker 1996). These figures have not only caused many problems in calculating accurately Latino turnout and registration, but also problems for candidates seeking office.

For non-western and southwestern states, the geographical location of Hispanics changes quite a bit. For the three states with the largest percentage of Hispanics, they can be found more or less in every corner of the states. However, in Illinois, New Jersey, New York, and Florida, the larger concentration of Hispanic citizens tend to be found in the larger cities or specific regions of the state, despite an increasing number of

Table 11-1 States with the Largest Hispanic Populations (1999)

State	% Hispanic Pop.	Tot. # of Leg.	Hispanic Rep.	% Hispanic Rep.
Arizona	22.7%	90	11	12%
California	31.6	120	24	20
Colorado	14.9	100	9	9
Florida	15.4	160	14	9
Illinois	10.5	177	6	3
New Jersey	12.6	120	4	3
New Mexico	40.7	112	41	37
New York	14.6	211	12	6
Nevada	16.8	63	1	.02
Texas	30.2	181	35	19%

Source: Http://www.census.gov/population/estimates/state/rank/hisp.txt.

Table 11-2 Hispanic Voter Registration and Turnout

	Registration	Turnout
1998	33.7	20.0
1996	26.7	35.7
1992	28.9	35.0
1988	28.8	35.5
1984	32.6	40.1
1980	29.9	36.3
1976	31.8	37.8
1972	37.5	44.4%

Source: Day, Jennifer C. and Avalaura L. Gaither. 2000. "Voting and Registration in the Election of November 1998." U.S. Census Bureau. Washington D.C.

them working in the agricultural sector. In Florida for example, the vast majority of Hispanics are found in the southern region of the state. The same is true for New York City, and Chicago (Moore and Pachon 1985).

Table 11-2 shows Hispanic voter registration and turnout rates from 1972-1998. The table shows that both registration and turnout rates have declined over the entire period of this analysis. The one exception was 1998 when registration increased by 7 percentage points. However, the turnout rate dropped by 15 percentage points from the previous election. Although the Voting Rights Act of 1965 was not directed toward Hispanic citizens, they have in fact benefited from the legislation. Prior to 1965, Hispanic registration and turnout rates were comparable to those of African Americans (Menifield and Julian 1998) (For a detailed account of the affects of the Voting Rights Act of 1965 on the Latino community, see Garcia 1986; de la Garza and DeSipio 1993).

Instead of centering the analysis on the aggregate, Table 11-3 examines the nine states that have the largest percentage of Hispanic citizens relative to the entire population in the state. As seen, the registration and voting rates of Hispanics were not the same across states. In 1998, Hispanics in New Mexico had the highest voter registration levels among these states at 51.5%. Colorado followed New Mexico at 47.2%. At the other end of the spectrum, the table showed that Arizona and California Hispanics had the lowest registration levels at 25.2% and 27.9% respectively.

Voter turnout levels dropped precipitously from the existing low registration levels. Again, the Hispanic citizens in New Mexico had the highest levels of voter turnout at 39.3%. No other state was really close

Table 11-3 Voting Behavior of Hispanics by States with
Significant Hispanic Representation (1998 data)

	U.S. Registered	U.S. Voted	Hispanic Registered	Hispanic Voted
Arizona	51.1%	33.8%	25.2%	14.7
California	52.1	40.5	27.9	21.4
Colorado	68.5	52.1	47.2	28.4
Florida	59.0	39.0	35.8	22.9
Illinois	63.9	44.5	30.3	20.7
New Jersey	60.1	35.5	42.1	23.4
New Mexico	60.4	48.2	51.5	39.3
New York	57.0	42.4	35.2	23.4
Texas	59.0	32.9	39.7	15.3
U.S. Average	62.1%	41.9%	33.7%	20.0%

Source: U.S. Bureau of the Census. 2000.
Http://www.census.gov/population/socdemo/voting/cps1998/tab04.

to that level. Colorado was the closest at 28.4%. Arizona and Texas round out the bottom levels at 14.7% and 15.3% respectively. When compared to the U.S. average and individual states, Hispanic registration and voter turnout rates were very low. The U.S. average was 62.1% for registration and 41.9% for voter turnout while the Hispanic rates were 33.7% for registration and 20.0% for voter turnout in the entire nation. With a couple of exceptions, Hispanic voting behavior within states followed a consistent pattern with the overall behavior of the state. When a state had low registration and turnout levels, Hispanics had lower registration and turnout levels. When the state had a higher rate, so did the Hispanic population. The one exception was the Hispanics in Illinois.

Descriptive Statistics

The number of Hispanic elected officials at the state and local level continued to increase over the period of this study. This growth was not limited to any particular region, state or level of position (Table 11-4). In 1985, the number of state level executives and state legislators was 119. By 1994, that number increased to 199. State executives include the attorney general, auditor, treasure, etc. This group made up the smallest numerical group of the four groups that were included in this analysis. Judicial and Law Enforcement officials followed the State Executives and Legislators group.

Table 11-4 Hispanic State Officials by Year

	St. Executives, and St. Leg.	County and Municipal	Judicial and Law Enforcement	Education and School Board	Total
1994	199	2,197	651	2,412	5,459
1993	182	2,023	633	2,332	5,170
1992	150	1,908	628	2,308	4,994
1991	151	1,867	596	1,588	4,202
1990	144	1,819	583	1,458	4,004
1989	143	1,724	575	1,341	3,783
1988	135	1,425	574	1,226	3,360
1987	138	1,412	568	1,199	3,317
1986	132	1,352	530	1,188	3,202
1985	119	1,316	517	1,185	3,147

Source: Http://www.census.gov/prod/99pubs/99statab/sec08.pdf.

The most rapid growth occurred at the education and school board level where the number of officials have grown from 1,185 in 1985 to 2,412 in 1994. This was not surprising given the increased growth of Hispanic children in the U.S. Overall, the number of Hispanic officials have increased by over 2,400 persons between 1985 and 1994.

Table 11-5 shows Hispanic state officials by region. As expected, the west and south had the most Hispanic officials by region. The west included California, New Mexico, Texas, Colorado and Arizona. The south region included Florida, Texas and the rest of the Deep South[3]. These two regions represented 80% of the total number of Hispanic officials. One notable difference between the south and west was the larger number of Judicial and Law Enforcement Officials in the South.

Table 11-5 Hispanic State Officials by Region (1994)

	St. Executives, And St. Leg.	County and Municipal	Judicial and Law Enforcement	Education and School Board	Total
Northeast	28	42	13	73	156 (3%)
Midwest	15	43	8	851	917 (17%)
South	61	1,059	410	768	2,298 (42%)
West	95	1,053	220	720	2,088 (38%)
Total	199	2,197	651	2,412	5,459

Source: U.S. Bureau of the Census. 1998. Statistical Abstract of the United States. Washington, D.C..

Table 11-6 Hispanic State Officials by Selected States (1994)

	St. Executives, and St. Leg.	County and Municipal	Judicial and Law Enforcement	Education and School Board	Total
Arizona	11	144	50	136	341
California	16	349	50	381	796
Colorado	9	140	10	42	201
Connecticut	12	9	0	5	26
Florida	16	33	12	3	64
Illinois	7	26	3	845*	881
New Jersey	2	17	1	17	37
New Mexico	50	410	105	151	716
New York	12	13	11	47	83
Texas	41	1,022	389	763	2,215
Total	*176*	*2,163*	*631*	*2,390*	*5,360*
U.S. Total	*199*	*2,197*	*651*	*2,412*	*5,459*

*Includes local school councils in the Chicago area.

Source: U.S. Bureau of the Census. 1998. Statistical Abstract of the United States: Washington, D.C.. The Book of the States. *1998. The Council of State Governments: Lexington, KY.*

Table 11-6 shows that Texas, by far, had the largest number of HEOs in 1994 with 2,215. Almost half of these were County and Municipal Officials. Illinois and California round out the top three states. Despite having the largest percentage of Hispanic residents in 1994, New Mexico finished 4th in this category. Connecticut had the lowest number of Hispanic officials. However, the state also had the smallest percentage of Hispanic citizens in the total population for these states in 1994.

Illinois had an exorbitant number of Education and School Board officials in 1994. However, the data also included the local school councils in the Chicago area. The researcher assumed that similar data were not available for the other states. Hence, it was assumed that these local school councils made up a large percentage of the 845 officials in this category.

Hispanic State Legislators

In 1985, there were 114 Hispanic state legislators in the United States (see Table 11-7). New Mexico's General Assembly consistently had the largest contingency of Hispanic legislators. These 34 Hispanic members represented 30% of their assembly in 1985. However, the

Table 11-7 Hispanic State Legislators by State

	1985	% of Leg.	1990	% of Leg.	1995	%of Leg.	2000	% of Leg.
Arizona	12	13%	12	13%	9	10%	11	12%
California	7	6	6	5	14	12	24	20
Colorado	9	9	11	11	6	6	9	9
Connecticut	1	<1	3	2	7	4	6	3
Delaware	0	0	0	0	0	0	1	2
Florida	7	4	11	7	14	9	14	9
Hawaii	1	1	0	0	2	3	1	1
Idaho	0	0	0	0	1	1	0	0
Illinois	2	1	2	1	7	4	6	3
Indiana	1	1	1	1	2	1	1	2
Kansas	3	2	3	2	4	2	2	1
Louisiana	1	1	0	0	2	1	1	1
Massachusetts	0	0	1	1	0	0	3	2
Michigan	0	0	0	0	0	0	2	1
Minnesota	1	<1	0	0	2	1	1	<1
Montana	2	1	0	0	0	0	0	0
New Jersey	1	1	1	1	1	1	4	3
New Mexico	34	30	38	34	43	38	41	37
New York	7	3	7	3	10	5	12	6
Nevada	0	2	1	2	1	2	1	2
Oregon	0	0	0	0	0	0	1	1
Pennsylvania	1	<1	1	<1	0	0	1	<1
Rhode Island	1	1	1	1	1	1	1	1
Tennessee	0	0	0	0	0	0	1	1
Texas	23	13	27	15	33	18	35	19
Utah	0	0	0	0	1	1	2	2
Washington	0	0	2	1	3	2	3	2
Wisconsin	0	0	0	0	0	0	1	1
Wyoming	0	0%	0	0%	0	0%	1	1%
Total	*114*		*128*		*163*		*186*	

Source: NALEO Educational Fund. 2000. National Roster of Hispanic Elected Officials. *Washington, D.C.*

number of Hispanic legislators in Texas had also continued to grow. Hispanic legislators made up 19% of the Texas General Assembly in 2000. This was a 6% increase since 1985. Hispanics seeking office in California have also continued to increase. The state elections held in 2000 witnessed ten new members from the 14 in 1995. This brought the delegation to 24, thereby making up 20% of the General Assembly.

As expected, the western and southwestern states had the largest number and percentage of Hispanic state legislators. With the exception of Florida, the Deep South was the most under represented group of states. These states did however, with the exception of Florida, have the smallest percentages of Hispanic residents in their state. Of the remaining states that had Hispanic representatives, the midwest had the smallest number of Hispanic state legislators. Most states in this area had only one Hispanic representative.

Although New York and Illinois have a large number of Hispanic citizens, they have not been able to elect a large number of Hispanic legislators. There were a couple of reasons that may explain this occurrence. First, the majority of Hispanic citizens in both states reside in the large cities. In this case, Chicago and New York City. More specifically, these residents tended to concentrate in certain neighborhoods/barrios within these two cities. Essentially, Hispanics were able to overwhelmingly elect three or four persons of their ethnic background. Areas where they made up a smaller percentage of the population have not proven to be fertile electoral grounds. A second possible reason for these small numbers was that non-Hispanic citizens did not tend to do well in voting districts where they were not the majority. One may argue that non-Hispanic voters were reluctant to support a Hispanic candidate when a non-Hispanic was on the ballot. This negative repercussion was fostered by the low voter turnout rate for Hispanic citizens. This phenomenon was not just indigenous to those states or groups, but also to other states as well.

Party identification was considered in Table 11-8. In 1985, 61% of all Hispanic legislators identified with the Democratic Party while 32% identified themselves as independents. Only 9 members ran under the Republican label. By 1990, 88% of Hispanic legislators identified with the Democratic label while less than 1% identified as independents. In 1995, 83% of the group identified as Democrats while 13% identified as Republican and 4% identified as Independent. The most recent data in 2000 shows that 86% of all Hispanic legislators identified with the Democratic Party label while none identified themselves as independent (see also DeSipio 1996; Hero 1992).

It is interesting to note that Florida was the only state that had a large number of Republican Hispanic legislators. In fact, the ratio had

Table 11-8 Hispanic State Legislators by State and Party ID

	1985			1990			1995			2000		
	D	R	O	D	R	O	D	R	O	D	R	O
Arizona	8	0	4	12	0	0	9	0	0	11	0	0
California	6	0	1	6	0	0	14	0	0	20	4	0
Colorado	4	0	5	11	0	0	5	1	0	8	1	0
Connecticut	0	0	1	2	0	1	6	1	0	5	1	0
Delaware	0	0	0	0	0	0	0	0	0	0	1	0
Florida	1	6	0	1	9	1	2	11	1	2	12	0
Hawaii	0	0	1	0	0	0	2	0	0	1	0	0
Idaho	0	0	0	0	0	0	0	1	0	0	0	0
Illinois	1	0	1	2	0	0	5	1	2	6	0	0
Indiana	1	0	0	1	0	0	2	0	0	1	0	0
Kansas	1	0	2	1	1	0	2	2	0	1	1	0
Louisiana	0	0	1	0	0	0	2	0	0	0	1	0
Massachusetts	0	0	0	1	0	0	0	0	0	3	0	0
Michigan	0	0	0	0	0	0	0	0	0	1	1	0
Minnesota	1	0	0	0	0	0	2	0	0	1	0	0
Montana	1	0	1	0	0	0	0	0	0	0	0	0
New Jersey	0	1	0	1	0	0	0	0	0	4	0	0
New Mexico	28	2	4	38	0	0	38	2	3	39	2	0
New York	7	0	0	6	1	1	10	0	0	12	0	0
Nevada	0	0	0	1	0	0	1	0	0	1	0	0
Oregon	0	0	0	0	0	0	0	0	0	1	0	0
Pennsylvania	1	0	0	1	0	0	0	0	0	1	0	0
Rhode Island	0	0	1	1	0	0	1	0	0	1	0	0
Tennessee	0	0	0	0	0	0	0	0	0	1	0	0
Texas	9	0	14	27	0	0	32	1	0	34	1	0
Utah	0	0	0	0	0	0	1	0	0	2	0	0
Washington	0	0	0	1	1	0	1	2	0	2	1	0
Wisconsin	0	0	0	0	0	0	0	0	0	1	0	0
Wyoming	0	0	0	0	0	0	0	0	0	1	0	0
Total	69	9	36	113	12	3	135	22	6	160	26	0
Percent	61%	7%	32%	88%	11%	1%	83%	13%	4%	86%	14%	0%

Note: D=Democrat, R=Republican, O=Other.

Source: NALEO Educational Fund. 2000. *National Roster of Hispanic Elected Officials.* Washington, D.C.

never been less than 5 Republicans for every 1 Democrat legislator. A large percentage of Florida's Hispanic legislators were of Cuban descent. Similar party identification can be found more recently at the

Table 11-9 Hispanic State Legislators by State and House Membership

	1985		1990		1995		2000	
	H	S	H	S	H	S	H	S
Arizona	6	6	7	5	7	2	7	4
California	4	3	3	3	10	4	17	7
Colorado	5	4	7	4	4	2	7	2
Connecticut	1	0	3	0	6	1	5	1
Delaware	0	0	0	0	0	0	1	0
Florida	7	0	8	3	11	3	11	3
Hawaii	1	0	0	0	2	0	1	0
Idaho	0	0	0	0	1	0	0	0
Illinois	2	0	2	1	5	2	4	2
Indiana	1	0	1	0	2	0	1	0
Kansas	2	1	2	1	2	2	1	1
Louisiana	1	0	0	0	0	2	0	1
Massachusetts	0	0	1	0	0	0	3	0
Michigan	0	0	0	0	0	0	2	0
Minnesota	0	1	0	0	2	0	1	0
Montana	2	0	0	0	0	0	0	0
New Jersey	1	0	1	0	1	0	4	0
New Mexico	22	12	25	13	27	16	26	15
New York	5	2	5	2	6	4	8	4
Nevada	0	0	0	1	0	1	0	1
Oregon	0	0	0	0	0	0	0	1
Pennsylvania	1	0	1	0	0	0	1	0
Rhode Island	1	0	1	0	1	0	1	0
Tennessee	0	0	0	0	0	0	1	0
Texas	19	4	22	5	26	7	28	7
Utah	0	0	0	0	1	0	1	1
Washington	0	0	1	0	1	2	2	1
Wisconsin	0	0	0	0	0	0	1	0
Wyoming	0	0	0	0	0	0	1	0
Total	81	33	90	38	115	48	135	51
Percent	71%	29%	70%	30%	71%	29%	73%	27%

Source: NALEO Educational Fund. 2000. *National Roster of Hispanic Elected Officials.* Washington, D.C.

congressional level as well for the Florida Hispanic delegation (Menifield 1998).

When House and Senate membership were considered, the data show that the vast majority of Hispanic legislators were elected to the House of Representatives (Table 11-9). The percentages have been very stable over the 15 year period. The House consistently had about 70% of

Table 11-10 Hispanic Committee Leaders in State Legislatures, House 2000

	# in House	% of House	Av. Serv.	# of Dem.	# of Rep.	# of. Chairs	# of V-Chairs	Tot. # of Standing Comm.
Arizona	8	13	4	8	0	0	0	25
California	17	22	3	13	3	11	5	30
Florida	10	8	4.2	2	8	3	3	40
New Mexico	26	37	-	25	1	4	11	17
New York	8	5	7.25	8	0	2	0	31
Texas	27	19	-	26	1	5	0	46

Source: Various State Government websites

the entire Hispanic delegation. Among the states that had more than five Hispanic legislators, Arizona and California had the best ratio of House and Senate Hispanic members over the period of this study.

Nevada had only one Hispanic legislator in the General Assembly and he has been in the Senate since he was elected (Sen. Bob Coffin). In four cases (states), the number of House members equaled the number of Senators and in eight cases the number of Senators exceeded the number of House members. The latter occurred more often in the 2000 election than any other election.

Table 11-10 contains the results of the analysis for Hispanic committee leaders in the House of Representatives for 2000. California had the highest number of committee chairs at 11, followed by a distant Texas at 5. New York Hispanic House members have the longest tenure of this group, but have only 2 committee chairs. New Mexico had the most vice chairs at 11, followed by California at 5. The number of standing committees in each House also varied. Texas had a high of 46 while New Mexico had a low of 17.

Table 11-11 Hispanic Committee Leaders in State Legislatures, Senate 2000

	# in Senate	% of Senate	Av. Serv.	# of Dem.	# of Rep.	# of. Chairs	# of V-Chairs	Tot. # of Standing Comm.
Arizona	4	10	9.5	4	0	0	1	11
California	9	18	3.9	9	0	5	1	25
Florida	3	7	7	0	3	2	0	19
New Mexico	15	36	-	14	1	4	10	10
New York	4	6	12.5	4	0	0	0	34
Texas	6	19	12	6	0	4	4	13

Source: Various State Government websites

New York Hispanic Senators have the longest tenure at 12.5 years, followed closely by Texas at 12 years and Arizona at 9.5 years (Table 11-11). California however had the most Hispanic committee chairs at 5, followed by New Mexico and Texas at 4. New Mexico had 10 vice chairs followed by Texas with 4. Arizona and New York had no Hispanic committee chairs.

Table 11-12 provides the most recent party positions held by Hispanic leaders in these states. The table shows that Hispanic legislators in California currently hold four leadership positions despite the fact that the average years of service for Hispanics was 3 years in the House and 3.9 years in the Senate. Senator Richard Polanco was the Speaker of the House. In addition, the Lieutenant Governor of California was also Hispanic, Cruz Bustamante.

Raymond Sanchez was the Speaker of the New Mexico House for the second time. He was first elected in 1978. The Pro Tempore was Manny Aragon and the Majority Whip was Mary Jane Garcia. Hispanic leaders in the Arizona General Assembly occupied both Minority Whip positions. There were no Hispanic leaders in the Florida, New York and Texas General Assemblies.

Table 11-12 Leadership Positions of Hispanic State Legislators 2000-2001

	Legislator	*Position*
Arizona	John Loredo	House Minority Whip
	Peter Rios	Senate Minority Whip
California	Richard Polanco	Senate Majority Leader
	Gloria Romero	House Dem. Whip
	Gil Cedillo	House Asst. Majority Leader
	Richard Alarcon	Senate Majority Whip
Florida	None	
New Mexico	Mary Jane Garcia	Senate Majority Whip
	Raymond Sanchez	Speaker of the House
	Ben Lujan	House Majority Floor Leader
	Manny Aragon	Senate Pro Tempore
New York	None	
Texas	None	

Source: Various State Government websites: Http://janus.state.me.us/states.htm

State and Local Hispanic Organizations

There are quite a few Hispanic/Latino organizations at the federal, state and local levels that seek to benefit their super constituency. However, this discussion is most interested in the formation of state legislative caucuses and other formal organization created by Hispanic legislators since legislators. California and Texas were the only two states, of the seven states that have the largest number of Hispanic legislators, which have a caucus specifically designed to promote the social and economic prosperity of Hispanics in their states.

The Texas Caucus is called the, *Mexican American Legislative Caucus* and it is currently composed of the 37 Hispanic House Members. The Caucus was formed in 1977 with the sole purpose of promoting the Hispanic community in the state (http://www.malc. org/home__page.htm). It was interesting that the 7 Democratic Hispanic Senators from the state were not members of the Caucus. The Caucus has a small staff that handles the day to day administrative activities of the organization.

The *Latino Legislative Caucus* was formed in 1973 in California with five members. Their chief objective was to write a legislative agenda highlighting the priorities needed to protect the rights of Latinos in California and avidly pursue that agenda. In 2000, the Caucus had 27 members from both Houses of the Assembly (http://www.assembly.ca. gov/latinoCaucus/history.htm).

The analysis reveals that both of these organizations laid out an agenda at the beginning of each legislative. These caucuses meet regularly during the month to discuss legislative strategies and to handle any administrative matters. The *Latino Legislative Caucus* appears to be the more active of the two. They meet once a week and hold regional meetings with other public officials to discuss issues on their agenda.

Connecticut, Minnesota, North Carolina, Ohio, Oregon, Utah, New York and Washington have Hispanic/Latino Councils, Commissions, Advisory Boards and Task Forces set up to educate the Governor, legislators and the community on the needs of Hispanic residents in their states. These organizations work under the auspices of and were created by either the Governor or the state legislative assembly. In some case, members included Hispanic legislators. Although their goals are many, there are some common themes that run through these organizations. They make recommendations for changes in programs and laws that affect Hispanics, they advise the Governor, state legislators and state agencies on the development of relevant policies, plans and programs and most importantly, they helped to define issues concerning the rights and needs of Hispanic citizens.

Implications and Conclusions

This analysis clearly shows the growth of Hispanic elected officials at the state and local level despite the poor voting patterns exhibited by Hispanic citizens. With consideration to the Hispanic growth pattern, continued success is highly dependent upon the mobilization of non-participants and children who will become eligible to vote in the very near future. If previous election models hold true, that is, Hispanics are more likely to vote for a Hispanic that a non-Hispanic, the only way for a Hispanic to win an election would be in a super majority Hispanic district. States that have a large percentage of Hispanic residents have the potential to control the governments in those states at every level. However, it is very questionable given past history whether this potential will be realized. DeSipio (1996) and many other scholars provide ample evidence to the socialization process of Hispanic American and the many problems that they encounter as immigrants and as citizens. These problems have more or less hindered Hispanics from participating in government. If the U.S. Bureau of the Census is correct in their estimates, the Hispanic population is going to have to change their behavior pattern if they expect to receive an increase in descriptive and substantive representation in the future.

Further, the literature and data in this research show that one of the key problems within the Hispanic community is mobilization. It will take more organizations like state level caucuses and other grass root organizations to push the agenda and register new voters. Most importantly, the Hispanic residents of these states who are eligible to vote are going to have to utilize this right if they expect to reap the benefits of representation. The number of state Hispanic Caucuses is considerably low. This is abundantly true in states that have a large number of Hispanic legislators. The formation of a caucus does not necessarily have to be a formal process. However, working together with individuals who share the same goals as you do is very important to achieving goals (Mansbridge 1999). Again, history suggests that strength lies in numbers. This lack of cohesiveness among Hispanic state legislatures is revealed by the lack of legislation that benefits their constituents. In addition, non-Hispanic legislators are obviously not supportive of redistributive economic policies to groups who do not participate in the political process. However, I am not arguing that all of the woes of Hispanic residents are the results of non-participation. On the contrary, I am merely strongly suggesting that this lack of participation has not helped them in their battle for political parity in states where they make up a large percentage of the population.

The problems of Hispanic legislators are also further damaged by institutions that are beyond their control. That is, the Supreme Court and the Governors who are credited with signing or vetoing favorable Hispanic legislation. Research shows that the disposition of the Court has not been favorable toward the creation of minority districts. Further, Democrats, are also not favorable towards these super majority minority districts because they have not only lost seats, but also lost control of Congress because of them (see also Brischetto 1998). This evidence should serve as a catalyst to Hispanic observers that the only alternative is formal political activity.

References

Abalos, David T. 1986. *Latinos in the United States: The Sacred and the Political.* Notre Dame, Indiana: University of Notre Dame Press.

Affigne, Tony. 2000. "Latino Politics in the United States: An Introduction." *PS: Political Science & Politics* 23: 523-528.

Arvizu, John R. and F. Chris Garcia. 1996. "Latino Voting Participation: Explaining and Differentiating Latino Voting Turnout." *Hispanic Journal of Behavioral Sciences* 18: 104-128.

Baker, Susan Gonzalez. 1996. "Su Voto Es Su Voz: Latino Political Empowerment and the Immigration Challenge." *PS: Political Science and Politics* 29: 465-468.

Bass, Loretta A. and Lynne M. Casper. 1999. "Are There Differences in Registration and Voting Behavior Between Naturalized and Native-Born Americans?" Population Working Division Paper No. 28: U.S. Bureau of the Census, Washington, D.C.

Brischetto, Robert R. 1998. "Latino Voters and Redistricting in the New Millenium." In *Redistricting and Minority Representation: Learning From the Past, Preparing for the Future.* ed. David A. Bositis. Landham, MD: University Press of America.

Blank, Robert. 1974. "Socio-economic Determinants of Voting Turnout: A Challenge." *The Journal of Politics* 36: 731-752.

Browning, Rufus. and Dale R. Marshall and David Tabb. 1984. *Protest is Not Enough: The Struggle of Blacks and Hispanics for Equality in Urban Politics.* Berkeley: University of California Press.

Campbell, Angus, Philip E. Converse, Warren E. Miller and Donald E. Stokes. 1960. *The American Voter.* Chicago: University of Chicago Press.

Cassel, Claes and David Hill 1981. "Explanations of Turnout Decline: A Multivariate Test." *American Politics Quarterly* 9: 181-195.

Casper, Lynne M. and Loretta E. Bass. 1998. "Voting and Registration in the Election of November 1996." U.S. Bureau of the Census: U.S. Department of Commerce. http://www.census.gov/prod/www/abs/vote.html.

Conway, M. Magaret. 1991. *Political Participation in the United States.* 2nd ed. Washington: CQ Press.

Day, Jennifer C. and Avalaura L. Gaither. 2000. "Voting and Registration in the Election of November 1998." *U.S. Census Bureau.* Washington D.C. http://www.census.gov/prod/2000pubs/p20-523.pdf.

de la Garza, Rodolfo O. 1984. "And Then There Were Some...." Chicanos as National Political Actors, 1967-1980." *Aztlan* 15: 1-24.

de la Garza, Rodolfo O, and Louis DeSipio. 1993. "Save the Baby, Change the Bathwater, and Scrub the Tub: Latino Electoral Participation After Seventeen Years of Voting Rights Act Coverage." *Texas Law Review* 71: 1479-1538.

DeSipio, Louis. 1996. *Counting on the Latino Vote: Latinos as a New Electorate*: Charlottesville: University of Virginia Press.

_____. 1996. "Making Citizens or Good Citizens? Naturalization as a Predictor of Organizational and Electoral Behavior Among Latino Immigrants." *Hispanic Journal of Behavioral Sciences* 18: 194-213.

Diaz, William A. 1996. "Latino Participation in America: Associational and Political Roles." *Hispanic Journal of Behavioral Science* 18: 154-174.

Falcon, Angelo. 1988. "Black and Hispanic Politics in New York City." In *Latinos in the Political System.* ed. F. Chris Garcia. Notre Dame: University of Notre Dame Press.

Falcon, Angelo. 1992. "Time to Rethink the Voting Rights Act? New York City's 12th Congressional District." *Social Policy* 23: 17-22.

_____. 1996. "Puerto Ricans in Postliberal New York: The 1992 Presidential Elections." In *Ethnic Ironies: Latino Politics in the 1992 Elections.* eds. Rodolfo de la Garza and Louis DeSipio. Colorado: Westview Press.

Garcia, F. Chris, and Rodolfo O. de la Garza. 1977. *The Chicano Political Experience: Three Perspectives.* MA: Duxbury Press.

Garcia, F. Chris, and Rodolfo O. de la Garza. 1985. "Mobilizing the Mexican Immigrant: The Role of Organizational Movement." *Western Political Quarterly* 38: 551-564.

Garcia, F. Chris, Angelo Falcon and Rodolfo O. de la Garza. 1996. "Introduction: Ethnicity and Politics: Evidence From the Latino National Political Survey." *Hispanic Journal of Behavioral Sciences* 18: 91-103.

Garcia, John. 1986. "The Voting Rights Act and Hispanic Political Representation in the Southwest." *Publius: The Journal of Federalism* 16: 49-67.

Garcia, John. 1997. "Hispanic Political Participation and Demographic Correlates." In *Pursuing Power: Latinos and the Political System.* 2nd Ed. ed. F. Chris Garcia. Notre Dame: University of Notre Dame Press.

Gilliam. Franklin D. 1985. "Influences on Voter turnout for U.S. House Elections in Non-Presidential Years." *Legislative Studies Quarterly* 10: 339-352.

Hero, Rodney. 1989a. "Multiracial Coalitions in City Elections Involving Minority Candidates: Some Evidence From Denver's Election of Federico Pena." *Urban Affairs Quarterly* 25: 342-351.

_____. 1989b. "The Elections of Federico Pena as Mayor of Denver: Analysis and Implications." *Social Science Quarterly* 70: 300-310.

_____. 1990. "Hispanics in Urban Government and Politics: Some Findings, Comparisons and Implications." *The Western Political Quarterly* 43: 403-414.

_____. 1992. *Latinos and the U.S. Political System: Two-tiered Pluralism.* Philadelphia, PA: Temple University Press.

_____. 1996. "An Essential Vote: Latinos and the 1992 Elections in Colorado." In *Ethnic Ironies: Latino Politics in the 1992 Elections.* eds. Rodolfo de la Garza and Louis DeSipio. Colorado: Westview Press.

Hero, Rodney, F. Chris Garcia, John Garcia, and Harry Pachon. 2000. "Latino Participation, Partisanship, and Office Holding." *PS: Political Science & Politics* 23: 529-534.

Hero, Rodney E. and Anne G. Campbell. 1996. "Understanding Latino Political Participation: Exploring the Evidence From the Latino National Political Survey." *Hispanic Journal of Behavioral Sciences* 18: 129-141.

Hritzuk, Natasha and David K. Park. 2000. "The Question of Latino Participation: From an SES to a Social Structural Explanation." *Social Science Quarterly* 81: 151-166.

Inglehart, Ronald. 1997. *Modernization and Postmodernization Cultural, Economics, and Political Change in 43 Societies*. N.J.: Princeton University Press.

Jewell, Malcolm and David M. Olson. 1988. *Political Parties and Elections in American States*. 3rd ed. Chicago: Dorsey Press.

Leighley, Jan E. and Jonathan Nagler. 1992. "Individual and Systemic Influences on turnout: Who Votes? 1984" *The Journal of Politics* 54: 718-740.

Lewis, Pierce, Casey McCracken, and Roger Hunt. 1994. "Politics: Who Cares?" *American Demographics* 16: #10.

Mansbridge, Jane. 1999. "Should Blacks Represent Blacks and Women Represent Women? A Contingent "Yes."" *The Journal of Politics* 61: 628-657.

Marquez, Benjamin and James Jennings. 2000. "Representation by Other Means: Mexican American and Puerto Rican Social Movement Organizations." *PS: Political Science & Politics* 23: 51-546.

Mejias, Victor. 1999. "Voting Campaign Celebrates Anniversary." *Hispanic* 12: 17.

Menifield, Charles E. 1998. "A Loose Coalition or a United Front: Voting Behavior Within the Congressional Hispanic Caucus." *Latino Studies Journal* 9: 27-44.

Menifield, Charles E. and Frank H. Julian. 1998. "Changing the Face of Congress: African-Americans in the Twenty-First Century." *The Western Journal of Black Studies* 22: 18-30.

Michelson, Melissa R. 2000. "Political Efficacy and Electoral Participation of Chicago Latinos." *Social Science Quarterly* 81: 136-150.

Moore, Joan and Harry Pachon. 1985. *Hispanics in the United States*. Englewood Cliffs, N.J.: Prentice Hall.

Montonya, Lisa J., Carol Hardy-Fanta and Sonia Garcia. 2000. "Latino Politics: Gender, Participation, and Leadership." *PS: Political Science & Politics* 23: 555-562.

Moreno, Dario and Christopher Warren. 1992. "The Conservative Enclave: Cubans and Community Power in Florida." In *From Rhetoric to Reality: Latinos in the 1988 Elections*. eds. Rodolfo de la Garza and Louis DeSipio. Boulder: Westview Press.

NALEO Educational Fund. 2000. *National Roster of Hispanic Elected Officials*. Washington, D.C.

Pachon, Harry and Louis DeSipio. 1992. "Latino Elected Officials in the 1990s." *PS: Political Science & Politics* 25: 212-217.

Patterson, Samuel. C., and Gregory A. Caldeira. 1983. "Getting Out the Vote:

Participation in Gubernatorial Elections." *American Political Science Review* 77: 675-689.

Radelat, Ana. 2000. "Road to Power." *Hispanic* 13: 22-28.

Sales Jr., William W., and Rod Bush. 2000. "The Political Awakening of Black and Hispanics in New York City: Competition or Cooperation?" *Social Justice* 27: 19-42.

Shaw, Daron, Rodolfo O. de la Garza and Jongho Lee. 2000. "Examining Latino Turnout in 1996: A Three-State, Validated Survey Approach California, Florida, Texas." *American Political Science Review* 44: 338-346.

Sierrra, Christine M., Teresa Carrillo, Louis DeSipio, and Michael Jones-Correa. 2000. "Latino Immigration and Citizenship." *PS: Political Science and Politics* 23: 535-540.

Squire, Perville, Raymond E. Wolfinger and David P. Glass. 1987. "Residential Mobility and Voter Turnout." *American Political Science Review* 81: 45-65.

The Book of the States. 1998. The Council of State Governments: Lexington, KY.

Tostado, Ricardo. 1985. "Political Participation." In *Hispanics in the United States: A New Social Agenda.* eds. Pastora San Juan Cafferty and William C. McCready. New Brunswick: Transaction Books.

U.S. Bureau of the Census. 1998. *Statistical Abstract of the United States*: Washington, D.C..

Verba, Sidney, and Norman H. Nie. 1972. *Participation in America: Political Democracy and Social Equality.* New York: Harper and Row.

Vigil, Maurillo E. 1984. "The Election of Toney Anaya as Governor of New Mexico: Its Implications for Hispanics." *The Journal of Ethnic Studies* 12: 81-98.

Wrinkle, Robert D., Joseph Stewart and J.L Polinard. 1996. "Ethnicity and Nonelectoral Political Participation." *Hispanic Journal of Behavioral Sciences* 18: 142-153.

Notes

1 The term Hispanic is used rather than Latino because it appears to be a bit more comprehensive than the term Latino. All persons who fit this designation are not of Latin American descent. In fact, quite a few citizens of Spanish speaking descent are from the Caribbean region.

2 Data projections over the next decade can be found at the following web address http://www.census.gov/population/www/projections/popproj.html.

3 The Deep South States include Arkansas, Alabama, Mississippi, Tennessee, Georgia, Florida, South Carolina and Louisiana.

CHAPTER 12

New Black Women in the Old White Confederacy: An Analyses of Occupational Status in State and Local Government

Patricia Jernigan and Mfanya Tryman

Studies of political representation proliferate journals, books and many conference themes. However, there is a paucity of research analyzing women in the bureaucracy. Within this discipline, studies of wage and occupational differentials between black and white women and men in the public and private sectors have received considerable attention over the years (Solberg and Laughlin 1995; Davis 1994; Kelly et al. 1991; Idson and Price 1992). Researchers have investigated the wage differentials between women and men with the same qualifications, the high concentration of black and white women in low paying occupations, and structural barriers that hinder black women from moving into management and administrative occupations. The majority of research in this area has focused on women in the federal government and the private sector. However, these research issues must be addressed at all levels of government in order to promote equal employment opportunities for all working individuals, including black women.

This chapter examines the labor market status of black women in state and local government in the South by comparing the wage and occupational status of them to that of white women, white men and black men. It will be argued that a comparison of the labor market status of these groups will reveal that while black women may be represented in the public sector overall, they are under-represented in supervisory and managerial positions (Daley 1996).

Trends in Black and White Women Employment

A historical analysis of women in the labor market reveals that black women have lagged behind men in general over most of recorded history and specifically behind white women. Black women have long been considered one of the most poorly paid groups in the United States (U.S. Commission on Civil Rights 1990). Moreover, black women have been traditionally more concentrated in low wage and undesirable jobs (King 1992; Nelson 1973). In 1940, three-fourths of the employed black women were in agriculture or domestic jobs compared to 13% of white women (King 1992). King's (1995) research found the vast majority of black working women concentrated in agricultural labor and domestic service. This was the trend for nearly 100 years after emancipation from slavery.

During this period, black women were largely employed in unskilled occupations, while white working class women were largely employed in skilled occupations (Cunningham and Zalokar 1992). Moreover, black women lacked representation in clerical and sales occupations as well as professional, technical or managerial occupations. Cunningham and Zalokar (1992) reported that in 1940 black women were nearly non-existence in professional or managerial occupations compared to white women. While one in four white women occupied these occupations, one in twenty black women were employed in these occupations. Furthermore, white women occupied a variety of professional occupations while black female professionals were almost exclusively teachers.

Although the occupational status of black women has changed drastically since the 1940s, black women are still over-represented in low-paying jobs (King 1992). Black women began to penetrate the labor market by moving into positions not traditionally held by blacks in the 1960s. In the first half of the 1960s, only a third of all employed black women were private household workers (Cunningham and Zalokar 1992; and Fosu 1987) compared to three-fourths during the 1940s (Fosu 1987). These positions constituted the lowest paying occupations. Median earnings for private household positions were 25% of the median earnings of female professional and technical workers. Service workers represented the next lowest paid positions. These two occupational categories constituted at least 55% of all employed black women for the period from 1958-1964 (Fosu 1987), whereas 6% of all working white women were in domestic positions and 16% in other service positions (Fosu 1987).

Domestic and service occupations are located in the secondary labor market. Both black and white women are concentrated in secondary sector occupations. However, a greater percentage of black women are in secondary sector occupations than white women (Fosu 1987).

The greatest gain for black women in the 1960s occurred when black women moved into clerical occupations where both black and white women are now concentrated (Fosu 1993; King 1992). According to Cunningham and Zalokar (1992), gains for black women included movement into clerical, professional and technical positions. They state that "the proportion of black women employed as clerical workers increased almost fourfold, and the proportion employed in professional and technical occupations doubled" (p. 543).

Albelda's (1986) research found the clerical field to be the fastest growing occupation for women of color. It is noteworthy to point out that with these vast improvements in the labor market, the status of black women still lagged behind white women in 1980 (Cunningham and Zalokar 1992). King's (1995) comparative study of the labor market status of black women in the public sector in the United States to black women in Great Britain revealed the same findings. She stated that black women and other women of color are on the bottom of the wage and occupational scale and still lag behind white women in spite of the decrease in the gender wage gap.

Between 1974 and 1980, the occupational status of black women steadily improved (Fosu 1992; King 1978). In the public sector, the number of black women entering the labor market showed a marked increase. Black women, white women, and black men out-paced white men during this period. Although black women improved their numbers in the market, salaries for black women, white women, and black men did not parallel those of white men. And despite the accelerated increase in salary for black women, white women, and black men, their salary increases still did not out-pace that of white men (Madhavan, Green and Jung 1985; Cayer and Sigelman 1980). According to the U.S. Civil Rights Commission (1990), by the mid-1980s, black women earned about 57% as much as white men, 83% as much as black men, and 88% as much as white women.

Cunningham and Zalokar (1992) concluded that by 1980, the relative differences in wage and occupation between black women and white women could be attributed to discrimination and human capital (education) differences. Black women, compared to white women, have been segregated in lower paying occupations, thus perpetuating differences in the labor market status of the two groups in public as well as the private sector of the labor market.

In spite of the vast labor market problems black women encounter, historically more black women have participated in the labor market than white women (Farley 1979; King 1978; Malveaux 1985; Jones 1985-1986), and are more likely to be full-time workers (Malveaux 1985-1986). Black women have exhibited comparatively high levels of labor force participation (U.S. Civil Rights Commission, 1990). During the 1960s and 1970s a significant number of black women entered the labor market compared to white women (Jones 1985-1986). However, the 1980s showed a steady slowing down of black women entering the labor market and a decline in wages earned during the previous decades (Davis 1994). King (1995) reported that in 1990, 76% of the black working women were full-time, whereas 68% of the white working women were full-time.

Trends in Black Women Education

Education has been affirmed as a key factor in shaping the environment in which black women are employed (Critzer and Rai 1998). Education provides black women the means to accelerate in the labor market, especially into high level occupations (Wilkerson 1985-86; Winegarden 1972). As women penetrate the labor market, those with specific educational training have been successful in obtaining employment, but they have encountered difficulty in obtaining management positions where job requirements are subjective (King 1992). It appears that white males, who dominate management positions, are still reluctant to elevate black women into management and administrative positions.

Stiglitz (1973) describes education as a process for obtaining better jobs. The more education, the more likely one will find employment and earn higher wages. Education provides leverage for black women in the labor market, but it does not guarantee them the same returns as white women (Jones 1985-86). Belman and Heywood (1991) showed that a college degree increased black women's occupational status, whereas a high school diploma resulted in smaller increases for black women than white women. Wilkerson (1985-86) concluded that education is not a guarantee of success in the labor market, nevertheless many jobs stipulate a high school diploma or college degree as a prerequisite for employment. This symbolizes the importance of education in the pursuit to gain employment. Sigelman and Karnig (1977) noted that a lack of education is a major stumbling block for blacks seeking employment.

Sigelman and Karnig's (1977) investigation found that "any educational requirement, …automatically screens out a higher proportion of minority group members than others. Such requirements may often be pegged at unreasonably high levels, but the clear implication is that the prospects for a more racially representative public service are effectively frustrated by educational requirements" (p. 898). Suitable educational credentials are essential for black women hoping to penetrate the higher level labor market jobs. The lack of educational credentials by blacks job candidates, especially a college degree, impedes efforts to recruit a labor force for high level positions (Sigelman and Karnig 1977).

During the 1970s - mid 1980s black women's educational status significantly improved, however, they did not surpass white women during this time period. Wilkerson (1985-86) states the proportion of white women who were high school graduates increased 11% (76 % to 87%); black women increased 26% (53% to 79%); but from 1982 to the mid-eighties the rate of black high school graduation rates has declined to about 60%.

Methods and Research Design

This research concentrates on the wage and occupational status of black women in state and local government in the South in comparison to white males, white females, and black males over a 20 year period using five year intervals. The study uses data from the Equal Employment Opportunity Commission from 1975, 1980, 1985, 1990 and 1995. For purposes of this inquiry, the South consists of those states of the Old Confederacy along with three border states: Alabama, Arkansas, Florida, Georgia, Kentucky, Louisiana, Mississippi, North Carolina, Oklahoma, South Carolina, Tennessee, Texas, Virginia, and West Virginia.

State and local governments are the largest employers of black women in the labor market. Black women have penetrated the public sector labor market, but they are under-represented in high level, decision-making, and policy making occupations encompassing Officials/Administrators and Professionals as designated by the U.S. Equal Employment Opportunity Commission. Jobs in these occupational categories not only represent high status occupations, but the highest annual median salaries.

Table 12-1 Workforce Representation of State and Local Government in the South, Race/Gender and Year

Race/Gender	1975	1980	1985	1990	1995
White Males	53%	45%	42%	42%	41%
Black Males	10	13	12	12	12
White Females	28	32	33	33	33
Black Females	8	11	12	13	14
	100%	100%	100%	100%	100%

Note: Percent may not total 100% due to rounding error.

Source: *Minorities and Women In State and Local Government*, 1977. *Job Patterns For Minorities and Women In State and Local Government*, 1996, 1991, 1985 and 1982.

Workforce Participation Rate

Table 12-1 shows the racial and gender composition of employees in state and local government in the South from 1975 to 1995. White males have dominated the workforce throughout this period. In 1975, white males constituted 53% of the total workforce population in state and local governments in the South. In each subsequent five-year interval, the percentage of white males in state and local governments in the South has steadily declined. Despite the overall percentage decline of white males for each interval, they still represent the largest group of workers in state and local government in the South. During the twenty-year period, the percentage of white males in state and local governments in the South has decreased from 53% in 1975 to 41% in 1995.

In 1975, black males were the third largest group of employees in state and local government in the South. This group represented 10% of the employees in state and local government in the South. This is 2% more than black females in state and local governments in the South in 1975. In 1980, the percentage of black males in state and local governments in the South rose to 12%. From 1980 through 1995 the percentage of black males in state and local governments remained constant at 12%.

White females represent the second largest group of workers in state and local government in the South. This group constituted 28% of the workforce in 1975. White females in state and local governments showed a slight increase from 1975 to 1995. From 1975 to 1980, their participation rate increased by four percentage points. In 1980, white females made up 32% of all those working in state and local governments in the South. From 1980 to 1985, white females increased from

Table 12-2 Labor Force Participation Rate in the South, Race/Gender and Year

Race/Gender	1975	1980	1985	1990	1995
White Males	54%	50%	50%	46%	46%
Black Males	9	8	8	8	8
White Females	30	34	34	37	37
Black Females	7	8	8	9	9
	100%	100%	100%	100%	100%

Source: U.S. Bureau of Census, 1970, 1980, and 1990.

390,787 (32%) to 33%. This represented a 1% increase during this interval. From 1985 to 1995 the percentage of white females in state and local government remained at 33%.

Black females were the only group that showed an increase in the workforce for each five-year interval. In 1975, black females represented 8% of the workforce in state and local government in the South. Between 1975 and 1980, black females had their largest percentage increase which was three percentage points, from 8%to 11% Black females had a 1% increase in their representation in state and local government in the South each five year interval after 1980, which resulted in 14% in 1995.

Table 12-2 shows the labor force participation rate in the South by race, gender, and year. White males represented the largest group of workers in the labor force in the South throughout this period. However, the participation rate of white males did decrease from 54% in 1975 to 50% in 1980 and 1985, and in 1990, the rate declined to 46%.

The black male participation rate in the labor force also declined during the 1980's and remained constant throughout the 1990's. In 1975, black males represented 9% of the labor force. By 1980, black males participation rate in the labor force declined by one percentage point, from 9% to 8% and remained at this rate in 1990 and 1995.

The white female employment rate in the labor force increased by 4% from 1975 to 1980. White and black women were the only groups that increased during this period. In 1975, white females represented 30% of the total labor force in the South and increased to 34% by 1980 and 1985. White females showed a three percentage point increase in the labor force by 1990. In 1990 and 1995, white females represented 37% of the total labor force.

The black female labor force participation rate increased from 7% to 8% between 1975 and 1980. In 1990 and 1995, this percentage rate

Table 12-3 Percentage Differences Between Workforce Representation In State and Local Government and Labor Force Participation Rate By Race/Gender and Year

Race/Gender	1975	1980	1985	1990	1995
White Males	-1	-5	-7	-4	-5
Black Males	+1	+4	+4	+4	+4
White Females	-2	-2	-1	-4	-4
Black Females	+1	+3	+4	+4	+5

Note: The data are the result of the difference between the results in Table 12-2 and Table 12-1

rose another point from 8% to 9%. In 1995, black females represented 9% (3,206,368) of the South's labor force.

A comparison of the labor force population to the state and local government workforce (Table 12-3) shows that white males have been under-represented in state and local governments every period during this study. In 1975, white males were under-represented by 1% in state and local government in the South. In 1980, they were under-represented by 5 percentage points. The highest under-representation occurred in 1985 when white males represented 50% of the labor force and 43% of the workforce in state and local governments. White males were under-represented in state and local governments in the South by 4% in 1990 and 5% in 1995. Although white males in southern state and local governments are under-represented in the workforce when compared to the labor force, they still constitute the largest group of workers in state and local government in the South in absolute numbers.

Conversely, black males were over-represented in state and local government when compared to the labor force during every five-year interval in this inquiry. In 1975, black males represented 10% of the workforce in state and local government in the South and 9% of the total labor force population in the South. From 1980 to 1995, black male workforce representation in state and local government increased to 12% and the labor force participation rate declined to 8%. These rates remained constant for the remainder of the research. Black males showed 4% over-representation in state and local governments in the South from 1980-1995.

White females were under-represented in state and local government in the South when compared with their total labor force population throughout the study period. In 1975 and 1980, white females were under-represented by 2 percentage points. By 1985, the percentage difference

Table 12-4 Workforce Representation In State and Local Government by High Level Occupations: Officials/Administrators and Professionals

Race/Gender	1975	1980	1985	1990	1995
White Males	57%	51%	47%	44%	40%
Black Males	3	4	5	5	6
White Females	35	38	40	41	42
Black Females	5	7	8	10	12
	100%	100%	100%	100%	100%

Note: Percent may not total 100% due to rounding.

Sources: *Minorities and Women In State and Local Government*, 1977. *Job Patterns For Minorities and Women In State and Local Government*, 1996, 1991, 1985 and 1982.

decreased by one point, from 2 to 1. In 1990 and 1995, the percent declined and white females were under-represented by 4% for each five-year interval. This was the largest gap for white females during the inquiry.

Black females were actually over-represented in state and local governments compared to the workforce throughout the study period. Black female participation rates steadily increased each five-year interval resulting in a low over-representation rate of 1% in 1975 to a high of 5% in 1995.

Occupational Participation Rate

Table 12-4 contains the workforce representation in state and local government in the South in high level occupational categories only. Officials/Administrators and Professionals have been designated as high level occupational categories for the purpose of this study. White males represent the largest group of workers in these occupational categories. In 1975, they represented 57% of the total workforce in high level occupational categories. The percentage of white males in high level occupational categories declined after 1975. In 1980, white males represented 51%, 47% in 1985, 44% in 1990, and 40% in 1995.

Black males have the lowest representation rates in high level occupational categories of the four groups. Black males represented 3% of the total workforce in high level occupational categories during 1975, 4% in 1980, 5% in 1985, 5% in 1990, and 6% in 1995.

White females constituted 35% of the total workforce in high level occupations in state and local governments in the South in 1975. These females represented the second largest group of workers in these categories. White females in high level occupational categories showed a small but steady increase for each five-year interval. In 1980, white females represented 38% of the high level occupational categories workforce, 40% in 1985, 41% in 1990, and 42% in 1995. In 1995, white females represented the largest group of employees in high level occupational categories in state and local governments in the South.

Black females represented 5% of the workforce population in high level occupational categories in state and local government in the South in 1975. In 1980, their percentage rate increased by two points, from 5% to 7%. In 1985, their representation rate in high level occupational categories increased to 8%. Black females increased two more percentage points in 1990, from 8% to 10%. They increased another 2 percentage points in 1995, from 10% to 12%. Black female representation rates in high level occupational categories increased each five year interval.

Table 12-5 shows the workforce representation rate in state and local governments in the South by the highest occupational category in state government, which is Officials/Administrators. White males dominated this category throughout the study period. They represented over 50% of this workforce occupation for each five-year interval. In 1975, white males represented 77% of the workforce population, 71% in 1980, 66% in 1985, 62% in 1990, and 58% in 1995. Although this group showed a steady percentage decline in each five-year interval, they still had much larger absolute numbers employed in the highest level of government than all other gender-race groups combined.

Black male representation in this occupational category increased from 3% in 1975 to 7% in 1995. In each year, their representation rate increased by one percentage point.

Table 12-5 Workforce Representation In State and Local Government by Top Level Occupational Category: Officials/Administrators

Race/Gender	1975	1980	1985	1990	1995
White Males	77%	71%	66%	62%	58%
Black Males	3	4	5	6	7
White Females	19	22	26	28	29
Black Females	2	2	3	4	6
	100%	100%	100%	100%	100%

Note: Percent may not total 100% due to rounding.

Sources: *Minorities and Women In State and Local Government*, 1977. *Job Patterns For Minorities and Women In State and Local Government*, 1996, 1991, 1985 and 1982.

Table 12-6 Demographics Composition of the Graduates with a Bachelor's Degree or Higher in the Labor Force

Race/Gender	1975	1980	1985	1990	1995
White Males	55%	53%	53%	50%	50%
Black Males	3	3	3	4	4
White Females	38	39	39	41	41
Black Females	4	5	5	5	5
	100%	100%	100%	100%	100%

Note: Percent may not total 100% due to rounding.

Source: U.S. Bureau of Census, 1970, 1980, and 1990.

White females increased their representation rate in this occupational category by 10 percentage points during the twenty-year study period. In 1975, white females represented 19% of the total workforce population in the Officials/Administrators occupational category. In 1980, the percentage rate increased to 22%, 26% in 1985, 28% in 1990, and 29% (25,411) in 1995.

Black female representation in the Officials/Administrators occupational category increased by four percentage points during the twenty-year study period. In 1975 and 1980, they represented 2%, 3% in 1985, 4% in 1990, and 6% in 1995. Black female participation rates in the top level occupational category was the lowest of the demographic groups throughout the study.

Table 12-6 provides data on the educational status of the labor force in the South. From 1975 to 1995, at least 50% of the labor force with a Bachelor's degree or over were white males. Although the percentage decreased from 55% in 1975 to 50% in 1995, white males still held the largest percentage of graduates with a Bachelor's degree or higher in the labor force. Black males represented 3% of the total graduates with a Bachelor's Degree or above in the labor force from 1975 to 1985. For 1990 and 1995 their rate increased to 4%.

In 1975, 38% of the college graduates in the labor force with a bachelor' Degree or above were white females. This group improved their number of baccalaureates to 41% by 1995. This represents a 3% increase from 1975 to 1995. The educational status of black females with bachelor's degrees or better improved from 4% in 1975 to 5% in 1980, where it remained through 1995.

Tables 12-7 and 12-8 reflect the differences in educational status of the demographic groups and their participation rate in high level

Table 12-7 Differences In Educational Status and Workforce Representation In High Level Occupational Categories: Officials/Administrators and Professionals

Race/Gender	1975	1980	1985	1990	1995
White Males	+2	-2	-6	-6	-10
Black Males	0	+1	+2	+1	+2
White Females	-3	-1	+1	0	+1
Black Females	+1	+2	+3	+5	+7

Note: The data are the result of the difference between the results in Table 12-4 and Table 12-6.

occupational categories and the top level occupational categories. Table 12-7 shows the differences between the percentage of the labor force with a bachelor's degree or higher and the workforce representation rate of each group in the Officials/Administrators and Professionals occupational categories. According to Table 12-7, more black females were in the government workforce in high level occupations than the percent of black females with a bachelor's degree or above in the labor force. More white females in the labor force held a bachelor's degree or higher than the percent of white females in high level occupational categories in the early years. White females with a bachelor's degree or better were under-represented in high level occupational categories in 1975 and 1980; in 1985 and 1995 they were over-represented by 1 percentage point; and in 1990 they showed parity in representation.

Black males with a bachelor's degree or better had parity in representation in 1975 and were slightly over-represented each of the following years. White males with a bachelor's degree or above were over-represented only in 1975. From 1980 to 1995 white males were under-represented in high level occupational categories based on their educational level. In 1975, the differences were a plus 2% to a -10%.

Table 12-8 provides the differences in the labor force with a bachelor's degree or above and the employment rate in government for the occupational category of Officials/Administrators, the highest occupational category designated by the EEOC. This occupational category constitutes the top level jobs in state and local government, in which policy development and decision making are essential components of the position. White males were over-represented in each five-year interval from 1975 to 1995. The differences ranged from a high of 22 percentage points in 1975 to a low of 8 percentage points in 1995. The percentage steadily decreased for each interval after 1975. Black males were equally

Table 12-8 Differences In Educational Status and Workforce Representation In the Top Level Occupational Category: Officials/Administrators

Race/Gender	1975	1980	1985	1990	1995
White Males	+22	+18	+13	+12	+8
Black Males	0	+1	+2	+2	+3
White Females	-19	-17	-13	-13	-12
Black Females	-2	-3	-2	-1	+1

Note: Result of differences between percentages in Tables 12-6 and 12-7.

represented in 1975 and over-represented for the remaining years. White females were under-represented from 1975 to 1995. Black females were also under-represented from 1975 to 1990. In 1995, black females were over-represented by one percentage point.

Annual Median Salary

To further analyze black women's status in state and local governments in the South, a comparison of their salary to white females, black males, and white males will be conducted. Table 12-9 shows the annual median salary of all state and local government employees in the southern states by race and gender. This table indicates that white males have the highest annual median salaries of the groups in this study from 1975 to 1995. Black females have the lowest annual median salary of the groups (except in 1975).

White males annual median salaries have increased from $8,828.00 in 1975 to $27,875.00 in 1995. The salary of black males increased from $5,687 in 1975 to $22,517 in 1995. Black males had the lowest annual median salary of the groups in this study for 1975. White females annual median salary in 1975 was $7,080 and increased to $24,754 by 1995. Black female's salary increased from $6,046 in 1975 to $21,357 in 1995. Black female's annual median salary represented the lowest of the groups in state and local government after 1975.

Data presented in Table 12-10 compares black women's annual median salary for high level occupational categories to the other demographic groups in state and local government in the South. For each of the five year intervals, black women's annual median salary has been less than the other groups. The wage gap between black females and white males appears to have narrowed over time, though black females still earn less than white males, black males, and white females. In 1975, black females annual median salary was equal to only 79%

Table 12-9 Annual Median Salary Of Southern State and Local Governments Employees By Year

Race/Gender	1975	1980	1985	1990	1995
White Males	$8,828	$12,530	$18,120	$21,722	$27, 875
Black Males	5,687	9,843	14,145	17,412	22, 517
White Females	7,080	10,097	15,208	18,809	24, 754
Black Females	6,046	8,797	13,250	16,453	21, 357
Average	$6,910	$10,317	$15,181	$18,599	$24,126

Source: *Job Patterns For Minorities and Women In State and Local Government*, 1996, 1991, 1885, and 1982. *Minorities and Women In State and local Government*, 1977, Volumes IV-VII.

Table 12-10 Annual Median Salary By Race and Gender For State and Local Government Employees In High Level Occupational Categories: Officials/Administrators and Professionals

Race/Gender	1975	1980	1985	1990	1995
White Males	$13,126	$18,433	$26,780	$32,728	$42,586
	(79%)	(74%)	(81%)	(83%)	(83%)
Black Males	11,305	15,307	22,670	28,408	36,795
	(91)	(89)	(96)	(96)	(96)
White Females	11,023	15,040	22,922	28,577	37,727
	(93)	(91)	(95)	(95)	(93)
Black Females	10,360	13,618	21,779	27,224	35,161

Note: Number in parenthesis is the percent of that particular annual salary that black females receive.

Source: *Job Patterns For Minorities and Women In State and Local Government*, 1996, 1991, 1885, and 1982. *Minorities and Women In State and local Government*, 1977, Volumes IV-VII.

($10,360/$13,126) of white males. In 1995, the wage gap declined to 83% ($35,161/$42,586) of white males. Although black women's annual median salaries were closest to black males and white females, they still represented the lowest paid of the groups.

A comparison of the annual median salaries of black women in the top level occupational category to their counterparts is shown in Table 12-11. In 1975, black women's annual median salary was 24% below white males, 11% below black males, and 7% below white females. There was only a slight variation between the salary of black males and black females, and white females and black females, which was prevalent

Table 12-11 Annual Median Salary of State and Local Government Employees In The Officials/Administrators Occupational Category

Race/Gender	1975	1980	1985	1990	1995
White Males	$14, 479 (76%)	$20, 096 (71%)	$29, 457 (82%)	$36, 283 (84%)	$47, 776 (83%)
Black Males	12, 429 (89)	16, 824 (84)	24, 509 (98)	31, 551 (96)	41, 396 (95)
White Females	11, 970 (93)	15, 991 (89)	25, 129 (96)	31, 551 (97)	41, 396 (95)
Black Females	11, 074	14, 201	24, 107	30, 438	39, 492

Note: Number in parenthesis is the percent of that particular annual salary that black females receive.

Sources: *Job Patterns For Minorities and Women In State and Local Government*, 1996, 1991, 1985, and 1982. *Minorities and Women In State and Local Government*, 1977, Volumes IV-VII.

throughout the interval years. Black citizens have been successful in obtaining positions in state and local governments, but they have not been as successful in obtaining comparable salaries in high salary positions.

By 1995, the wage gap between black females and black males and white females had narrowed. Black female's annual median salaries were only 5% below these two groups, whereas they were 17% below white males.

It does appear, nevertheless, that black women have made significant gains in their salary ratio in comparison to white males, black males, and white females over the years in most of the states. For example, in West Virginia, black females had a salary ratio higher than that of white females for four of the five reporting periods.

Implications and Conclusions

This research assessed the labor market status of black women in state and local governments in the South by comparing their status to that of white males, black males and white females. Studies have shown that black women have always participated in the labor market, however, they have largely been relegated to jobs and positions in the secondary job sector. Positions in the secondary job sector usually have lower wages, minimum wage benefits, undesirable working conditions, and less job security.

White males have monopolized upper level and mid-level positions in the southern workforce in state and local government from 1975 to 1995. Data from this study shows that white males make-up the majority of workers in state and local. It appears that the "good old boy" system is still alive and prevalent with the dawning of the new millennium. Although the percentage of white males in state and local governments decreased, they still represent the largest group of workers in state and local government in the South.

White females have managed to retain the position of the second largest group of workers in the workforce in state and local government in the South. During the twenty-year study period, this group averaged about 30% of the state and local government labor force. Black males represented between 10% and 12% of the workforce from 1975 to 1995, whereas black females represented between 8% and 14% of the workforce for this same period.

When race and gender are considered, black women made the greatest gains in state and local government representation in the South from 1975 to 1995, going from 8% of the workforce to 14%. White males decreased from 53% to 41% during this period. However, white females had the greatest increase in the general labor force during this time period, going from 30% to 37%, while black women went from 7% to 9%.

Black women have made considerable progress in state and local government over the years, going from domestic workers and housemaids in the fifties, to protesters and marchers for civil rights and women's rights in the sixties, to occupying low, middle and high positions in state and local government in the seventies, eighties, and nineties. However, their white female counterparts continue to outpace them in top level positions as well as salaries. It would be difficult to argue that any one of the theoretical explanations put forth earlier has the greatest credence at this point. Surely, as black females have become more qualified and better educated, they have obtained better positions in state and local government as well, as the Human Capital theory suggests. The Institutional Discrimination theory suggests that black females are still discriminated against in the workforce, and it is clear from all of the data presented here that they remain behind their gender and racial counterparts. Last, but not least, the Dual Labor Market theory suggests that there are two labor markets, in which black females reside in the secondary market. This is no longer true, either. It is true, nevertheless, that black females occupy more of the lower level positions in state and local government than the other groups in this study. But one could argue that they were also the last group to enter government service.

The study shows that black women have a significant presence in state and local government in the South. However, their involvement in high level occupational categories in state and local government in the South is limited. Black women's annual median salary in state and local governments in the South still lag behind other groups. Black women's annual median salary may exceed the other demographic groups in some instances, but this is not the norm.

Discrimination in the South as a region has dissipated. However, there are southern states where black women with the proper credentials may still be under-represented in state and local governments. Public policies that will change the mindset of southern legislators and bureaucrats can not be legislated. Therefore, remedies that will solve the issue of job and gender discrimination and equity that is more than 200 years old are highly sought.

References

Albelda, Randy P. 1986. "Occupational Segregation by Race and Gender, 1958-1981." *Industrial and Labor Relations Review* 39: 404-11.

Alexis, Marcus. 1973. "A Theory of Labor Market Discrimination with Interdependent Utilities." *American Economic Review* 63: 296-302.

Belman, Dale, and John S. Heywood. 1991. "Sheepskin Effects in the Returns to Education: An Examination of Women and Minorities." *Review Of Economics and Statistics* 73: 720-24.

Bergmann, Barbara R.1974. "Occupational Segregation, Wages and Profits When Employers Discriminate by Race and Sex." *Eastern Economic Journal* 1: 103-10.

Cayer, N. Joseph, and Lee Sigelman. 1980. "Minorities and Women in State and Local Government: 1973-1975." *Public Administration Review* 40: 443-50.

Critzer, John W., and Kul B. Rai. 1998. "Blacks and Women in Public Higher Education. Political and Socioeconomic Factors Underlying Diversity at the State Level." *Women & Politics* 19: 19-38.

Cunningham, James S., and Nadja Zalokar. 1992. "The Economic Progress of Black Women, 1940-1980: Occupational Distribution and Relative

Wages." *Industrial and Labor Relations Review* 45: 540-55.

Daley, Dennis. 1996. "Paths of Glory and the Glass Ceiling: Differing Patterns of Career Advancement Among Women and Minority Federal Employees." *Public Administration Quarterly.* 20:143-162.

Davis, Theodore J. 1994. "Income Inequities Between Black and White Populations in Southern Nonmetropolitan Counties." *Review of Black Political Economy* 22: 145-58.

Farley, Jennie. 1979. *Affirmative Action and the Woman Worker.* New York: AMACOM.

Fosu, Augustin Kwasi. 1987. "Explaining Post-1964 Earnings Gains by Black Women: Race or Sex?" *Review of Black Political Economy* 15: 41-55.

_____. 1992. "Occupational Mobility of Black Women, 1958-81: The Impact of Post 1964 Antidiscrimination Measures" *Industrial and Labor Relations Review* 45: 281-94.

_____. 1993. "Do Black and White Women Hold Different Jobs in the Same Occupation? A Critical Analysis of the Clerical and Service Sectors." *Review of Black Political Economy* 21: 68-82.

Idson, Todd L., and Hollis F. Price. 1992. "An Analysis of Wage Differentials by Gender and Ethnicity in the Public Sector." *Review of Black Political Economy* 19: 75-97.

Joint Center for Political and Economic Studies. 1997. *Black Elected Officials: A National Roster.* Washington, D.C.: University Press of America, Inc.

_____. 1993. *Black Elected Officials: A National Roster.* Washington, D.C.: University Press of America, Inc.

_____. 1990. *Black Elected Officials: A National Roster.* Washington, D.C.: University Press of America, Inc.

_____. 1985. *Black Elected Officials: A National Roster.* Washington, D.C.: University Press of America, Inc.

_____.1980. *National Roster of Black Elected Officials.* Volume 10. Washington, D.C.: University Press of America, Inc.

_____. 1975. *National Roster of Black Elected Officials.* Volume 5. Washington, D.C.: University Press of America, Inc.

Jones, Barbara A. 1985-86. "Black Women and Labor Force Participation: An Analysis of Sluggish Growth Rates." *Review of Black Political Economy* 14: 11-31.

Kelly, Rita Mae, et al. 1991. "Public Managers in the States: A Comparison of Career Advancement by Sex." *Public Administration Review* 51: 402-12.

King, Allan G. 1978. "Labor Market Racial Discrimination Against Black Women." *Review of Black Political Economy* 8: 325-35.

King, Mary C. 1992. "Occupational Segregation by Race and Sex, 1940-88." *Monthly Labor Review*115: 30-36.

_____ 1995. "Black Women's Labor Market Status: Occupational Segregation in the United States and Great Britain." *Review of Black Political Economy* 24: 25-43.

_____. 1990. "The Impact of Affirmative Action Regulation and Equal Employment Law on Black Employment." *Journal of Economic Perspective* 4: 47-63.

Madhavan, M.C., Louis Green, and Ken Jung. 1985. "A Note on Black-White Wage Disparity." *Review of Black Political Economy* 13: 39-50.

Malveaux, Julianne.1985-1986. "Comparable Worth and its Impact on Black Women." *Review of Black Political Economy* 14 : 47-62.

Nelson, Charmeynne D. 1975. "Myths About Black Women Workers in Modern America." *Black Scholar* 6: 11-15.

Sigelman, Lee and Albert K. Karnig. 1977. "Black Education and Bureaucratic Employment." *Social Science Quarterly* 57: 858-63.

Solberg, Eric and Teresa Laughlin. 1995. "The Gender Pay Gap, Fringe Benefits, and Occupational Crowding." *Industrial and Labor Relations Review* 48: 692-708.

Stiglitz, Joseph E. 1973. "Education and Inequality." *Annals of the American Academy of Political and Social Science* 409: 135-45.

U.S. Bureau of the Census. 1990. Census of Population: General Social and Economic Characteristics: U.S. Department of Commerce.

U.S. Bureau of the Census. 1980. Census of Population: General Social and Economic Characteristics: U.S. Department of Commerce.

U.S. Bureau of the Census. 1970. Census of Population: General Social and Economic Characteristics: U.S. Department of Commerce.

U.S. Commission on Civil Rights. 1990. *The Economic Status of Black Women: An Exploratory Investigation.*

U.S. Equal Employment Opportunity Commission. 1996. *Job Patterns For Minorities and Women in State and Local Government, 1995.* Washington, D.C.

_____. 1991. *Job Patterns For Minorities and Women in State and Local Government, 1990.* Washington, D.C.

_____. 1985. *Job Patterns For Minorities and Women in State and Local Government, 1985.* Washington, D.C.

_____. 1982. *Job Patterns For Minorities and Women in State and Local Government, 1980.* Washington, D.C.

_____. 1977. *Minorities And Women In State and Local Government,*

1975 Volume III State Statistical Summary Alabama-Georgia. Washington, D.C.

_____. 1977. *Minorities And Women In State and Local Government, 1975* Volume IV State Statistical Summary Idaho-Massachusetts. Washington, D.C.

_____. 1977. *Minorities And Women In State and Local Government, 1975* Volume V State Statistical Summary Michigan-New Mexico. Washington, D.C.

_____. 1977. *Minorities And Women In State and Local Government, 1975* Volume VI State Statistical Summary Idaho-Massachusetts. Washington, D.C.

_____. 1977. *Minorities And Women In State and Local Government, 1975* Volume VII State Statistical Summary South Dakota-Wyoming. Washington, D.C.

_____. 1977a. *Black Experiences Versus Black Expectations (A Case for Fair-Share Employment)*. Washington, D.C.

Wilkerson, Margaret. 1985-1986. "A Report on the Educational Status of Black Women During the UN Decade of Women, 1976-85." *Review of Black Political Economy* 14: 83-96.

Winegarden, C.R. 1972. "Barriers To Black Employment in White Collar Jobs: A Quantitative Approach." *Review of Black Political Economy* 2-3: 13-24.

CHAPTER 13

Representative Government and Affirmative Action in Mississippi: An Oxymoron in the Making?

Mfanya Donald Tryman

In the state of Mississippi, the concept of affirmative action seems like an oxymoron. This is due, in part, to the egregious nature of racial discrimination and racism in the past that stigmatized Deep South states like Mississippi. Because racial discrimination was so blatant, little attention has been given to the progress and representation of African Americans in state and local government in agencies and bureaucracies in Mississippi. Title VI and Title VII of the 1964 Civil Rights Act dramatically transformed and opened the doors of equal opportunity for women and people of color in the workforce and provided some degree of representation for African Americans and women. Title VI forbids the federal government from awarding contracts or providing funds to employers that discriminate on the basis of race, gender, religion, nationality, or color. Title VII mandates that employers take actions to ensure affirmative action in the recruiting, hiring, and promoting of such categories in the workforce (Congressional Quarterly Almanac, 1964.). Mississippi, like every other state, is subject to the same federal regulations. The U.S. Equal Employment Opportunity Commission (EEOC) was established as a part of the 1964 Civil Rights Act as an agent to monitor these provisions, insuring that African Americans would have a representative voice.

The purpose of this paper is fourfold: 1) to briefly discuss the various administrations of governors starting with Ross Barnett that set the political and racial climate for state and local government, 2) to investigate the progress that African Americans have made in employment representation in Mississippi state and local government starting in 1975 utilizing the standardized EEOC job categories and data, 3) to analyze the vertical occupational mobility of these employees starting in 1975 and culminating in 1995, and 4) to peruse and dissect those policymaking positions that African Americans have achieved during this same 20 year period, since policymaking is a critical component in the political process and public policy outcomes. These are strategically significant positions in influencing policy outcomes.

A Methodological Note

Little of a scholarly nature has been written on African Americans and affirmative action in administrative and bureaucratic capacities in the state of Mississippi, although a number of studies have been conducted related to the problems and progress that African Americans have experienced in the political arena and voting (Ladner 1970; Coleman and McLemore 1982; Hester 1982; Parker 1990; Coleman 1993). Specifically, scholarly literature on gubernatorial administrations and affirmative action in Mississippi are virtually nonexistent, although there are a number of studies related generally to blacks in state and local government and the influence of black political officials in influencing black appointments and hiring (Beyle 1998; Hawkins 1992; Singell 1991; Rehfuss 1986; Riccucci 1986; Dye and Renick 1981). Hence, there is a greater reliance on newspapers in this section of the paper to account for issues and events related to affirmative action and representative government. The primary data for the uniform job classifications in state and local government were obtained from the EEOC's EEO-4 five-year published reports in 1975, 1980, 1985, 1990, and 1995.

Gubernatorial Administrations in Mississippi, 1960-1996

It is important to note that the issues of social and political equality took precedence over other aspects of equality in the South. That is to say, the question of whether African Americans would be able to enjoy the fruits associated with the principles of freedom, justice, and equality in the U.S. Constitution was more important than the question of jobs and economic development, which would flow from ascertaining the former rights. Hence, jobs took a back seat in the early gubernatorial administrations fighting racial integration in the sixties. These governors were more concerned with racial segregation than job integration. As Lea has pointed out ".... the politics of class, race, and a traditional political culture explain why Mississippi's powerful position in Congress was historically more often used to fight civil rights and expanded social programs than to improve the racial atmosphere and the economic lot of the common people in the state." (1993, 10).

Yet, African Americans began making progress on several fronts in the fifties and sixties, which not only included steps toward social equality, but political power involving elected representatives as well as isolated appointments in various positions of state and local government. Several Civil Rights Acts aided the struggle for racial equality.[1] While political grandstanding in the name of racial segregation took place on several occasions, the social and political pressures, particularly from the federal government, would also influence gubernatorial administrations in opening the doors to black representation in the public sector of state and local government.

Thus, progress in state and local government jobs did not occur in a vacuum for black residents. It is a pejorative argument that a number of factors converged to open the doors for better job opportunities. This included the 1964 Civil Rights Act, the 1965 Voting Rights Act (the guaranteed right to vote that closed loopholes southern officials exploited to deny blacks the right to vote, followed by the election of black elected officials), political and legal pressure and sanctions from the federal government, protest marches and violence, and effective lobbying. Dye and Renick, in a study of 111 cities utilizing EEO-4 reports, found that black employment in administrative and professional positions was directly tied to representation on city councils and the size and percent of the black population of the city (Dye and Renick 1981).

While the data for this study originates in 1975, the focus on governors starts in 1960 because the first crack in the door of *de jure* racial segregation began during the gubernatorial term of Ross Barnett. One of Governor Barnett's most notable "accomplishments" during his tenure in office from 1960-64 was the debacle with James Meredith, who integrated the University of Mississippi in 1962 after a confrontation and bloodbath between college students, non-student segregationists, and the National Guard that had to be called out by President Kennedy. Barnett was a symbol of southern resistance to racial integration at any and all levels, including higher education. Barnett had campaigned for office on the basis of maintaining racial segregation while pursuing industrial expansion. While he condemned the North and the federal government for intrusion upon states' rights, he had no problems in pursuing economic development by wooing northern industry (Sumners 1980).

Governor Paul B. Johnson, who was a strong advocate of a research and development center for the colleges and universities of the state, succeeded Barnett in office. During his tenure in office from 1964 to 1968, Mississippi became a state in transition. Johnson had become a symbol of segregation by physically attempting to block the entrance to Ole Miss by James Meredith and federal authorities as Lieutenant Governor under Barnett, and used the slogan "Stand Tall With Paul" as part of his successful campaign for governor in 1964. Nevertheless, it was during his administration that a number of events occurred that would incrementally change the social and economic fabric of Mississippi. Desegregation as the result of civil rights legislation in the mid-sixties combined with the quest for economic and industrial expansion. The state began to accept federal aid, which had non-discrimination stipulations. For the first time, the state began to employ more workers in industry than in agriculture. The Education and Research Center in Jackson, now known as the Universities Center, was established and funded under the administration of Governor Johnson (Sumners 1980).

John Bell Williams (1968-72), who came to office in January of 1968, succeeded Johnson. Just as Johnson had stood as a symbol of segregation, one of the first symbolic actions of desegregation by Williams started in his inaugural parade, in which he banned the Americans for Preservation of the White Race float, a float which attempted to move into parade formation anyway, only to be stopped by police. Accomplishments during William's administration included a pay raise for school teachers, which he strong-armed through the legislature, a massive highway building program, and the establishment of the Medicaid program in Mississippi, which benefited a large number of black and white Mississippians. The Governors Office of Federal State Programs was established in 1968 to handle federally funded programs for state agencies (Wheat 1993). The state NAACP, however, called for the impeachment and removal of Williams, who had supported the shooting of two black students on the campus of Jackson State College (now University) by highway patrolman in 1970, claiming that they were responding to sniper fire during campus protests (Pittmay 1970).

William Waller was elected governor of Mississippi and served from 1972-76 after unsuccessfully attempting to succeed himself by changing the state constitution. During his administration, he became the first Mississippi governor to appoint blacks in representative positions in state government. This included appointments to the state Board of Corrections, the Prison Parole Board, and the College Board. Waller had, earlier in 1963, unsuccessfully prosecuted Byron de la Beckwith, who had been charged with the 1963 assassination of NAACP leader Medgar Evers.[2]

Michael Raft, Executive Director of the Mississippi Council on Human Relations, noted in 1974 that two investigations of state agencies showed that most of them still practiced blatant discrimination, deliberately attempting to keep blacks in menial positions, and that blacks constituted only 6 percent of state agencies in Mississippi, although the state was 40 percent black at the time. Of 69 letters sent to state agencies requesting information on job opportunities, only 17 responded, and of these, 9 stated that there were no openings while the other 8 continued to notify the council of its openings. At the beginning of 1974, in spite of Waller's efforts to employ blacks through appointments, 44 state agencies still had no black representation in any capacity.(The Commercial Appeal 1974).

Cliff Finch succeeded Waller as governor of Mississippi, and served from 1976-80. Like Waller, Finch also appointed blacks to representative positions in state government. Just as importantly, he projected the image of a populist politician in his campaign for governor as well as during his gubernatorial administration. By identifying with class rather than racial interests, he was successful in getting the vote of "redneck" whites as well as most blacks. His down home political style appealed to the average Mississippian. With his concocted buffoonery, political stunts, and awkward syntax, which reflected his lack of education, his political style provided relief at a time when Mississippi had just experienced the racial turmoil of the sixties and the school busing and integration of the seventies. A number of scandals were associated with his administration. Nevertheless, more than any other person, Finch is credited with the creation of the current Democratic party in Mississippi, bringing some degree of racial harmony and representation in a conflict-ridden political structure. As with the incremental actions of the previous two governors, Finch was responsible for black advancement as well. He brought programs such as Head Start, food stamps, and

Job Corps to the state. Before his administration, there were no young people enrolled in Job Corps, which reached over 1,000 in 1986 (Salter 1986).

During Finch's administration controversy arose in the Governor's Office of Job Development and Training over the placement and representation of black and white youngsters in the Youth Incentive Entitlement Project. A black minister who had been terminated by the program had alleged that black youth were given menial clean-up jobs while white youth were given more meaningful jobs. The minister alleged that the governor's office ignored the investigative findings of the EEO officer and that he was terminated for "blowing the whistle" (Jackson 1978).

In 1980, William Winter succeeded Cliff Finch as governor. Winter is considered to be one of the most progressive governors that the state of Mississippi has ever had. Winter served from 1980 to 1984. Because of the scandals and corruption associated with the previous administration of Governor Finch, the campaign for governor in 1979 revolved, not around the issues and political rhetoric of the past, but around the question of what candidate could best restore political trust, effectiveness, and efficiency to state government. Winter is credited with the first uniform personnel act in Mississippi state government, which has a number of attributes necessary for efficient, effective, and representative government. The act meant the creation of a single personnel system to handle more than 27,000 state employees, civil service protection from political interference and protection for those under the classification commission. It also provided employees working with federal programs with a merit system, and provided protections for 2,000 other employees who were exempt from any personnel system. Black representation was achieved on the classification commission through a Winter appointment in his first year in office, which served as the forerunner for the new Personnel Board, and he appointed a black as director of the Governor's Office of Human Resources. Strangely enough, Winter called for abolishing the Voting Rights Act, which was due to expire in 1982, arguing that it was no longer needed since everyone now had the right to vote (Mould 1981). But his crowning achievement was the Education Reform Act, which provided for state-funded kindergartens, compulsory school attendance, and upgrading schools and curricula. A record tax increase was passed to finance his educational reforms (Shaw 1983).

Bill Allain succeeded William Winter as governor in 1984 and served until 1988. Allain was the first governor to appoint an African American to the Mississippi Supreme Court. Although Waller had been unsuccessful in changing the state constitution in order to succeed himself in office, and Winter refused to support such an amendment when he took office, Allain supported and took credit for a constitutional amendment, which allowed the governor to serve another term. Among other accomplishments, Allain also took credit for the full implementation and funding of the 1982 Education Reform Act, and appointed a number of black and women residents to various boards and commissions proportionate to the state population (McIntosh 1988). It was clear that African American were achieving representation in a number of spheres.

In 1988, Ray Mabus became one of the youngest governors in the nation at the age of 39, beating Jack Reed, a Republican businessman, who in defeat received 47% of the vote. Mabus pledged to deliver Mississippi from its tradition of backwardness and racial politics. At the same time, while Mississippi was electing a progressive governor in 1987 who pledged never for Mississippi to be last again, voters narrowly repealed by an embarrassing 52-48 percent margin a 97-year-old ban on interracial marriages (Winbush 1987). Mabus pushed for educational reform, economic development, and political reform. Like previous governors, he appointed a number of African Americans to public positions.

In 1990, it was reported that the 1991 Mississippi legislature would be required to provide $6.16 million to end a 20-year-old discrimination suit against the state employment agency. Of this amount, $4.79 million would go to 766 African Americans and/or women and the remaining amount of money to lawyers for the class action suit. The Mississippi Employment Security Commission in Bolivar County (in northwest Mississippi) was found guilty of race and sex discrimination and upheld by the Fifth U.S. Circuit Court of Appeals after two appeals by the state. The suit charged racial discrimination in 1969-70 and sex discrimination from 1969-73. The discrimination suit included referrals of blacks to job openings below their qualifications and referrals of whites to positions above their qualifications, acceptance of job orders from businesses who wanted only males, and referrals of women to low paying jobs and men to high paying jobs at a pharmaceutical company. Plaintiffs initially filed discrimination complaints with the EEOC in 1970, and four African Americans followed with a suit in 1972 (Kraft 1990).

Ray Mabus was defeated in the first attempt by an incumbent

Mississippi governor to successfully succeed himself by Kirk Fordice, a Republican businessman who garnered 51% of the vote to 47% for Mabus. Mabus suggested that his lost to Fordice was a victory for the "Old Guard." (Campbell 1991).

The election of Kirk Fordice in 1991 in many ways represented a setback for racial progress and representative government. In fact, Fordice fought the *Ayers* college desegregation suit in 1992, and stated that he would call out the National Guard before instituting a tax increase, even if directed by the U.S. Supreme Court, to fund black universities in the state (Shaffer 1994).[3] Unlike recent Democratic governors, Fordice only grudgingly appointed a few blacks (conservatives) to boards and commissions. In 1998 Mississippi was the only state in the union that had not complied with the National Voter Registration Act of 1993, which is often referred to as "Motervoter." This act allows citizens to register to vote at a number of social service agencies and eliminates dual voter registration roles. Fordice, a vocal critic of the act, referred to this legislation as "Welfare Voter" (Wagster 1998). While former Mississippi governors had promoted diversity in appointments going back to Waller's election in 1972, Fordice continued to ignore the trend in 1996 by appointing four all-white male businessmen to replace outgoing College Board members, one of whom was a woman and one of whom was black. Further, he accused African Americans of using the issue of race when they opposed his initial appointments, which were turned down by the legislature (Shaffer and Breaux 1997). Fordice also questioned plans to open the files of the Sovereignty Commission, a state-sanctioned agency created in the 1950s to enforce racial segregation (Jackson 1996). He attempted, unsuccessfully, to stop state funding of a minority business loan program, arguing that the U.S. Supreme Court had ruled against such funding (*The Clarion Ledger* 1999). Fordice had been re-elected in 1996. His term expired in 2000.

Equal Employment Opportunity Job Descriptions

The EEOC utilizes eight job categories to standardize equal employment opportunities in the public workforce for the federal government and the 50 states. The top five includes official and administrative, professional, protective services, para-professional, and technical. Official and administrative positions include those who participate in setting broad policies and are responsible for carrying out such policies. They direct particular departments or provide specialized consultation on a district, regional, or area basis (e.g., department heads, bureau chiefs, division chiefs and directors). Professionals are those with specialized training or theoretical knowledge, usually obtained from going to college, work experience, or other training which provides them with equivalent knowledge (e.g., accountants, social workers, dieticians, doctors, engineers). Technicians occupy those positions required to have a combination of basic scientific or technical knowledge and manual skills that can be acquired through specialized post-secondary school education or through the equivalent of on-the-job training (e.g., computer programmers, drafters, survey and mapping technicians, licensed practical nurses). Protective services include employees trusted with public safety, security, and protection from destructive forces (e.g., police patrol officers, fire fighters, guards, and deputy sheriffs). Para-professionals constitute those workforce members who have some of the duties of a professional or technician in a supportive role, and which usually requires less formal training and or experience normally required for professional or technical status (e.g., research assistants, medical aids, child support workers) (Equal Employment Opportunity Commission Reports, 1975-1995).[4]

Data Analysis

The first year in which systemic data is available for full-time employees in state and local government in Mississippi was 1975, collected by the EEOC in EEOC-4 Reports. A number of points should be kept in mind when examining the data in the following tables from 1975 to 1995.[5] First, employment gains by African Americans began to occur after the civil rights legislation in the mid-sixties. Specifically, the 1964 and 1965 Civil Rights Acts had the greatest impact. Second, Mississippi's population is 37% African American, which gives it a diverse minority base. Third, since black elected officials began to increase in dramatic numbers in the seventies, it is not unusual to think that there would also be an increase in black appointments and employees. (This would be especially true in mostly black or majority black towns. But one would also expect black elected state officials to begin to exert their collective political muscle in the legislature to influence job hiring and black appointments). Beyle (1998) in *Congressional Quarterly* notes this point in an introductory essay. He stated that "politically, it makes sense to open up jobs for women and minorities; they are becoming more active in politics and their support often is needed to win elections" (117). Fourth, as noted earlier, Mississippi began to accept and receive some of the largesse of the federal government grants and contracts, which had anti-discrimination clauses attached. While Mississippi, like other southern states, continued to posture with rhetoric regarding states' rights in the sixties, they also begin to open their state treasuries to the federal aid available, which stipulated equal opportunity, at least on paper, in the recruitment and hiring of more people of color and women in state government. Fifth, since Mississippi has a number of black colleges and universities that pre-dated the civil rights era and racial integration, it is not unexpected that a large number of college educated and trained workers would be available for employment in state and local government. This includes three black public colleges and universities and two private ones.[6] Lastly, since the data is not broken down by the level of government, it has implications that will be explored in greater detail.

As Table 13-1 shows, in 1975, 3% of the administrative positions were held by black males compared to 67% for white males and only 1% for black women in contrast to 28% white women. Similarly, black

Table 13-1 Mississippi State and Local Government Full-Time Employees 1975*

	WM	BM	WF	BF
Official/Administrative	891	42	373	17
	(67%)	(3%)	(28%)	(1%)
Professional	1,086	51	1,162	75
	(45%)	(2%)	(48%)	(3%)
Technician	622	84	1474	312
	(24%)	(3%)	(59%)	(12%)
Protective Service	2,084	397	96	22
	(80%)	(15%)	(4%)	(1%)
Para. Professional	384	312	1,050	799
	(15%)	(12%)	(41%)	(31%)
Total	5,067	886	4,155	1,225

Source: Equal Employment Opportunity Commission, *State and Local Government Information, EEO-4 Report for 1975.*

*Data and totals for each report do not include Hispanics, Asian, or Native Americans, who constitute less than 1 percent of state employees. Percents may not equal 100 due to rounding.

males constituted only 2% in the professional ranks while white males made up 45% of the professionals in state and local governments. Three percent of the professional wage employees were black females while white women made up 48% of this category.

In the technical area, 24% or almost one-fourth of the 2492 technical employees were white males compared to just 3% for black males. At the same time, white females made up 59% of technicians in contrast to 12% for black females. In the area of protective services, white males constituted a higher percent (80) of this category than any other positions of the top four categories, making up 2084 of the employees in this area. Black males made up only 15% or 397, and black females were just 1% or 22 of the employees while white women were 4% or 96 of the protective service employees. White females (41%) and black females (31%) combined for 72% of the total employees in the paraprofessional ranks. Of the 11,333 full-time employees in the five occupations in 1975, 2,111 or 19% were black.

In 1985, ten years after the first report in 1975, white males continued to represent two-thirds of the officials and administrators in state and local government with 66%. Black males represented 4%, and white women reflected 26% of the total, a decrease of 2% over 1975. Black females increased to 4%, up 3% from 1975.

In the professional realm, white males dropped from 45% in 1975 to 39% in 1985, but increased in absolute numbers from 1,086 to 5,963. Black males increased among professionals from 2% in 1975 to 5% in 1985. White females dropped from 48% to 45% during this time period, yet increased their numbers from 1162 to 6970. Black females increased from 3% of the professional class in 1975 to 11% in 1985. These results are found in Table 13-2.

White males represented a slight majority (51%) of all technicians in 1985, which more than doubled the 24% they held in 1975. Black males slightly increased their numbers from 3% to 5% during this same time period. White females reflected a dramatic decrease among technicians, going from 59% to 33% during this ten-year period, a percentage decrease of almost half. Black females remained almost constant, dropping slightly from 12% in 1975 to 11% in 1985. In 1985, the number of workers in the five occupations almost quadrupled, going from 11,333 in 1975 to 43,913 in 1985. African Americans constituted 21% of the workers. Protective services continued to be dominated by white males in 1985, where they constituted 74% of the entire group, a drop of 6%

Table 13-2 Mississippi State and Local Government Full-time Employees-1985

	WM	BM	WF	BF
Official/Administrative	2512	157	995	142
	(66%)	(4%)	(26%)	(4%)
Professional	5963	718	6970	1688
	(39%)	(5%)	(45%)	(11%)
Technician	4028	433	2636	837
	(51%)	(5%)	(33%)	(11%)
Protective Services	7283	1676	553	315
	(74%)	(17%)	(6%)	(3%)
Para. Professional	1070	1289	2464	2184
	(15%)	(18%)	(35%)	(31%)
Total	20,856	4,273	13,618	5,166

Source: Equal Employment Opportunity Commission, *State and Local Government Information, EEO-4 Report for 1985.*

over 1975. Black males represented 17% in 1985, an increase of 2% over 1975. White females reflected 6% of the protected services in 1985, an increase of 2 above the 4% in 1975. Black females made up 3% in 1985, 2% more than 1975. Among paraprofessionals, white males made up 15% in 1985, the same percent as in 1975. Black males were 18% of this category in 1985 compared to 12% in 1975. White females constituted 35% of this occupation in 1985 in contrast to 41% in 1975. Black females were 31% of this class in 1985, no change from 1975.

By 1995, (Table 13-3) white males represented 50% of the officials and administrators in state and local government compared to 8% for black males. White females constituted 34% of these positions while black females made up 7% of the positions. Among professionals, white males were 32% of the total group in contrast to only 7% for black males. White females constituted almost half B 6074 (47%) B of the total employees in this category while black females were 1906 (15%) of the total.

In the technical classification, white males were roughly one third of the employees in state and local government, which totaled 2273 of the workers, while black males constituted 13% of the group. White females reflected just over one third of the personnel in this category at 36% of the total, while black females made up 18% of technical professionals. In the category of protective workers, 50% were white males

Table 13-3 Mississippi State and Local Government Full Time Employees-1995

	WM	BM	WF	BF
Official/Administrative	1660	283	1156	240
	(50%)	(8%)	(34%)	(7%)
Professional	4169	896	6074	1906
	(32%)	(7%)	(47%)	(15%)
Technician	2273	872	2451	1238
	(33%)	(13%)	(36%)	(18%)
Protective Services	3800	2362	425	1086
	(50%)	(31%)	(6%)	(14%)
Para. Professional	634	1069	2357	3788
	(8%)	(14%)	(30%)	(48%)
Total	12,536	5,483	12,463	8,258

Source: Equal Employment Opportunity Commission, *State and Local Government Information, EEO-4 Report for 1995.*

and 31% were black males. Six percent were white females and 14% were black females. Finally, among paraprofessionals, white males made up only 8% of these workers in contrast to 14% for black males.

At the same time, white females made up 30% of the paraprofessionals in state and local government while black females reflected 48% or almost half of the total. In 1995, the number of full-time workers in state and local government in the five occupations actually decreased by 5,174, dropping to 38,739.

It is, of course, at the upper level of management that policy is made and implemented. Hence, it is significant to examine the progress that African Americans have made at this level. Table 13-4 pulls together the data from tables 13-1 through 13-3 in the upper level management category. This provides a better perspective of such progress from 1975 to 1995.

In 1975, black males made up only 3% of the officials and administrators and just 2% of the professionals. They continued to make progress in both of these categories from 1975 to 1995. By 1995, they represented 8% of the administrators and 7% of the professionals in state and local governments. Black women had similar numbers in the administrative realm, holding just 1% of the official and administrative positions in 1975 and 7% of these positions in 1995. Among professionals, black women made up 3% of the total in 1975 and had reached 15% by

Table 13-4 Mississippi State and Local Government Upper Level Management Full Time Employees- 1975-1995

	WM	BM	WF	BF
Official/Administrative	891	42	373	17
	(67%)	(8%)	(34%)	(7%)
Professional	1086	51	1162)	75
	(45%)	(2%)	(48%)	(3%)
1975 Total	1,977	93	1,535	92
Official/Administrative	1902	107	795	63
	(66%)	(4%)	(28%)	(2%)
Professional	3740	348	3864	656
	(43%)	(4%)	(45%)	(8%)
1980 Total	5,642	455	4,659	719
Official/Administrative	2512	157	995	142
	(66%)	(4%)	(26%)	(4%)
Professional	5963	718	6970	1688
	(39%)	(5%)	(45%)	(11%)
1985 Total	8,475	875	7,965	1,830
Official/Administrative	2792	223	1256	242
	(62%)	(5%)	(28%)	(5%)
Professional	6372	919	8787	2289
	(35%)	(5%)	(48%)	(12%)
1990 Total	9,164	1,142	10,043	2,531
Official/Administrative	1660	283	1156	240
	(50%)	(8%)	(35%)	(7%)
Professional	4169	896	6074	1906
	(32%)	(7%)	(47%)	(15%)
1995 Total	5,829	1,179	7,230	2,146

Source: United States Equal Employment Opportunity Commission, *State and Local Government Information, EEO-4 Reports for 1975, 1980, 1985, 1990, 1995.*

1995. While black men and black women represent similar percentages among officials and administrator, and have made similar progress in this area, this is not the case among professionals. Black women have made significantly greater progress in this job classification, in which they represent 15% of the total compared to only 7% for black men.

By contrast, white males and females overwhelmingly occupied most of the positions in official/administrative capacities and professional occupations in 1995. Combined, they held 85% of all official/administrative positions in state and local government compared to 15% for black men and women; whereas in 1975 white males and females combined held 95% of these positions. In the professional category, white men and women together held 79% of all positions in 1995 compared to 22% for black men and women; in 1975 white males and females held 93% of these positions.

Implications and Conclusions

African Americans have made significant progress in state and local government since the EEOC began to collect data in a systemic manner in the mid-seventies. This is especially true when one considers that there was virtually no black representation in state government and only a handful in elected or official capacities in Mississippi until the late sixties. This dramatically changed in the years after the 1964 Civil Rights Act and 1965 Voting Rights Act. In the early sixties, less than 10% of eligible black residents were registered to vote compared to 70% in 1990. In the early sixties, only about 5% of all registered voters were black, by 1990 this figure had reached almost 35%. In 1968 there was only one black representative in the state legislature, by 1993 there were 42 and by 1997 there were 45 out of a total of 174 (35 in the House of a total of 122 and 10 in the Senate of a total of 52). In 1968, there were only 4 black county supervisors, 78 in 1992, and 95 in 1997 out of a total of 410. In 1964, there were only 6 black elected state and local representatives, by 1990 there were 690 and by 1997 there were 803 out of a total of 4,754 (Coleman 1993; Joint Center for Political and Economic Studies, 9; Clark 1997). In 1968, there were no black representatives who held legislative committee chairmanships in the state house or senate; in 1996 there were 8 African American who held committee chairs in the state senate alone (Shaffer, Sturrock, Breaux, Minor, 277 1999). While these gains in voting, politics, and representatives in state and local government have been incremental in nature, it is a substantial change compared to the period of *de jure* segregation.

However, the greatest gains in black representation in state and local government have not been in obtaining administrative and professional positions, a major subject of this paper. It is here that policymaking and administrative discretion occurs which affects not only the agency, but the state as a whole and local governments. These positions not only have the most administrative influence in an agency or town, but they also provide better pay and benefits than lower level positions in state and local government. While it could be argued that white males no longer dominate official/administrative and professional occupations to the extent of 15-20 years ago, they, along with white women, still held 85% of the former positions and 79% of the latter positions in 1995. White females, a protected class like blacks, have more than achieved parity at this level, occupying 35% of the official/administrative positions and 47% of the professional positions. White females appear to have penetrated, or perhaps eluded, the glass ceiling in state and local government in Mississippi. *Congressional Quarterly*, in a 1998 publication, reaches a similar conclusion in stating that "A recent study of state government agency heads suggests that women in state government are circumventing the so-called glass ceiling or administrative lid rather than trying to break through it. They are doing this by moving into expanded state government activities, such as consumer affairs and arts agencies, by involvement in governmental and political activism, and by reaching parity with men in terms of education, experience, and professionalism." (Beyle 1998, 117).

Black males in 1995 had their greatest representation (31%) in the protective services occupation, the same category as 1975 (15%), followed by paraprofessional (14% in 1995). Black females were most represented among paraprofessionals in 1995, holding 48% of the occupational positions; the comparable figure in 1975 was 31%. In most occupations, black males and females are still greatly under-represented. The greatest gains of blacks have been in secondary positions that include technical, paraprofessional, protective services, and paraprofessional occupations.

Former conservative governors, while their motives may have been suspect, made bold appointments of blacks to commissions and boards when racial integration was still a laboratory experiment for Mississippi in the 1970s and 1980s. In addition, the fact that no blacks served in appointive positions as agency heads in the Fordice administration in 1999 is a step backward for representative government in Mississippi. Fordice had the opportunity to appoint African Americans to a number of positions since 1992, but seldom exercised such a prerogative. Even more importantly, the statements and actions of Fordice suggest some degree of hostility toward representative government and racial diversity. Undoubtedly, for political reasons, Democratic governors will continue to appoint blacks as agency heads. Yet, such appointments may well be tempered by the fact that an overwhelming majority of white Democrats (83%) statewide opposed affirmative action in a 1996 statewide poll (Shaffer, Sturrock, Breaux, Minor, 1999). Since Fordice is the only Republican governor since Reconstruction in Mississippi, it is too early to suggest a trend with the GOP with regard to the appointment of blacks to high level political and administrative positions. V.O. Key noted in his classic work on politics in the South in 1949 that the traditionalistic political orientation in this region was characterized by disenfranchisement, malapportionment, a one party system, and Jim Crow (Key 1949). Overt and egregious manifestations of this invidious system have disappeared from the political and administrative landscape. Nevertheless, the legacy of the past will still require time, programs, and aggressive governors to overcome past discrimination in the quest of African Americans to achieve a more representative stature in the upper echelons of state government in Mississippi. It should also be kept in mind that the data in this study does not break down the number of African Americans employed by the state compared to local governments. Mississippi has more black elected officials than any other state, in part, because they have a large number of black majority towns and counties, which increases the opportunities to appoint African American in administrative and official positions. Hence, it is reasonable to assume that a large number and percent of African Americans holding positions in policymaking as well as secondary occupations are at the city and county level rather than in state government.[6] The number of African Americans holding administrative and policymaking positions in state government is further compromised by this reality.

Finally, while African Americans have obviously made progress, this progress may be tempered in the future as a result of recent Supreme Court rulings on affirmative action, and ongoing litigation that probably will have a chilling effect in recruiting and hiring that employ aggressive methods to diversify the public sector, particularly at the managerial and administrative level. Because of the foregoing discussion and analysis, in all likelihood a great deal of the progress in creating a representative government will continue. However, more of this progress will probably be the result of political influence and racial considerations in majority-black towns and counties rather than at the state level in affirmative action or other special programs designed to diversify the government workforce at various levels.

This study has a number of implications for state and local government in general and southern state and local government in particular. Progress in the number of black elected officials in southern state and local government has not been limited to Mississippi; nor, for that matter, has it been limited to the South (Bositis 1998). Black Americans have also made substantial gains in various bureaucratic capacities as well in state and local government in other states (*Equal Employment Opportunity Commission* 1995).

Other southern states have witnessed the advent of the two party system in state politics in the latter half of the twentieth century, as Republicans have made gains in gubernatorial and legislative capacities as well as the judiciary in state and local government. The two party system in southern politics raises a number of interesting research questions for the state of Mississippi as well as other state and local governments in the region. To begin with, has there been a concomitant gain in administrative and bureaucratic positions as black Americans have made advances in the political arena? While this study did not address this question in detail with regard to Mississippi, it is clear that the two factors are related. Or, put another way, to what extent have black elected officials used their power and influence to appoint blacks to administrative positions and pressure local and state government officials to hire more blacks in state and local government positions?

A second research question that will be proffered here is to what extend has affirmative action programs influenced the recruitment, hiring, and promotion of blacks in southern state and local government, and what role have political parties played in this process? Mississippi witnessed progress in the number of blacks in state and local government primarily during the era of Democratic governors in Mississippi, with more limited success under a Republican governor. Has this pattern held true in other southern states, or have other factors been responsible for such progress?

As noted earlier, EEOC data does not break down what percent of the positions, race, and gender are located in state government as opposed to local government. While it has been theorized here that a great deal of progress for blacks in Mississippi bureaucracies and agencies may indeed be more at the local level rather than at the state level, a third important question to be researched is whether this pattern holds true in other states as well? Succinctly put, is most of the racial progress at the local level in majority black towns and municipalities where blacks control political power?

The fourth and final research question is related to salary and agency type. Are the salaries of blacks in Mississippi and other southern states commensurate with their white counterparts in state and local government with an equal number of years of service in similar position classifications? Finally, a corollary of this research question is one related to the type of agency that blacks are hired and promoted in. Are they going into local and state government in positions that have a substantial public policy impact on the citizenry in critical areas of well-being, or are these positions in agencies that have little significance to the public?

References

Beyle, Thad L. 1998. *State Government: Congressional Quarterly's Guide to Current Issues and Activities. 1998-99,* Washington, D.C.: Congressional Quarterly, Inc.

Bositis, David A. 1998. *Black Elected Officials: A Statistical Summary 1993-1997.* Washington, D.C.: Joint Center for Political and Economic Studies.

Campbell, Sarah C. 1991. "Futuristic Mabus Regrets not Staying in Present." *The Clarion Ledger.* November 8, p. 1A.

Clark, Eric. 1997. *Mississippi Official and Statistical Register, 1996-2000.* Jackson, MS: Secretary of State Office.

Coleman, Mary D., and Leslie B. McLemore. 1982. "Black Independent Politics in Mississippi: Constants and Challenges." In *The New Black Politics: The Search for Political Power.* eds. Michael Preston , Lenneal Henderson, and Paul Puryear. 2nd Ed., New York: Longman.

Coleman, Mary. 1993. "Black Politics and Political Change in Mississippi." In *Politics in Mississippi.* ed. Joseph P. Parker. Salem, Wisconsin: Sheffield Publishing Co.

Congressional Quarterly Almanac. 1964. Congressional Quarterly Service. 20: 338-380. Washington, D.C..

Davis, Dan. 1987. "Waller Says State is Ready for Back to the Future." *The Clarion Ledger.* April 26.

Dye, Thomas R., and James Renick. 1981. "Political Power and City Jobs: Determinants of Minority Employment." *Social Science Quarterly* 62: 475-486.

Hawkins, Robert. 1992. "Diversity and Municipal Openness. *Public Management* 74: 3-35.

Hester, Kathryn Healy. 1982. "Mississippi and the Voting Rights Act: 1965-1982." *Mississippi Law Journal* 52: 803-76.

Key, V.O. 1949. *Southern Politics in State and Nation.* New York: Alfred Knopf.

Kraft, Beverly P. 1990. "Job-bias to Cost States $61 million." *The Clarion Ledger.* August 22, p. 1A.

Ladner, Joyce. 1970. "What Black Power Means to Negroes in Mississippi." in *The Transformation of Activism.* ed. August Meier. Chicago: Aldine Publishing Co.

Lea, James F. 1993. "The Political Culture of Mississippi: Tradition and Change." In *Politics in Mississippi.* ed. Joseph P. Parker, Salem, WI: Sheffield Publishing Co.

McIntosh, Shawn. 1988. "Allain Laces His Farewell with Advice." *The Clarion Ledger.* January 7, p. 3B.

Mississippi Employment Security Commission. 1999. *Mississippi: Labor Market Information for Affirmative Action Programs.* Jackson: Labor Market Information Department.

Mould, David. 1981. "Winter Calls for Abolishing Voting Rights Act." *The Commercial Appeal.* April 29.

Parker, Frank. 1990. *Black Votes Count: Political Empowerment in Mississippi After 1965.* Chapel Hill: The University of North Carolina Press.

Pittmay, Paul. 1970. "Patrols Role: What is it?" *Delta Democrat Times.* June 7, p. 5.

Rehfuss, John A. 1986. "A Representative Bureaucracy? Women and Minority Executives in California Civil Service." *Public Administration Review* 46: 454-460.

Riccucci, Norma M. 1986. "Female and Minority Employment in City Government: The Role of Unions." *Policy Studies Journal* 15: 3-16.

Riley, Steve. 1986. "Finch Chronology." *The Clarion Ledger.* April 23. p. 12A.

Salter, Sid. 1986. "Mississippi Will Remember Finch for Contributions to Racial Harmony." *The Clarion Ledger.* April 27, p. 3H.

Shaffer, Stephen D. 1994. "Mississippi: Friends and Neighbors Fight the "Liberal" Label." In *The 1992 Presidential Election in the South.* eds. Robert P Steed, Laurence W. Moreland, and Todd A. Baker. Westport: Praeger.

Shaffer, Stephen D., and David Breaux. 1997. "Mississippi Politics in the 1990s:

Ideology and Performance," *Paper Presented at the American Political Science Association Meeting*, Washington, D.C..

Shaffer, Stephen P., David E. Sturrock, David A. Breaux, and Bill Minor. 1999. "Mississippi: From Pariah to Pacesetter?" In *Southern Politics in the 1990s*. ed. Alexander P. Lamis, Baton Rouge: Louisiana State University Press.

Shaw, Robert. 1983. "Governor Recalls Toughest Decision." *Starkville Daily News*. December 31. p. 14.

Singell, Larry. 1991. "Racial Differences in the Employment Policy of State and Local Governments." *Southern Economic Journal* 58: 430-444.

Starkville Daily News, "Fordice Questions Plan to Open Sovereignty Records." June 18.

Sumners, Cecil L. 1980. *The Governors of Mississippi*. Gretna, LA: Pelican Publishing Co.

The Commercial Appeal. 1974. "State Agencies May Face Racial Suits." September 21.

The Daily Corinthian, 1978. "Governor's Office Denies Racism in Job Loss." August 10.

United States Equal Employment Opportunity Commission. 1975. *State and Local Government Information, EE0-4 Reports*. Washington, D.C.: Government Printing Office.

United States Equal Employment Opportunity Commission. 1980. *State and Local Government Information, EE0-4 Reports*. Washington, D.C.: Government Printing Office.

United States Equal Employment Opportunity Commission. 1985. *State and Local Government Information, EE0-4 Reports*. Washington, D.C.: Government Printing Office.

United States Equal Employment Opportunity Commission. 1990. *State and Local Government Information, EE0-4 Reports*. Washington, D.C.: Government Printing Office.

United States Equal Employment Opportunity Commission. 1995. *State and Local Government Information, EE0-4 Reports*. Washington, D.C.: Government Printing Office.

Wagster, Emily. 1998. "Delta Residents at Capitol Rally Show Opposition to Votes." *The Clarion Ledger.* January 21, p. 3B.

Wheat, Edward M. 1993. "The Bureaucracy: Mississippi's Fourth Branch." In *Politics in Mississippi*. ed. Joe B. Parker. Salem, WI: Sheffield Publishing Co.

Winbush, Don. 1987. "Mississippi Rises Again." *Time Magazine* November 16, p. 32.

Notes

1. Beginning with the 1957 Civil Rights Act, the 1960 Civil Rights Act, the 1964 Civil Rights Act, and the 1965 Voting Rights Act. The latter two Acts were major ones in the struggle for full equality.

2. Byron de la Beckwith has since been retried and convicted in the assassination of Medgar Evers in 1963 and is serving a life sentence in prison.

3. A conservative U.S. Supreme Court ruled in 1992 in Ayers vs. Fordice that Mississippi still operated a dual system of higher education in four areas and ordered a number of remedies to be carried out by the federal district court in Mississippi.

4. This study only examines the first five occupations listed. The last three categories of administrative support, skilled craft, and service maintenance are occupations African Americans were always resigned to, though not in state government, under de jure segregation.

5. The Equal Employment Opportunity Commission publishes employment data related to this study in five-year intervals. Hence, the data for this study begins in 1975, and includes 1980, 1985, 1990 and 1995.

6. Two of the state universities in Mississippi, Jackson State University (historically Black) and Mississippi State University (historically white), offer the Master of Public Policy and Administration degree, designed for employment in state government at the entry level. Between the two universities, it is estimated here that 10-15 black students matriculate every year and work in state and local governments. In addition, the Stennis Institute at Mississippi State University offers workshops and training sessions for state and local administrators and professionals, of whom a large number who participate are black.

7. Of the 82 counties in Mississippi alone, 23 of them are majority black counties, 2 are 49% black, and 4 more are 42- 46% black. This does not automatically translate into a majority of black elected county officials (due to gerrymandering and redistricting) or a majority of black administrators and professionals (that may be appointed or elected) but it does give some indication of the representation at this level. (Mississippi Employment Security Commission. March, 1999).

CHAPTER 14

Legislative Collaboration and Descriptive Representation

Kathleen Bratton

To a large degree, scholars engaged in the study of minority groups in legislatures have focused on one minority group or another. While there are exceptions (e.g., Barrett 1997; Bratton and Haynie 1999; Endersby and Menifield 2000), one set of research focuses on the role of gender in policy making (e.g., Diamond 1977; Dolan and Ford 1998; Kathlene 1994; Leader 1977; Reingold 1992; Rosenthal 1998; Saint-Germain 1989; Tamerius 1995; Thomas 1991, 1994; Thomas and Welch 1991; Vega and Firestone 1995; Welch 1985), whereas another set of research focuses on the role of race in policy making (Herring 1990; Lublin 1997; Meier and England 1984; Menifield 1998; Miller 1990; Mladenka 1989; Swain 1993; Whitby 1997). Moreover, scholars engaged in the study of race and legislative behavior or of gender and legislative behavior generally have focused on the influence of *individual* legislators on policy agendas and outcomes. This focus on a single group – and within groups, on the behavior of individual legislators – overlooks an important element of the representation of minority interests: cooperation within and across minority groups. In this study, I investigate whether cosponsorship in four state legislatures – Arkansas, California, Illinois and Maryland – is patterned along racial and gender lines, and I examine the effect of cosponsorship on the individual legislative effectiveness of black and of female state legislators.

Cosponsorship patterns in legislatures offers an opportunity to study the collaborative behavior of representatives. In each of the four legislatures studied, while bills could be introduced by a single sponsor, typically (and in some cases, most) legislation is introduced by multiple sponsors.[1] The meaning of cosponsorship, of course, can range from true collaboration to merely a show of support for the measure. However, sponsorship in general entails costs; legislators must pick and choose among legislation to sponsor (Schiller 1995). Thus cosponsorship of legislation is an appropriate measure of the degree to which legislators support each other's interests.

Collaboration on legislation is likely one way for minority and female legislators to increase their effectiveness within legislatures. There is some debate over the purposes and effectiveness of cosponsorship in the U.S. Congress (see, for example, Kessler and Krehbiel 1996; Krehbiel 1995; Wilson and Young 1997); at the state level, prior evidence suggests that black legislators in particular may be less successful at passing legislation than white legislators, but that cosponsorship increases the likelihood that legislation will pass (Bratton and Haynie 1999). More generally, it is likely that collaborating on legislation and lending support to legislation sponsored by others allows representatives to build networks and gain influence within the legislative institution.

Why might legislative minorities such as African Americans and women be expected to cooperate within and across minority groups? In the following section, I will discuss several possible frameworks that can be applied to the study of how working relationships within a legislature can be patterned according to race and gender.

Cooperation Within Minority Groups: Social Identity Theory

Social identity theory posits that individuals rely on salient social categories such as race and gender as cues to compatibility in values, preferences, and interests (Kanter 1977). Research indicates that female legislators and black legislators have distinct policy interests (Bratton and Haynie 1999), and that female legislators and black legislators tend to be more liberal than their white male colleagues (Frankovic 1977; Leader 1977; Lublin 1997; Welch 1985; Whitby 1997). Thus, it is reasonable to expect that within the legislature, female legislators may collaborate with and support other female legislators, and black legislators may collaborate with and support other black legislators.

A number of scholars have found that in the work world outside the legislature, even in ostensibly gender-integrated environments, informal groups tend to be sex-segregated and race-segregated (e.g.,

DiTomaso, Thompson and Black 1988; Lorber 1989, 1994; Irons and Moore 1985; Miller 1986; Morrison and Von Glinow 1990; O'Leary and Ickovics 1992). Scholars examining the role of gender in the workforce have found that women in predominantly male environments face obstacles in finding effective mentors (Goh 1991; Ragins and Cotton 1991; Struthers 1995). From this perspective, women may be less likely than men to work with men, and African-American legislators may be less likely than white legislators to work with white legislators.

Cooperation Across Minority Groups: Balance Theory and Sociocultural Theories

There has been a substantial amount of debate in the scholarly literature regarding the likelihood that minority groups will cooperate with each other. Theories such as balance theory (Heider 1958) would suggest that minority groups that are the object of prejudice and discrimination should be attracted to each other. Both African Americans and women have a history of political, social, and economic discrimination, and both groups share a relatively recent entry into state legislatures. Therefore, each group may be sympathetic to issues salient to each other. Alternatively, sociocultural theories would suggest that minority groups might adopt the dominant attitudes of majority groups, including stereotypes of and discrimination against other minorities.

Theories of interethnic tensions among minority groups in the mass public have been supported by a number of empirical studies (Dyer, Vedlitz, and Worchel 1989). However, at the elite level, the empirical evidence strongly suggests that African Americans and women share policy interests, and thus it is reasonable to expect that they are likely to collaborate with each other. Prior research indicates that African-Americans and women are more likely than their white male colleagues to focus on policies involving women, involving minorities, and involving welfare policy (Bratton and Haynie 1999). Moreover, it is likely that working relationships formed when working on legislation pertinent to women's interests and to minority interests carry over to collaborative efforts regarding other policy areas. Panning (1982) and Campbell (1982) argue that legislative cosponsorship depends on ideological proximity; as noted above, some research indicates that black legislators and female legislators may be more liberal than their white male counterparts (Frankovic 1977; Leader 1977; Lublin 1997; Welch 1985; Whitby 1997). Furthermore, the organizational behavior literature suggests that working relationships outside the legislature are often divided upon racial and gender lines (Lorber 1989, 1994); there is little reason to expect otherwise within the legislature. Women are socialized in a fundamentally different way than men, and such differences in socialization may be reflected in the informal organization of the workplace (Lorber 1989).

Differences Between Minority Groups: Social Distance Theory and Integrative Styles

-Social Distance Theory

Workplace divisions may be particularly pronounced in terms of race. Within the mass public, women and men live in the same neighborhoods with each other, are educated together, and create families together. The economic and social connections between men and women lead to an acceptance by men and women of common values (Brickman et al. 1980; Gurin 1985) and reduces the likelihood of conflict between men and women (Coser 1956). Perceived cultural differences and conflicts of interest between African-American legislators and white legislators may be far greater than those between men and women. Social distance has been defined as "feelings of unwillingness among members of a group to accept or approve a given degree of intimacy in interaction with a member of an outgroup" (Williams 1964, 29). Emory Bogardus' (1958) social distance study demonstrated that Americans accept or reject other ethnic groups in direct proportion to perceived cultural differences. Though social distance between the races is slowly decreasing, social distance and racial segregation in American society persists (Hacker 1992; Massey and Denton 1993; Owen, Eisner, and McFaul 1981).

This social distance may be reflected in the fact that racial differences in public opinion within the mass public tend to be more marked than gender differences (Kinder and Sanders 1996); African-Americans at the elite level of politics are particularly likely to be liberal (Lichter 1985). Legislation sponsored by African-Americans may reflect these ideological differences. Thus it is likely that cosponsorship may be patterned more along racial lines than gender lines.

-Integrative Styles

A second reason why workplace divisions may be less pronounced in terms of gender is that women tend to have more collaborative styles than men, and thus may be more likely than their male counterparts to collaborate not only with other women, and with other minorities, but also with white men. Prior research has indicated that women in particular may be more likely than men to approach policy-making from a collaborative perspective. Applying work by Kenneth Thomas (1975) to a study of gender differences among legislative leaders, Rosenthal (1998) argues that women are more likely to adopt 'integrative' leadership styles, including, among other characteristics, a team orientation (p. 57). She argues that because of cultural norms and socialization, and in part because of their prior experience in organizations that emphasize what Putnam (1995) labels 'social capital', women are more likely to develop legislative styles that incorporate collaboration, inclusivity, and team-building. Rosenthal's work focuses on leadership styles, but the logic extends to legislative styles in general; from this perspective, women are more likely than men to collaborate with women, but also more likely than men to collaborate with men.

Collaboration on legislation is likely one way for minority and female legislators to increase their effectiveness and influence within legislatures. One important question is whether collaboration within and across minority groups in legislatures serves as a complement to or a substitute for collaboration with white men. If members of minority groups within legislatures are more likely to cosponsor with each other – but less likely to cosponsor with white men – these legislators risk losing influence, and being categorized as speaking for general interests. If collaboration within and across minority groups serves as a complement to collaboration with white male legislators, members of minority groups may more effectively increase their influence.

Hypotheses

Although many questions may arise from the previous theories, I center my research on six hypotheses. Each of these hypothesis are outlined below.

H_1:   Legislators that sponsor legislation involving health, education, welfare, children's interests, black interests, and women's interests will cosponsor a relatively large proportion of legislation with black legislators and with female legislators.

H_2:   Women will cosponsor a relatively high proportion of legislation with each other even after controlling for the percentage of bills sponsored involving health, education, welfare, children's interests, black interests, and women's interests.

H_3:   Women will cosponsor a relatively high proportion of legislation not only with each other, but also with male legislators (although note that H_2 suggests that the greatest degree of cosponsorship will be with other women).

H_4:   Black legislators will be more likely to cosponsor legislation with other black legislators, even after controlling for the percentage of bills sponsored involving health, education, welfare, children's interests, black interests, and women's interests.

H_5:   Racial divisions in cosponsorship will be more marked than gender divisions in cosponsorship.

H_6:   Black and female legislators will cosponsor a relatively high percentage of legislation with each other.

Data and Methods

The data for this chapter are drawn from the Arkansas, California, Illinois, and Maryland state legislatures in 1999. These states provide geographical diversity, as well as diversity in terms of the percentage of women and African-Americans serving within the legislature, and diversity in terms of the average degree of cosponsorship. Information regarding the composition of these legislatures as well as the degree of cosponsorship within these legislatures is presented in Table 14-1.

OLS regression analysis is used to examine the effect of gender and race on cosponsorship within the legislature. OLS regression analysis is a statistical technique that provides estimates for the effect of various factors (in this case, gender and race) on political phenomena (in this case, cosponsorship with members of various groups within a legislature). Twenty regression analyses are presented, five for each state; the analyses examines the effect of gender and race on the degree of overall cosponsorship, as well as on the degree of cosponsorship with black women within the legislator's political party, with black men within the legislator's political party, with white women within the legislator's political party, and with white men within the legislator's party. The unit of analysis is the individual legislator, and each dependent variable is coded as the percentage of legislation sponsored by the legislator that is cosponsored by at least one legislator of the group in question. To better restrict the analysis to bills on which some real collaboration took place

Table 14-1 Cosponsorship in Arkansas, California, Maryland, and Illinois

	Arkansas	California	Illinois	Maryland
Number of Legislators in Analysis	99	80	118	142
Average (Range) of Percentage of Bills Cosponsored	45.4 (0-100)	43.0 (7 – 83)	74.2 (13 – 100)	76.6 (0 – 100)
Average (Range) Percentage of Bills Cosponsored with Black Females in Legislator's Party	00.2 (0 – 8)	N/A	13.5 (0 – 67)	11.2 (0 – 100)
Average (Range) Percentage of Bills Cosponsored with Black Males in Legislator's Party	5.4 (0 – 43)	6.3 (0 – 21)	9.3 (0 – 44)	19.8 (0 – 100)
Average (Range) Percentage of Bills Cosponsored with White Females in Legislator's Party	12.5 (0 – 67)	16.6 (0 – 58.8)	25.1 (0 – 64)	29.0 (0 – 100)
Percentage of Bills Cosponsored with White Men in Legislator's Party	25.8 (0 – 80)	31.3 (7 – 75)	55.6 (10 – 100)	51.7 (0 – 100)
Number of Black Female Legislators	1	0	7	10
Number of Black Male Legislators	10	4	8	16
Number of White Female Legislators	19	18	25	36
Number of White Male Legislators	69	58	78	80
Average (Range) Percentage of Bills Focusing on Education, Health, Welfare, Children's Interests, Women's Interests, or Black Interests	31.2 (0 – 61)	40.6 (7 – 67)	40 (6 – 100)	49 (0 – 72)
Number of Republican Legislators	24	32	56	35
Average (Range) Percentage Black in Legislator's District	16 (0 – 77)	8 (1 – 46)	15 (0 – 79)	27 (0 – 99)
Average (Range) Average Income in Legislator's District	27,136 (17,470 – 56,455)	45,515 (23,822 – 81,288)	40,706 (19,285 – 104,981)	49,063 (22,274 – 99,999)
Average (Range) Percentage of Individuals in Legislator's District with College Degree	17 (7 – 55)	30 (7 – 54)	27 (7 – 71)	31 (11-99)

(as opposed to bills which large numbers of legislators simply cosponsor as a show of support), only bills with five or fewer sponsors were
used in calculating cosponsorship measures.[2]

Recall that the first hypothesis was that individuals who introduce
a relatively high degree of legislation involving education, health, welfare, children's interests, black interests, and women's interests would
be more likely to cosponsor with black and female legislators.[3] In order
to test this hypothesis, I include the percentage of such legislation that is
sponsored by each legislator as a predictor in each regression analysis.[4]

In addition to the race and gender of the legislator, and to the policy interests of the legislator, I control in each analysis for several other
likely influences on cosponsorship. It is likely that representatives who
hail from particular types of districts – for instance, districts with a highly educated population, or districts with a majority black population –
may share policy interests with black and/or female legislators, and be
more likely to cosponsor legislation with African-Americans and women.
Therefore, I include controls for demographic characteristics within the
legislator's district: the percentage black in the legislator's district, the
average income of individuals residing in the legislator's district, and the
percentage of residents within the legislator's district who have received
a college degree. These data are gathered from *The Almanac of State
Legislatures* (Lilley, DeFranco, and Diefenderfer 1994). It is also possible that cosponsorship patterns vary across political parties; I thus control
for the party affiliation of the legislators. Finally, in the analyses of
cosponsorship with subgroups of legislators, I control for the percentage
of bills that are cosponsored overall.[5] The means and ranges of the dependent and independent variables by state are presented in Table 14-2.

Results

The results are presented in Tables 14-2 through 14-5. The parameter estimates for each variable indicate the increased (or decreased)
degree of cosponsorship for that type of legislator *compared to the reference group of white male legislator.* For instance, in Illinois, relative
to white males, all other things equal, an additional 13.70% of the bills
introduced by black males are cosponsored with black females.
Similarly, in Arkansas, relative to white males, all other things equal, an
additional 12.41% of the bills introduced by black males are cosponsored with black males.

Recall that the first hypothesis was that individuals who introduce a relatively high degree of legislation involving education, health, welfare, children's interests, black interests, and women's interests would be more likely to cosponsor with black and female legislators. Moderate support is found for this hypothesis, but only with respect to cosponsorship with white women. In Arkansas and California, legislators focusing on these policy areas cosponsored a significantly higher percentage of legislation with white women. Interestingly, in California and Illinois, legislators focusing on these policy areas cosponsored a relatively high percentage of legislation overall. In Maryland, legislators focusing on these policy areas cosponsored a relatively high degree of legislation with black men and with white women, although the parameter estimates are not statistically significant.[6]

In the second hypothesis, I outlined the expectation that women would be more likely to cosponsor legislation with other women, even after controlling for policy interests. Again, moderate support is evident for this hypothesis. The findings are particularly strong for Illinois; women, regardless of race, are more likely to cosponsor with other women. The effects are of substantial magnitude and are generally statistically significant. In Arkansas, black women are predicted to be relatively likely to cosponsor legislation with white women, although it should be noted that there is only one black female legislator in Arkansas (Wilma Walker of College Station). In Maryland, black women cosponsor a significantly higher proportion of legislation with other black women, and a slightly higher proportion of legislation with white women (although this latter result is not statistically significant). Contrary to expectations, white women in Maryland cosponsor significantly less legislation with other white women than do white men. In California, cosponsorship does not appear patterned according to gender.

In the third hypothesis, I expected that women would be more likely to cosponsor legislation than their male counterparts. Again, moderate support is found for this hypothesis; white women in Arkansas and Maryland cosponsor more legislation than their white male colleagues. In Arkansas, black women are predicted to cosponsor less legislation than white men, although, again, this estimate is based on the analysis of one black female legislator.

The fourth hypothesis was that black legislators would cosponsor a relatively high proportion of legislation with other black legislators. This expectation appears to be supported for both black men and women. In every state, with few exceptions black legislators, compared to their white colleagues, are significantly more likely to cosponsor with other black legislators. The effects are generally quite substantial. In Arkansas, for instance, compared to white men, black men are predicted to cosponsor approximately 12% more legislative measures with other black male legislators. In Maryland, compared to white men, black male legislators are predicted to cosponsor approximately 26% more legislative measures with black female legislators. There are only two exceptions to this pattern. First, in Arkansas, there is no difference between black women and white men in the proportion of legislation cosponsored with black men. Recall, however, that the results for Arkansas are based on one black female legislator. Second, in Maryland, black male legislators cosponsor only marginally more legislation with other black male legislators than do white male legislators. Aside from these two findings, the results are clear: cosponsorship is patterned on race.

An examination of the actual bills introduced provides more evidence for this hypothesis. Some, but certainly not all, of cosponsorship among African-Americans is derived from shared interests. In Arkansas, three multiple-sponsored measures are introduced by a majority of African Americans.[7] One deals with affirmative action, one with support programs for at-risk high school students, and one with regulating terminal use fees at banks. In California, five such measures were introduced, including one establishing community-based alcohol programs for youth, and one establishing job training programs for disadvantaged youths. In Illinois, and Maryland, forty-three and twenty-seven such measures respectively are introduced, and collaboration often transcends the limits of policy areas generally associated with African-American representatives. While some measures reflect policy areas commonly thought to be of particular interest to African-Americans (for instance, measures establishing support programs for low-income individuals, measures regulating foster care, or measures directing benefits to specific predominantly black Maryland communities), many do not (for instance, allowing mortgage brokers to collect finders fees for procuring insurance for borrowers, regulating securities transactions, protecting the rights of those injured in accidents, and requiring a home inspection license).

The fifth hypothesis was that racial differences in sponsorship patterns would be more marked than gender differences. This hypothesis is strongly supported as well. For instance, in Maryland, black male legislators cosponsor approximately 8% more legislation than do black

Table 14-2 Cosponsorship Patterns Among State Legislators in Arkansas

	Parameter Estimates (Robust Standard Errors)				
	% of Bills Cosponsored	*% of Bills Cosponsored with Black Women*	*% of Bills Cosponsored with Black Men*	*% of Bills Cosponsored with White Women*	*% of Bills Cosponsored with White Men*
Independent Variable					
Black Male Legislator	3.99	.32	12.41***	26.39***	-21.91***
	(13.81)	(.27)	(5.42)	(6.24)	(8.13)
Black Female Legislator	-32.94***	N/A[a]	-4.58	9.31**	-.85
	(8.77)	(	3.80)	(4.87)	(6.36)
White Female Legislator	14.13***	-.21	6.67**	-1.45	-9.81***
	(5.04)	(.19)	(3.83)	(3.88)	(4.30)
Republican Legislator	11.06***	N/A[b]	N/A[b]	-11.33***	-12.11***
	(4.87)			(2.83)	(3.64)
Percentage of Bills Focusing on Education, Health, Welfare, Children, Women's Interests, or Black Interests	-.22	~ .00	.03	.28**	-.02
	(.27)	(.01)	(.08)	(.14)	(.13)
% Black in Legislator's District	.04	-.01	.12**	-.22***	.02
	(.17)	(.01)	(.06)	(.09)	(.11)
Average Income in Legislator's District (in thousands)	-.24	.05*	.16	-.13	.51***
	(.56)	(.04)	(.35)	(.29)	(.37)
% of Individuals in Legislator's District with College Degree	-.12	-.03	.08	.17	-.53*
	(.37)	(.02)	(.23)	(.20)	(.23)
% of Bills Cosponsored	N/A	~ .00	.07**	.32***	.62***
		(.01)	(.04)	(.06)	(.08)
Intercept	54.59***	-.72	-9.60	-5.88	.34
	(15.47)	(.64)	(7.72)	(6.26)	(9.34)
R^2	.11	.06	.40	.46	.59
Number of Legislators	95	71	71	95	95

***: significantly different from 0, $p \leq .01$ (one-tailed test)

**: significantly different from 0, $p \leq .05$ (one-tailed test)

*: significantly different from 0, $p \leq .10$ (one-tailed test)

Dependent Variable: Percentage of measures cosponsored with legislator in the same party

[a]: only one black female legislator serving

[b]: No black Republican legislators serving

Table 14-3 Cosponsorship Patterns Among State Legislators in California

	% of Bills Cosponsored	% of Bills Cosponsored with Black Men	% of Bills Cosponsored with White Women	% of Bills Cosponsored with White Men
	Parameter Estimates (Robust Standard Errors)			
Independent Variable				
Black Male Legislator	1.75 (14.91)	7.60" (4.07)	-1.20 (7.47)	-.48 (4.55)
Black Female Legislator[a]	N/A	N/A	N/A	N/A
White Female Legislator	4.43 (5.24)	1.61 (1.90)	.96 (2.87)	1.64 (1.55)
Republican Legislator	-5.24 (4.91)	N/A[b]	-8.92''' (2.61)	-1.03 (2.24)
Percentage of Bills Focusing on Education, Health, Welfare, Children, Women's Interests, or Black Interests	.29" (.16)	~ .00 (.05)	.12' (.08)	.07 (.07)
% Black in Legislator's District	-.32 (.40)	.11 (.13)	.08 (.19)	-.17 (.14)
Average Income in Legislator's District (in thousands)	-.01 (.30)	-.02 (.13)	.10 (.15)	-.15 (.15)
% of Individuals in Legislator's District with College Degree	.13 (.31)	.10 (.11)	-.01 (.16)	.02 (.14)
% of Bills Cosponsored	N/A	.16''' (.06)	.44''' (.07)	.80''' (.05)
Intercept	30.96''' (12.28)	-4.76 (6.11)	-8.15 (6.77)	1.80 (6.36)
Adjusted R^2	.17	.45	.65	.84
Number of Legislators	79	47	79	79

''': significantly different from 0, $p \leq .01$ (one-tailed test)

": significantly different from 0, $p \leq .05$ (one-tailed test)

': significantly different from 0, $p \leq .10$ (one-tailed test)

Dependent Variable: Percentage of measures cosponsored with legislator in the same party

[a]: no black female legislators serving

[b]: No black Republican legislators serving

Table 14-4 Cosponsorship Patterns Among State Legislators in Illinois

	Parameter Estimates (Robust Standard Errors)				
	% of Bills Cosponsored	*% of Bills Cosponsored with Black Women*	*% of Bills Cosponsored with Black Men*	*% of Bills Cosponsored with White Women*	*% of Bills Cosponsored with White Men*
Independent Variable					
Black Male Legislator	.87 (9.71)	13.70** (7.02)	7.17** (3.56)	7.42* (5.37)	1.33 (5.59)
Black Female Legislator	-.81 (9.43)	18.51*** (6.51)	10.49*** (3.75)	6.69 (5.46)	1.07 (4.99)
White Female Legislator	-.66 (3.62)	5.59** (3.32)	1.00 (2.48)	15.27*** (3.70)	-6.40*** (2.81)
Republican Legislator	-2.40 (3.35)	N/A[a]	N/A[a]	.45 (2.46)	-5.57*** (2.05)
Percentage of Bills Focusing on Education, Health, Welfare, Children, Women's Interests, or Black Interests	.29*** (.10)	-.09 (.12)	.03 (.07)	.11 (.11)	.06 (.08)
% Black in Legislator's District	-.19** (.10)	.07* (.04)	.03 (.04)	-.02 (.07)	-.11* (.08)
Average Income in Legislator's District (in thousands)	.10 (.18)	-.17 (.13)	.08 (.07)	.24*** (.11)	-.05 (.11)
% of Individuals in Legislator's District with College Degree	-.13 (.21)	.02 (.16)	-.17* (.11)	-.08*** (.15)	-.12 (.11)
% of Bills Cosponsored	N/A	.31*** (.12)	.15*** (.06)	.40*** (.07)	.85*** (.05)
Intercept	66.44*** (6.17)	-6.42 (9.35)	-5.06* (3.71)	-20.64 (6.11)	.51 (5.94)
Adjusted R²	.11	.47	.38	.50	.72
Number of Legislators	118	62	62	118	118

***: significantly different from 0, $p \leq .01$ (one-tailed test)

**: significantly different from 0, $p \leq .05$ (one-tailed test)

*: significantly different from 0, $p \leq .10$ (one-tailed test)

Dependent Variable: Percentage of measures cosponsored with legislator in the same party

[a]: No black Republican legislators serving

female legislators with black female legislators; black female legislators cosponsor approximately 17% more legislation than white female legislators with other black female legislators; only marginal differences exist between white men and white women in the proportion of legislation cosponsored with black women. In Illinois, black male legislators cosponsor about 1% more legislation than black female legislators with white female legislators; white female legislators cosponsor approximately 8% more legislation than black female legislators with white female legislators. Among black legislators, substantial gender differences occasionally are evident. For instance, in Illinois, white women cosponsor approximately 15% more legislation than do white men with other white women. In Maryland, black women cosponsor approximately 16% more legislation than do black men with white women. But, generally, gender differences are rarely as large as racial differences among women or among men.

Finally, the sixth hypothesis was that black and female legislators would sponsor a relatively high proportion of legislation with each other. This hypothesis receives moderate support. In Illinois and Arkansas, black men cosponsor a significantly higher proportion of legislation with white women than do white men; similarly, white women in Arkansas cosponsor a significantly higher proportion of legislation with black men.

Importance of Cosponsorship

In general, the results presented in this chapter demonstrate that the race and the gender of a legislator generally affect their choice of legislators with whom to cosponsor. Earlier in this chapter, I speculated that cosponsorship facilitated representation on the part of black legislators and female legislators. Here, I present a set of analyses that demonstrates the importance of cosponsorship to one measure of legislative effectiveness, bill passage. The unit of analysis in these analyses is the bill.[8] The dependent variable in this logit regression analysis is coded 1 if a bill passes, and 0 otherwise.[9] The primary independent variables of interest are five dummy variables: a variable coded 1 if the bill has multiple sponsors, and 0 otherwise; a variable coded 1 if the bill has multiple black sponsors, and 0 otherwise; a variable coded 1 if the bill has multiple female sponsors, and 0 otherwise; a variable coded 1 if the bill has only one sponsor, and the sponsor is female, and 0 otherwise; and a variable coded 1 if the bill has only one sponsor, and the sponsor is

Table 14-5 Cosponsorship Patterns Among State Legislators in Maryland

	Parameter Estimates (Robust Standard Errors)				
	% of Bills Cosponsored	% of Bills Cosponsored with Black Women	% of Bills Cosponsored with Black Men	% of Bills Cosponsored with White Women	% of Bills Cosponsored with White Men
Independent Variable					
Black Male Legislator	-2.16 (7.86)	25.92" (14.07)	1.74 (17.51)	-11.77 (11.53)	-19.69" (12.08)
Black Female Legislator	-4.64 (10.68)	17.52' (13.35)	16.99 (17.68)	3.99 (13.65)	-16.77 (13.90)
White Female Legislator	6.86" (4.24)	1.24 (2.72)	-3.43 (5.44)	-8.45 '(5.33)	-2.29 (4.77)
Republican Legislator	-4.22 (5.49)	N/Aª	N/Aª	-18.76''' (5.25)	-12.47" (5.84)
Percentage of Bills Focusing on Education, Health, Welfare, Children, Women's Interests, or Black Interests	-.09 (.22)	.08 (.15)	.29 (.26)	.11 (.27)	.25 (.25)
% Black in Legislator's District	.18" (.10)	.14 (.18)	.30' (.23)	-.08 (.14)	~ .00 (.11)
Average Income in Legislator's District (in thousands)	.27 (.23)	.25 '(.19)	.16 (.31)	.34 (.31)	-.46" (.23)
% of Individuals in Legislator's District with College Degree	-.16 (.22)	-.24' (.18)	-.27 (.31)	-.03 (.29)	.51''' (.18)
% of Bills Cosponsored	N/A	.09' (.07)	.33''' (.11)	.37''' (.09)	.67''' (.09)
Intercept	67.89''' (11.62)	-13.82' (9.13)	-29.94" (15.48)	-10.88 (13.56)	1.22 (12.38)
Adjusted R^2	.06	.40	.33	.22	.37
Number of Legislators	135	101	101	135	135

''': significantly different from 0, $p \leq .01$ (one-tailed test)

": significantly different from 0, $p \leq .05$ (one-tailed test)

': significantly different from 0, $p \leq .10$ (one-tailed test)

Dependent Variable: Percentage of measures cosponsored with legislator in the same party

ª: No black Republican legislators serving

black. The estimate for the first variable provides an estimate of the effect on passage of cosponsorship, regardless of race and gender. The estimates for the second and third variables provide estimates for any *additional* effect on passage of having multiple female sponsors and multiple black sponsors, respectively. Finally, the estimated effects of the fourth and fifth variables provide estimates for the effect on passage of having a single female sponsor and single black sponsor, respectively. In these analyses, I control for several other factors, which likely influence passage, such as the percentage of sponsors in the majority party, the percentage of sponsors in the leadership, and the average seniority of sponsors. The results are presented in Table 14-6.

Table 14-6 Influences on Passage in Arkansas, California, Illinois, and Maryland

	Parameter Estimates (Standard Errors)			
	Arkansas	*California*	*Illinois*	*Maryland*
Independent Variable				
Bill Has Multiple Sponsors	.20	.49***	1.52***	.65***
	(.20)	(.17)	(.10)	(.18)
Bill Has Multiple Female Sponsors	1.23***	.29	.40***	-.04
	(.54)	(.37)	(.14)	(.31)
Bill Has Multiple Black Sponsors	-.88	.72	.61***	-.51
	(.93)	(1.08)	(.26)	(.41)
Single-Sponsored Bill with Female Sponsor	.07	-.12	-.04	-.24*
	(.19)	(.15)	(.11)	(.19)
Single-Sponsored Bill with Black Sponsor	-1.02***	.03	-.10	-.19
	(.31)	(.23)	(.14)	(.23)
% of Sponsors in Majority Party	.26	1.42***	-.77***	.25
	(.22)	(.14)	(.11)	(.25)
% of Sponsors in Leadership	.43**	.12	.11	.36*
	(.21)	(.15)	(.25)	(.28)
Average Seniority of Sponsors	.14***	.01	-.02***	.01
	(.05)	(.04)	(.01)	(.02)
Intercept	-.45**	-.69***	-1.20**	-.83***
	(.21)	(.19)	*(.25)	(.26)
Pseudo R^2	.05	.08	.13	.02
Number of Bills	774	1,311	3,043	673

***: significantly different from 0, $p \leq .01$ (one-tailed test)
**: significantly different from 0, $p \leq .05$ (one-tailed test)
*: significantly different from 0, $p \leq .10$ (one-tailed test)
Dependent Variable: Coded 1 if Passed, 0 Otherwise

In three of the four states analyzed (the exception is Arkansas), a bill with multiple sponsors is more likely to pass than a single-sponsored measure. Most important, from the perspective of this chapter, is that measures with multiple female sponsors are particularly likely to pass in Arkansas and Illinois. Bills with multiple black sponsors are particularly likely to pass in Illinois. Measures introduced by black legislators in Arkansas and by female legislators in Maryland are less likely to pass, but only if they are single-sponsored measures.

Implications and Conclusions

Moderate to strong support was found for the hypotheses regarding patterns of cosponsorship outlined in this chapter. In particular, we can conclude that cosponsorship is patterned along gender and racial lines, and that the effects are particularly strong for race. Only moderate support was found for the expectations that women would demonstrate a more collaborative style than men in their cosponsorship behavior, and only moderate support was found for the expectations that cosponsorship would be particularly likely not only within minority legislative groups, but also across minority legislative groups.

It is important to note that the results differ substantially across states. More research should be done to examine what institutional differences may contribute to these varying cosponsorship patterns. Moreover, more research should be done to investigate whether differences in cosponsorship change depending on the gender and race of primary versus secondary sponsors.

Cosponsorship is an important way in which minority and female legislators can facilitate their effectiveness. Collaboration with other minority and other female legislators is likely more effective when used as a complement to rather than a substitute for collaboration with white male colleagues. As we have seen in this chapter, collaboration increases legislative effectiveness, and in some states that is particularly true for black legislators and for female legislators. More generally, it is likely collaboration allows legislators to build networks and gain influence within the institution, and can be an important part of the representation of African-Americans and women.

References

Barrett, Edith. 1997. "Gender and Race in the State House: The Legislative Experience." *The Social Science Journal* 34: 131-44.

Bogardus, Emory. 1958. "Racial Distance Changes in the United States during the Past Thirty Years." *Sociology and Social Research* 43: 127-135.

Bratton, Kathleen A. and Kerry L. Haynie. 1999. "Agenda-Setting and Legislative Success in State Legislatures: The Effects of Gender and Race." *Journal of Politics* 61: 658-679.

Brickman, Philip, Robert Folger, Erich Goode, and Yaacov Schul. 1980. "Micro and Macro Justice." In *The Justice Motive in Social Behavior*, ed. M.J. Lemer. New York: Plenum.

Coser, Lewis A. 1956. *The Functions of Social Conflict*. New York: Free Press.

Diamond, Irene. 1977. *Sex Roles in the State House*. New Haven, CT: Yale University Press.

DiTomaso, Nancy, Donna E. Thompson, and David H. Blake . 1988. "Corporate Perspectives on the Advancement of Minority Managers." In *Ensuring Minority Success in Corporate Management*, ed. Donna E. Thompson and Nancy DiTomaso. New York: Plenum Press.

Dolan, Kathleen, and Lynne E. Ford. 1998. "Are All Women State Legislators Alike?" In *Women and Elective Office*, eds. Sue Thomas and Clyde Wilcox. New York: Oxford University Press.

Dyer, James, Arnold Vedlitz, and Stephen Worchel. "Social Distance among Racial and Ethnic Groups in Texas: Some Demographic Correlates." *Social Science Quarterly* 70: 607-616.

Endersby, James W. and Charles E. Menifield. 2000. "Representation, Ethnicity, and Congress: Black and Hispanic Representatives and Constituencies." In *Black and Multi-Racial Politics in America*, ed. Yvette Alex-Assensoh and Lawrence Hanks. New York: New York University Press.

Frankovic, Kathleen A. 1977. "Sex and Voting in the U.S. House of Representatives 1961-1975." *American Politics Quarterly* 3: 315-330.

Goh, Swee C. 1991. "Sex Differences in Perceptions of Interpersonal Work Style, Career Emphasis, Supervisory Mentoring Behavior, and Job Satisfaction." *Sex Roles: A Journal of Research* 24: 701-710.

Gurin, Patricia. 1985. "Women's Gender Consciousness." *Public Opinion Quarterly* 49: 143-163.

Hacker, Andrew. 1992. *Two Nations: Black and White, Separate, Hostile, Unequal.* New York: Scribner's.

Heider, Fritz. 1958. *The Psychology of Interpersonal Relations*. New York:

Wiley.

Herring, Mary. 1990. "Legislative Responsiveness to Black Constituents in Three Deep South States." *Journal of Politics* 52: 740-58.

Irons, Edward D. and Gilbert Moore. 1985. *Black Managers: The Case of the Banking Industry.* New York: Praeger.

Kanter, Rosabeth M. 1977. *Men and Women of the Corporation.* New York: Basic Books.

Kathlene, Lyn. 1994. "Power and Influence in State Legislative Policymaking: The Interaction of Gender and Position in Committee Hearing Debates." *American Political Science Review* 88: 560-576.

Kessler, Daniel and Keith Krehbiel. 1996. "Dynamics of Cosponsorship." *American Political Science Review* 90: 555-566.

Kinder, Donald R., and Lynn M. Sanders. 1996. *Divided By Color.* Chicago: University of Chicago Press.

Krehbiel, Keith. 1995. "Cosponsors and Wafflers from A to Z." *American Journal of Political Science* 39: 906-23.

Leader, Shelah Gilbert. 1977. "The Policy Impact of Elected Women Officials." In *The Impact of the Electoral Process,* edited by Joseph Cooper and Louis Maisel, pp. 265-284. Beverly Hills: Sage.

Lichter, Linda S. 1985. "Who Speaks for Black America". *Public Opinion* 8: 41-44, 58.

Lilley, William, Laurence J. DeFranco, and William M. Diefenderfer III. 1994. *The Almanac of State Legislatures.* Washington, DC: Congressional Quarterly.

Lorber, Judith. 1989. "Trust, Loyalty, and the Place of Women in the Informal Organization of Work." In *Women: A Feminist Perspective,* ed. Jo Freeman. 4th ed. Mountain View: CA: Mayfield.

Lorber, Judith. 1994. *The Paradox of Gender.* New Haven, CT: Yale University Press.

Lublin, David. 1997. *The Paradox of Representation.* Princeton: Princeton University Press.

Massey, Douglas S. and Nancy A. Denton. 1993. *American Apartheid: Segregation and the Making of the Underclass.* Cambridge: Harvard University Press.

Meier, Kenneth, and Robert E. England. 1984. "Black Representation and Educational Policy: Are They Related?" *American Political Science Review* 78: 392-403.

Menifield, Charles E. 1998. "A Loose Coalition or a United Front: Voting Behavior Within the Congressional Hispanic Caucus." *Latino Studies*

Journal 9: 26-44.

Miller, Cheryl M. 1990. "Agenda Setting by State Legislative Black Caucuses: Policy Priorities and Factors of Success." *Policy Studies Review* 9: 339-54.

Miller, Jon. 1986. *Pathways in the Workplace: The Effect of Gender and Race on Access to Organizational Resources*. Cambridge, MA: Cambridge University Press.

Mladenka, Kenneth R. 1989. "Blacks and Hispanics in Urban Policy." *American Political Science Review* 83: 165-92.

Morrison, A.M. and M.A. Von Glinow. 1990. "Women and Minorities in Management." *American Psychologist* 45: 200-208.

O'Leary, Virginia E. and Jeanette R. Ickovics. 1992. "Cracking the Glass Ceiling: Overcoming Isolation and Alienation." In *Womanpower: Managing in Times of Demographic Turbulence*, ed. Uma Sekaran and Frederick T.L. Leong. Beverly Hills, CA: Sage Publications.

Owen, Carolyn A., Howard C. Eisner, and Thomas R. McFaul. 1981. "A Half-Century of Social Distance Research: National Replication of the Bogardus Studies." *Sociology and Social Research* 66: 80-98.

Putnam, Robert D. 1995. "Bowling Alone: America's Declining Social Capital." *Journal of Democracy* 6: 65-78.

Ragins, Belle Rose, and John L. Cotton. 1991. "Easier Said than Done: Gender Differences in Perceived Barriers to Gaining a Mentor." *Academy of Management Journal* 34: 939-51.

Reingold, Beth. 1992. "Concepts of Representation Among Female and Male State Legislators." *Legislative Studies Quarterly* 17: 509-537.

Rosenthal, Cindy Simon. 1998. *When Women Lead; Integrative Leadership in State Legislatures*. New York: Oxford University Press.

Saint-Germain, Michelle A. 1989. "Does Their Difference Make A Difference? The Impact of Women on Public Policy in the Arizona Legislature." *Social Science Quarterly* 70: 956-68.

Schiller, Wendy J. 1995. "Senators as Political Entrepreneurs: Using Bill Sponsorship to Shape Legislative Agendas." *American Journal of Political Science* 39: 186-201.

Struthers, Nancy J. 1995. "Differences in mentoring: A function of gender or organizational rank?" *Journal of Social Behavior and Personality* 10: 265-272.

Swain, Carol. 1995. *Black Faces, Black Interests: The Representation of African-Americans in Congress*. Cambridge, Mass: Harvard University Press.

Thomas, Kenneth. "Conflict and Conflict Management." 1975. In *The Handbook of Industrial and Organizational Psychology*, ed. Marvin Dunnette. Chicago: Rand McNally.

Thomas, Sue, and Susan Welch. 1991. "The Impact of Gender on Activities and Priorities of State Legislators." *Western Political Quarterly* 44: 445-56.

Thomas, Sue. 1991. "The Impact of Women on State Legislative Policies." *Journal of Politics* 53: 958-76.

Thomas, Sue. 1994. *How Women Legislate.* New York: Oxford University Press.

Vega, Arturo, and Juanita M. Firestone. 1995. "The Effects of Gender on Congressional Behavior and the Substantive Representation of Women." *Legislative Studies Quarterly* 20: 221-222.

Wallace, T. Dudley, and J. Lew Silver. 1988. *Econometrics: An Introduction.* Reading, MA: Addison-Wesley.

Welch, Susan. 1985. "Are Women More Liberal than Men in the U.S. Congress?" *Legislative Studies Quarterly* 10: 125-134.

Whitby, Kenny J. 1997. *The Color of Representation.* Ann Arbor: University of Michigan Press.

White, Halbert. 1980. "A Heteroscedasticity Consistent Covariance Matrix Estimator and a Direct Test of Heteroscedasticity." *Econometrica* 48: 817-818.

Williams, Robin. 1964. *Strangers Next Door: Ethnic Relations in American Communities.* Englewood Cliffs, NJ: Prentice-Hall.

Wilson, Rick K. and Cheryl D. Young. 1997. "Cosponsorship in the U.S. Congress." *Legislative Studies Quarterly* 12: 25-43.

Notes

1 In this chapter, no distinction is made between primary sponsors and secondary sponsors.

2 In three of the four states, some bills are introduced which receive such a consensus of support that dozens of legislators may cosponsor them; in these cases, it is unlikely that true collaboration occurred. In Arkansas, approximately 19% of introduced measures have a between two and five sponsors (66% of all measures are single-sponsored). In California, approximately 18% of introduced measures have between two and five sponsors (70% are single-sponsored). In Illinois, approximately 44% of introduced measures have between two and five sponsors (55% are single-sponsored). In Maryland, approximately 34% of introduced measures have between two and five sponsors (35% are single-sponsored).

3 Black interest legislation included measures which would improve the socioeconomic status of black Americans and/or promote equity of black Americans, such as: affirmative action legislation, voting protections designed to increase black participation and representation, anti-discrimination measures, establishment of Martin Luther King and Black American holidays, measures requiring divestiture from South Africa. Women's interest legislation included measures which would improve the socioeconomic status of women and/or promote equity of women, such as: anti-discrimination measures; alimony, child support, and child custody regulations; affirmative action legislation; measures liberalizing divorce law, or protecting property rights and pensions for divorcees or widows; measures involving women's health issues (sex education, pregnancy, childbirth, mammography, fertility); measures addressing domestic violence; measures establishing displaced homemaker programs; child care regulations; measures establishing family leave or flex time; measures addressing sexual assault and sexual harassment; measures addressing equal pay legislation and comparable worth; and measures establishing programs for female inmates; measures regulating pornography. Education legislation included such matters as curriculum, educational programs, school board elections; regulations of schools and colleges; education bonds, school board and educational personnel administration, salary, and benefits; appropriations to schools, colleges, and universities; school district mergers; vocational and technical education; adult education and literacy programs; school construction; school insurance; transportation to education programs; powers and responsibilities of governing bodies of colleges and universities; general-purpose libraries; workforce education efforts; general continuing education. Health legislation included such matters as: regulations, salary, and benefits of medical personnel; policies regarding disease prevention and treatment; disabilities; occupational health and safety; workmen's compensation for injury and disease; health and disability insurance provision and regulation; health science education; emergency services; health institutions; health equipment; chiropractic; dentistry; food safety regulations; pesticide regulations; regulation of economic poisons. Children's legislation included such matters as: foster care regulations; child care provision and regulation; child custody and support; child welfare regulations; children's health legislation; juvenile courts and court proceedings; child abuse. Welfare legislation included such matters as: public assistance provision and regulation; creation of low-income housing; Medicaid regulations; establishment and regulation of orphanages; urban renewal programs; unemployment policy; public defenders; administration of departments of public aid; foster care regulations; regulations of migrant labor; social work regulations; urban renewal programs; minimum

wage legislation; payroll deductions or charity; aid to displaced homemakers.

4 Supplementary analyses not presented here indicate that there continue to be gender differences in policy interests. Racial differences were less marked. In Arkansas, white women were significantly more likely to sponsor legislation focusing on black interests, women's interests, education, health, welfare, and children's interests. In Illinois and Maryland, women, regardless of race, were significantly more likely to sponsor legislation focusing on these policy areas.

5 In all analyses, White's robust standard errors are calculated to correct for heteroscedasticity (Wallace and Silver 1988; White 1980). Heteroscedasticity is a violation of the OLS assumption of constant variance of the error terms. Put simply, heteroscedasticity implies that the predicted relationship systematically fits some cases better than others.

6 Collinearity may inflate the standard errors and reduce statistical significance, particularly given the relatively low number of legislators analyzed. Therefore, throughout the chapter, interpretation will focus on both the magnitude of the estimated effects and the statistical significance.

7 Again, only bills with fewer than six sponsors are considered.

8 Again, bills with more than five sponsors are eliminated from the analysis.

9 Logit regression analysis is similar to OLS regression analysis, but is used when the dependent variable is coded 1 (for the presence of some phenomenon) and 0 otherwise.

CHAPTER 15

Representation of Minorities in the Next Century

Charles E. Menifield

From the outset, the main objective of this research was to provide the reader with a guided tour of representation from the perspective of individual minority groups in the U.S. at the federal, state and local levels. These chapters provide detailed records of the historical growth of these groups throughout the latter half of the 20th century along with a discussion of the propensity of the group to secure legislation that will benefit minority citizens.

This research has revealed and accomplished several things. First, the research has continued to broaden the definition of representation. From a descriptive perspective, the research has reinforced and further validated the arguments espoused by Mansbridge (1999). From a substantive view, the research showed that some minority legislators recognize the need to form racial coalitions and cosponsor legislation with those outside of their ranks in order to get the policies that they deem as necessary for the groups that they represent. Lastly, the research provided the reader with a foundation on which other scholars of minority political behavior can continue to conduct research of this nature.

The remainder of this chapter considers each minority group individually because the results of each set of analysis do not necessarily apply to the aggregate. There were six key questions posited in the introduction. All of these questions were not addressed in each chapter, but rather on a minority group basis. The questions addressed were:

1)   Have minority groups achieved descriptive representation in Congress, state legislatures, state executive offices, and local governments and in the bureaucracy?

2)   Have minority elected officials been able to substantively represent minority constituents?

3)   Have non-minority elected officials represented minority groups effectively?

4)   How successful are the coalitions that minority group form with those in the majority?

5)   From an ideological perspective, are all minority groups the same? If so, do these groups pursue similar legislation?

6)   What is the future of minority representation in the twenty-first century?

African Americans in Government

The authors of chapters two and nine found a lot of similarities between the political behavior of African American elected officials at the federal and state levels of government. First, the descriptive findings showed that the number of African American elected officials has increased with each election. However, growth has somewhat stabilized at the congressional level. The only negatives were the poor voter registration and voter turnout levels.

Specifically, at the congressional level, Menifield and Jones found that the role of the CBC is pivotal to achieving substantive representation of African Americans in the country. From an ideological and partisanship view, most African Americans, both elected and non-elected, tend to be liberal Democrats. These two homogenous factors have made it quite easy for African Americans officials to coalesce on legislation. This was particularly true when social and economic policy legislation were considered. The analysis clearly shows that African Americans vote as the most cohesive bloc in Congress. The effect of this voting bloc became more important as the number of African Americans increased and the number of other Democrat lawmakers shrank. If the current level of African American representation continues and the number of Democrat legislators begins to increase, there will be a number of African American leaders who will chair important committees. Obviously, the acquisition of these leadership positions will put African American decision-makers in a much better position to pursue policies that will benefit their constituents.

At the state level, King-Meadows and Schaller found that the growth of African American legislators has kept pace with other minority groups. Tryman's case study analysis of African Americans in the Mississippi bureaucracy also revealed an increase of minority officials since 1975. Southern states in particularly have the largest black legislative delegations in the country. This was not surprising given the large percentage of African Americans in the south. Using a case study model, King-Meadows and Schaller examined the Maryland and North Carolina's black caucuses and found that despite some constituency diversity, voting cohesion was very high when compared to other groups in the legislatures. Hence, the ability to substantively represent constituents was very high among African American legislators. Utilizing theories espoused by other scholars, they concluded that this behavior pattern allowed African Americans to circumvent the collection action problem that is often encountered in politics. Individuals were motivated to pursue those highly sought after benefits. Further, they found that cohesion facilitated the coalition building process for these two groups. Other Democrats found them to be one of the most reliable groups in the political arena. Therefore, they negotiated and formed coalitions as needed. Bratton furthered these finding with her analysis of bill cosponsorship at the state level in Arkansas, California, Illinois and Maryland. She found that patterns of cosponsorship were high when race was taken into account. However, there were some variations across these states. Lastly, women were found to slightly less likely to collaborate with men.

Women in Government

Although women can be considered a minority group when compared to men, the roles that they played and their political behavior at any level were not the same as other minority groups. McCurdy showed that women have made some inroads into the government that other minority groups have not. For example, the number of women in Congress has increased at a much faster rate than that of all other ethnic minority groups. They were the fastest growing and largest minority group in Congress in the 1990s. Unlike other minority groups, their growth was not limited to the House of Representatives. On the contrary, women have made up nearly 10% of the Senate for the last five years. Despite fluctuating tenure averages in both Houses, women have also acquired a power base. Women in the 1990s had more committee chairs and ranking minority members than any other period of time. However, committee leadership advances have been more limited in the Senate than in the House. In terms of party leadership, the 1990s were also the most fruitful time period for women in Congress. In fact, women achieved leadership positions in the Senate for the first time during this period. On the surface, an increase in the number of leadership positions would suggest that the propensity to secure legislation for women would be higher. However, party identification essentially dominated this process. Women in Congress were the most partisan diverse minority group in Congress. As a result, the achievement of their goals were somewhat unrealized because they tended to vote with their party rather than with members of the Women's Issues Caucus. However, voting cohesion among women did increase when social policy that affected women in general were considered. It was estimated that as their seniority increased and as they moved up the party hierarchy, their ability to represent should likewise increase.

Menifield and Gray and Jernigan and Tryman examined representation among women at the state and local level and found similar findings to that of McCurdy on the descriptive data. The number of women in state legislatures increased by no less than 130 new women for each five-year election cycle since 1975. Similarly, the number of black women in the South saw increased growth patterns. In terms of party identification, there were more women legislators who identified with the Democratic Party. The largest contingency of women legislators were found in Washington where they made up 41% of the legislature. Overall, women made up almost 25% of all state legislatures in 2000. Committee chair assignments and party leadership positions were highly correlated with the number of women in office. However, the case study analysis of women in the Mississippi and Vermont legislatures showed that the acquisition of committee chair assignments did not necessarily increase the success rate of women's legislation. In fact, bill cosponsorship was a more important factor in determining the success of female legislation. Specifically, when bills were cosponsored with men, the chances of success improved dramatically. Despite having a much larger female delegation, women legislators in Vermont were no more successful than the women in the Mississippi General Assembly were in passing legislation.

Hispanics in Government

Santos and Huerta examined Latinos in Congress and found that the number of Latino congressmen has continued to increase over the past thirty years. With respect to these increases in descriptive representation, they sought to determine whether substantive representation increased as well. They found that Latino representatives were very similar to non-Latino representatives in their ability to represent their constituents. Specifically, Latino representatives introduced a comparable number of bills and had similar success rates to non-Latinos. However the ability to represent and representing were not interchangeable.

Although the regression analysis findings suggested that Latino congressmen supported legislation that was beneficial to Hispanics, Latino congressmen as a group did not introduce enough legislation that was geared specifically toward improving the economic standing of Hispanic citizens. In fact, few of the laws sponsored by Latino representatives affected the Hispanic population in a positive fashion. Using the bills and amendments that the "NHLA identified as issues that were of interest to Latinos, the vast majority had a negative impact on Latinos. One implication of this behavior is that Latino members of Congress are relegated to a position of *reactionaries* – reacting to the actions of the majority party rather than acting first, and forcing the Majority party to react to their concerns." Three major problems can be noted. First, Latino congressmen lack organizational cohesion and a clear agenda despite having a formal Hispanic Caucus with a complete organizational structure and mission. Second, party diversity within the group has had an overwhelming negative affect on group behavior. Hence, ideological differences were also present. Menifield found similar data suggesting this problem at the state level. Lastly, the finding suggests that Hispanic voters have not held these elected officials accountable at the polls given their severe lack of participation in the political process.

Menifield's research on Hispanic state legislators furthered this particular section of Santos and Huerta's research. Hispanic citizens have one of the worse voter turnout rates on record. This lack of political involvement, at any level, has been a detriment to improved descriptive and substantive representation. Similar to Congress, Hispanic growth at the state and local level in all elected positions has been nothing short of a phenomenon given their political behavior. However, the potential growth has yet to be seen. All of the evidence suggested that Hispanic elected officials have not actively sought to recruit Hispanic non-participants. Nor have the elected officials, as a group, sought to organize and plan their future. For example, there were very few Hispanic caucuses in the states that have large Hispanic communities. In fact, only two of the states considered had a caucus. One of these two did not involve the Hispanic Senators in the caucus. These trends have furthered exasperated the problems of Hispanic citizen involvement in the political process. History would clearly suggest that Mayhew (1974) is correct when he indicated that legislators want to be re-elected and they will engage in behavior that will facilitate that process. One part of the process is courting voters and potential voters. Unfortunately Hispanic non-voters are likely to remain in-active and thus are unlikely to be courted by elected officials or candidates seeking office. As a result, Hispanic citizens are likely to maintain their current economic and social levels.

Lastly, this lack of participation is further worsened by other political institutions that have sought to eliminate/lower the number of minority elected officials. In order to utilize fully their majority minority status in the next century, the solution is quite clear. Hispanic voters and elected officials will have to completely modify their behavior pattern if they expect to receive an increase in substantive representation. Otherwise, they will continue to remain at their current economic levels.

Asian Americans in Government

There was very little formal data available on Asian Americans in elected offices in the United States. Takeda found that the problem lies in the lack of data rather than data collection techniques. From a descriptive point of view, the research showed that Hawaii is the only state that epitomized Asian American representation at the congressional and state and local level. California and Oregon were the only two continental states that have Asian American representation in Congress. Hence, they were under represented in Congress, and to a lesser extent, in state legislatures. However, there were not a lot of Asian American elected officials at the state and local levels. This included areas where there were large communities of Asian Americans.

Unlike African and Hispanic Americans, the key factor to this under representation at the federal level was dispersion within and among congressional districts. In addition, there was a lot of ethnic diversity among Asian Americans. Economically, Asian Americans were better off than African Americans and Hispanics. Their participation levels were also higher. If Asian Americans are successful in arguing for the creation of Asian congressional districts in California and New York in 2001, where they are fairly geographically cohesive, they should be able to increase their numbers in Congress. Further, they may also be able to improve the relationships among the different Asian groups by identifying the issues that affect all of them.

Despite arguments to the contrary, Takeda argued that a lack of descriptive representation at the state and local level was a function of historical, political and structural conditions. Asian Americans residential patterns, immigrant status, ethnic differences, and overt discrimination provided clear evidence explaining their political behavior.

From the substantive perspective, Takeda found that Asian Americans were much more divided in their partisan views, but tended to be more liberal. Given the lack of Asian Americans in Congress it was very difficult to gauge whether or not Asian Americans were achieving substantive representation. In most cases, legislation that benefited them also benefited African and Hispanic Americans. In the 1980s and 1990s only a few bills were introduced that were specifically geared towards the Asian community. Using a bill cosponsorship model, Takeda considered H. Con. Res. 124, a bill addressing Asian American loyalty to the country, to try and determine substantive representation. He found that the percentage of Asian residents in a district and membership in the Congressional Asian Pacific Caucus played a positive role in determining cosponsorship. Race, gender and seniority were not found to be significant. The future of Asian Americans is more or less still unknown. It is quite possible, as it is with most minority groups, that an increase in descriptive representation will improve the chances of substantive representation, but only the future will provide those answers.

American Indians in Government

American Indians were clearly the most distinct group among these five. Generally speaking, they were the most underrepresented group. However, the dynamics of American Indian behavior was drastically different from that of other groups. Peterson and Duncan found that a "lack of national representation is likely a consequence of localized populations, dispersed interests and a lack of interest in national policy. For most American Indians, the decisions made by state and local governments are as important, if not more so, than those decisions made by the federal government." As a result, they have had very low voter turnout rates. As history shows us, the vast majority of the American Indian population were placed into reservations hundreds of years ago and they still primarily live on those reservations where the tribal governments are more or less autonomous. It was within this tribal institution where they are the most active. However, the role of the Bureau of Indian Affairs has become increasingly more important in seeking national benefits to American Indians.

As gaming and other economic activities have become more and more popular on reservations, the amount of political activity has increased among the American Indian population. They have lobbied and made campaign contributions at the state and national level. However, most of them have choose to work within the parameters of their tribe rather than involving outsiders. Lastly, they concluded that the future for American Indians was bright given their improved economic and educational systems.

The Future of Minority Groups in Government

There are a couple of things that are likely to occur based on the cumulative research findings. First, all of the research conducted suggests that minority groups in general will have an increasing role in politics in the twenty-first century. The magnitude of that role is largely within their control. Models and research designs seeking to explain political behavior, coalition building, campaigns and so forth will have to take these changes into account. As the number of minorities increase, the ability to achieve substantive representation is likely to improve.

Second, to some extent, it is hard to make an argument that ethnic minority groups receive "adequate" representation from non-minority elected officials when political behavior and economic status are considered. However, it is certainly not impossible for them to receive adequate from non-minority elected officials. The evidence presented here and in previous research suggests a high correlation between economic status and political behavior. That is, it is highly unlikely that a group will reap the economic benefits of legislation when their participation rates are low. If this is true, one could make a pretty reasonable argument that Hispanics are economically worse off than other Americans are because they do not participate in the political process. With most things, there are exceptions to the rule. Menifield and Jones show that African Americans in Congress unquestionably seek the collective good of African Americans in the entire U.S. despite diminishing registration and turnout rates among them.

Third, it is very questionable what sort of litigation may be filed and what state legislatures will likely do with regards to legislative redistricting. If Menifield and Julian are correct in their prognosis, the creation of more minority districts is highly unlikely in areas where minority growth is not abundant. However, it is much more likely to occur in the areas where minorities have a super majority. The down side to the creation of those districts is that they will more than likely be packed with as many minorities as possible so that the number of other minority districts will be minimized. Additional lawsuits challenging the creation of majority minority districts are likely to occur. If appealed to the U.S. Supreme Court, they are not likely to be viewed favorably given the ideological and partisan cleavages that have been seen since 1993. This is furthered with the recent election of a Republican President who is likely to appoint more conservative justices to the Court.

Hence, the only variable that can assure continued representation over time is political participation. These groups are going to have to mobilize at every single level in order to achieve and expand representation. This is particularly true for the Hispanic population.

References

Mansbridge, Jane. 1999. "Should Blacks Represent Blacks and Women Represent Women? A Contingent "Yes." *The Journal of Politics* 61: 628-657.

Mayhew, David. R. 1974. *The Electoral Connection*. New Haven, CT: Yale University Press.

Appendixes

Appendix 1-1

African Americans Who Have Served in the U.S. House 1960-2000

State	House	Tenure		House	Tenure
Alabama					
Earl Hilliard	House	1993-			
California					
Ronald Dellums	House	1971-	Julian Dixon	House	1979-
Maxine Waters	House	1991-	Juanita McDonald	House	1996-
Barbara Lee	House	1998-			
Connecticut					
Gary Franks	House	1991-96			
Dist. Of Columbia					
Walter Fauntroy	House	1971-91	E. Holmes-Norton	House	1991-
Florida					
Alcee Hastings	House	1993-	Carrie Meek	House	1993-
Corrine Brown	House	1993-			
Georgia					
Andrew Young	House	1973-77	John Lewis	House	1987-
Cynthia McKinney	House	1993-	Sanford Bishop	House	1993-
Illinois					
George Collins	House	1971-72	Ralph Metcalfe	House	1971-79
Cardiss Collins	House	1973-96	Bennett Stewart	House	1979-81
Gus Savage	House	1981-93	H. Washington	House	1981-83
Charles Hayes	House	1983-93	Bobby Rush	House	1993-
Mel Reynolds	House	1993-95	Danny Davis	House	1996-
Jesse Jackson Jr.	House	1996-			
Indiana					
Katie Hall	House	1983-85	Julia M. Carson	House	1996-

African Americans Who Have Served in the U.S. House 1960-2000 (cont'd.)

State	House	Tenure		House	Tenure
Louisiana					
W. Jefferson	House	1991-	Cleo Fields	House	1993-95
Maryland					
Parren Mitchell	House	1971-87	Kweisi Mfume	House	1987-96
Albert Wynn	House	1993-			
Michigan					
John Conyers	House	1965-	George Crockett	House	1980-91
B. Rose Collins	House	1991-96	Carolyn Kilpatrick	House	1996-
Mississippi					
Mike Espy	House	1987-93	Bennie Thompson	House	1993-
Missouri					
William Clay	House	1969-	Alan Wheat	House	1983-93
New Jersey					
Donald Payne	House	1989-			
New York					
Shirley Chisholm	House	1969-83	Charles Rangel	House	1971-
Ed Towns	House	1983-	Major Owens	House	1983-
Floyd Flake	House	1987-	Gregory Meeks	House	1998-
North Carolina					
Eva Clayton	House	1993-	Melvin Watt	House	1993-
Ohio					
Louis Stokes	House	1969-	Stephanie Tubbs	House	1998-
Oklahoma					
J. C. Watts	House	1995-			
Pennsylvania					
William Gray	House	1979-91	Lucien Blackwell	House	1991-
Chaka Fattah	House	1995-			
South Carolina					
James Clyburn	House	1993-			
Tennessee					
Harold Ford Sr.	House	1975-96	Harold Ford Jr.	House	1996-
Texas					
Barbara Jordan	House	1973-79	Mickey Leland	House	1979-89
C. Washington	House	1989-93	Eddie B. Johnson	House	1993-
Shelia Jackson-Lee	House	1994-			
Virginia					
Robert Scott	House	1993-			

Appendix 3-1: Numbers of Women Serving in the United States Congress 1917-2000

Congress	Year	# of Women Senate	% of Senate	# of Women House	% of House	Total Congress	% of Total
65th	1917-1919	0		1 (0D, 1R)	.002	1	.002
66th	1919-1921	0		0		0	
67th	1921-1923	1 (1D, 0R)	.01	2 (0D, 2R)	.005	3 (1D, 2R)	.01
68th	1923-1925	0		1 (0D, 1R)	.002	1 (0D, 1R)	.002
69th	1925-1927	0		3 (1D, 2R)	.007	3 (1D, 2R)	.01
70th	1927-1929	0		5 (2D, 3R)	.011	5 (2D, 3R)	.01
71st	1929-1931	0		9 (4D, 5R)	.021	9 (4D, 5R)	.02
72nd	1931-1933	1 (1D, 0R)	.01	7 (4D, 3R)	.016	8 (5D, 3R)	.02
73rd	1933-1935	1 (1D, 0R)	.01	7 (4D, 3R)	.016	8 (5D, 3R)	.02
74th	1935-1937	2 (2D, 0R)	.02	6 (4D, 2R)	.014	8 (6D, 2R)	.02
75th	1937-1939	2 (1D, 1R)*	.02	5 (4D, 1R)	.011	7 (5D, 2R)	.01
76th	1939-1941	1 (1D, 0R)	.01	8 (4D, 4R)	.018	9 (5D, 4R)	.02
77th	1941-1943	1 (1D, 0R)	.01	9 (4D, 5R)	.021	10 (5D, 5R)	.02
78th	1943-1945	1 (1D, 0R)	.01	8 (2D, 6R)	.018	9 (3D, 6R)	.02
79th	1945-1947	0	.00	11 (6D, 5R)	.025	11 (6D, 5R)	.02
80th	1947-1949	1 (0D, 1R)	.01	7 (3D, 4R)	.016	8 (3D, 5R)	.02
81st	1949-1951	1 (0D, 1R)	.01	9 (5D, 4R)	.021	10 (5D, 5R)	.02
82nd	1951-1953	1 (0D, 1R)	.01	10 (4D, 6R)	.023	11 (4D, 7R)	.02
83rd	1953-1955	2 (0D, 2R)	.02	11 (5D, 6R)**	.025	13 (5D, 8R)**	.02
84th	1955-1957	1 (0D, 1R)	.01	16 (10D, 6R)**	.037	17 (10D, 7R)**	.03
85th	1957-1959	1 (0D, 1R)	.01	15 (9D, 6R)	.034	16 (9D, 7R)	.03
86th	1959-1961	2 (1D, 1R)	.02	17 (9D, 8R)	.039	19 (10D, 9R)	.04
87th	1961-1963	2 (1D, 1R)	.02	18 (11D, 7R)	.041	20 (12D, 8R)	.04
88th	1963-1965	2 (1D, 1R)	.02	12 (6D, 6R)	.028	14 (7D, 7R)	.03
89th	1965-1967	2 (1D, 1R)	.02	11 (7D, 4R)	.025	13 (8D, 5R)	.02
90th	1967-1969	1 (0D, 1R)	.01	11 (6D, 5R)	.025	12 (6D, 6R)	.02
91st	1969-1971	1 (0D, 1R)	.01	10 (6D, 4R)	.023	11 (6D, 5R)	.02
92nd	1971-1973	2 (1D, 1R)	.01	13 (10D, 3R)	.030	15 (11D, 4R)	.03
93rd	1973-1975	0	.00	16 (14D, 2R)	.037	16 (14D, 2R)	.03
94th	1975-1977	0	.00	19 (14D, 5R)	.044	19 (14D, 5R)	.04
95th	1977-1979	2 (2D, 0R)	.02	18 (13D, 5R)	.041	20 (15D, 5R)	.04
96th	1979-1981	1 (0D, 1R)	.01	16 (11D, 5R)	.037	17 (11D, 6R)	.03
97th	1981-1983	2 (0D, 2R)	.02	21 (11D, 10R)	.048	23 (11D, 12R)	.04
98th	1983-1985	2 (0D, 2R)	.02	22 (13D, 9R)	.051	24 (13D, 11R)	.04
99th	1985-1987	2 (0D, 2R)	.02	23 (12D, 11R)	.053	25 (12D, 13R)	.05
100th	1987-1989	2 (1D, 1R)	.02	23 (12D, 11R)	.053	25 (13D, 12R)	.05
101st	1989-1991	2 (1D, 1R)	.02	29 (16D, 13R)	.067	31 (17D, 14R)	.06
102nd	1991-1993	4 (3D, 1R)⁺⁺	.04	28 (19D, 9R)⁺	.064	32 (22D, 10R)⁺	.06
103rd	1993-1995	7 (5D, 2R)⁺⁺⁺	.07	46 (34D, 12R)⁺	.106	53 (39D, 14R)⁺	.10
104th	1995-1997	9 (5D, 4R)R	.09	47 (30D, 17R)⁺	.108	56 (34D, 21R)⁺	.10
105th	1997-1999	9 (6D, 3R)	.09	54 (37D, 17R)ᴿᴿ	.124	63 (43D, 20R)ᴿᴿ	.12
106th	1999-2001	9 (6D, 3R)	.09	56 (39D, 17R)ᴿᴿᴿ	.129	65 (45D, 20R)ᴿᴿᴿ	.12

Note: The table shows the maximum number of women elected or appointed to serve in that Congress at one time. Some filled out unexpired terms and some were never sworn in.

* A total of four women (3D, 1R) were appointed or elected to the Senate in the 75th Congress, but no more than two served together at one time. Gladys Pyle (R, SD) was elected to, but never sworn in to the 75th Congress.

** Does not include Mary Elizabeth Pruett Farrington, a Republican Delegate to the House from the Territory of Hawaii (pre-statehood). Delegate Farrington succeeded her husband who died in office.

+Does not include a Democratic Delegate to the House of Representatives, Eleanor Holmes Norton, from Washington, D.C.

++On election day 1992, three women served in the Senate, two were elected and one was appointed. On November 3rd, Dianne Feinstein won a special election to complete two years of a term, she was sworn in on November 10, 1992.

+++Includes Kay Bailey Hutchison (R-TX), who won a special election on June 5, 1993 to serve out the remaining year and one half of a term.

R Includes Sheila Frahm (R-KS), who was appointed on June 11, 1996 to fill a vacancy caused by resignation. She was defeated in her primary race to complete the full term.

RR Does not include two Democratic Delegates to the House of Representatives, Eleanor Holmes Norton from Washington D.C., and Donna M. Christian-Green from the Virgin Islands. Also does not include Susan Molinari (R-NY) who resigned August 1, 1997. Includes 4 women (2 Democrats and 2 Republicans) who won special elections in March, April, and June 1998.

RRR Does not include two Democratic Delegates, Eleanor Holmes Norton from the District of Columbia, and Donna M. Christian-Green from the Virgin Islands.

Sources: Center for the American Woman and Politics. 2000. "National Information Bank on Women in Public Office." Eagleton Institute of Politics, Rutgers University. http://www.rci.rutgers.edu/~cawp/facts/cawpfs.html;   United States Congress. 1989. Biographical Directory of Congress 1776-1989. Senate Document 100-34 (Washington DC: U.S. Government Printing Office);   Congressional Quarterly. 1991. Guide to Congress. 4th ed. Washington DC: Congressional Quarterly Press;   Michael Barone and Grant Ujifusa. 1999. The Almanac of American Politics 2000. Washington DC: National Journal. Percentages calculated by the author.

Appendix 3-2: Women Who Have Served in Congress 1960-2000

State	House	Tenure		House	Tenure
Alabama					
Maryon Allen	Senate	1978	Elizabeth Andrews	House	1972-73
Arizona					
Karen English	House	1993-1995			
Arkansas					
Catherine Norrell	House	1961-63	Blanche Lincoln	House	1993-97
				Senate	1999-
California					
Yvonne B. Burke	House	1973-79	Shirley N. Pettis	House	1975-79
Bobbi Feilder	House	1981-87	Sala Burton	House	1983-87
Nancy Pelosi	House	1987-	Maxine Waters	House	1991-
Dianne Feinstein	Senate	1992-	Barbara Boxer	Senate	1993-
				House	1938-93
Lynn Woosley	House	1993-	Anna G. Eshoo	House	1993-
Lucille Roybal-Allard	House	1993	Jane Harman	House	1993-99
Lynn Schenk	House	1993-95	Zoe Lofgren	House	1995-
Andrea Seastrand	House	1995-97	Juanita McDonald	House	1996-
Ellen Tausher	House	1997-	Loretta Sanchez	House	1997-
Barbara Lee	House	1998-	Lois Capps	House	1998-
Mary Bono	House	1998-	Grace Napolitano	House	1999-
Colorado					
Patricia Schroeder	House	1973-97	Diana DeGette	House	1997-
Connecticut					
Ella T. Grasso	House	1971-75	Barbara B. Kennelly	House	1982-99
Nancy L. Johnson	House	1983-			
Florida					
Paula Hawkins	Senate	1981-87	Ileana Ros-Lehtinen	House	1989-
Corrine Brown	House	1993-	Tillie Fowler	House	1993-
Karen L. Thurman	House	1993-	Carrie Meek	House	1993-
Georgia					
Cynthia McKinney	House	1993-			
Hawaii					
Patsy T. Mink	House	1965-77	Patricia Saiki	House	1987-91
		1990-			
Idaho					
Helen Chenowith	House	1995-			

Appendix 3-2: Women Who Have Served in Congress 1960-2000 (cont'd.)

State	House	Tenure		House	Tenure
Illinois					
Charlotte T. Reid	House	1963-71	Cardiss Collins	House	1973-96
Lynn M. Martin	House	1981-90	Carol Moseley-Braun	Senate	1993-99
Jan Schakowsky	House	1999-	Judy Biggert	House	1999-
Indiana				'	
Katie Hall	House	1982-85	Jill Long	House	1989-95
Julia Carson	House	1997-			
Kansas					
Martha Keys	House	1975-79	Nancy Kassebaum	Senate	1978-97
Jan Meyers	House	1985-97	Shelia Frahm	Senate	1996-
Kentucky					
Anne Northup	House	1997-			
Louisiana					
Elaine S. Edwards	House	1972-	Corinne C. Boggs	House	1973-91
Cathy Long	House	1985-87	Mary Landrieu	Senate	1997-
Maine					
Olympia Snowe	House	1979-95	Susan Collins	House	1997-
	Senate	1995-			
Maryland					
Marjorie S. Holt	House	1973-87	Gladys Spellman	House	1975-81
Beverly Byron	House	1979-93	Helen Benley	House	1985-95
Constance Morella	House	1987-	Barbara Mikulski	House	1977-87
				Senate	1987-
Minnesota					
Margaret Heckler	House	1967-83	Louise Day Hicks	House	1971-73
Missouri					
Joan Kelly Horn	House	1991-93	Pat Danner	House	1993-
Karen McCarthy	House	1995-	JoAnn Emerson	House	1997-
Nebraska					
Virginia Smith	House	1975-91			
Nevada					
Barbara Vucanovich	House	1983-97	Shelley Berkley	House	1999-
New Jersey					
Millicent Fenwick	House	1975-83	Helen S. Meyner	House	1975-79
Marge Roukema	House	1981-			
New Mexico					
Heather Wilson	House	1998-			

Appendix 3-2: Women Who Have Served in Congress 1960-2000 (cont'd.)

State	House	Tenure		House	Tenure
New York					
Shirley Chisholm	House	1969-83	Bella S. Abzug	House	1971-77
Elizabeth Holtzman	House	1973-81	Geraldine Ferraro	House	1979-85
Louise Slaughter	House	1987-	Nita M. Lowey	House	1989-
Susan Molinari	House	1990-97	Nydia M. Velazquez	House	1993-
Carolyn B. Maloney	House	1993-	Sue W. Kelly	House	1995-
Carolyn McCarthy	House	1997-			
North Carolina					
Eva Clayton	House	1993-	Sue Myrick	House	1995-
North Dakota					
Mary Rose Oakar	House	1977-93	Jean Ashbrook	House	1982-83
March Kaptur	House	1983-	Jocelyn Burdick	Senate	1992-
Deborah Pryce	1993-		Stephanie Jones	House	1999-
Oregon					
Maurine Neuberger	Senate	1960-67	Elizabeth Furse	House	1993-99
Darlene Hooley	House	1997-			
Pennsylvania					
Marjorie Mezvinsky	House	1993-95			
Rhode Island					
Claudine Schneider	House	1981-91			
South Carolina					
Corinne B. Riley	House	1963-71	Elizabeth Patterson	House	1987-93
Tennessee					
Louise Reece	House	1961-63 I	Rene Baker	House	1964-65
Marilyn Lloyd	House	1975-95			
Texas					
Lera M. Thomas	House	1966-67	Barbara Jordan	House	1973-79
Eddie B. Johnson	House	1993-	Hay Hutchison	Senate	1993-
Shelia J. Lee	House	1995-	Kay Granger	House	1997-
Utah					
Karen Shephard	House	1993-95	Enid G. Waldholtz	House	1995-97
Virginia					
Leslie L.Byrne	House	1993-95			
Washington					
Julia B. Hansen	House	1960-74	Jolene Unsoeld	House	1989-95
Maria Cantwell	House	1993-95	Jennifer Dunn	House	1993-
Patty Murray	Senate	1993-	Linda Smith	House	1995-99

Appendix 3-2: Women Who Have Served in Congress 1960-2000 (cont'd.)

State	House	Tenure	House	Tenure
Wisconsin				
Tammy Baldwin	House	1999-		
Wyoming				
Barbara Cubin	House	1995-		

*Assumed office after the death of her husband, either through appointment, or special election.

†Serving in the 106th Congress at time of publication.

Sources: Center for American Women and Politics. 2000. "National Information Bank on Women in Public Office." Eagleton Institute of Politics, Rutgers University. http://www.rci.rutgers.edu/~cawp/facts/cawpfs.html;   United States Congress. 1989. Biographical Directory of Congress 1776-1989. Senate Document 100-34 (Washington DC: U.S. Government Printing Office); Congressional Quarterly. 1991. Guide to Congress. 4th ed. (Washington DC: Congressional Quarterly Press); Michael Barone and Grant Ujifusa. 1999. The Almanac of American Politics 2000. Washington DC: National Journal.

Index

Editor's Biographical Sketch

Charles E. Menifield is an assistant professor of political science and public administration at Mississippi State University in Starkville, Mississippi. His research interests lie primarily in the area of voting behavior, minority group behavior, PAC contributions, public administration and budgeting and fiscal management. His research has appeared in *Public Choice, Western Journal of Black Studies, Latino Studies Journal, Journal of Black Studies, Congress and the Presidency, Deviant Behavior* and the *Policy Studies Journal*. Charles received his Ph. D. from the University of Missouri-Columbia.

About the Contributors

Kathleen Bratton is an assistant professor at Louisiana State University where she teaches, Women and Politics, Congress and the Presidency, State and Local Politics, Research Methods, and Campaigns and Elections. Her research has appeared in the *Journal of Politics* and *American Politics Quarterly*. Kate received her Ph. D. from the University of North Carolina-Chapel Hill.

Robert Duncan teaches American History and American Government at Redlands Community College in El Reno, OK. He has a master's of Educational Social Sciences from Southwestern Oklahoma State University. His main areas of emphasis are the sixties, the civil rights movement, and Vietnam. He received his bachelor's degree at William & Mary in political science.

Patrick Ellcessor is a Ph. D. candidate at Texas A&M University at College Station where he is studying political behavior, immigration and the courts. He received a masters and bachelors degree in political science from Appalachian State University in Boone, NC. Patrick has published his work on immigration in *Proteus: A Journal of Ideas*.

Regina C. Gray is a Ph. D. candidate in the department of government and politics at the University of Maryland-College Park, where she specializes in State and Local Politics, Public Policy, and Urban Policy Studies. She received a M.A. in political Science, at George Washington University in Washington D.C. and a bachelor's degree from Emory University in Atlanta, Georgia in Political Science.

Juan Carlos Huerta is an assistant professor of political science at Texas A&M University at Corpus Christi, TX where he teaches courses in Latino/Ethnic Politics, Public Opinion and the media, Latin American Politics, Democratization and Comparative Politics. His research has centered on Latino politics, voting behavior and representation. Carlos received his Ph. D. at the University of Houston. His research has appeared in *Social Sciences Quarterly*.

Patricia Jernigan is a Ph. D. candidate in the department of political science at Mississippi State University in Starkville, MS where she is writing her dissertation on women in the bureaucracy in southern states. She received the master's degree at Jackson State University in Public Policy and Administration and the bachelor's degree at Tougaloo College in Sociology.

Charles E. Jones is an associate professor of African American Studies at Georgia State University in Atlanta, Georgia. His research has appeared in *Legislative Studies Quarterly, National Political Science Review, Journal of Black Studies, Western Journal of Black Studies, Phylon: The Review of Race and Culture, Review of Public Personnel Administration, Readings in American Political Issues*, and *Dilemmas of Black Politics: Issues of Leadership and Strategy*. Professor Jones is one of the leading experts in the United States on the Congressional Black Caucus. He received his Ph. D. from Washington State University in Pullman, WA.

Frank Julian is a professor of legal studies at Murray State University in Murray, KY where he teaches a variety of classes in the legal studies program. Although his teaching interest lie in legal studies, his research has appeared in the *Journal of Business and Public Affairs, South Texas Law Journal, Western Journal of Black Studies, Journal of College Student Affairs, PS: Political Science and Politics, The Accounting Educators' Journal* and *NASPA Review*. Frank received his Law degree from West Virginia University in Morgantown, WV.

Tyson King-Meadows is an assistant professor at Middle Tennessee State University in Murfreesboro, TN. Although his research interests are primarily in African American Politics, he also has an interest in budget systems. His research has appeared in *Public Budgeting and Finance* and *The Minority Voice*. Tyson received his Ph. D. from the University of North Carolina at Chapel Hill.

Jan Leighley is an associate professor of political science at Texas A&M University at College Station, TX. She has published widely in the *Journal of Politics, American Political Science Review, American Journal of Political Science, American Politics Quarterly, Public Choice, Political Research Quarterly* and *Political Geography Quarterly*. Jan received her Ph. D. at Washington University.

Karen McCurdy is an assistant professor of political science at Georgia Southern University in Statesboro, GA. Although her research focuses on committees in Congress, she has conducted numerous research projects analyzing environmental policy. Her work has appeared in *Legislative Studies Quarterly* and the *Encyclopedia of Women in American Politics*. Karen received her Ph. D. from the University of Wisconsin-Madison.

Geoff Peterson is an assistant professor of political science at the University of Wisconsin-Eau Claire. Geoff has articles appearing in *Political Behavior, American Indian Quarterly* and *Congress & The Presidency*. His central research focus is Native American Politics. Geoff received his Ph. D. from the University of Iowa.

Adolfo Santos is an assistant professor of political science at the University of Houston-Downtown where he teaches a number of courses in American Politics, Minority Politics, Policy and Planning, Political Theory and Comparative Politics. His work on minorities in Texas has been published in *Texas Politics Today*. Adolfo received his Ph. D. from the University of Houston Downtown.

Thomas F. Schaller is an assistant professor of political science at the University of Maryland-Baltimore County where his focus lies mainly in the study of the Presidency and Public policy. His research has appeared in *Public Choice, Publius: The Journal of Federalism*, and *Constitutional Political Economy*. Tom received his Ph. D. from the University of North Carolina at Chapel Hill.

Okiyoshi Takeda is a Ph. D. candidate in the department of Politics at Princeton University where he is writing a dissertation on bill passage in the U.S. House of Representatives. He has taught courses on Asian American politics at the University of Pennsylvania, New York University and Columbia University. He received bachelors and masters degrees from the University of Tokyo in political science. He has published an article on divided government in *Thought*, an article on Asian American student political identity in *American Review* and an article on the development of Asian American studies in the *Annual Review of Migration Studies*.

Mfanya Tryman is a professor of political science at Mississippi State University in Starkville, MS. He is widely published in the field of African American politics. His works have appeared in *American Review of Politics, American Justice, National Political Science Review, Western Journal of Black Studies, Journal of Social and Behavioral Sciences, Journal of Public Affairs and Issues*, and the *Journal of Third World Studies* to name a few. He has countless book chapters and other manuscripts examining subjects from affirmative action to the Soweto Riots of South Africa. Mfanya received his Ph. D. from Florida State University.